'TWAS *Arnold's* POST fir *Harry* fought,
   Arnold ne'er enter'd in his thought,
How ends the bargain? let us fee,
The fort is fafe, as fafe can be,
Ӊ is favourite *per force* muft die,
His view's laid bare to ev'ry eye;
His money's gone—and lo! he gains
One fcoundrel more for all his pains.
ANDRE was gen'ro—ඁ and *brave*.
And in his room ᐧ
'Tis fure ordain'
All thofe, of coᐧ
Now let the *De*ᐧ
Or *Arnold* cheaᐧ

Mothers fhall ftill ᐧ
Arnold fhall be the bug-bear of their ye—
Arnold!---vile, treacherous, and leagued with Satan.

THE TRAITOR AND THE SPY

JAMES THOMAS FLEXNER

THE TRAITOR
AND THE
SPY

Benedict Arnold and John André

Newly Illustrated and with a New Foreword

LITTLE, BROWN AND COMPANY

BOSTON   TORONTO

T 08/75

The Traitor and the Spy was originally published in 1953
by Harcourt, Brace and Company. It was subsequently published in a shortened version under the title *The Benedict
Arnold Case.*

Library of Congress Cataloging in Publication Data

Flexner, James Thomas, 1908–
  The traitor and the spy.

  Bibliography: p.
  Includes index.
  1. Arnold, Benedict, 1741–1801.　2. André, John,
1751–1780.　I. Title.
[E236.F57　1975]　　　973.3′092′2　　　75-11909
ISBN 0-316-28606-0

*Published simultaneously in Canada
by Little, Brown & Company (Canada) Limited*

PRINTED IN THE UNITED STATES OF AMERICA

TO BEATRICE

Foreword to the New Edition

A DRUGGIST and disreputable horse trader, Benedict
Arnold made himself, through inborn talents, the greatest combat general who fought on either side during the
American Revolution. He married as his second wife Peggy Shippen, a disgruntled Philadelphia aristocrat, beautiful and much
younger than he. Hardly were they married before they got
secretly in touch with a poetic English soldier with whom Peggy
had flirted when the British had occupied Philadelphia. John André
was rising with startling rapidity to the important post of adjutant
general of the British army.

In coded letters carried at great risk by secret agents, Arnold
offered to sell his soldiers with the key fortress of West Point, to
deliver to the enemy, dead or alive, the indispensable commander
in chief of the American cause, George Washington. The plot
promised to destroy the American battle for freedom with all its
implications that were to ring down the corridors of history.

On September 22, 1780, André rowed ashore from a British
warship for a secret rendezvous with Arnold. Thus was set in
motion ten days of wild action which proved again that truth is
stranger than fiction.

Here is a story which could have been chanted, exactly as it
was inscribed by Nature on the authentic tablets of history, in
ancient times by some heroic bard. Even blind Homer might not
have scorned a drama so rich in events and personalities. On an

ix

exalted stage where moved the destinies of empires and perhaps the future liberties of all mankind, two able men and a gifted woman were drawn, by flaws in the very characteristics that had raised them high, into mortal danger. And Nature, not like lesser artists afraid of the extremest melodrama, lavishly interwove into her saga coincidence, extended suspense, struggles to escape, and exalted tragedy.

For years before I dared undertake the subject, I had eyed the Benedict Arnold story wondering whether I could possibly carry off so epic a theme. Apart from doubts of my personal skill there was the fact that I had no intention of abandoning the basic conception of modern historical writing: fidelity to fact as recorded in primary sources. Could this method be applied effectively to a narrative brimming with dramatic action?

I was in the end emboldened to write *The Traitor and the Spy*, which was originally published in 1953, by the realization which grew on me with every book I completed that the requirements of accurate biography by no means mark out a strait road to limited effects. True, no modern biographer can be expected to function as an epic poet. But fiction is now an accepted epic form. And I had become convinced that the possibilities of sound, factual biography are, although occupying a somewhat different ground, as various as the possibilities of the novel.

At the two extremes of their span, biography and fiction do not overlap. There is a kind of biography which is purposefully unliterary, the volumes being the practical (and often extremely valuable) end products of a different kind of endeavor: they codify, as directly as possible, discoveries of research. Such works are as far outside the scope of creative expression as impressionistic narratives, in which fact becomes almost completely secondary to emotion, are outside legitimate intentions of historical writing.

In the extensive middle ground, the two genres are by no means as far separated as is commonly supposed. The novelist creates characters from his own reactions to real life and joins them in a story that could have actually taken place in the exterior world. The biographer finds his characters in the exterior world and then follows their careers through the examination of documents. The best of these documents closely parallel what the novelist hears in his association with living men, for they are speech preserved in letters. It could be argued that the letters are more revealing, since they convey to the reader intimacies which are in ordinary social intercourse hidden. Unless he secretes tape recorders in bridal suites, the novelist is only present at amorous interchanges in which he himself is one of the principals, while the biographer reads many a love letter intended for eyes not his own. As for the insight gained from the personal experience of living, the biographer need have no less of this than the novelist.

According to often accepted theory, the novelist has complete mastery of his characters, who may be visualized as robots entirely subject to his command. But robots do not make for good fiction. The truth is that soon as a novelist has set up his characters, he has abandoned a good deal of his original freedom. Now he can only make his actors behave in the manner which his experience and insight tell him would actually be the case for those specific persons in the world outside his brain pan. To use an old critical cliché: when a novel comes to life, the characters run away with the author. The novelist is then very much in the situation of the biographer, whose characters also have imperious wills of their own.

However, the indulgences permitted by his craft do permit the novelist extra freedoms. He can banish in the middle of the game characters who refuse to carry out his will, substituting new characters specifically designed for his present purposes. If a climax to which he believed he was advancing proves to be off his course, he can fashion a different climax. But the biographer cannot revise his dramatic personae or alter their acts. He must comprehend, and through comprehension justify, the course which his characters actually took in life. Despite contrary conclusions axiomatic to present critical thinking, it is possible to argue that discerning the basic patterns, the fundamental emotions in the undoctored turmoil of living, is no less creative than the practice of the novelist's greater freedom. Indeed, the imaginative insight demanded of the biographer more closely resembles the creativity of scientists who fathom the secrets of nature by the coordination of observed facts into inclusive systems. It may well be that the biographer's art is particularly well suited to the age of science we all inhabit.

Like the novelist, the biographer is free, before he starts a new project, to go anywhere. He, too, may select at will the horses that are going to run away with him. Shall he concentrate on a single protagonist or try to depict the interweaving in a specific milieu of various lives? What protagonist or what milieu? As a novelist floundering between books frantically matches possible characters and situations to his own interests and possibilities, so the biographer haunts libraries, seeking the subject to which he will devote several years of labor.

I have upon occasion thrashed around for months in the unhappiness and frustration of a man dedicated to a craft who is blocked from practicing it. More than once, I have started on a biography and, after going beyond first acquaintance with the protagonist, decided to abandon the relationship.

The most conspicuous example was Aaron Burr. After I had completed my account of Arnold's treason, it seemed a natural progression to deal with the man usually considered to be the major villain associated with the early years of the nation. But Burr proved for me an impossible subject. Where Arnold had grandeur, Burr was sleazy throughout. Unless a writer is willing to reverse the historical record, showing white as black and black as white, the Burr story narrates how a cheap and shoddy individual with no real convictions or abilities beyond the push to elbow himself ahead could successfully insert himself on the same stage with great men at one of the great moments of history. A truthful account of Burr could prove a fruitful subject only for a Balzacian biographer, and my interests are not Balzac's.

Even Benedict Arnold presented me with problems. Being not myself an admirer of warfare and the acts of death (I turned with dismay from John Paul Jones, a born killer who had already committed murder before war gave sanction to his sanguinary proclivities), I could not have written a full-length biography devoted exclusively to Arnold. Yet I was fascinated by Arnold.

He seemed to me a classic example of the hero in the Wagnerian sense, a man of physical prowess and derring-do who finds his consummation in that activity which most tests bodily skill and fortitude: battle. Battle not war: There were many aspects of war to which Arnold was unsuited and which he resented because they interfered between the hero and the exalted exercise of his gifts. Arnold could not understand policy beyond the scope of his eyes and his sword, nor could he feel idealism beyond the idealism of the body. He could kill the strong, spare the weak, succor the wounded. He protected women (eventually to the further souring of his entire career), but he could not understand what the American Revolution was all about. He was like a great tower that had been built to withstand gales from only one direction. When the hurricane shifted, the mighty structure crashed to the ground.

Even as a tree can only reach its ultimate dimensions in an open field, so Arnold was born in a place and time that uniquely permitted the characteristics of such a man to develop without check. He was among the first officers in a previously nonexistent army that was serving a nation not yet born. Any traditions he followed had to be applied from other contexts. His loyalties could not be due to habit and training; they had to come from circumstance and will. He taught himself to fight and his military rise was beyond the most extreme possibilities in organized armies. The span of time from the day he joined the Continental Army as a captain to his commission as major general was less than two years—but even at that he had reason to feel aggrieved because officers of lesser ability had risen in this improvised army even more rapidly. Hardly sustained or molded by any institutions outside himself, Arnold remained solitary on a crowded scene.

There have been modern generals with many psychological resemblances to Arnold. But how different their development! At an age when Arnold captained small merchant ships as an over-aggressive businessman, such modern fighters were gathered into a military establishment, educated at institutions like the United States Military Academy at West Point. They moved on routinely into the long-established army of a long-established nation, a meticulously charted world where there were laid out roads designed by generations of experience to take maximum advantage of the gifts that a born fighter possesses. There were roads of promotion up which they could travel with little resentment or controversy.

Men especially trained for such occupations handled aspects of war with which the fighters were not equipped to cope. "Heroes" did not find themselves, as Arnold did, their own recruiters and supply officers, commandants of cities without aides trained in military government.

Such modern fighters were sustained on the sides of their natures where their own foundations were weak not only by elaborate organizations, but by conditioning and traditions often stronger than their characters. They have broken out in little ways, but they were isolated from such excesses as brought Arnold down.

In ancient times, Achilles shared much of Arnold's temperament. He brooked little interference with what he pleased to do—but his passions were sustained, as Arnold's were not, by social structure. Although he was titularly under the command of Agamemnon, he was the leader of his own tribe in what was a loose alliance. When Agamemnon preempted a slave girl he felt he had a right to, he sulked in his tent in a manner that would in a modern army have made him liable for a court martial for disobeying orders. But his own followers felt that they were insulted by the insult to him. He could have marched to his "tall ships," perhaps even made his own peace with the Trojans, without being guilty of treason.

Since Arnold represents the full flowering of aggressive characteristics that exist to some extent in us all, all can to some extent identify with him. He is far from being an unsympathetic character. His bravery, his ability to lead men are sure and clear, and the picture of the wounded hero struggling with ingratitude and injustice which he lacked weapons to overcome would be touching were it not for his final, desperate act of betrayal.

Yet, for all the grandeur and drama of his career, I felt that a biography in which he would be the sole protagonist would not do for me. It would be a perpetual leaning tower, as lopsided as his own character was.

The addition to the book of John André as a second major actor added balance, the more satisfactorily because Nature, in arranging complicated events, does not act at random. Despite great and obvious variations of experience and character, the young British officer had weaknesses that dovetailed with Arnold's even as their tragedies eventually dovetailed. Thus on a psychological as well as a historical plane, the two lives drew together.

Where Arnold was from the start a physical man designed for derring-do, André began life as a delicate dabbler in the arts whose friends could not imagine him as a soldier. Yet he chose, although there was no such tradition in his background, to be a soldier. This was partly a conscious posturing in the presence of the old heroic tales that Arnold was from his own inner nature to reenact. André also had worldly motives similar to Arnold's. He was, it is true, an inheritor of money as Arnold was not, and his family was higher in the mercantile scale, yet trade was considered in eighteenth-century English aristocratic circles an occupation unworthy of gentlemen. André's military achievements brought him, as Arnold was brought, into contact with social superiors who would otherwise not have countenanced him. Yet, like Arnold, he was resented by some as an upstart. He had failed, when ambition led him into his final gamble, really to achieve acceptance.

Fighting, killing, conquering came naturally to Arnold, but when the pageantry of British military life swung over into actual warfare, André was far from edified. He became, after unhappy experiences as a prisoner of war, a soldier by intellectual conversion. Not a fighter but a staff officer, he was nonetheless more brutal than Arnold. Where Arnold killed as an aspect of the game of battle, André schemed killing as terror. Yet he held on to romantic ideas that Arnold never consciously harbored, setting out with a blithe sense of adventure to a rendezvous that was for Arnold soul's torture. If André (as seems possible) gained his ascendancy over the British commander in chief, Sir Henry Clinton, partly through homosexuality, this adds to the picture a not incongruous note.

With André added to Arnold, the story still lacked the beautiful villainess who heightens any such story. Not wishing to stint her epic saga, Nature designed Peggy Shippen expertly, if cynically, for perfect effect. Although Peggy was young and small and fair and femininely appealing, there was more iron in her makeup than in either of the men's. The treason may well have been, in the first instance, her creation. Her closest literary prototype was Lady Macbeth. But her sleepwalking scene was not the result of a "mind diseased" by horror and guilt. It was the calculated playacting of a woman who had long used hysteria to achieve her ends. Not for her the lines, "All the perfumes of Arabia cannot sweeten these little hands." She put those hands to work to make the best of the situation in which the treason threw her and her children. Alone of the three protagonists she triumphed.

Trying to do justice in a factual biography to events so dramatic involves violating the conception, fondly held in some circles, that a true telling of past happenings must be a stolid piling of fact on fact. Practitioners of this methodology view excitement as an exterior ingredient poured on, as if it were a French chef's sauce, by a "popularizing" author. In actuality, not excitement but dullness is, in any human chronicle, the additive from outside.

There breathes not a man with soul so dead that he does not find his own life exciting, even if the drama lies in the drab despair that makes him weep in a lonely room over the emptiness of his existence. People who, by making a mark in the world, become biographical subjects believe in their own stars, often bringing to their visions dreams as perfervid as the creations of the most extreme romantic poets. To distill this excitement out of historical writing is to apply censorship as distorting as any other effort to force fact into a preconceived mold.

Nature is a fierce creator. She begins every life with an act of the greatest mystery and melodrama. And she lurks as an assassin at the end of every biographical road. In between, she throws aloft ardors and crises with all the lavishness of an artist gone wild.

Looked at in this broad context, the lives narrated in this book are not in essence different from every life story. What is unusual is that the events here told fall with such fidelity into patterns which the human imagination has accepted as fraught with the highest drama. From a scholarly point of view, this kinship to legend should be no deterrent, since the historian must, like the reporter or the detective, be able to go anywhere his trade calls him. But from a literary point of view, recounting a saga (whether in fiction or biography) presents serious problems.

The resemblance of the events portrayed to traditional epics

xvi

cannot be ignored. It will be in the reader's mind and must therefore be in the writer's. Passages that would not seem flat in some other kind of narrative fall flat in such a work. The writer must sometimes do his best to buckle on the wings of Pegasus. Yet those wings are dangerous appendages, paradoxically the more so when the call for them is so obvious. The writer has every reason to fear that in dealing with events supremely romantic he will fly too high. Verisimilitude can easily disappear into what will seem conventional posturing.

All the great universals of humanity are clichés, and thus the closer a literary passage approaches exalted themes, the greater the danger of sideslipping into the sentimental, the shrill, the obvious. Yet an amulet exists against this danger. Although there is no greater cliché than love, no such thought will occur to a lover who is holding in his arms the woman he most desires. Love can be reborn in all its original ardor by the immediacy of the situation. The universal ceases to be a cliché when it is specifically applied.

It follows that the requirements of historical scholarship can be of great assistance in achieving elevated effects, for such scholarship depends primarily on the establishment of specific facts. There exist hardly any authentic details relevant to his subject which cannot contribute, if properly handled, to the ends of a biographer. Yet some details strike more powerfully than others. The more voluminous (within reason) the record, the more fortunate the biographer, since he is given more alternatives to choose from.

I found Nature endlessly indulgent when I wrote *The Traitor and the Spy*. As the narrative became more exciting, requiring therefore to be more firmly rooted to detail, the record expanded to satisfy the immediate international concern with what had happened. Long letters were written by those who had been on the scene, and there were not less than three court trials with recorded testimony, questions and answers.

The personalities as well as the action that were revealed surpassed my greediest hopes. Not even Shakespeare could have conceived a more effective and perfectly integrated comic relief than that supplied by the two yokels who resentfully rowed the boat

xvii

that brought André and Arnold together. It was a perfect stroke to have the brutish shrewdness of these low-comedy boatmen warp dangerously the elevated conspirators' history-threatening plans.

In addition to clinging doggedly to detail, the biographer dealing with events of the most throbbing emotion should (like a novelist in the same situation) use extreme literary restraint. Although the great scenes must be carefully prepared for, so that their significance will be completely manifest, once the horses start galloping, the author must step backwards. His style should become stark, laconic, purely factual. It would be courting disaster to report with more than the greatest sobriety Peggy's hysterics during which she ran around almost naked and bamboozled Washington into believing her a victim not a promoter of the treason. It would be a desecration for the author to interpose his own sentiments between his readers and the nobility with which John André, when the hangman's rope swung above and toward him, conducted the fatal ritual of his own execution.

The republication of this book after the passage of twenty-two years must raise in the reader's mind, as it did in the author's, concern as to whether the text is now out of date. I was gratified to discover that during the interval no publication has brought to light any facts which change, to any significant degree, the story as here presented.

This volume is fully illustrated, unlike its predecessor, which contained only a frontispiece. The Source References were originally published in a separate pamphlet. They have been incorporated into this volume.

CONTENTS

CONTENTS

Book Four: LOVE

Book Five: TREASON

ILLUSTRATIONS

ILLUSTRATIONS

Book One

PEACE

CHAPTER ONE

Morning Shows the Day

AS BRAVE on the battlefield as any man who lived, Benedict Arnold told a patriot leader that "his courage was acquired, and that he was a coward till he was fifteen years old."

Arnold came from a proud though depressed line. His great-great-grandfather had been associated with Roger Williams in the founding of Rhode Island, and the immigrant's son, the first Benedict Arnold, had started the procession of very rich men who have walked Newport's streets. However, Benedict II lost most of the family fortune. His son, Benedict III, the father of the traitor, was apprenticed to a cooper and moved to the inland Connecticut port of Norwich under humble circumstances. All his neighbors knew how he had lifted himself. He had entered the employ of Absalom King, who navigated his own ships to Europe and the West Indies from the town docks on New England's Thames River. When King died at sea, Benedict III married his widow, the former Hannah Waterman. Since she belonged to a leading local family and had inherited King's fortune, Arnold rose with a single bound into the social and financial aristocracy of a community extremely conscious of rank. Every Sunday in church Benedict III strutted down the aisle to a front pew, leaving far in the rear his brother Oliver Arnold, who had accompanied him to Norwich but had remained a cooper.

Benedict III's first son, Benedict, was born in 1738 and died less than a year later. When on January 14, 1741, another boy appeared, he too was named after his father. The child toddled out onto the street as an inheritor of wealth and position. Fascinated with his change of fortune, the elder Benedict had expanded King's business in a series of bold strokes, even building alongside the family residence a retail shop in which he sold the wares he brought from overseas. Artisans bowed respectfully to his little son, and the parents of Benedict's playmates were pleased to have him in their parlors.

The boy's privileged position lasted just long enough to make clear to him, when the family prestige vanished, what he had lost. His father overexpanded the business, and as the inevitable reckoning came, tried to cheat his creditors, sacrificing his reputation without saving his fortune. The Arnold store and ships, the family luxuries, were swept away by a rising tide of failure. Soon, when it was necessary to serve on the debtor yet another paper, the sheriff did not bother to go to the countinghouse; it was quicker to seek him in the taverns. That the elder Benedict responded with a sense of persecution was revealed when he promised payment to one man to reward him "for your ingenuity in waiting on me, when almost all my other creditors were severe to me."

As her husband's infirmities became increasingly clear, Mrs. Arnold became ever more dominant in the household. And in the village, everyone pitied her; her celebrity as a pious, long-suffering woman mounted. When little Benedict met her fine relations on the street, they either looked the other way or greeted him too effusively. Even the prominent pew in church which, out of respect for Mrs. Arnold, had not been taken from her, was an embarrassment to her son since it made more conspicuous the raggedness of his clothes.

Benedict spent his winters in nearby Canterbury, Connecticut, where he had been sent to a school kept by his mother's kinsman, the Reverend James Cogswell. Mrs. Arnold bombarded her son with good advice by letter: "Keep a steady watch over your thoughts, words, and actions, be dutiful to superiors, obliging to equals, and affable to inferiors, if any such there be. Always choose that your companions be your betters, that by their good examples you may learn." She urged him to spend the shillings she sent to him "prudently, as you are accountable to God and your father." *

When Benedict was twelve, Norwich was struck by yellow fever. His mother wrote to him in Canterbury that the entire family was infected, and two of his sisters were dying. "My dear, God seems to be saying to all, 'Children, be ye also ready!' Pray, take the exhortation, for the call to you is very speaking, that God should smite your sisters and spare you as yet. . . . Pray, improve your time and beg God to grant His spirit, or death may overtake you unprepared, for His commission seems sealed for a great many, and for aught you know you may be one of them. My dear, fly to Christ! If you don't know the way, tell Him. He is the way; He only is the door. Plead for the guidance of the Holy Spirit to guide you to that only shelter from death eternal, for death temporal we must all try sooner or later. . . . Your groaning sisters give love to you. God may mete you with this disease wherever you be, for it is His servant, but I would not have you come home for fear it should be presumption. My love to you—beg you will write us. I have sent you one pound chocolate."

The mother's anguish was justified, for two of her daughters soon died. While a comparatively young woman, she had lost her first husband; of her seven children, only Benedict and a younger sister, Hannah, remained. If we may judge from her letters, Mrs. Arnold was permanently saddened, obsessed by death and fear of what might come after. Her first duty, she felt, was to prepare her surviving children to "step off the banks of time" by urging them to submit cheerfully to God's will in all things, so that they might receive His grace. The same message was dinned into Benedict's ears by his preceptor, who, famous throughout Connecticut as a logician, expounded in the classroom and from the pulpit the doctrines of Old Light Congregationalism. The exhortations Benedict gave his own children reveal that he was deeply impressed.

The winged death's heads on the gravestones of Arnold's sisters grimaced at the little boy, and he had been taught no solution but to say, "Thy will be done." Yet he could not say it in his heart, could hardly think it, for submission was completely alien to his

* The spelling and punctuation have been modernized in all documents quoted.

temperament. For him the word "philosopher" was synonymous with "weakling." Trembling, he despised himself as a coward. Then gradually, painfully, he worked out solutions of his own.

As with the other neighborhood boys he waited beside the mill for the grain they had brought to be ground, Arnold eyed the great wheel that turned in the flood. It was terrifying in its fierce energy, and suddenly he knew what he had to do. Clambering up on the dam, he threw himself on the wheel, and, hugging the slimy wood to his chest, went round and round through the violent water. When finally he dived into the lower stream, clearing with ease the thundering blades, he saw admiration on the faces of his companions.

Even after his neighbors had decided he was annoyingly brave, he still had to force himself on such occasions as the evening when the whole town turned out to watch a house burn. The firemen had given up and were standing in the crowd, their painted leather buckets dangling at their sides, when a dark figure appeared high up, in the very center—or so it seemed—of the flames. Benedict strolled out along the already cracking ridgepole, lit by the splendor of fire.

Such exploits, which every month came more easily until at last he hardly felt a tremor, made him a leader in the semiautonomous society of boys; and there he displayed gifts that were to bring him greatness in that other semiautonomous world, the army. His childhood companions respected his ingenuity in thinking up pranks, his skill at skating, riding, shooting at the mark. Benedict tolerated no insubordination, but, so some of his neighbors remembered, he was not a bully. No authentic record from any period of his life shows him torturing the weak—he preferred to cast himself as their protector. Yet he always enjoyed toppling the strong. He picked fights with bigger boys.[1]

When on Thanksgiving, evening succeeded to the morning sermons and the afternoon athletic contests, the boys traditionally lighted bonfires. "The high hills in Norwich," an old inhabitant wrote, "are in fine vantage ground, from which these tall and vivid volumes of flame send forth a flood of light over the woods and

[1] Text notes begin on page 409.

valleys, houses and streams below, producing a truly picturesque effect." Benedict felt called on to build a fire that would be long remembered, but all really satisfactory fuel belonged to his elders. The tar barrels he fixed on had to be stolen from a shipyard. He had almost got them to the top of the highest hill when the constable came puffing up, "a stout, grave man," grim with adult authority. The only solution Arnold could think of was to throw off his coat and dare the officer to fight.

As Benedict dashed through the town on high-spirited and antisocial errands, it was impossible not to notice that he was more vital and energetic than the better-behaved boys. Short but powerfully built, muscular, with a strong hook nose, dark skin, and light blue eyes, he was recognized as "bold, enterprising, ambitious, active as lightning." Not all the inhabitants of Norwich were, like Mrs. Arnold, primarily concerned with preparing for another world. They enjoyed amassing property in this one and could use able assistants. Shrewd merchants stared after the bad boy, wondering whether he could be tamed.

The town's most distinguished citizens, Drs. Daniel and Joshua Lathrop, decided to make the experiment, perhaps because they were kinsmen of Mrs. Arnold. Growing herbs in huge gardens and greenhouses, importing in a single shipment drugs to the value of £8,000, they dominated the apothecary trade of southern New England. "At an early age," Benedict became their apprentice.

At first he found it hard to settle down. During 1755, a drummer pounded out a march on the main street of Norwich, and then a recruiting officer in a noble uniform called for volunteers to fight the French on the northern frontier. Without asking anyone's permission, Benedict signed up. Neither his mother nor the Lathrops were impressed. Mrs. Arnold wept and said he was too young; the Lathrops produced indentures to prove he was bound to them. Soon he was again sweeping out the store.

"It is said," James Stedman of Norwich wrote Jared Sparks in 1834, "that not long after this he ran away again and enlisted in the army and went to Ticonderoga and other places on the lines. Being employed in garrison duty, and finding no fighting which his soul seemed to long after . . . he deserted." Although this story has been repeated until it has become American legend, a complex of evidence indicates that it is false. What Stedman himself considered an unsubstantiated rumor seems to have been a garbled version of an appeal published in the New York *Gazette* on May 21, 1759, for the apprehension of a deserter called Benedict Arnold. The deserter was almost certainly the future general's distant cousin.[2]

The Lathrops released their apprentice for military service only on one occasion of great emergency. In August 1757, Fort William Henry was besieged by the French and many Indians; if this strong point on Lake George fell, an easy route to New England would be open to the savage tribes. Benedict and the other young men of Norwich galloped northward. He was probably on the road when word came that the fort had fallen and its garrison—1,500 men, the excited messenger reported—had been massacred by the Indians. The young warrior's heart beat high with anger and excitement, but the only result was frustration. As thousands of farm boys poured into the woods north of Albany, the enemy returned to Canada. Now Arnold saw for the first time how unruly the militia could become. Uncomfortable without tents and cooking utensils, furious at not being allowed to chase after the vanished foe, they rioted, threatened to shoot their officers, and deserted in disgust. Benedict's company returned to Norwich after he had served thirteen days.

Although Benedict undoubtedly longed to join the fighting, this abortive gallop seems to have constituted his entire military experience during the French and Indian War. The Lathrops had legal control over their apprentice, and he could comfort himself with the thought that, since they filled major contracts for the army, he was making a contribution to the cause. At the same time, he was learning an art that was always to fascinate him, the art of making money. His masters did not limit their activities to their highly profitable traffic in drugs. Their European agents bought whatever could be secured at a bargain, and thus Benedict was concerned with the sale of goods that ranged from French wines to silks woven in India. Although his enemies were to accuse him, after he became famous, of having been "a half-bred apothecary," he was actually being trained in handling large-scale affairs.

He lived in Dr. Daniel Lathrop's Georgian mansion, surrounded by formal gardens; he was served by colored slaves. His employer, who had studied medicine in London, was as cultured as he was rich; the newest books from abroad appeared in his library as a matter of course. Mrs. Lathrop was the daughter of Joseph Talcott, the first native-born governor of Connecticut. Like the English aristocrats whose way of life they admired, the Lathrops felt their eminence had placed upon them social responsibility; they combined pride with benevolence. The Congregational Church, Yale College, and the Norwich Free School profited by their largess.

When Benedict was sent out on errands, he often rode in their chaise, a long, low, dun affair, studded thick along the edges with brass nails. Such equipages were rare in inland Connecticut, and this one, which flaunted its grandeur by bearing a coat of arms, was criticized by Norwich democrats as "a lamentable proof of aristocratic pride." Benedict received many annoyed and envious looks as he rattled along in splendor. He sat all the straighter because his own family was falling to pieces.

When Benedict was eighteen, his mother made the departure from time for which she had so long been preparing. No force remained to keep his father from the gutter. On May 26, 1760, "one of his Majesty's grand jurors" swore out a warrant for the elder Benedict's arrest, stating that he "was drunken in said Norwich, so that he was disabled in the use of his understanding and reason, appearing in his speech, gesture, and behavior, which is against the peace of Our Lord, the King, and the laws of this Colony." The sheriff duly reported that he had "arrested the body of the within named Benedict Arnold," but whether the derelict was jailed or not no record reveals. The family homestead was sold for debt, and, during 1761, the father died.

As the Arnold family dropped away, Mrs. Lathrop poured on the apprentice her frustrated motherhood. Her own three children had died in a single epidemic, and, although the tragedy was years old, she meditated on it daily. Once more, Benedict heard endless sermons on the imminence of dissolution, the need for grace. His reaction shocked all Norwich, for it involved blasphemy.

One morning the sky darkened as for the Last Judgment, and there burst over the town such a tremendous thunderstorm as roars from the Connecticut hills only once in a generation. The air was green with live leaves torn from the thrashing trees. Convinced that God manifested His displeasure in natural calamities, the citizens knew He was angry. In houses all over town, men and women were on their knees. But in the Lathrops' shop Arnold leaped up on a counter, and raised his flushed face to the heavens. At each tremendous flash and blast, he waved the hat he held in his hand. He cheered in unison with the thunder, defying his mother's God with "profane exclamations."

Such behavior did not detract from his efficiency in business. Behind the Lathrops' mansion, a still gurgled as it made elixirs; men delved and wrangled in the greenhouses and herb gardens; heavy carts rumbled up from the water front; lighter carts set out for the countryside; warehouses filled up and emptied and filled up again; pens scratched in ledgers; clerks displayed goods; money poured into the tills. Through this domain, Benedict walked each year with a more self-confident stride; his voice began to ring out, giving orders. When his apprenticeship was over, he was so useful to the Lathrops that they did not wish to let him go. He stayed for a few months, but he was restive; he wanted to set up a business for himself. Finally, his employers thanked him for his services—or so he always claimed—by giving him £500 with which to establish an apothecary shop in New Haven. Carrying letters of recommendation from the Lathrops, he departed for London to buy goods with which to stock his store.

CHAPTER TWO

A Warlike Merchant

IN LONDON, Benedict Arnold found elegant lodgings at Holborn. "Exceedingly fond of dress," he was careful to appear in the style of a great Colonial gentleman when he visited the merchants to whom he had letters. Men who could buy and sell him a hundred times over bowed low at his approach and pressed goods upon him. Since the pro-English commercial laws that were causing revolutionary agitation in America drained hard money from the Colonies, London wholesalers, if they were to ship across the ocean, had to extend credit. Arnold was enchanted to accept it.

The fledgling merchant intended to sweep New Haven off its feet. Every day timid men opened little shops that vanished again because no one noticed them, but people would notice his store. The first apothecary shop in the city, it would be crowded with English goods. He was doing a favor to the London sellers by using every bit of credit they would give him, since he thus assured his own success and their eventual payment. The Connecticut minister, Samuel A. Peters, heard that Arnold bought "apothecary wares and dry goods to the value of three or four thousand pounds, and a chariot."

Soon a new sign appeared near New Haven's water front: "B. Arnold, Druggist, Bookseller, etc. From London." To this utilitarian message the youth added his motto, *"Sibi Totique"*—for himself and for all. According to Peters, Arnold "flourished away as an apothecary and merchant, kept ten horses and as many servants, and broke in two years. His creditors threw him into jail." After about six weeks of imprisonment, he was released by an act for the relief of debtors passed in May 1763, which enabled him to settle for a few shillings on the pound.

A few months more and he was ready to revive the family reputation in Norwich. Writing himself down as "of New Haven, merchant," he bought back the homestead which his father had lost. Standing by his side as he flourished his signature down on the deed, his sister Hannah looked on with admiring eyes.

Hannah, who occupied the reclaimed house, was "pleasing in her person, witty, and affable." On first meeting her, men wondered why she was not married, but they soon found out. She talked endlessly of the virtues of her brother. When Benedict came for a visit, how gaily she amused him by making fun of her suitors! On one occasion, however, she seemed constrained. Then there walked through the door, with easy familiarity, a dark man who spoke with an accent. That his sister should encourage any suitor was bad enough, but this creature was a Frenchman! Benedict forbade him the house, on pain of bodily injury. Hannah was docility itself, but when he was back in New Haven he began to wonder. He galloped to Norwich, and sure enough, he heard the Frenchman's voice in the parlor. He stationed himself on the lawn, and commanded a servant to beat on the door. When the suitor came leaping out of the window, Arnold fired at him but—perhaps on purpose—missed. The suitor thereupon left town. Arnold, so it is said, later met him in Honduras and severely wounded him in a duel. As for Hannah, she never married.

Arnold soon needed the money he had put into the Norwich house; he sold it and brought Hannah to New Haven, where she tended his store. By hook and by crook, he again collected an expensive stock. The volumes he offered were in themselves an education: Plutarch and Rousseau; Smollett and Milton; histories, both sacred and secular; English, French, Latin, and Greek grammars; complete letter writers; and books with such fine titles as *Virtue the Source of Pleasure*. Among the drugs were Frances's Female Elixir, Greenough's Tincture for the Teeth, Spirits of Scurvy Grass, and all kinds of pomatum and cold cream. He sold "neat watches," painters' colors, necklaces and earrings, "a very elegant assortment of metzotinto pictures," stationery, tea, rum, sugar, mustard.

However, Arnold was restless behind a counter. First in partnership and then, as he grew more prosperous, on his own, he bought ships. Almost every spring he watched New Haven shrink at the end of a rollicking plain of water; autumn had come when he saw his sister and the shop again. Leaving transatlantic trade to bigger vessels out of larger ports, he sailed his sloops and brigantines, which were less than 100 feet over-all, through estuaries and coastal waters from Canada to the Indies.

When he started from home, the hold of his boat was fitted like a stable and filled with horses; lumber was lashed on deck. Putting in at the Windward Islands, he tried to dispose of his cargo for cash or rum. If he got cash, he expended it on European goods at Antigua or the Bay of Honduras, at St. Croix or St. Eustatius. He was in effect traveling around Europe, since these bits of land belonged to different nations. Moving easily from one currency and customs system to another, a man who was not inclined to confide in revenue officers found many ways to make quick profits.

For the home voyage, Arnold loaded such European goods as he had secured, and crammed the remaining space with rum, sugar, and molasses. Stopping off wherever there was a pound to be made, he came at last to New Haven, where he unloaded his cargo and filled up again with woolen goods and the cheese that brought a great price to the northward. Sometimes he tacked up the Hudson to the Dutch settlers around Albany; more often he skirted the coast to Canada. In Quebec and Montreal, he traded his goods for the horses he would take to the Indies the following spring. When, a few years later, he appeared in Canada commanding an invading army, the ballad-makers of Quebec remembered him as "that famous jockey."

To keep his New Haven store going, Arnold was buying again from London factors. In 1768, six firms started action against him for £1,766.5.6. This time he was able to satisfy even so large a judgment. He turned over his sloop *Sally* as security and paid slowly, wrangling all the time about rates of exchange. When he had cash on hand, he hated to use it to pay his bills; he preferred to spend it on new speculations. He was, a contemporary wrote, "a bold adventurer in all his undertakings."

Since currency was scarce and not uniform; since, in the absence of banks, debts were paid by drafts on business associates, even the most cautiously managed affairs ran clumsily. Dealing with plungers as aggressive and as precariously established as himself, Arnold was always in controversy. When he saw a chance of persuading, he employed a robust good humor, but when he was crossed, his wrath swelled: "I assure you that it is with the utmost indifference I observe the unjust and false aspersions your malice could invent . . . as a consciousness of my uprightness and fairness in regard to our concerns will never suffer the opinion of you or any other blockhead to give me any uneasiness. And it is with equal indifference I observe your threats in regard to the contract which will rather induce me to come to New York than otherwise; as I should take a pleasure in convincing the world that your unjust aspersions are equally false, cruel and ungrateful." Indeed, he planned to have his correspondent arrested "which I hope will prevent any more of your impertinency."

In 1764, the enactment of the Sugar Act fell so heavily on the Indies trade that no New Haven merchant, as an official admitted, had "the most distant intention of paying the duties." Smuggling, however, became a ticklish business, since the law made offending ships liable to confiscation. Anger mounted on the water front and then was fanned to fury by the Stamp Act, but the town's conservative, agricultural aristocracy remained unmoved: they regarded the traders who were being hard hit as undesirable upstarts. Rioting did not begin until Arnold returned from a voyage.

When Peter Boles, one of his sailors, tried to inform against him, Arnold, so he admitted openly, gave the informer "a little chastisement." Under his captain's burning eyes, Boles agreed that he had been "instigated by the devil," and that "I justly deserve the halter for my malicious and cruel intentions." He promised to leave New Haven—but did not do so. "I then made," Arnold wrote, "one of the party that took him to the whipping post, where he received near forty lashes with a small cord, and was conducted out of town."

Horrified to find the violence that they deplored in other communities kindling in their own, the New Haven grand jurors swore out a warrant for Arnold and his companions. The water-front mob replied by burning two of the jurors in effigy. Calling a town meeting, the conservative citizens agreed to "assist one another and particularly the civil authorities in restoring order." A street fight seemed imminent when the justices of the peace achieved a compromise by finding against the whipping mob but awarding Boles the insulting damages of fifty shillings.

Arnold then published his account of the affair which contains the earliest known statement of his political philosophy: "Is it good policy, or would so great a number of people in any trading town on the continent, New Haven excepted, vindicate, caress and protect an informer, a character—particularly at this alarming time—so justly odious to the public? . . . One would imagine every sensible man would strive to encourage trade and discountenance such useless, such infamous informers."

In 1767, Arnold married Margaret Mansfield. Her father, Samuel Mansfield, had inherited from his own father the post of high sheriff; he came from one of New Haven's few old merchant families and was considered "a very respectable character." Our querulous informant Peters insists that Mansfield opposed his daughter's marriage to a nobody. However, father and son-in-law were soon in partnership; the older man attended to the business in New Haven, while the younger sailed their boats and managed their overseas trade.

The twenty-two-year-old bride was certainly handsome, for Arnold was too conscious of the eyes of the world to marry an unattractive woman. Three sons appeared in quick succession: Benedict, Richard, Henry. Since Arnold lodged several of his own and his wife's relations, his house became full of voices; yet he was desperately lonely. Peggy Mansfield comes down through history as a silence. Always her husband appealed to her for understanding, for sympathy, for emotional support; always he appealed in vain.

"I am now in the greatest anxiety and suspense," he wrote her from Quebec, "not knowing whether I write to the living or the dead, not having heard the least syllable from you this four months. I have wrote you almost every post somehow." He wondered why she had not sent him the cash he had asked for. "My dearest life, you cannot imagine the trouble and fatigue I have gone through since here." Two of his sailors had informed against him to the customs authorities, and he had almost lost his vessel. No sooner had he adjusted this matter than he was arrested on the complaint of a New York merchant for a debt which he insisted he had settled eight years before. To prevent a costly lawsuit, he had promised to pay and had put up a bond. Although he should sail at once for Barbados, he would await the next post, "and shall be very unhappy if I have not the pleasure of hearing you and our dear ones are well." In a postscript he speaks of his "anxious and aching heart"; there had been no letter.

From New York, he wrote, "Was I not the most unfortunate man living, you would hardly believe me when I tell you I have been laid up with a severe fit of the gout. . . . The dear Providence seems to frown on us in every respect. Be not discouraged, but bear our misfortunes with fortitude and without repining, since the race is not to the swift, etc. We may daily see objects more miserable than ourselves, who, perhaps, are less deserving [of misery]. Time and patience, which overcomes all things, will, I hope, produce fairer prospects and a happier day for us both. . . . Pray, take care of yourself and do not worry too much."

He tried by letters to his associates to shield his Peggy from the importunities of his creditors which might cause her "trouble and uneasiness"; he sent paragraph after paragraph of love to her and "our dear little prattlers"; he described his forlorn condition in long passages of eloquent self-pity; but the end was always the same: "I assure you I think it hard that you have wrote me only once when there have been so many opportunities." "You cannot imagine how anxious I am to see you and be once more among my friends," he exclaimed—but when he reached home, he found no comfort there.

One winter his wife would not let him touch her. A rumor was circulating that Arnold had contracted "the venereal disease at Jamaica and the Bay"; that he had kept bad company and been perpetually drunk; that his duel with Mr. Brookman was "occasioned by a dispute about a whore I wanted to take from him." Asserting that "the peace and reputation of an innocent and injured family is at stake," Arnold sued one of his associates for slander, and sent to the tropics for evidence. When his envoy brought back depositions so carelessly worded that they would not hold in a Connecticut court, Arnold refused to pay him, and was thrown into another lawsuit.

All this public screaming did not placate his Peggy or improve his reputation; nor did the many appeals to heaven with which he interlarded his conversation keep the Puritan statesman, Roger Sherman, from considering him "an irreligious and profane character. . . . I remember he sued a man at New Haven for saying he had the foul disease."

Although Arnold was making money, he had not won the respect of his neighbors; in New Haven as in Norwich, he felt undervalued. He could no longer escape into a special world of boys; now his sanctuary was the unpopulated ocean. Although on his short and cargo-encumbered decks he could pace hardly further than an animal in its cage, he felt almost free. He was undisputed master of the five or six sailors who were his only fellow men; he had no enemy but tempest, which fought fair and without rancor. Concerning strong weather, he noted impassively: "Fresh breeze until 6 P.M. The remainder of the day blows excessively hard in squalls from south to west, and plenty rain. Large sea."

When trees, whether palms or pines, appeared over the horizon, tranquillity vanished. People closed in on him again; he had to prove his worth, often with senseless violence. At the Bay of Honduras he forgot to attend the party of a British trader, Captain Croskie, and when he rowed over to explain, the captain, who was suffering from a hangover, cursed him as a damned American without breeding. The next morning, the two men met in mortal combat. Croskie, who had the first shot, missed. Arnold wounded him, but only slightly. After surgeons had stemmed the blood, Arnold stated that he was ready to receive another shot, but "gave notice that if his opponent missed again, he would kill him." Croskie apologized. In such personal encounters, the future general, who had never seen a battle, was becoming used to gunfire.

He was getting less experience in politics. During those years, private letters were commonly crammed with discussions of constitutional matters, but it took a major event like the Boston Massacre to deflect Arnold from his personal affairs. He had been "shocked," he wrote from St. George's Key at "the most cruel, wanton, and inhuman murders. . . . Good God! are Americans all asleep and tamely giving up their glorious liberties, or are they all turned philosophers, that they don't take immediate vengeance on such miscreants? I am afraid of the latter and that we shall all soon see ourselves as poor and as much oppressed as ever heathen philosopher was. But enough of politics."

When he was home in New Haven, Arnold was concerned not with discussions of human rights but with action. He led one of the "trained mobs," made up mostly of men disfranchised by the property requirements, that poured from taverns to terrorize conservative voters. When the Reverend Peters, driven from Windham, arrived in New Haven, Arnold's ruffians visited him. The preacher was to claim that he had proved Arnold a coward by frightening him with a pistol, but actually, when Arnold led his men away, he was following the policy of the Sons of Liberty, who kept the Tories moving by threats, but preferred not to injure them. Peters soon fled to London.

As the winds of civil conflict rose, Arnold forgot the winds of ocean. In December 1774, the sons of leading New Haven families banded together to form a company of the elite Governor's Foot Guard, and invited the aggressive water-front raider to join them. Soon he was parading on the green in "a scarlet coat of common length, the lapels, cuffs, and collar of buff and trimmed with plain silver buttons; white linen vest, breeches and stockings; black half-leggings; and a small, fashionable and narrow ruffled shirt." His military bearing so impressed his elegant companions that they elected him their captain; he found himself shouting orders to the sons of families that had despised him.

To make visible his rise in worldly eminence, Arnold began to build on Water Street a house in the very latest style, with a central hallway, gambrel roof, and pediments over the windows. He put a hundred fruit trees in the two-acre lot, and erected "neat stables" for ten or twelve horses, and a coach house for two carriages. Peters considered this establishment "by far the grandest in New Haven." Although Arnold, as he asserted, spent £1,800, the inside was only half finished when every bell in town clamored.

At Lexington and Concord, redcoats and Minute Men had fired at each other; Massachusetts was at war. Arnold gleefully sharpened his sword, but his neighbors gathered dejectedly on street corners. Conservative New Haven felt even more conservative on that grievous day; even men who had signed angry petitions were frightened. A town meeting voted neutrality and appointed a committee to see that no warlike acts were undertaken. As the members paced to their first meeting, they had to dodge Arnold's men running full tilt to a rendezvous on the green.

The sixty militiamen answered with wild cheering when Arnold asked whether they were ready to fight the British. However, the committeemen had the keys to the powder house. Drums boomed and fifes tweetled as Arnold led his first command on its first military mission: to terrify the town fathers. He paraded his company before the tavern where the committee was sitting; then he stormed into the conference. When the officials, including his superior in the Connecticut militia, Colonel David Wooster, pointed out that the town meeting had legally voted neutrality, Arnold damned the town meeting. Wooster, hoping the troops would be more reasonable than their captain, went out and advised them in a fatherly manner to wait for orders. Arnold interrupted, threatened to break down the door of the powder house, and shouted, "None but Almighty God shall prevent my marching!" The committee released the keys.

For thirty-three years of peace Arnold had been unhappy; now he marched jubilantly to war.

CHAPTER THREE

Dear Julia and Her Enchanting Friend

EVENING sank murkily in Warnford Court, behind London's Throgmorton Street. The clerks closed the ledgers in which all day they had been copying figures, blew out their candles, and shuffled away. In one office, a young man of nineteen sat longer over his labors, his brown eyes staring heavily from under sullen brows. Into his window came the sound of home-going feet, but no exclamations, no laughter, none of the gaiety he had recently known at Buxton and Lichfield. Gathering up his documents with a weary sigh, he placed letter paper before him, and then his supple features came alive.

"From the midst of books, papers, bills, and other implements of gain," he wrote, "let me lift up my drowsy head awhile to converse with dear Julia. And first, as I know she has a fervent wish to see me a quill-driver, I must tell her that I begin, as people are wont to do, to look upon my future profession with great partiality. . . . Instead of figuring a merchant as a middle-aged man, with a bob wig, a rough beard, in snuff-colored clothes, grasping a guinea in his red hand, I conceive a comely young man, with a tolerable pigtail, wielding a pen with all the noble fierceness of the Duke of Marlborough brandishing a truncheon upon a signpost, surrounded with types and emblems, and canopied with cornucopias that disembogue their stores upon his head; Mercuries reclined upon bales of goods; Genii playing with pens, ink, and paper; while, in perspective, his gorgeous vessels, 'launched on the bosom of the silver Thames' are wafting to distant lands the produce of this commercial nation. . . . I see sumptuous palaces rising to receive me; I see orphans, and widows, and painters, and fiddlers, and poets, and builders, protected and encouraged; and when the fabric is pretty nearly finished by my shattered pericranium, I cast my eyes around and find John André, by a small coal fire, in a gloomy countinghouse in Warnford Court, nothing so little as what he has been making himself, and, in all probability, never to be much more than he is at present. But oh! my dear Honora!—it is for thy sake only I wish for wealth.—You say she was somewhat better at the time you wrote last. I flatter myself that she will soon be without any remains of this threatening disease." [1]

It had all started a few months before, during the summer of 1769, when his mother had taken the family to Buxton so that they might recover from the shock of his father's death, by drinking the mineral waters that bubbled there in healing springs. The town was not, like Bath, a center of fashion: instead of the Pump Room there were primitive stone domes over the wells; instead of the Parade, the stuffy parlors of gray inns, where the sick talked unceasingly of symptoms. Those were depressing days: his father just dead; he himself, as the oldest son, tied to the countinghouse, his dreams of military glory fading. When he tried to escape from his thoughts by walking outside the town, he entered an endless moor cut by fissures and dominated by cliffs; all was as barren as his existence promised to be.

But it was in Buxton, this waste place inhabited, as he thought, by whining invalids, that he met Anna Seward, the poetess whom he alone called by the sentimental name of Julia. She was a little stout perhaps, but commandingly handsome: her hair was red-gold and her eyes mirrored every emotion of her burning heart. Particularly when she recited her own verses, they enlarged until you hardly heard the words as you experienced the woman. In conversation, she poured forth everything she felt in an energetic stream; her talk was not of pounds and cargoes, but of art, literature, music, virtue, love.

Always with his dear Julia was his beloved Honora Sneyd, the blonde, blue-eyed ward of the Seward family who drooped silently on the poetess' arm like—the simile was inevitable—a bruised flower. Her cheeks were touchingly blanched by consumption, yet if André, as he argued with his Julia, turned to Honora for approval, her transparent skin ruddied in a blush.

The two ladies were as impressed by John as he was by them; indeed, the young man was to charm almost every person, male or female, he ever met. He was remembered as "well-made, rather slender, about five feet nine inches high, and remarkably active. His complexion was dark, his countenance good and somewhat serious." He "excelled" in "drawing, painting, and dancing; and professed the modern languages, particularly French, Italian, and German, to an uncommon degree of perfection. . . . His manner was so affable and attractive that he was pointed out as a man possessing those elegant and pleasing accomplishments so well known under the name of *the graces*." We have the word of a Connecticut militiaman that he was "the handsomest man I ever laid eyes on."

John's dark skin and his vivacity testified to Gallic ancestry. His father, Anthony André, belonged to a Swiss merchant family which had scattered over Europe for the purposes of trade. Born in Genoa, Anthony was raised at the family headquarters in Geneva. As a young man, he had come with a brother to London, where the two were naturalized in 1748. They set up a prosperous countinghouse, and soon Anthony married Marie Louise Giradot, a Parisian who had been visiting an aunt in Bristol.

A portrait of the bride, by a minor French painter, has come down in the family. Never was a picture conceived in terms more gaily elegant. Mrs. André wears a silk dress frothing with lace and brocade, and from neck to hip there is looped a tremendous sash of flowers. More flowers entwine her brow, and her dark hair flies free with fashionable abandon behind sloping shoulders and a swanlike neck. Yet, when the artist came to her features, he could not make them accord with his frivolous composition: her eyes were less coquettish than competent. The portrait reveals an uneasy dichotomy between two ways of life: Mrs. André's pose is aristocratic; but the expression on her face belongs to the *bourgeoisie*.

John André was not born in 1751 as all books state and even his tomb in Westminster Abbey implies. According to the records of St. Martin Orgars, a French Protestant Church in London, he was born on May 2, 1750, and baptized there on May 16. Thus he was a year older than has always been believed. He was the eldest of a family of five: three sisters and a baby brother ten years his junior.

The record of his baptism is in French. The family spoke that language at least some of the time, and kept close connections with the Continent, yet John was to write home in English, and he never struck his British companions as having a foreign air. At first the family lived over the shop in Warnford Court from which Anthony traded with the Levant and handled his properties in the West Indies; but they soon escaped to the suburb of Clapton, where Anthony bought the "Manor House," a residence large enough to be later used as a school. Here Anthony lived the life of a country gentleman, as far as was possible for a newcomer who was engaged in trade.

John's early schooling was entrusted to a minister in nearby Hackney. Half-senile, afflicted with "gout, rheumatism, and the stone," the Reverend Thomas Newcomb would drowse in his chair as the boy danced around him; then the heavy lids would lift to reveal eyes still touched with fire, and from the old man's lips would come tales of how he had cut down Defoe in a satire; how Pope had stolen whole passages from him to include in the *Dunciad;* how he had helped Young compose his *Night Thoughts.* Critics, Newcomb insisted, had considered his long paean to religion, *The Last Judgement of Men and Angels,* as great as Milton; but now he was old and forgotten, times were mean, the giants were all buried. His pupil should read the great monuments of the past, and, with the prejudices and reminiscences of the old poet running along as a gloss, John found them fascinating. When André himself scribbled verses, Newcomb grudgingly admitted that they were not bad for an infant in those feeble modern times.

According to the earliest account of his childhood, the boy moved on from Newcomb to St. Paul's School, Westminster; however, the records of that fashionable institution are innocent of his name, and he certainly received the major part of his training on the Continent. The Swiss miniaturist Pierre Eugene Du Simitière regarded him as "a countryman of mine, although born in London, his family being of Geneva and himself sent there very young to be educated. Our tastes were similar, and we both learned to draw under the same master."

A sketch John made to commemorate the death of his brother's pet dog reveals a schoolboy's confusion of styles. A naked grave-digger in the center of the composition shows that he had drawn from the nude—a practice not encouraged in England; a cupid is based on memories of baroque painting; but the grieving family group is altogether boyish and altogether charming. His fashion-ably dressed sisters and he himself weep decorously over the still corpse, while his brother raises on a pole a legend of mourning. The tone is amazingly high-spirited for so macabre a subject.

In the manner of eighteenth-century gentlemen, John thought art no more than an agreeable accomplishment. As for the pursuit on which his family prosperity was based, he considered trade de-meaning. Since he was not rich enough to be a landed proprietor or pious enough for the ministry, the obvious career was the army, which also appealed to his romantic temperament. At the University of Geneva, he specialized in mathematics and military draw-ing. His father was not impressed. When sixteen or seventeen, the boy was called home and firmly sentenced to the countinghouse.

It was an active place, for the family business prospered—André despised the activity. He was scheming for escape when, on April 14, 1769, his father died. The passing of so influential a merchant was recorded in the *Gentleman's Magazine*; Anthony André's will showed that he was wealthy. In addition to providing for his wife, he placed £25,000 in the public funds to be divided among his five children. On John's twenty-first birthday, the young man would inherit what would be in modern currency at least $100,000. Yet, as the oldest male in his branch of the family, he was more than ever tied to the firm which was now under the direction of his uncle.

André was rebellious and his new friends, particularly his dear Julia, sympathized. The poetess was enchanted by the graceful and talented young man. But he was nineteen, and she, alas, was twenty-six. They were saved from having to exclude from their relationship the noblest of all emotions by the seventeen-year-old blonde who hung on the poetess's arm.

Dear Julia and Her Enchanting Friend

To Anna, her seventeen-year-old friend Honora was less an independent individual than an extension of herself. As a disciple of Rousseau, the poetess believed that human beings could be perfected by education, and years before she had resolved to make the family ward into a combination of her own personality and her sister's. The sister, so she wrote, would supply "the sweetness, the unerring discretion, and the self-command," while she herself contributed "the imagination, the sensibility, and the warm disdain of groveling propensities." As a result, Honora would, "by all those who know how to appreciate excellence, be acknowledged, like Miranda, 'to have been formed of every creature's best.'" When her sister died, Anna took completely into her own hands the shaping of her friend.

The child had at first been robust, but Anna had never trusted "the clear health which crimsons her cheeks and glitters in her eyes. Such an early expansion of intelligence and sensibility," she explained, "partakes too much of the angelic, too little of mortal nature to tarry long in these low abodes of frailty and pain." Then tuberculosis made Honora in fact the sickly angel Anna had always imagined her.

Anna had concluded that she herself would never experience romantic love that matched her imaginings. When her father, canon of Lichfield Cathedral and himself a poet, had inflated his pride by urging Anna to read Milton at the age of three, he had little suspected what a flood he was loosing. He was still pleased when at nine she could recite by heart the first three books of *Paradise Lost*, nor was he alarmed until, when Anna was fifteen, the famous Dr. Erasmus Darwin told him that his daughter was writing better verse than he. It struck him suddenly that she would be a scribbling old maid; he forbade her pen and paper, condemned her to needlework. But it was as useless as to command the ocean to stand still.

Although many men were attracted by Anna's intelligence, few could visualize the handsome bluestocking gracing a domestic hearth. The poetess thus described her final disillusionment. "When my attachment for General, then Cornet, V—— sunk in the snowdrifts of his altered conduct, Honora Sneyd . . . was commencing woman . . . more lovely, more amiable, more interesting than anything I ever saw in female form. . . . When disappointed love threw all the energies of my soul into the channel of friendship, Honora was its chief object. The charms of her society . . . made Lichfield an Edenic scene to me."

Anna and John decided he was in love with Honora; Honora agreed to be in love with him. Years later, the poetess wrote that the girl's affection had been "a mere compound of gratitude and esteem," but at the time everything was carried out according to the rules of high romance. In one of her poems, Anna tells how John succumbed to his lady's charms as he painted her miniature:

> *While with nice hand he mark'd the living grace,*
> *And matchless beauty of Honora's face*
> *Th' enamour'd Youth the faithful traces blest,*
> *That barb'd the dart of beauty in his breast;*
> *Around his neck th' enchanting Portrait hung*
> *While a warm vow burst ardent from his tongue.*

The Sewards invited the Andrés to return with them to Lichfield, where the youth was introduced to one of the nation's busiest literary coteries. Reacting against Dr. Johnson's earthy rationalism, Anna and her friends dedicated themselves to high emotion. The books they wrote, although today read only by scholars, were in those first years of the romantic movement enthusiastically praised. Dr. Darwin's *The Botanic Garden* was so successful that Wordsworth, whose own work was less admired, was irritated into writing his essay on poetic diction. And Anna herself, as the beloved "Swan of Lichfield," became England's most popular poetess.

Canon Seward's family lived within the cathedral close, and there, under the trees which he called "those good green people," John came to know Anna's enthusiastically artistic friends. He talked poetry with them where the shadows of the spires darkened the well-clipped lawn, and played his flute as they sang to their reflections in the minster pool. But he was to remember with the greatest excitement the headquarters of the movement, Anna's dressing room, where the poetess presided over a "select" group "united in the soft bonds of friendship," whose hearts were formed "of those affectionate materials so dear to the ingenuous tastes of

Julia and her Honora." As they amused themselves with "the sensible observation, the tasteful criticism, or the elegant song," they seemed, John continued, "combined together against the inclemency of the weather, the hurry, bustle, ceremony, censoriousness, and envy of the world."

André and his friends subscribed to optimistic humanitarianism. Unlike Arnold, who was taught that an individual could be saved from original sin only by the intervention of divine grace, they believed that man was naturally good. If man did not show it, that was because he had been corrupted by worldly luxuries; simple people were pure. "It is not to you," John wrote Anna, "I need apologize for talking in raptures of an higler whom we met on our road." When André's post chaise broke down, the peddler "ran up and with a face full of honest anxiety, pity, good nature, and every sweet affection under heaven, asked if we wanted anything. . . . My benevolence will be the warmer while I live for the treasured remembrance of this higler's countenance."

Writing humorous verses and drawing caricatures, John rocked the select circle with laughter; he was as gay as he was high-minded, and his physical vitality spilled from graceful dances into grotesque boyish capers. Anna's friends welcomed eagerly his romance with the wilting Honora, who had long been to them a source of sentiment and tears.

Honora sat mostly silent. Having no sense of humor, she joined automatically in the laughter. Occasionally she allowed herself to wonder whether all her friends, even her protectress Anna, were not a little silly: they talked so much about life, and yet ignored— or so it seemed to her—reality. However, her eyes remained soft and her brow smooth, and when she opened her little mouth she talked like the others. John was delighted when she called the spires of the cathedral "the ladies of the valley," or referred to Anna's dressing room as "the dear blue region." He proposed marriage. Anna and her friends were lyrical: Honora acquiesced.

However, Mrs. André and Honora's elders took a more practical view. Not wishing to "provoke romantic resistance," they agreed to let the engagement stand, but they insisted that John should see his fiancée only rarely until he was in a position to support her: the £5,000 he was to inherit was a tidy sum, but not adequate for a lifetime. When the select circle learned of this sordid development, the faces around Anna's fireplace turned glum, but their indefatigable leader soon righted everything by discovering a romantic angle. Lovers were supposed to go through ordeals to prove themselves worthy of their ladies; John's ordeal was to abandon his military ambitions, and, although he hated trade, win Honora by making his fortune in the family business. Enthralled by this interpretation of his affairs, the young man returned to the countinghouse at Warnford Court with a new enthusiasm.

Before he departed, he brought up the subject of letters. Anna was all eagerness—they would correspond wonderfully and on a high plane—but Honora drooped more than usual and said it hurt her side to write. She would add postscripts.

The contrast between life with the ladies and his mercantile labors was the underlying theme of all André's letters. "I have now," he writes, "completely subdued my aversion to the profession of merchant, and hope in time to acquire an inclination for it. Yet God forbid that I should ever love what I am to make the object of my attention, that vile trash which I care not for, but only as it may be the future means of procuring the blessing of my soul. Thus all my mercantile calculations go to the tune of *dear Honora*. When an impertinent conscience whispers in my ear that I am not of the right stuff for a merchant, I draw my Honora's picture from my bosom, and that sight of that dear talisman so inspirits my industry that no toil seems oppressive."

Sometimes he was allowed to visit Lichfield. "With what eager delight my eyes *drank* in their first view of the spires! What rapture did I not feel on entering the gates, in flying up the hall steps, in rushing into the dining room, in meeting the gladdened eyes of dear Julia and her enchanting friend. That instant convinced me of the truth of Rousseau's observation 'that there are *moments* worth ages.' "

For thirteen months John remained intimate with Anna, engaged to Honora, and enslaved to the family business. Then we find him at a Christmas party in Lichfield. He is talking as always with his dear Julia, while Honora sits beside them, less frail than formerly but equally beautiful. For once, she is not silent, for a newcomer,

John André. A miniature probably painted when, as an artistic youth in his early twenties, André was studying on the Continent. *Courtesy, James André.*

Drawing by André made before he came to America. Whether a scene in a church or a courtroom, this drawing reveals the elegant young man following Hogarth into high-spirited depictions of low life. *Courtesy, Dorothea K. André.*

Anna Seward and Honora
Sneyd. The two women
who formed with the young
John André so strange a
triangle. From contemporary
engravings.

Richard Lovell Edgeworth (who was to be the father of the novelist, Maria Edgeworth), has engaged her in conversation. He is rich, handsome, and witty; but, since he is married, the select circle is not concerned for Honora's heart. No one can know that Edgeworth, afflicted with a "cheerless" wife, is deciding that "for the first time in my life I saw a woman that equaled the picture of perfection which existed in my imagination."

"She conversed with me with freedom," Edgeworth continued in his *Memoirs*, "and seemed to feel that I was the first person who had seen the value of her character." Since "Miss Seward shined so brightly that all objects in her sphere were dimmed by her luster," it took close observation to recognize Honora's "power of reasoning," her "uncommon understanding and clear judgment." As for her relationship with André, Edgeworth "did not perceive from his manner, or from that of the young lady that any attachment subsisted between them. On the contrary, from the great attention which Miss Seward paid to him, and the constant admiration which Mr. André bestowed upon her, I thought that, though there was considerable disproportion in their ages, there must exist some courtship between them."

As John's visit was drawing to a close, Honora seems to have rebelled against Anna's dominance. In any case, her elders broke the news to André that he was no longer betrothed. "From all I then saw or have since known," Edgeworth commented, "I believe that Honora Sneyd was never much disappointed. . . . Mr. André appeared to me to be pleased and dazzled by the lady. She admired and estimated highly his talents, but he did not possess the reasoning mind that she required."

His love affair shattered, John revived an older ambition. Fame, honor, glory called him to the profession of arms. It is quite possible that after the breaking of his engagement he never sat at his countinghouse desk again. In almost exactly a month, on January 25, 1771, he bought a second lieutenant's commission in the Royal Welsh Fusiliers.

CHAPTER FOUR

A Poetic Soldier

AFTER almost eight months as a second lieutenant, André bought a first lieutenancy in the Seventh Foot, the Royal Fusiliers. But he was soon dissatisfied and bored. In peacetime, a warrior had no opportunities for romantic glory, and André's fellow officers were more concerned with drinking, gambling, and wenching than with his own hobbies of music, literature, and art. His mind flew back to the happy years he had spent on the Continent. Since Göttingen was an excellent place to secure advanced military training, a trip there, he decided, would further both his ambition and his pleasure.

With George Rodney, son of the famous admiral, he crossed the channel early in 1772. Theirs was a high-spirited expedition. André had been in Göttingen for several months before he matriculated at the university, giving as his major mathematics, the basis of military science. After a short stay in the student lodgings, he moved to quarters more suited to his tastes.

English gentlemen commonly supplemented their university courses by hiring tutors, who also took off their hands the bother of buying tickets and planning tours. André engaged a young poet, Heinrich Christian Boie, who introduced him to Johann Heinrich Voss, Ludwig Hölty, Johann Friedrich Hahn, and the rest of the group of impecunious scholars who were that very summer to hold a meeting that is famous in the history of German culture. Under their special goddess, the moon, in an oak grove

(*Hain*) that symbolized for them wild nature, they organized the Göttingen Hain, a poetic fellowship dedicated to making German letters national, noble, and pure. Modeling themselves on heroic bards who had inspired ancient Teutonic knights, they were self-consciously masculine. They met in a tavern redolent of tobacco and wine, yet André heard there, as he had done in that "dear blue region," Anna Seward's dressing room, high talk of Rousseau and "the rights of the heart." Again sophistication was denounced, eyes filled with tears at the virtue of uncorrupted savages. As Anna's circle had reacted against the rationalism of Dr. Johnson, the Hain despised the rationalism of Molière and Corneille. Anna herself could have conceived no gesture more touching than their conceit of decorating with flowers, at each meeting, an empty chair in honor of their inspiration, Klopstock.

The Hain were enchanted with John André. Not only was he a messenger from the England they admired—the land of King Arthur, Shakespeare, and Ossian—but he seemed to the poor scholars marvelously socially correct, delightfully rich. The poets so sang his praise that Georg Christoph Lichtenberg, a satirist who enjoyed the worldly literature of France, was piqued: "Do you already know the Englishman André? He is supposed to paint well(!) as Mr. Boie, who does not paint well, has written me."

Although André, who had been merely an apprentice in Anna's circle, was regarded by the Hain as a hero, he was not so charmed by the new group of poets as he had been by the old. It was not only that there was no blonde Honora to moon over—the change was deeper. He was now a man of the world and an officer in His Majesty's service. The Rousseauian cult of simplicity, which had once seemed to him revealed truth, now seemed suited only to sentimental females and poets like these, whose experience was limited by their humble social station. When, after his return to England, he spoke of his German months, he did not dwell on the rising young writers who had honored him. He boasted of his visits to "most of the [princely] courts in that part of Europe."

A miniature of André painted at about this time shows him as handsome, but young for his years, the cheeks still boyishly plump. He looks cocky and spoiled. There is too much sensitivity in the delicate nose and the small, well-formed mouth, yet the eyes stare with firmness, and the whole gives an impression of strong will, of clear intelligence. The viewer is both fascinated and disturbed—there are tensions within, fierce contradictions that make it impossible to guess what sort of a man, when he reaches belated maturity, John André will be.

After about nine months in Germany, he was called home because his regiment had been ordered to America; he forgot to notify the poets. When the Hain heard by chance that he was going, Voss, Hölty, and Hahn resolved to write, in competition with each other, poems of farewell. "We first made merry and then each went to a separate alley and composed by the light of the moon." As the young men who were to be famous in German literature gesticulated and scribbled, André sat in a drawing room, oblivious of the honor being paid him.

On his last day in Göttingen, each poet copied out his effusion in his finest hand, but no opportunity arose to present the sheaf of odes. The farewell party which Rodney gave that evening at the König von Preussen was limited to Englishmen, but Boie finally found the courage to go there, the papers in his hand. Voss, who considered André "one of my best friends" and whose poem had been judged the best, waited at his lodgings, hardly listening to the chatter of some aesthetic visitors banded together as the "Parnassus." There was a knock on the door and a liveried servant "came directly to me." Abandoning the Parnassus, Voss hurried to the party. "Never in my life have I felt prouder than when the Englishmen all came to meet me and embraced me. André, in particular, pressed me to his heart, and said, 'You are a noble fellow; you love your fatherland!'"

"We sat drinking champagne and burgundy until midnight," Voss continued, "and then went out, with music, to serenade. Many friends of André's joined us in the serenade, and four, among whom was Count Wallersdorf, remained with us. Then we held a *Landesvater* [ceremony of brotherhood], the first for me. In half an hour, I had counts and barons, and my dear Boie for brothers. You should have seen the latter, with his sheathed sword in one hand, and his hat in the other, when he sang forth his

Landesvater. He never could keep the tune, so I sang it with him. At three o'clock, we both slipped off, and slept until half-past six, when the other brothers woke us, because André was on the point of starting. He took leave of us with tears, and I was obliged to promise that I would accept a position in England if he could get one for me. May one not indeed be a little proud of the affection of an intelligent and honest Englishman?"

André left Göttingen on November 1, 1772, but he did not accompany his regiment to Canada. Since exile at a crude Colonial post did not appeal to him, he arranged for an extension of his leave.

While he was in England, Honora announced her engagement to Edgeworth, whose "cheerless wife" had obligingly died. Anna was crushed: "The precious established habits of my life were broken, and the native gaiety of my spirit eternally eclipsed. . . . No sprightly parties did I promote or, when I could help it, join through the years 1773-4-5-6." André, she insisted, was also "a major sufferer." Of course, "Honora's attachment for him never had the tenderness of her friendship for me," yet his despair at her marriage made him court self-destruction in the army. This sublime inaccuracy is often repeated by grave writers, although André had since boyhood longed for a military career and he had joined the army more than two years before. Edgeworth, indeed, tells us that John had lost his interest in Honora, and André's own relations are quoted as accusing Anna of "a nonsensical falsehood." Anna would have us believe that the vision of his lost blonde made André forever immune to other women. On the contrary!

Back in Göttingen during the spring of 1773, he inscribed in Voss's album a poem called *Parting*. If it referred to Honora and her imminent marriage, it did so in the most vague metaphor, since there is no hint, in this description of a ladylove sailing away in a boat, of an engagement or a successful rival. The phrasing, furthermore, is more conventional than deeply felt:

> *I urged the land, in phrensy'd mood*
> *To follow with the tide;*
> *And, as the land more backward stood.*
> *The river's course I chide. . . .*

33

Despair'd, I stagger'd from the strand
And sought this silent grove
Where these sad lines my fault'ring hand
Has pencil'd unto love.

That summer in Germany, André continued to shuttle back and forth between literary and aristocratic circles. He visited his distant cousin, Johann André, the famous composer who had collaborated with Goethe, and, indeed, he had so many friends in common with that genius that they may well have met. In the autumn, he settled in Gotha, where he so fascinated the Grand Duke and his Duchess that they posed while he painted them "for his own pleasure." This was a considerable concession since, like most amateurs, André could not carry the charm of his line drawings into depicting a head in the round. In a miniature self-portrait he had recently executed for his mother, he was at ease with the flat image of his uniform, but lost when it came to doing more than indicate in a pedestrian style the contours of his face.

The Frenchified Lichtenberg, who sometimes served as a minister of state, now met André, and was enchanted to discover that he did not, as might be assumed from the Hain's praises, make a fetish of simplicity. Instead, he proved to be one of the two "most distinguished Englishmen" who had visited Göttingen in sixteen years, and certainly "the most sympathetic and engaging." He spoke many languages, had a "penetrating understanding" and "a lively feeling for the beautiful." However, Lichtenberg was worried when his friend was again called to the army. He could not imagine as a soldier this "man of nearly womanlike modesty and gentleness."

André lingered on his way home, visiting Metz and Soudan. In London, he sought out connections who would soften the rigors of military life in exile by introducing him to the best society of the New World. When he embarked at last on the *St. George*, he accompanied Samuel Smith, the son of a rich Baltimore merchant; instead of going directly to Quebec, where his regiment was stationed, he sailed for the most sophisticated of Colonial cities. On September 2, 1774, three days before the First Continental Congress met there, he landed in Philadelphia.

In the England he had left, American unrest was taken lightly, but he found America gripped by anti-British frenzy. He had hardly set foot on shore when Israel Putnam, of the Connecticut militia, relayed a dispatch that British warships were bombarding Boston; before the report proved false, the streets filled with armed men. Then the regiment that garrisoned the city, the Royal Irish, marched onto transports and sailed away to reinforce General Thomas Gage in that plague spot, Boston. A report in the *Pennsylvania Journal* stated that André's regiment was leaving Canada for the same rendezvous. He decided to hurry to Massachusetts. However, he found the soldiers around Gage drinking and amusing themselves almost as unconcernedly as if they had been in London. The Colonials, he was told, were like little dogs; the louder they yapped, the less likely they were to attack the British lion. André's regiment would remain in Quebec.

Although boats sailed for Canada from Salem and Marblehead, André took the less easy but more picturesque route overland to Lake Champlain and then down that wilderness waterway. His circuitous travels did not mean, as some have assumed, that he was serving as a spy; he was composing, for possible publication, a book about the exotic Colonies.[1] Several years later, he showed his old Geneva friend Du Simitière "the curious journal he kept of all his travels and campaigns in America wherein were drawn in the most lively and picturesque manner the dresses, customs, amusements of the Canadians, Americans, and Indians; the curious animals, birds, insects, plants, etc., all in their proper colors, together with landskips, prospects, and plans of places." The volume, Du Simitière believed, displayed "superior talents."

André had been with his regiment at Quebec for some time when in March 1775 he wrote his sister, Mary, "My acquaintances thicken and I begin to sort them and select those whom I choose to be connected with. Among the English, I have several morning visit and cap acquaintances, and a few tea-drinking and occasional supper-dinner houses. With the French, I every now [and] then make parties into the country in which I, with my equipage, join the string and drive out a lady. We dine, dance rondes, toss pancakes, make a noise, and return, sometimes overturn, and sometimes are frostbit." To this cheerful account of civilian society, he adds nothing of his association with his fellow soldiers, mentioning them only to explain that he had built "an exceeding good library" by adding the books of absent officers to his own.

The ground, he continued, was covered by five feet of snow. "We are to see nature wear the twelfth-cake-like appearance a couple of months longer. I own I am not tired of it. The spirit of society, which reigns here during this season, and the dress we wear, banish the idea of cold, and the brightness of the weather cheers our spirits. Imagine a heaven of the purest blue, and an earth of the purest white, and over the country trace out roads above enclosures, through rivers, etc., planted on either side with branches of fir to work them, and numberless carioles, sleighs, etc. driving about, and you will have some notion of the appearance of the country."

"Very busy" collecting drawings for his journal, André wished in particular to have more chance to study the Indians. He had only attended one savage ceremony: "You would have been highly delighted to have seen the gentlemen, almost as lightly clad as our grandpapa Adam, smeared over with vermilion, blue, black, etc., from head to foot, throw themselves into the most horrid contortions and represent with the wildest yellings and howlings the history of a warlike expedition from their first going out to the scalping and mutilating their enemy. The undress of the ladies is a blanket tolerably impregnated with bears' grease and vermilion, which they wear capuchin fashion. Their finery is a man's shirt copiously besprinkled with vermilion, fine bead necklaces, earrings, etc., a little sort of winding blue kilt or petticoat coming down to their knees, and blue cloth leggings—a sort of trousers—with fine shoes worked with porcupine quills, black, red, yellow, etc., with fringes of red hair (not carroty locks) but scarlet horsehair or something of the kind."

Reversing the formula of the noble savage, André mocks the Indians by describing them as ignoble gentlefolk. In a surviving drawing, he shows them satirically, in the manner of Hogarth. We see stolid French Canadians and amazed British soldiers watching the antics of drunken aborigines. One Indian rocks on a table, nursing a jug, while others, clad mainly in breechcloths and scalp locks, throw their knobby bodies into grotesque attitudes. Raised high above the scene, an old lady in a nightcap holds up a candle, while her face, framed in scraggly locks, registers ridiculous consternation.

André was far from pleased when his regiment was ordered to march into the woods and learn under savage tutors how to "encamp in the Indian fashion" by digging pits in the snow and roofing them into crude huts. "Branches of firs are the foundation of your bed. . . . The amusements of the day are to be hunting upon snowshoes or large rackets tied to one's feet. In short, we are to take humanity a peg lower, and in proportion as our beds are bad we are to fatigue ourselves the more. Such, dear Mary, is the life of Quebec: today silken dalliance clothes our limbs and we wreath the bow and wind the dance; tomorrow we hut in a style little above the brute creation."

John André foresaw nothing more rigorous than an uncomfortable hunting trip; he was soon to face a Rebel army led by Benedict Arnold.

Book Two

BATTLE

CHAPTER FIVE

Two on First Base

THE MARCH to Cambridge of the New Haven Company of the Governor's Foot Guards was a triumphal progress. Down the elm-shaded streets of every town they paraded before a cheering populace. The Battle of Lexington had brought out many militia units; the others were straggles of lads who might have been in pursuit of the local deer. The townsfolk trembled to think of such troops meeting British regulars. The New Haveners could have been British regulars. Their scarlet coats trimmed with buff moved in neat ranks, while their black half-leggings swung with a single motion: the sound of forty-eight feet hitting the ground together seemed enough to make King George tremble on his throne. At the head of the column, an impressive officer rode on a noble horse. As he turned to bark a command, he appeared to ignore everything but the grim trade of battle, yet Benedict Arnold was conscious of the sensation he was making.

When the dazzling New Haven Company joined the American army at Cambridge, impressed officials quartered them in a mansion. They were chosen to deliver to the enemy the body of a soldier who had died of wounds received at Lexington. Drilling his men under the eyes of professional officers, Arnold had the pleasure of being complimented in the crisp accents of British aristocrats.

Arnold had already appeared before the Massachusetts Committee of Safety to say that he knew where the patriots could secure ordnance needed for a successful siege of Boston. There were "at

Ticonderoga eighty pieces of heavy cannon, twenty brass guns—from four- to eighteen-pounders—and ten to twelve large mortars," with small arms in proportion and a large sloop on the lake. Undermanned, in ruinous condition, "the place could not hold out an hour under vigorous attack." Since his information was in the main correct, Arnold had undoubtedly spied out, during one of his trading trips, the old fort near the southern tip of Lake Champlain. He now offered to storm the British post and bring back the cannon.

Although the committeemen expressed excitement, after Arnold had left they succumbed to doubts. Like most Americans at this time, they hoped that the British ministry would back down. To attack a royal fort from which no hostile action had emanated would carry the American protest much closer to outright war. Furthermore, Ticonderoga was in New York, which might resent a Massachusetts invasion. In the end, the committee wrote their New York counterpart, expressing a longing for cannon and asking what to do.

For two nights, the committeemen tossed in their sleep, dreaming of mortars, and then their restraint broke. On May 3, 1775, they appointed Arnold to what their minutes discreetly called "a secret service." His private orders made him a colonel, and "commander in chief over a body of men not exceeding 400," that he was to enlist in "the western part of this and neighboring colonies." Having captured Fort Ticonderoga and "the vessel and other cannon and stores on the lake," he was to garrison the fort and hurry back with the cannon. Delighted with his overnight promotion from captain to colonel, Arnold did not consider that a Connecticut man who accepted a Massachusetts commission would have to be very careful lest he become a man without a country. Nor did he realize the gravity of the situation when he heard that a rival expedition was in motion. Leaving his lieutenants behind to recruit troops, he galloped off, accompanied only by an orderly, to take command in the name of Massachusetts of an already existing force which had sprung up in another colony.

Unwittingly he had himself been responsible for his competitors, since, during his march to Cambridge, he had talked about Ticonderoga to a Connecticut leader, Samuel H. Parsons. Parsons had galloped to Hartford, where he had plotted with Silas Deane and other local firebrands to attack the fort without the knowledge of the Connecticut Committee of Safety, which would undoubtedly object to the expansion of the war. The conspirators made Edward Mott, a militia captain familiar with Ticonderoga, the leader of a secret and illegal party which hurried off to raise troops in the very area to which Arnold's orders had directed him for the same purpose.

In the Berkshire village of Pittsfield, Mott picked up some farm boys and two politicians who were to cast a baleful shadow on Arnold's future: sly James Easton, militia colonel, deacon, and tavernkeeper; voluble John Brown, late member of the Massachusetts Congress and secret emissary to the Canadians. The augmented party climbed further into the mountains until they saw, raised high above their heads on a pole, a stuffed wildcat snarling in the direction of New York. The rambling, two-story building before them was the Catamount Tavern, headquarters for the band of outlaws who ruled an illegal colony, the New Hampshire Grants. In a noisy bar, changed into a capitol by the words "council room" rudely scratched into a stone over the fireplace, they found many men, clad in fringed leather. Rum was circulating, but against the walls firelocks were neatly stacked.

Both New Hampshire and New York had once claimed jurisdiction over the surrounding area, which is now Vermont. After New York had won the litigation, settlers who had bought New Hampshire deeds were deprived of farms their labor had made productive. They sought legal relief, but, when a New York judge ruled against them, a tremendous woodsman named Ethan Allen rose in the back of the Albany courtroom to shout, "The gods of the valleys are not the gods of the hills!" He organized an illegal army, the Green Mountain Boys, who by force of arms kept New York officials out of the mountains. It was to this partisan commander that the delegation from Hartford now addressed themselves.

The Green Mountain Boys, so Allen wrote, were delighted to "annihilate the old quarrel with the government of New York by swallowing it up in the general conflict of liberty." They marched from the Catamount Tavern in Bennington to another tavern some twenty miles below Ticonderoga, where Allen was chosen commander in chief, and Easton his deputy. Allen hurried ahead, while his followers drank deep to their glorious adventure.

Suddenly the tavern door opened to admit an officer and a soldier in red coats. The Boys had reached for the tomahawks before they realized that the intruders were not Englishmen but a Massachusetts colonel and—of all things—his servant. At first, the half-drunken outlaws were "extremely rejoiced" by this indication of official support; a minute more, and they were "shockingly surprised." The newcomer had stated coolly that he had come to take command. When everyone objected at once, he displayed a commission appointing Benedict Arnold commander in chief of a force to take Ticonderoga. He looked around the taproom triumphantly, as if this had settled the matter, but the backwoodsmen howled with laughter at the idea that this dandy, who traveled with a valet, wished to command real men. As they beat each other's backs, and, crowing derisively, danced on the tables, they did not notice that their leaders were in serious discussion with the popinjay. Arnold's orders, if honored, would change a private adventure that might have disastrous repercussions into an act of state. The leaders pounded for order and advised the Boys to accept the command of the smiling outsider. But the frontiersmen "were for clubbing their firelocks and marching home."

The altercation continued until the Boys sank into drunken sleep. On waking groggily, they discovered that Arnold had gone off to find Allen. Abandoning their provisions in their haste, they chased after, afraid that this strangely tough city slicker would browbeat their "colonel." It was finally agreed that Allen and Arnold should serve as joint commanders.

The expedition disappeared under high-towering branches that strained day into twilight; only rarely did the sun pour blindingly down on a clearing where furrows snaked between tree stumps, and among the lairs of animals a log house smoked. Lonely settlers stared as the armed band passed rapidly by behind strangely contrasting leaders. The gigantic one was an ebullient backwoodsman who shouted a coarse greeting; his companion, a short, stocky officer in a fine uniform, held himself as stiffly as if he were on a parade ground. Yet the manner of both was histrionic, and each clearly wished even the smallest child to recognize him as the commander of the column.

On the evening of May 10, about 250 high-spirited men reached the eastern shore of Lake Champlain. A mile of water separated them from the fort, but no boats could be found until the middle of the night, and then a thunderstorm intervened. Only between eighty and ninety soldiers had been ferried to Willow Point, a third of a mile from Ticonderoga, when the darkness began to soften. The men's whispering shredded into silence, and Arnold and Allen, not wishing to lose the advantage of surprise, ordered the first attack the emerging United States ever made against a hostile fortification.

After the little army had hurried through a thick forest, "great and surprising works" appeared above them, dim in the morning mists: redoubts, a glacis, walls and bastions pierced with cannon. The woodsmen slipped silently along the banks of the lake, but when they came to a path that mounted the precipice, Arnold and Allen shouted and began to race each other: each was to claim he reached the fortification first. As their two heads rose above the cliff, they saw that the wicket gate in a huge portal hung open. A sentry drooped over a musket. He came suddenly to life, lifted his weapon, aimed, and pulled the trigger. Nothing happened. He dropped the musket and fled through the gate. Arnold and Allen, who had not broken their run, charged after him down the covered way and reached the inner court in time to see him disappear into a bomb-proof. A second sentry came at them, holding his bayonet before him. Allen's sword descended, scratching him on the cheek. He threw down his gun and put his hand to his face.

The rest of the Americans came in at a gallop and gathered on the British parade ground. Surrounding them were a bewildering assortment of buildings, but only the one disarmed redcoat was in sight. Not knowing what else to do, the Boys war-whooped. Arnold ordered them to secure the barracks. Allen menaced the prisoner with his sword and demanded to be led to the commanding officer. "Come out, you damned skunk," he shouted at the blank windows, "or I will sacrifice the whole garrison!"

Lieutenant Jocelyn Feltham, of His Majesty's Twenty-sixth Foot, had been wakened, so he tells us, "by numbers of shrieks and the words, 'No quarter! No quarter!' " In another instant, the cries were coming from inside the fort. Leaping naked from his bed, he ran down the hall and pounded on the door of his commander, Captain William Delaplace. When that warrior's snores continued their exasperating rhythm, Feltham darted back into his room, leaped into his waistcoat and coat, but did not wait to put on his trousers. With the trousers flying behind him, he sped along the hall and opened the door of a stairway that led down to the parade. He found himself face to face with a tremendous backwoodsman and a shorter gentleman in uniform. Behind these were "an armed rabble," shouting, waving tomahawks and firelocks.

"I endeavored to make them hear me, but it was impossible." When Arnold and Allen had finally silenced their followers, Feltham launched on a series of questions, hoping "to amuse them until our men fired." With as much scornful superiority as is possible to a royal officer without trousers, he demanded by what authority they had entered the fort. "In the name of the Great Jehovah and the Continental Congress!" was Allen's famous reply.

Further questioning revealed that Feltham was facing joint commanders. Arnold explained courteously about his Massachusetts commission; Allen broke in about Connecticut, and shouted, "I must have immediate possession of the fort and all the effects of George III!" Feltham waved his trousers nervously, wondering why his men did not fire, but kept the talk going. The ruder Allen became, the courtlier Arnold; the more Arnold played the punctilious officer, the louder Allen cursed as he brandished his sword over Feltham's head. To Allen's threat that if a single gun were fired, he would slaughter every man, woman, and child in the fort, Arnold added that the officers who surrendered "might expect to be treated like gentlemen."

When Feltham became convinced that his soldiers would never fire—they had all been surprised in their beds and disarmed—he admitted he was not the commander and introduced Delaplace, who officially surrendered the fortress. Behind crumbling bastions on the banks of a wilderness lake, a British sword passed into American hands, and history turned a page.

"The sun seemed to rise that morning with a superior luster," wrote Allen, "and Ticonderoga and its dependencies smiled on its conquerors, who tossed about the flowing bowl," toasting "Congress and the liberty and freedom of America." With their companions who had by mid-morning all streamed across the lake, the captors got royally drunk on some ninety gallons of rum they found in the storehouse. While the wives and children of the British soldiers cowered, the reeling backwoodsmen rifled their possessions: one carried off a washstand; another slapped a bonnet on his head to the uncontrolled hilarity of his companions. What was too heavy to lift, they smashed. Through the mounting Saturnalia, Arnold strode in fury, quoting military law on the illegality of stealing the private property of prisoners. He even snatched prizes from the hands of the victorious backwoodsmen and returned them to the vanquished enemy. Eventually Allen, his face as red with anger as with rum, confronted Arnold to deny that he had ever agreed to a joint command. He ordered the interloper to leave the fort. When Arnold countered by showing his Massachusetts commission, Mott drew up a commission for Allen that sounded even more impressive. Triumph and liquor had made the illegal army forget their concern with governmental backing.

Now the Green Mountain Boys took drunken shots in Arnold's direction, and one of them, placing a loaded musket against Arnold's chest, said he would shoot through him unless he admitted Allen's authority. Arnold replied that he would never betray the responsibility placed on him by Massachusetts. The two men stared in each other's eyes for a moment. Then the assailant lowered his gun and shambled off for another drink. Although no one obeyed his commands, Arnold continued to give them.

To his employers in Cambridge, he reported, "Colonel Allen is a proper man to head his own wild people, but entirely unacquainted with military service; and, as I am the only person who has been authorized to take possession of this place, I am determined to insist on my right, and I think it my duty to remain here against all opposition until I have further orders." He was "extremely sorry that matters have not been transacted with more prudence and judgment. I have done everything in my power. . . . I hope soon to be properly released from this troublesome business, that some proper person may be appointed in my room." The troops, he continued, were "in the greatest confusion and anarchy,

47

destroying and plundering private property, committing every enormity, and paying no attention to the public service." It was impossible to do anything about forwarding the needed cannon to Cambridge, and he was afraid that a hundred British soldiers could without difficulty recapture the fort.

For four days Arnold wandered about the camp, and then a sail appeared on the lake. The lieutenants Arnold had left behind to recruit troops appeared with some fifty men on a schooner confiscated from a Tory trader. Now that he had soldiers of his own, Arnold set about establishing order in the fort and protecting the local inhabitants. On a trip of inspection for the Connecticut patriots, Barnabas Deane wrote his brother Silas that but for Arnold, "no man's person would be safe who was not of the Green Mountain party." A war was going on within the war, Deane explained: the Vermonters persecuted the New Yorkers who were now in their power, and planned, by holding the Lake Champlain area, to force their land claims on New York.

While the Green Mountain Boys, whose experience with navigation was limited to fishing in mountain streams, watched sullenly, Arnold armed the schooner with captured cannon. He intended to obey his orders to seize the British naval sloop even if he had to navigate into Canada and attack the fort at St. Johns. The Boys had no intention of letting him get exclusive credit for such an exploit. They climbed into bateaux and rowed passionately after the sailboat, not slackening their efforts after it vanished over the horizon.

Arnold was becalmed about thirty miles from his objective. With thirty-five men in two rowboats, he crossed the border for the first invasion by the United Colonies of a foreign land. At 6 A.M. on May 18, he reached St. Johns, where, as he reported, he "surprised and took a sergeant and his party of twelve men, the King's sloop of about seventy tons with two brass six-pounders and seven men, without any loss on either side." The English had risen from their beds to find themselves captured. Since he was told that they expected reinforcements at any moment, Arnold reasoned that Providence must be watching over the Americans "that we arrived at so fortunate an hour." (The British force marching down from Canada probably included the poetic young lieutenant, John André.)

Having destroyed all the military equipment he could not carry off, Arnold immobilized the enemy—cannon could not be transported through the tangled wilderness that bordered Lake Champlain—by sailing away in their sloop, dragging their rowboats behind him.

Sails pulled powerfully in the sunshine; water gleamed and gestured; it was so quiet that you could hear the birds on shore singing; and then from the distance came the clank and splash of oars. Soon Arnold moved effortlessly abreast of the Boys who were making such headway in their bateaux as their exhaustion allowed. He saluted with a salvo on the King's cannon: the Boys replied with a rattle of small arms. Always tolerant in moments of triumph, Arnold smiled affectionately at the "mad fellows," whose virtues he could appreciate since many aspects of their characters were echoed in his own: he would have made just such a crazy dash down the lake had he been in their shoes. He shouted that he had rum on board and wondered whether they were thirsty. Instantly, a flood of Boys swept across the deck. Allen remembered with pleasure the "several loyal Congress healths" that were drunk.

Anxious to right the balance with their rival, the Boys announced that they would proceed to St. Johns and hold it against all comers. Arnold explained about the British reinforcements, adding that it was "a wild, impracticable scheme, and provided it could be carried into execution, of no consequence, so long as we are masters of the lake, and of that I make no doubt, as I am determined to arm the sloop and schooner immediately." When the backwoodsmen laughed at such craven advice, Arnold gave them provisions—in their hurry they had come off with none—and watched as they rowed away toward Canada. Then he sailed back to Ticonderoga.

Four days later, he saw the Boys come tearing down the lake as if the whole British army were after them. On reaching the neighborhood of St. Johns, they had fallen into an exhausted sleep, only to be awakened by "a discharge of grapeshot from six field pieces and of small arms from about 200 regulars." The Boys ran as fast as they could, but three were captured. The misadventure persuaded most of them that they were needed on their farms, and

49

Allen was so "cooled down" that Barnabas Deane induced him publicly to surrender the leadership to Arnold. True, Allen remained at the post, and was soon again signing letters "the principal commander of the army," but the situation had reversed itself: Arnold, who was attracting new recruits while Allen's force dwindled, wielded the real power.

Fearing that the reinforced British would attack, he put the sloop and schooner "in the best posture for defense," and sailed to Crown Point, some thirty miles down the lake, where a ruined fort gave some shelter, and there were narrows that could easily be blocked. Had the enemy possessed boats in which to advance, they would have been warmly received, for Arnold had discovered a genius for making militiamen behave like regulars. His little fleet was perpetually ready; scouts threaded the woods; men prepared for shipment the guns needed at Cambridge; a doctor Arnold had imported took care of the sick. No longer fearing marauders, the local inhabitants slept soundly.

Arnold knew he was doing a good job, yet sometimes he was uneasy. "I have had intimations given me," he wrote the Massachusetts Committee of Safety, "that some persons had determined to apply to you and the Provincial Congress to injure me in your esteem by misrepresenting matters of fact. I know of no other motive they can have, only my refusing them commissions for the very simple reason that I did not think them qualified." He hoped "my conduct will not be condemned until I have an opportunity to be heard."

He was right to be worried. As soon as they had sobered up after Ticonderoga's fall, his rivals—the group that had set out from Hartford with Mott, the recruits they had secured at Pittsfield, and the Green Mountain Boys—schemed to get all the glory. Easton and Brown, being Massachusetts men, were selected to undermine Arnold's commission from that state. Before the Massachusetts Congress, Easton complained that Arnold had interfered with a successful expedition planned in Connecticut. Only too glad to place on other shoulders the responsibility for attacking a royal fort, Massachusetts gave official credit to Connecticut and resolved that Allen should "remain in possession of the command."

When Arnold's letter giving his version of the events finally reached the Massachusetts Committee of Safety, that body forwarded it to their superiors, the Massachusetts Congress, with the pious remark that the matter was "out of their province." By referring to Arnold as Captain, not Colonel, they in effect denied the commission they had given him, which had been the foundation of all his actions. The Massachusetts Congress thereupon wrote Arnold, whom they gave no title whatsoever, that, as their energies were committed to the siege of Boston, they had turned the campaign over to Connecticut.

However, the Connecticut authorities were not pleased to have the expansion of the rebellion laid at their door; Governor Trumbull started investigations to see whether the whole affair had not been fomented by Massachusetts and Arnold.

Brown, in the meantime, had reported to the Continental Congress; this central legislature of the United Colonies was dismayed. They voted that the attack had been a spontaneous uprising of Ticonderoga's neighbors—if they were told of Arnold's official orders they preferred to ignore them—and urged that the fort be restored forthwith to the Crown. The invaluable cannon were to be regarded as borrowed, and would be returned after "that restoration of former harmony" which the Congress "so ardently desired."

That news of Ticonderoga's fall was received by the public with jubilation helped the various legislatures to regain their calm. Although all agreed that any further American invasions of Canada, such as the attacks on St. Johns, would be fatal to hopes of peace, the northern Colonies, which were vulnerable should a British force advance down Lake Champlain, persuaded the Continental Congress to hold as much of that waterway as lay in New York. New York promised to supply the forts but would not man them; Connecticut offered to send 1,000 men, but not at once.

Finding they could not yet withdraw, the Massachusetts authorities warmed up their letters to Arnold. He was a colonel again; they "highly approved" of his conduct; they were "sorry to meet with repeated requests from you that some gentleman be sent to succeed you in command."

As the legislatures veered with the political wind, the commands they sent Arnold were contradictory; he did whatever he thought best. He had probably not received incontrovertible instructions to stay out of Canada when, early in June, he sailed again over the border. Anchoring his little fleet at Isles aux Noix, a safe distance below St. Johns, he ordered an advanced guard to spy on the enemy and, if possible, capture some royal troops from whom he could get information. No prisoners were taken, but a letter from André, who was stationed at Chambly, twelve miles up the Sorel River from St. Johns, reveals that the Americans succeeded in making a nuisance of themselves.

"We begin to have some notion of the forces of our enemy," André wrote, "and I am happy to say that they do not appear in a very formidable light." He explained how they "infest the woods opposite St. Johns, firing from the bushes on our bateaux which are constantly moving up and down the river to watch their motions. . . . We have, however, daily expeditions to the woods. I had this duty yesterday, and though I am not particularly keen after the pleasure of being shot at, had almost as leave have met the Yankees as been baked in the sun for the mosquitoes' dinner."

At Isles aux Noix, Arnold was conferring with some rebellious Canadians and an emissary he had sent to the Indians: he was dreaming that he might capture all Canada. The province was sparsely populated—most of the inhabitants were in the St. Lawrence River Valley as were the two cities, Montreal and Quebec—and had belonged to England for only a dozen years. To rule this shaky possession, Parliament had, in the Quebec Act, continued feudal French law. They had made no provision for free legislatures; they had strengthened the power of the higher Catholic clergy and the rich families who constituted the local noblesse. Only these few persons were pleased. The 60,000 French peasants were sullen, and the 2,000 Englishmen angry. Arnold was attempting to determine where the British regulars were stationed, how many Canadians would fight for the Crown, and what allies an invading army could expect.

When he sailed back to Crown Point, he found that Easton, returned from his political junketing, was reviving Allen's pretensions to command. Arnold had accused Easton of hiding during the assault on Ticonderoga on the excuse of drying his gun; he despised the boastful tavernkeeper. "I took the liberty of breaking his head, and on his refusing to draw like a gentleman, he having a hanger [short sword] by his side and a case of loaded pistols in his pocket, I kicked him very heartily and ordered him from the Point immediately."

Allen had already in a vaguely worded letter offered to capture Canada when Arnold suggested to the Continental Congress a detailed plan. The majority of the Canadians, he assured them, would remain neutral. To overcome the 550 British regulars and the few local allies, which he had discovered constituted the entire enemy force, he proposed an expedition of 2,000. The majority would march to Montreal, where there were only forty soldiers and Arnold's friends had promised to open the gates; while a detachment of 700 would immobilize and finally capture the 500 regulars at St. Johns and Chambly. Quebec, with a garrison of only 120, would then fall easily.

It would be more economical, he argued, for the patriots to take and hold Quebec, "a strong fortress built to our hand," than to renovate dilapidated Ticonderoga. Once Canada was given "a free government, agreeable to the English constitution, like the other Colonies," it could never be returned to despotism, and thus menace the rest of America, even if by George III's "treachery" it were given back to France. Conquest of the region would supply the United Colonies with "an inexhaustible granary," cut the British from the lucrative fur trade, and, by discouraging the enemies of American liberty in England, "be the means of restoring that solid peace and harmony between Great Britain and her Colonies so essential to the well-being of both. . . . Though at first view it might seem like going beyond our province to invade the rights of Great Britain, yet a due regard for our own defense, as well as the advantage of the inhabitants of that country, make it necessary."

Arnold was not expert at tact, but in this letter he did his best. "I hope the exigency of the times, and my zeal in the service of my country will apologize for the liberty of giving my sentiments so freely on a subject which the Honorable Congress are doubtless the best judges of, but which they in their hurry may not have paid that attention to [which] the matter requires. I beg leave to add, that if no person appears who will undertake to carry the plan into execution (if thought advisable), I will undertake and with

53

the smiles of Heaven answer for the success of it, provided I am supplied with men, etc., to carry it into execution without loss of time." A final paragraph, which lists the troops and supplies he would need, contains the plea, "no Green Mountain Boys."

Had Arnold's scheme been carried through before the arrival of winter, Canada might have fallen and the flow of history been deflected. Yet, when most Americans still hoped to avoid full-scale war, such action was not politically possible. Arnold would have been wiser if, instead of pursuing vast objectives, he had noticed the realities of his own situation.

A Connecticut colonel, Benjamin Hinman, soon arrived with a considerable force; he stated that he had come to take the top command. Although Arnold had been notified that the Massachusetts Congress wished to bow out in favor of Connecticut, he replied that Hinman's commission merely paralleled his own, and that, as senior officer, he remained in control. Hinman, who was a mild soul, did no more than grumble, even after Arnold ordered his small garrison at Ticonderoga to bar the much larger Connecticut unit from the fort unless they agreed to obey Massachusetts orders.

When a committee of the Massachusetts Congress appeared at Crown Point, Arnold treated them with the courtly condescension of a commander entertaining politicians, but he could not play this agreeable role for long. The committee stated that his commission was inferior to Hinman's. After he had indignantly questioned their authority, they showed him their orders to turn the top leadership over to Connecticut, and also to determine, "after having made yourselves fully acquainted with the spirit, capacity, and conduct of said Arnold," whether he should be continued as colonel of the Massachusetts Regiment or should be discharged. Arnold, the committee's chairman reported, "seemed greatly disconcerted."

Declaring that "he would be second in command to no person whatsoever," Arnold returned to his quarters, and "after some time contemplating upon the matter," wrote out his resignation, dated June 24, 1775. The appointment of "a younger officer" to take over the fortresses and vessels a senior had captured, was, he stated, "a most disgraceful reflection" on the superseded officer and his troops. As for empowering the committee to investigate his conduct, that was "unprecedented, and a very plain intimation that the Congress are dubious of my rectitude and abilities, which is a sufficient inducement to me to decline serving them any longer." Asserting that the regiment he had personally raised went out of existence with his commission, he told his men to go home.

When in command, Arnold had spent from his own pocket hundreds of pounds for necessary supplies. He now demanded that these sums be returned to him, but the committee answered that they had no such instructions: he would have to present his bills to the Congress. Then it developed that the committee had been empowered to pay only as many of Arnold's troops as they considered capable of fighting. Arnold protested "the very great hardship on the private men, who, having served well near two months, are now to be mustered, and if by sickness or hard labor they are reduced and not fit for service . . . they are to lose their former time and service, and reduced to the distress of begging their bread until they can get home to their friends." The order was, of course, extremely unfair; when it was rumored around Crown Point, there arose what the committee considered "a dangerous mutiny."

Mott gleefully repeated the rumor (he was not present) that Arnold gathered his troops on board the sailboats and threatened to "deliver the vessels" to the British. It was within Arnold's character to have shouted that if the committee thought what he and his men had done was so insignificant that they were to be tossed out unpaid and in disgrace, he would be glad to take them at their word and put the captured sloop back where he had found it: then, perhaps, the Congress would be really satisfied! If Arnold did speak in this manner, the committee regarded it as empty rhetoric, for they did not accuse him of any part in the mutiny.

Arnold's own story was that "not being able to pay off the people, who were in great want of necessities and much in debt" gave him "great trouble to pacify them." Perhaps he did not try too hard, since the troops who had trusted him were being unjustly handled. Furthermore, the cowardly Easton had succeeded him as commander of the Massachusetts Regiment and was trying to make a clean sweep by taking over Arnold's soldiers.

When Arnold went on board a boat for dinner, the crew, he asserted, locked him in the cabin to prevent him from interfering;

"I complained much of the insult offered me." The mutineers replied that they bore him no personal ill will, but were determined to oblige the committee, by force if necessary, to pay them enough so that they could "go home to their families with honor." In the end, the committee exceeded their instructions by agreeing that, whatever the men's physical condition, they would receive back pay. Arnold thereupon withdrew. Sullenly, he sailed down the lake up which he had so recently advanced in triumph.

With his departure, somnolence settled over the once bustling camp. Harmony reigned, but also inactivity. One of the sailboats, on which the defense of the lake depended, remained without a captain, and one of the forts, as a passing American officer complained, could have been taken "with a penknife only." It was lucky that the displaced commander had left the British no vessels in which to advance.

Arnold had been in the army of the United Colonies hardly more than two months, and already he was one of its best known and most controversial leaders. He had been brave, but, as his retreat from St. Johns shows, not foolhardy; he had been as concerned with defense as attack; he had never forgotten the importance of sound organization and adequate supply. In return for the complete subordination he demanded from those he considered his inferiors, he watched over them, even to the extent of paying for a doctor from his private purse. "The men who went under your care to Boston," his sister wrote him, "give you the praises of a very humane, tender officer. Hope those now with you may meet with an equal degree of tenderness and humanity." It seems clear that they did. In his official reports, Arnold did his best to be fair even to his enemies: he gave the Green Mountain Boys much more credit than they gave him, and his strictures were justified by his duty to write an accurate account. Many of his difficulties had been caused by his determination to protect civilians and prisoners: he received the thanks of the local inhabitants for having supplied them "with provisions in their distress," and of the captured British officers for the punctilio with which he had carried out military law.

Somehow Arnold had familiarized himself with the regulations, customs, and ideals of long-established Old World armies. Everyone, from Washington down, who tried to apply these rigid forms to the rapidly improvised American forces got into trouble with patriots who thought armies should be run by popular vote, like town meetings. That Arnold should irritate his undisciplined rivals was inevitable, yet he need not have made lifelong enemies. His method in a quarrel was not to persuade, but, as he had done with Easton, to break his opponent's head. Indeed, he sometimes revealed a disturbing similarity to the unruly militiamen he wished to reform. He had not always been scrupulous about obeying his superiors, and certainly he had not behaved like the regular officer of his dreams when, on being removed from command, he had disbanded his men.

More serious even than his ungovernable passions was his blindness to political reality. Absorbed in his role of an efficient officer, he ignored the structure of the governments which he represented, and tried to apply his sudden commission from one of thirteen Colonies as if it had been granted in a stable and unified military organization. Although his removal from the top command had been a necessary adjustment between Colonies, he took it as a personal insult.

He had been ordered to Cambridge to settle his accounts. Since large sums were owed him, it would have been to his advantage to obey, yet, as he always did when he was hurt, he hurried home. Riding down crooked streets to his house on the New Haven water front, Arnold hoped that now, at long last, his wife would give him sympathy and understanding. Although the world had treated him with the old unfairness, he had acted, while permitted, as a hero. She had seen his name in the public prints, heard his exploits on every tongue. Certainly, she would receive him warmly now.

With almost a hopeful heart, he opened the door of his home, but Peggy did not come to greet him. It was his sister Hannah who hurried down the stairs. A few words, and he knew the truth: the silent Peggy Mansfield Arnold had made the ultimate withdrawal, down to a grave beneath the pavement of the Congregational Meeting House. His marriage had ended in tragedy, as his military career seemed to have done.

Once again, Hannah had taken over his affairs. She tried to re-

57

fire life in her brother by pointing out that his business affairs had been at a standstill since he had marched away to Lexington. Although no word could be got to his brigantine on its way to Quebec—the boat that was named after his dead wife would certainly be confiscated because of his forays into Canada—a brig that was due back from the Indies would need a cargo. Arnold collected 60,000 barrel staves and hoops; but one morning he was so crippled with gout that he could hardly rise from his bed. Trapped by acute pain, he saw the brig shifting at its dock without sailing papers, the "quantity of lumber" weathering on the shore. This seemed to be the end of all ambition, the final blow to hope.

Yet, as the war darkened and the army grew ever larger, the two generals who had just been given top commands scanned the continent, searching for able officers. Philip Schuyler, entrusted with an augmented force facing Canada, inquired whether the equivocal hero of Ticonderoga had made too many enemies to be appointed his adjutant general. And the new commander in chief, George Washington, wondered, as the merchants of Norwich had done years before, how best to use the unpredictable but undeniable talents of Benedict Arnold.

CHAPTER SIX

Wilderness Adventure

WHEN Arnold was well enough to get about again, he did not dispatch his brig to the West Indies. Leaving that valuable asset moored at New Haven, he rode to Watertown, where a committee of the Massachusetts Congress was clamoring to settle his Ticonderoga accounts. On learning that Arnold, about whom they had heard all kinds of uncomplimentary rumors, insisted that they owed him money but had not kept careful records, the legislators became suspicious, nor were they mollified by his description of the confusions attendant on a hand-to-mouth campaign conducted by irregular forces under a perpetually disputed command. The insinuations of the committeemen only made Arnold bluster. He had been on the scene; he had spent what he considered necessary for the well-being and the safety of his troops; it was up to these civilians to accept his word. Did they doubt his honor?

From item to item the argument continued, to the sound of pens writing "disallowed." On August 19, 1775, Arnold was given £195.13.9, less than half what he said he had spent. This settlement was considered so unfair that the Continental Congress eventually paid Arnold the £245.14.0 Massachusetts had denied him.

While the dickering committeemen were lowering his opinion of legislators, Arnold met Washington. The commander in chief was a patrician, such as Arnold himself wished to be, and also an officer punctilious about rank. Had not Washington, during the

French and Indian War, resigned a commission rather than serve under one of his juniors, just as Arnold had recently done? Both combined urbane elegance with backwoods hardihood and love of physical adventure; both were born leaders of men. Arnold may well have seen in Washington a vision of what he himself might become; and Washington, although not blind to Arnold's less ex-alted social background, recognized in him many of the traits of his own young manhood. The general had not always possessed the hold on his emotions that was one of his great strengths, nor could he control himself now without an effort. "All his features," wrote Gilbert Stuart, "were indicative of the strongest passions, yet like Socrates his judgment and self-command made him appear a man of different cast in the eyes of the world." Since he had learned to hold himself in, perhaps Arnold would also learn. The two soldiers were equally pleased with each other; and Washing-ton decided that this was the man to carry out a rash maneuver that might, with a single blow, capture all Canada.

Although it had been several months since Arnold had left Ti-conderoga, the northern campaign was stalled. Still afraid to in-vade Canada lest so doing destroy all chances of a negotiated peace, Congress had tried to persuade the inhabitants to revolt. When it became clear that they would not rise unless an army were present to protect them, Congress handed the dilemma to General Schuyler, who was instructed to determine the sentiments of the Canadians, and, if he found an American force would be welcomed, to march in not as an attacker but as an ally. Patroon of the area north of Albany, one of the richest landowners in America, Schuyler was so conservative that some feared he was at heart a Tory. Doubting the constitutional right of the Colonials to do what he had been ordered to do, he dawdled indecisively at his headquarters near Ticonderoga.

Washington wished to push things along. He knew that between the ocean, closed to the Colonials by British naval superiority, and the inland way along Lake Champlain to Montreal that Schuyler was supposed to attempt, there was a third route to Canada occa-sionally traversed by missionaries or Indians in solitary canoes. They paddled up the roaring Kennebec River high into the Maine mountains where they came on three lakes that served as stepping-stones to the broad, sluggish flow of Dead River. Eventually, they abandoned this waterway, and, carrying their boats over the rocky and swampy waste known as the Height of Land, reached the headwaters of a river so violent that the French called it the Chaudière (cauldron). Pouring down declivities, the Chaudière joined the St. Lawrence opposite Quebec.

Since the seventeenth century, generals had eyed this route, and, after the close of the French and Indian War, it had been explored by an English engineer. All had feared that a passage possible for light canoes would prove the graveyard of an army carrying enough equipment to be effective. Greatly underestimating the difficulties, Washington reasoned that a force appearing from a forest considered impassable might capture by surprise the walled city of Quebec, practically immune to ordinary siege. And the nation that controlled Quebec controlled Canada.

When Washington asked him to lead such an expedition, Arnold was all eagerness. The service to the patriot cause would be great, and he knew that the only general who had ever captured Quebec, James Wolfe, had become an international hero. After "the Gibraltar of America" had surrendered to Benedict Arnold, all the congresses with all their foolish committees would be sorry that they had not recognized his worth.

There was need for haste. English reinforcements might well be crossing the Atlantic, and winter was certainly on the way, bringing to the northern mountains snow and ice more deadly even than hostile armies. However, Schuyler was slow in sending his approval and an assurance that, by advancing up Lake Champlain, he would draw from Quebec the few regulars in Canada. It was dangerously late when Arnold received his orders.

Although he was removed from the jurisdiction of any individual Colony by being commissioned a colonel in the Continental Army, Arnold found that, because he "had been traduced and had many prejudices to encounter," he could not secure commissions for his friends. Eleazer Oswald, who had been a lieutenant in his Ticonderoga force, and was now to be his secretary, was forced to go along as a volunteer.

The more than a thousand men who enlisted in his corps were all bold spirits, but few had ever navigated a mountain river. Only a regiment of riflemen from backwoods Virginia and Pennsylvania were truly qualified for the adventure. They wore, as forest camouflage, long capes the color of a dry leaf, and they carried rifles developed for the special needs of wilderness hunting which were the most accurate firearms known. The British called "these shirt-tail men with their cursed twisted guns . . . the most fatal widow- and orphan-makers in the world."

After a delay because the troops would not move until paid back wages, the column finally began on September 13 to march to Newburyport. Winter was so uncomfortably close that Arnold decided to risk an ocean voyage to the Kennebec, although a single English warship could have sunk his entire fleet of eleven small vessels.

Sole commander of a daring adventure, he felt confident, at peace with himself, and warm toward his fellow men. In Newburyport, he had prevented his troops from looting the Tories, and when, on one of his ships, a man was killed in a drunken fight, Arnold pitied the murderer who, so he wrote Washington, "appears to be very simple and ignorant, and in the company he belonged to had the character of a peaceable fellow. . . . I wish he may be found a proper object of mercy."

His fleet arrived unharmed at the Kennebec, where Arnold found waiting for him 200 bateaux: pointed, flat-bottomed barges "capable of carrying six or seven men each with their provisions and baggage." Made from heavy and leaky green pine, they were, he wrote Washington, "very badly built," but he could do no more than make up for their small size by ordering another twenty. His men were outraged. "Could we have come within reach of the villains who constructed these crazy things," wrote Private George Morison, "they would fully have experienced the effects of our vengeance. . . . Avarice or a desire to destroy us—perhaps both— must have been their motives." Actually, no seasoned boards had been available.

Some woodsmen appeared at Arnold's headquarters full of the excitement of bad news. British regulars, they reported, were guarding the Chaudière; the nearer woods were crawling with enemy spies who daily expected to be reinforced by bloodthirsty Mohawks. Arnold laughed at their concern, writing Washington that they had seen only one Indian, "a noted villain," who had frightened them with wild stories. However, Arnold detailed a group of riflemen to each brigade to act as scouts.

Instantly Daniel Morgan, the riflemen's colonel, appeared at headquarters. His men, he shouted, had enlisted on the understanding that they were to serve only under their own officers. Arnold could almost imagine himself back at Ticonderoga facing that other gigantic hunter Ethan Allen. Now he was wiser; he had learned that if you were to use backwoods troops, you had to respect their distrust of strangers. He gave in to Morgan, although his army would be much less well-guarded.

The best Arnold could do was to send ahead two scouting parties to look for enemies and mark the route. To avoid piling up at obstacles, he dispatched his main body in four waves, a day's journey apart. Some of the men operated the laden bateaux; others marched beside them along the shore, helping out at rapids and carries. The riflemen, who went first, were to cut roads at the carrying places, while the back contingents transported most of the supplies. When almost all had set out, Arnold started after them in a light canoe paddled by Indians. Coming to the head of the column, he waited for everyone to pass, and then made another dash, catching up with the riflemen at the Great Carrying Place from the Kennebec to the Dead River.

Under generally fair skies, he watched the "oak, elm, ash, beech, maple, pine, hemlock, etc." drop the colored leaves of autumn into whitely churning rapids. Waterfalls gleamed, and in the shallows sand was bright as a fish's belly. The surrounding hills rose ever higher, until his canoe advanced through a narrowing gorge cut in mountains on which the snow of winter had already fallen.

Coming round a bend, Arnold heard mingled with the splashy roar of rapid water, the yelling of men engaged in hard labor. Then he darted among his troops, moving dramatically fast as his Indians sweated at the paddles. Standing in their boats or half submerged beside them, the men cheered. Arnold was, one of them wrote, "beloved by the soldiery." He smiled and waved, happy in the comradeship of adventure.

So far, the invasion had resembled an arduous camping trip; there were many rigors but no serious accidents. "You would have taken the men for amphibious animals," Arnold wrote Washington, "as they were a great part of the time under water." In the rapids, they had waded waist-band high, pulling and heaving their clumsy boats. Sometimes they advanced a dozen times to be as often swept back. Then it was necessary to carry until the river became again navigable. Four men would stagger along with the gunwale of an upturned bateau cutting into their shoulders, while other groups of four bore barrels that swung from crossed poles. Several trips were required to get everything over. There were many spills on the uneven terrain, yet good humor reigned. A man who rose from a mud hole dripping from head to heel was asked how he had liked his board and lodging. When his tormentor tripped in turn and thrashed like a tadpole in a morass, the first victim would cry, "Come here, and I'll lift you out!" Arnold laughed as heartily as his men.

At the head of the Kennebec, he was sanguine. Although quantities of provisions had been destroyed in the leaky boats, his scouts reported no enemy activity in the woods, and, as far as natural obstacles went, he believed "the greatest difficulty is already past." The only danger he foresaw was that a trap might be sprung when his men appeared at the settlements, with the wilderness at their backs. Writing his friends at Quebec for information, he entrusted the letter to Eneas, whom he considered a faithful Indian, not knowing he was a British spy.

Arnold notified Washington that he would advance to the headwaters of the Chaudière, but not decide, until word came back from Canada, whether to invade the province or retire as he had come. To prepare for the latter contingency, he ordered that additional supplies be sent up the Kennebec and stored in a log house. "The expense will be considerable," he explained, summarizing his attitude toward military costs, "but when set in competition with the lives or liberty of so many brave men, I think it trifling." Always careful of the sick, he built a little hospital. Then he set out across the Great Carrying Place to Dead River.

In the journal he kept to show Washington, Arnold revealed a real-estate operator's eye for fertile soil, but his descriptions of nature were mostly laconic notations of landmarks that would enable others to follow his route. However, the lakes he now traversed inspired him to eloquence. "We soon arrived at the second pond, which makes as desolate an appearance as the first does bountiful, the lake being very irregular, long, and narrow, the trees all dead and full of moss, the water very thick and muddy." After a difficult carry of more than a mile, he reached the third pond. "There the prospect is very beautiful and noble, a high chain of mountains encircling the pond, which is deep, clear, and fine water, over which a forked mountain which exceeds the rest in height, bearing northwest and covered with snow in contrast with the others, adds greatly to the beauty of the scene."

He was encouraged when he reached Dead River to see that it was "about sixty yards wide, uniformly deep and gentle." With this watery highway before him, Arnold felt himself almost in Canada; he was not really worried at finding Colonel Greene's division short of flour, and most of their bread damaged. However, he cautiously delayed the march two days until supplies came from the rear.

On October 19, as the troops proceeded up Dead River after more than a month in the wilderness, Arnold noted, "Small rains the whole of this day. . . . N.B. Rained very hard all night." The 20th: "Rainy morning. . . . Continues rainy the whole of this day, wind to southward." The 21st: "Storm continues." The wind had risen almost to hurricane force, and falling trees made movement by land extremely dangerous, yet Arnold remained sanguine. When he recorded that the river had risen "upwards of three feet," he added that it had been unusually shallow.

Four times that day Arnold and his Indians carried their canoe around swollen waterfalls. They paddled upstream nearly twelve miles, passing many troops to come to the head of the column. After dark, they encamped, "very wet and much fatigued. . . . It was near eleven o'clock before we could dry our clothes and take a little refreshment, when we wrapped ourselves in our blankets and slept very comfortably until four o'clock in the morning." Arnold was waked by a multitudinous crashing. Gigantic dams of driftwood and fallen trees came groaning down the river bed as the water rose many feet in a few minutes. Before he could reach his belongings, they were awash. "Very luckily for us, we had a small hill to retreat to, where we conveyed our baggage and passed the remainder of the night in no very agreeable situation."

The next morning the sun glinted down from a clear, windswept sky on what Arnold considered "a very disagreeable prospect, the country round entirely overflowed, so that the course of the river, being crooked, could not be discovered; which, with the rapidity of the current, renders it almost impossible for the bateaux to ascend the river, or the men to find their way by land, or pass the small brooks, and arms of the river, etc. Add to this our provisions almost exhausted, and the incessant rains for three days past has prevented our gaining anything considerable, so that we have but a melancholy prospect before us. "But," he added, "in general high in spirits."

From his hillside, Arnold stared anxiously down the flood. He was relieved when at nine o'clock the riflemen appeared, wet but paddling valiantly. He dried his baggage for a full day while two more groups went by. The next morning, the commands of Enos and Greene, about half his army, had still not come up, but he was too impatient to wait longer or to seek them down river. Propelled by his Indian paddlers, he pushed ahead, and toward evening he came to a double bend below a waterfall where the current swirled passionately. There were broken boats in the stream, and many riflemen were drying themselves on the banks. "We had the misfortune," Arnold wrote, "of oversetting seven bateaux and losing all the provisions. Here the whole division encamped. The river continues high and rapid, and as our provisions are but short, and no intelligence from Canada, I ordered a council of war."

Thus briskly Arnold reported disaster. His journal reveals always the physical assurance of an athlete certain he possessed the strength to overcome all troubles. Energetic paragraphs which contain no repining, but imply that whatever must be done is being done with a minimum of fuss or worry, indicate why men cheerfully followed Benedict Arnold into danger.

By the pounding waters of the swollen river, the council of war discussed whether to go on or give up. Before them lay an arduous and unknown terrain and then enemy territory where savage Indians and trained European soldiers might be waiting to destroy them. Their munitions were reduced by loss and water. Weakened by exposure, the men were falling prey to rheumatism and dysentery. Ice now encrusted the shallows along the river banks; at nightfall, wet clothes froze rigid; winter was clearly deepening. Since most of the supplies they had brought with them had either gone overboard or been ruined in the leaky boats; since the disturbances inevitable to so large a party drove away game and kept fish clinging to the bottom of the river, "cooking," as one officer remarked, "had gone out of fashion." Soon actual starvation might begin. And every rigor was made more terrifying by the forest, "a direful, howling wilderness, not describable."

When all had been going well, Arnold had made preparations for retreat; in adversity, he persuaded his officers to boldness. Having sent home the sick, the feeble, and the faint of heart, they would proceed with as many men as could be given fifteen days' provisions. But supposing they did not escape from the forest in fifteen days, or that the last supplies were destroyed as the rest had been? To meet such contingencies, forty picked woodsmen, under Captain Oliver Hanchet, were ordered to dash for the French settlements and to return at once with whatever food they could buy. Arnold decided to accompany this advance party rather than investigate what had happened to the half of his army somewhere down river. The reasons for his decision are not clear. Perhaps he wanted to be present at the politically important first contact with the Canadians; perhaps he wished to share with his men the danger of meeting an ambush; perhaps he decided that securing food was the most important task that remained; perhaps his temperament urged him to stay in the lead. In any case, he set off, sped by his powerful Indian paddlers, and during the rest of the march most of his army did not see him again.

The rear divisions were ignorant of what was happening in front. At the height of the flood, Colonel Enos had paddled ahead in search of Arnold, but, failing to reach him, had returned to his frightened men. Then the invalids who had been ordered back came drifting down in several boats. They told "lamentable stories" of unbreastable torrents and famine ahead; they whispered that "the army were all returning home except a few who were many miles forward with Colonel Arnold." A dispatch retailing the decisions of the council of war was hardly reassuring. And to top everything, winter struck in a snow storm. Colonel Greene's soldiers courageously resolved to persevere, but Colonel Enos turned back, taking with him about a quarter of the army and most of the remaining provisions. Had Arnold been present, with his ability to inspire confidence and his power to command, he could undoubtedly have prevented this crippling desertion.

He was far ahead. Having pushed through increasing snow to the Height of Land, he left Dead River and cut across the Canadian boundary to the Chaudière. The region which most of Arnold's men, their bateaux wrecked, would have to traverse on foot, was an unmapped hodgepodge of lakes, streams, marshes, ravines, ridges, and tangled fallen trees. The most probable-seeming route usually ended in a quagmire or on the wrong side of a half-frozen river; it would be possible for an army to wander here for days, gradually starving and freezing into nothingness. Arnold himself lost his way several times on the intricate watercourses and had to rescue by boat a group of Hanchet's men who were marooned in a marsh to which "they had waded two miles through water to their waists."

Arnold had fortunately sent ahead other emissaries in addition to the treacherous Eneas. They were waiting at the headwaters of the Chaudière to report that "the French inhabitants appear very friendly and are rejoiced at our approach; that there is very few troops in Quebec." Since it was now clear that no enemy forces were posted between Arnold and the villages where he hoped to secure provisions, he reduced the advance party to the fifteen men who could float rapidly down river in the few remaining boats. Again Arnold was faced with the choice of staying behind to look after his soldiers or dashing ahead to find them food. Again he decided to keep the lead. He quieted his fears about the safety of his army on the treacherous Height of Land by composing a letter of directions, appointing guides, and ordering Captain Hanchet to wait. That officer was furious at having his command taken from him when its success seemed assured. To his protests, Arnold countered with a lecture on discipline, adding one more to his regiment of enemies.

The Chaudière, Arnold soon discovered, "is very rapid, full of rocks and dangerous, and the more so to us as we had no guides.

VIEW of the old FRENCH FORT, REDOUBTS and BATTERIES at TICONDEROGA on LAKE CHAMPLAIN and HIS MAJESTY'S SHIP INFLEXIBLE also the PIERS Constructed with the Trunks of large Trees by the AMERICAN ARMY for the conveying of their Troops to Mount Independence taken on the spot by H. Rudyard Lieu.t of Eng.rs Engineers in the year 1777.

Fort Ticonderoga: UPPER: The fort in 1777, drawn on the spot by H. Rudyard, a lieutenant in the Royal Engineers. On the right is a line of rafts used by the Americans for communication between the main fort and Mount Independence. LOWER: Fort Ticonderoga as it stands today, after accurate restoration. *Both: Courtesy, Fort Ticonderoga.*

Arnold's March to Quebec: UPPER: The great falls of the Chaudière River. When swollen by rains that accompanied a hurricane, these falls and the rapids associated with them destroyed the last of Arnold's batteaux. *Photograph by Robert Cummings.* LOWER: A replica of one of the batteaux, manned by members of the Arnold Expedition Historical Society. The vessels, of which Arnold had more than two hundred, had to be small, because the men carried them on their shoulders around impediments. *Both: Courtesy of the Arnold Expedition Historical Society.*

We lashed our baggage to the boats, and the current carried us down the stream at the rate of eight or ten miles an hour." As quick as galloping horses, the bateaux charged through white water, but unlike horses they could not be stopped. A man stood in each bow with a pole, fending off boulders, and in the sterns steering oars churned the already turbulent flood. The flotilla roared around bends without knowing what fallen trees waited to stave the boats, what waterfalls to toss them in the air. However, there was exhilaration in the dash, and every hour might save the life of a starving soldier.

After they had gone about fifteen miles, the pace grew even faster, and they found themselves in the midst of "a very long rapid." With a splintering crash, a boat went to pieces against a rock; but the others could not slow down to help. There was a second crash, and more driftwood in the stream. A third boat went over, but was not smashed. "Six men," Arnold noted, "were a long time swimming in the water and were with difficulty saved." He cursed his misfortune, but soon discovered that the accident had been "a kind interposition of Providence," for had they not been stopped by shipwreck they would have been carried over a falls, "which we had never been apprized of," and "dashed to pieces and all lost."

Although they now navigated the river "with more precaution than before," the remaining boats covered forty miles the next day, and on the third day they saw smoke rising against the evening sky. The forest faltered; cultivated fields slid into view, and then a mingling of Indian wigwams with French Canadian huts. For Arnold, the arduous journey was over. He leaped ashore, pointed at beef cattle, waved money in his hand.

During his absence, his men suffered the worst dangers of the march. Despite the directions Arnold had sent them, they lost their way on the Height of Land. They struggled up cliffs slippery with ice, through snowy thickets, along the banks of unfordable rivers. They sank to their armpits in marshes, and when they struggled up on tufts of solid soil, their clothes froze "thick as panes of glass." As they wandered day after day, trapped in a wilderness maze, provisions gave out. In an agony of hunger, soldiers cooked their moccasins for soup, chewed on the leather, and proceeded barefoot. A pet dog was eaten. Many men died, yet gaunt figures kept staggering to the headwaters of the Chaudière.

Then they were no longer lost, but miles of wilderness still lay before them. All pretense of military formation was abandoned, as each man plunged ahead as best he was able. If one who moved stumbled over another motionless in the snow, he increased his pace; no one was strong enough to help his companions. Stretched along forty miles of river bank, troops were advancing silently, too exhausted to talk or cry out, when a sound of cheering started at the head of the column and moved slowly upstream. As each soldier struggled with his personal nightmare, he looked up to see "a vision of horned cattle . . . hurried on by men with horses loaded with sacks." Every few miles, an animal was slaughtered and a pound of beef given to every sufferer. Arnold had come to the rescue.

He was spending money lavishly to supply the needs of his troops. When he saw a sixteen-year-old private sitting on a log, too ill to proceed, Arnold sprang from his horse, arranged for the boy's care in a nearby farmhouse, and pressed two silver dollars into his hand. But no memory of Congressional committees inspired him to make out a voucher.

The appearance of an army from a wilderness considered impenetrable sent wild stories flying through Canada. After rumor had changed the word *toile* (linen), used to describe the riflemen's capes, to *tole* (sheet iron), the habitants visualized a band of conquistadors, grim in medieval armor, marching on Quebec. *Les Bostonnois*, as the Canadians called the invaders, inspired as much terror as enthusiasm. Although Arnold distributed proclamations of friendship; although one very old lady danced Yankee Doodle to her own singing for the edification of the troops; most Canadians preferred to remain neutral. They would let the British and Rebels fight it out, selling provisions to either if the price was high.

Arnold, who believed in the importance of show and had taken good care of his baggage, probably wore full regimentals when he received a delegation of Indians in their best feathers. After a chief, "with all the air and gesture of an accomplished orator," had asked why the Colonials had come among them in a hostile manner, he explained, without the least regard for fact, "The King's army at Boston came out into the fields and houses, killed a great many women and children." Raising 50,000 men, the Colonials had killed or wounded 1,500 redcoats, driven the rest aboard their ships. Then Arnold came to Canada to protect the inhabitants from foreign troops who "make them pay a greater price for their rum, etc." This statement, coupled with Arnold's martial bearing, so impressed the Indians that about forty joined his force.

Men continued to straggle out of the wilderness. Some who had been left behind for dead appeared, pale and wavering as ghosts, to the momentary terror of their companions. About two-thirds of Arnold's original army gathered slowly around him; how many of the rest had died, how many turned back, reliable statistics do not reveal. Since the cautious British commander had decided, when apprised by Eneas of the invasion, to await Arnold behind the ramparts of Quebec, no enemy appeared. On November 8, almost two months after he had left Cambridge, Arnold led some 600 men to the banks of the St. Lawrence.

Across the river they could see Quebec casting the reflection of its high, fortified bluffs deep into the water. The warehouses of the Lower Town looked easily accessible, but the men who were at Arnold's orders making scaling ladders, wondered whether such instruments could ever top the towering walls of the citadel. It was with nervous hands that a detail hammered out iron spearheads with which to defy cannon. Even to approach the lethal ramparts would be dangerous—perhaps impossible—for a frigate of twenty-six guns and a heavily armed sloop were moored in the St. Lawrence, and guard boats rowed back and forth in perpetual patrol. Since the forewarned British had taken all shipping from the Americans' side of the river, Arnold's men had nothing but light canoes which they had carried from distant creeks, fragile envelopes of birch bark that would collapse under cannon shot and could be sunk even by muskets.

Arnold was determined to cross secretly at night, but for three days the wind blew so hard that the canoes would have been swamped. All along, the weather had behaved like an English agent: hurricane, flood, snow, and now a gale kept Arnold from finding Quebec virtually undefended. Had he arrived two weeks before, the troops behind the walls would have been Canadian militiamen, less inclined to fight than surrender. Since then, almost every day had brought British reinforcements. Major General Guy Carleton, the experienced soldier who was royal governor of Canada, slipped in to take command; and while the final wind blew, Lieutenant Colonel Allen Maclean appeared with 200 kilted Highlanders. As the crack troops marched through the streets, the spirit of the King's partisans rose, and Arnold's friends looked for cover. Quebec was now in posture of defense.

On the far side of the St. Lawrence, Arnold paraded the force with which he hoped to conquer the Gibraltar of America. The soldiers, who had not been all together since they had entered the wilderness, stared at each other in amazement. "A more pitiful and humorous spectacle was exhibited than I had ever before seen," wrote Private Abner Stocking. The fine uniforms of officers hung in ribbons and were faded until indistinguishable from the torn homespun of the farm boys. Shoes were clumsily stitched folds of rawhide, hats a rarity. Men remembered as fat were now thin, thin men walking skeletons. Long hair hung lankly over brows or stood up from skulls in bursts; unkempt beards of every color jutted from the 600 jaws. "I thought," continued Private Stocking, "we much resembled the animals which inhabit New Spain called the Ourang-Outang."

The scarecrow army strutted as they passed their nattily uniformed commander; they cheered and waved their guns. Arnold shouted to his "brave boys" that Quebec was almost in their hands.

CHAPTER SEVEN

Misfortunes and the Price of Honor

HAD human enemies joined with flood, cold, and starvation, Arnold's army could have been annihilated while still scattered and starving, but most of the regulars in Canada were facing Schuyler on the Lake Champlain route. The largest British detachment had for some months been stationed at St. Johns. During the warm summer days, an officer resplendent in the red coat with blue facings of the Royal Fusiliers had often sat in the shade of a tree with a watercolor box beside him. As he busily illuminated a manuscript, Indians leaned over his shoulder, watching with stolid awe: redmen were always amazed by white men's art. If a shape began to look three dimensional, John André had to watch lest a brown hand smudge the colors as it reached down to feel.

André and his companions had changed St. Johns from the weak post Arnold had raided. Sod walls rose around two compounds, each 100 feet square, one enclosing an old brick barracks, the other a brick house and wooden barn. A 300-foot passage joined the redoubts. On three sides, a stockade and moat guarded the entire works, while the fourth side was protected by the Sorel River which flowed, half a mile wide, northward from Lake Champlain. Directly in front of the fortification, a little shipyard dabbled in the water. Here, to oppose the boats Arnold had captured earlier that summer, a schooner and a row galley were building. André was quartermaster for the men from his regiment, who formed the

73

largest detachment in the garrison made up of other regulars, French Canadian volunteers, a few sailors and Indians.

After some abortive advances and ignominious retreats, the Rebels began to besiege the strong point on September 17, 1775. (Arnold, leading the other prong of the invasion, had just set out from Cambridge for the Kennebec.)

André signalized his sudden transformation into a fighting man by beginning a military diary in which he tried, with a determination that seems almost desperate, to present himself as an imperturbable soldier. Observation of human character is suppressed, wit appears only in rare flashes; sensibility even more rarely, and emotion only when he has not succeeded in suppressing it. The map he drew of the terrain is accurate, not decorative.

The immediate result of the Rebel landing, André noted, was overcrowding: the British were obliged to "encumber" the fort with eighty women and children who had been outside in huts. This raised to about 650 the persons "contained in a barrack built for twenty-five men, a barn, and a large house. . . . The men had neither bedding, straw, or blankets."

During the night, some 200 Rebels, under Arnold's enemy John Brown, slipped by the fort and cut the supply line to Canada. The first reaction of the British commander, Major Charles Preston, was "to bring in the cattle belonging to the neighboring farms." Only after the mooing herds had added to the confusion in the fort, did he send out a detachment to dislodge Brown. Firing sounded in the woods, and then a messenger appeared for more ammunition. At the head of twenty men, André was sent to deliver it. The terrain was not what he had imagined in his military dreams: branches poked at his eyes and mud sucked at his feet. Finally, he came out of the wilderness into a meadow where a dead soldier lay among the goldenrod, and four or five bleeding men squirmed on the ground. André's revulsion comes faintly through his comment, "In this affair, as there have since been throughout the campaign in Canada, there were Englishmen fighting against Englishmen, French against French, and Indians of the same tribe against each other."

The British, who had driven the Rebels into the forest, were expressing their disdain by calmly rebuilding a log bridge the enemy had torn up to make a breastwork. "Some noise was heard," André relates, "and an Indian who appeared at the edge of the wood was seized by two or three who were with us. A good many shot were then fired from behind the trees and bushes, but, upon our returning the fire very briskly, nothing more was heard of the enemy."

It had been an easy victory, but when the enemy again cut the supply line, Major Preston did not let his troops rout them once more. He dispatched three Indians to Montreal for help and then bolted shut the gates. A cold rain began to fall. During the soaking nights, even the regulars became jittery as they peered from their tiny fortress. On the 19th, André rushed with his companions to the ramparts when a sentry fired his piece, and on the 20th an alarm elicited "almost a general fire from the works. In the morning," André continues, "a horse was found dead: this was the enemy our out sentry had seen and challenged."

Daylight showed crowded, muddy compounds and, beyond the walls, a field of rank marsh grass that soon gave way to a choked forest. In occasional clearings, from which the stumps had not been drawn, deserted cabins sagged. The landscape was scarred with impassable quagmires and fallen timber. Across the river, "a perfect howling swamp" was framed by dark hemlocks and firs. A gentleman's house in a considerable clearing a mile to the north-wards seemed imported from another world.

Although outnumbered four to one, the British with their more and better cannon kept the besiegers far from the walls. Eight days passed before the Rebels succeeded in getting two mortars into position, and then the guns proved of such poor quality that they did hardly any damage. "We had our daily little cannonade," André wrote, "and seventeen shells burst among us in the evening without hurting anyone." More depressing was the weather; chilling rain alternated with clear days of bitter cold.

The monotony was finally relieved by some drunken Indians who reeled in to report that Ethan Allen had been captured during a farcical attempt to take Montreal. Disobeying all orders, the wild irregular had attacked with eighty men on the theory that the Canadians would rise. He was said to be on the way to England in irons.

75

When the little shipyard had completed the schooner and the row galley, André foresaw the end of the siege: "The universal cry was to go up with the vessels to attack the enemy, and to send a party by land at the same time to spike their guns." Although rumor reported that "some scheme for an attack was fixed upon," the fleet did no more than spray the shores with grapeshot, and the only sortie was the intrepid mission of Captain Monin and M. Moiquin who brought in eight cows that appeared at the edge of the wood.

Preston's policy, it became clear, was to block the Rebel advance as long as possible and hope that Governor Carleton would be able to enlist enough Canadians to relieve the fort. Every few nights, another messenger scuttled through the woods to call for help, but, so André wrote, no official word came back from the outside world. The defenders were, of course, ignorant of Arnold's expedition which was now mounting the Kennebec.

After three weeks of confinement in the tiny, freezing works the French Canadian volunteers began deserting by twos and threes. "They surely suffered a great deal," André commented, "but it was no time to complain. . . . We began to be more sparing of our ammunition to make it keep proportion with our provisions."

As he lived dirtily in 100-foot compounds with dirty crowds from whom there was no escape, able to walk only a few hundred yards, sentenced to food unworthy of beasts, and in perpetual danger as enemy guns barked and enemy shots fell, André could not comfort himself with the thought that he was engaged in a glorious adventure. The garrison, he realized, was able to hold out at all only because of the incompetence of the Rebels. "Had they understood, or been a fit people to carry on" a scientific siege, they might by proper approaches have brought their batteries "much closer to our redoubts, have overlooked us, destroyed our breast-works, and, by a slaughter from which there would have been no shelter, have rendered our holding out a mere sacrifice of men who might be reserved for better services."

Bravely André expressed the true military attitude; lives were only worth saving if they could be more usefully expended on another occasion. He tried to write of the enemy equally impersonally, but sometimes he could not help thinking of them as people.

He found it amusing that the Americans called a gigantic mortar they were bringing up "the sow," and when the mortar burst after a few shots, he noted, "The witty observed that the sow brought her pigs to a fine market. The enemy, on their side, were heard to laugh, and we afterward had reason to think that anything relating to the sow was a better joke to them than to us."

On October 10, after twenty-four days of siege, "we could see the enemy dragging cannon on the other side of the river." A day later, "men and gun carriages were seen crossing the river." On the 13th, "a great many men with packs on their backs" hurried by on the opposite shore. "Many thought the enemy were going to attack Chambly," the fortress that guarded their line of retreat. (Arnold had now crossed from the Kennebec to Dead River.)

The Rebel cannon had been creeping closer, and on the 14th the whole situation changed in a howl of powder. A thirteen-inch shell "made the inside of the house a pile of rubbish in which scarcely a habitable corner was to be found. The shell burst in falling," André continues, "and the experiment if our magazine was bombproof was not tried." However, "part of a barrel of powder blew up in the south redoubt." A lieutenant was killed, and six soldiers wounded, one fatally.

The next day, the cannonading killed more defenders and blasted the schooner to the bottom of the river. "The weather," André wrote, "grew very cold, and, as the windows of the house were all broken, as many as could find room in the cellars slept there. The rest, unable either to get a place or to bear the heat and disagreeable smell arising from such numbers being crowded together, slept above in cold and danger, or walked about the greatest part of the night." It rained. The enemy "thought fit to rouse us at midnight with a few shells and shot." A carpenter was hustled by him, with a bleeding stump where his arm should have been.

"We were constantly employed in throwing up traverses. These, from the hasty manner in which they were constructed and the bad weather, soon fell in; and were again propped and repaired, so that our shattered house, together with the ruinous traverses, mud ditches, broken platforms, etc., exhibited a very ragged scene. Within doors, if that could be called within doors where doors

77

and windows were broken in pieces, the appearance was no better: heaps of boards, earth, glass, brick, and other rubbish lay promiscuously scattered. The rooms, by the partitions being broke, were mostly laid together, and the roof and ceiling were open on every side. . . . The south redoubt was no better circumstanced: a thirteen-inch shell had fallen into the barn and many shot had struck the house. Our rum, wine, etc., were exhausted. Salt pork was our daily fare, with sometimes a few roots, and we reduced ourselves about this time to two-thirds the usual allowance."

The situation of the sick and wounded "was a very cruel one. They were neither out of the reach of danger nor were they sheltered from the inclemency of the weather, or provided with any of those things which might alleviate their sufferings." Each day, the little cemetery between the houses grew more extensive.

Firing was heard toward Chambly, and Preston sent out another plea for help. Then the forest opened to emit a British officer, but he was surrounded by Rebels. In spotless regimentals that contrasted with the bedraggled uniforms of St. Johns's defenders, the drum major of the Royal Fusiliers had come "to inform us that Chambly had surrendered and to request leave for bateaux to pass the forts with the prisoners and their baggage." André limited himself to this laconic statement, leaving it to the French diarist Foucher to express the indignation of the garrison that their fellow soldiers had given in after only two days' siege, while still copiously supplied, and without losing a man.

As the tragedy deepened, André trusted his pen less and less. The next day he noted briefly, "The garrison of Chambly passed the forts." Yet he must have been moved to see float by under Rebel guard eighty of His Majesty's crack troops, and—most humiliating to a soldier of André's cast—the standard of the Royal Fusiliers. There seemed little hope that he and his companions would not soon also be captured, for the drum major had informed them that Carleton had started to their relief with every soldier he could raise, but had been defeated, and was now helpless to relieve them. At this grievous moment, when the French volunteers were begging to be allowed "to capitulate for themselves," the doomed garrison received a touching reinforcement. André noted impassively: "A young man came into the forts with a flag of truce to bring three women whose husbands were in the fort."

The rain that was engulfing Arnold in flood fell incessantly. A sergeant received "a mortal wound from a splinter of a brick. Three balls," André commented, "have at different times entered the officers' guardroom at the South Redoubt, and, though there were never less than eight or ten people in the room, and once thirteen, no one was hurt, if we except Captain Stronge who received a slight contusion." However, "the weather began to be exceeding cold, and the men to fall sick. We were obliged to diminish the guards . . . for want of a sufficient number for a relief. Our ammunition became scarce, and we fired little and only small balls."

Shooting was heard toward Montreal, and then an Indian sneaked in to deny that Carleton had been defeated. On the contrary, 5,000 regulars had arrived from England, and a relief expedition was on the way. "We gave him a letter for General Carleton which was fastened in a silver tag he wore in his hair." To complete the jubilation, "nine fat pigs came running toward the fort and were received with great cordiality."

However, the Rebels were building a battery on a hill to the northwest that dominated the fort. (Schuyler's field commander, Brigadier General Richard Montgomery, had wanted to put it there weeks before but had been outvoted by his subordinates; "the privates," he complained, "are all generals.") When the battery finally spoke, "large pieces of the wall were knocked in. . . . The few corners where some little shelter from the weather was to be had were now no longer tenable. A great many shot passed through the parapets and some wounded men behind them." In all parts of the crowded fortification, soldiers dropped down.

Toward night, the enemy beat a parley. Across the frozen field there skipped a Montreal hairdresser who, on being admitted to the fort, assured Preston that Carleton had indeed been defeated. There was no hope, the bubbling Frenchman told the gray and silent British commander. However, Montgomery would be glad to accept surrender on honorable terms.

When Preston sent word to the Rebels that the hairdresser was not to be believed, as he was "frequently subject to fits of insanity," Montgomery offered to let them question a respectable Montreal citizen who was his prisoner. "An officer," André wrote, "was sent up to the Point"; we learn from Foucher that the officer was André. He was certainly blindfolded before he entered the American lines. Having groped his way up the side of the sloop Arnold had stolen, he was then allowed to see a little rocking room in which a Canadian grandee sat dejectedly. André listened as the voice, sometimes indignant and sometimes sad, complained that the peasants had been unfaithful to their overlords and their church. No one would fight except the possessors of estates, and they, alas, were too few. Not only had Carleton been defeated, but, as reinforcements had not actually arrived from England, he had no possibility of raising another army. André concluded, "There was now nothing left but to frame the best articles [of surrender] we could for the garrison."

Concerning the surrender ceremony on November 3, 1775 (Arnold was gathering his troops in the French settlements), André wrote only, "The troops marched out of the redoubts and embarked for an encampment of the Rebels, two miles above St. Johns." Yet there was much to describe. When Montgomery's army filed into the clearing before the forts, André saw for the first time the men who had defeated him. The New York Regiments looked almost military down to the waist—they were uniformed that far—but trousers of every material and color gave them away. Most of the others wore civilian clothes. Although Montgomery, who had once been a British officer, stood straight and was suitably accoutered, his staff slouched around him, many without epaulets and some lacking swords.

After this motley gang had drawn up in slovenly lines, the British, led by their music, marched from their shattered fortifications with rigid ceremony, as though changing guards at a palace: the Twenty-sixth in red coats faced with pale yellow; André's Fusiliers in red coats with blue facings and white lace; the Royal Artillery in blue and white; the sailors with tarred pigtails. Under his high grenadier cap decorated with a rose, a garter, a crown, and a galloping horse, André kept his face firm and moved with proud precision.

The regulars halted, facing their ragged captors, and Major

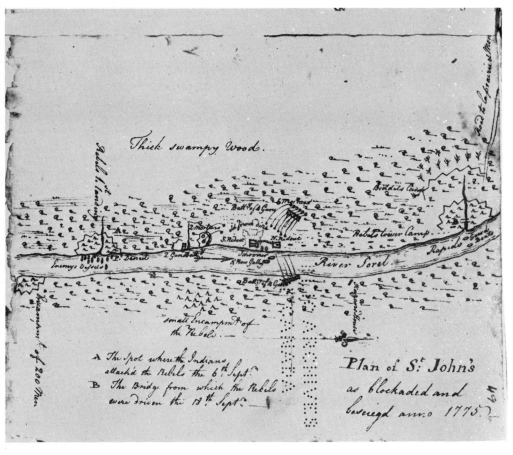

The siege of St. John's. A drawing, taken from André's diary, of the extended and frustrating action that introduced the elegant artist-poet to the grim realities of warfare. *Courtesy, Public Archives of Canada.*

Sir Charles Grey, the first general whom André served as aide, was a born killer. He taught the sensitive youth the arts and advantages of military murder. Engraving after a miniature from the *European Magazine*, 1797.

Sir Henry Clinton, the British commander in chief who, falling under the sway of André's ability and charm, promoted the junior officer, with dizzying and resented speed, to be adjutant general of the entire army. *Courtesy, Vincent Freedley. Photograph, Frick Art Reference Library.*

Preston barked an order; André's sword lay before him on the ground. Then Montgomery, the renegade English officer, spoke, "Brave men like you deserve an exception to the rules of war. Let the officers and volunteers take back their swords."

Eager to show him a perpetual slave of love, Anna Seward asserted that André wrote an unidentified friend, "I have been taken prisoner by the Americans and stripped of everything but the picture of Honora, which I concealed in my mouth. Preserving that, I consider myself fortunate." Actually, André kept his possessions; the garrison was not plundered.[1]

With his fellow quartermasters, André went to Montreal on parole to collect the soldiers' baggage. He found that even there the scepter of His Britannic Majesty cast but an evanescent shadow. The Indian allies had returned to their wigwams, the militia had deserted, subjects once faithful were turning their coats; Governor Carleton was preparing to flee, with the few regulars who were not dead or captured, to make a last stand at Quebec. Since whatever goods were left in Montreal would fall to the Rebels, André helped gather up everything that could possibly be considered private property of the soldiers. Montgomery heard that the baggage the quartermasters carried off filled "about twenty-two small bateaux."

André's little fleet soon met the advancing Americans. Shivering in torn clothes and with rags wrapped around their feet, the Rebels muttered to see British officers wearing warm, stylish coats pass by in vessel after vessel piled above the gunwales with goods destined for captured enemies. Finally, the quartermasters were halted at bayonet point.

Montgomery, who had just marched without opposition into Montreal, wrote Schuyler, "I wish some method could be fallen upon of engaging *gentlemen* to serve; a point of honor and more knowledge of the world, to be found in that class of men, would greatly reform discipline, and render the troops much more tractable. The officers of the First Regiment of Yorkers and Artillery Company were very near a mutiny the other day because I would not stop the clothing of the garrison of St. Johns. I would not have sullied my own reputation, nor disgraced the Continental arms, by such a breach of capitulation for the universe. There was no driving it into their noodles that the clothing was really the property of the soldier; that he had paid for it; and that every regiment, in this country especially, saved a year's clothing, to have decent clothes to wear on particular occasions." Finally, the general managed to bully his troops into letting the quartermasters go.

Eight days after the surrender, André was back at St. Johns with the baggage, which was now loaded on sixty carts. He looked wistfully at the fallen walls which had been so imperfect a shield. "We left in the fort about three days' provisions," he wrote, "scarce any loose powder, and three boxes of ammunition for each gun that was mounted; that is, the quantity kept in case of storm. . . . The men showed a cheerfulness under their fatigues which, [in] spite of events, can but reflect honor upon them, as few could be so devoid of reflection as not to see how slender our hopes of relief were, and, of course, to apprehend the most unfavorable issue. . . . Upon the whole, it may be said that the garrison of St. Johns suffered, in their misfortunes, danger and hardships which have often been the price of honor to more fortunate troops." It was small consolation.

According to the terms of the surrender, André was to join his companions in "Connecticut or such other province as the Honorable Congress shall direct, there to remain until our unhappy differences shall be compromised or till they are exchanged." André was sentenced, perhaps for years, to exile in some rural corner of this hostile land. His first war seemed to have come to an ignominious end.

CHAPTER EIGHT

A Proud City to Conquer

ARNOLD was still encamped on the far side of the St. Lawrence from Quebec, waiting for a chance to slip birch-bark canoes past warships. On November 13, 1775, the wind that had for three days made the river impassable blew itself out. When the night proved starless, Arnold lined up his troops without lights in the impenetrable black. After some thirty-five canoes had been eased into the tide, he led the long procession across dim water that reflected the distant glow of the city and nearer, two grills of brightness, the anchored men-of-war that could, with a few cannon shots, sink his whole flotilla. Elsewhere in the darkness, he knew, British rowboats moved ceaselessly on patrol.

A mile and a half of river separated the canoes from Wolfe's Cove, where that general had landed when he had captured Quebec. At first, the thundering of Chaudière Falls made it safe for Arnold to whisper orders, but mid-stream was so still that if water dripped from a raised paddle, his heart tightened. Then a rhythmic clanking approached, the oarlocks of a British barge. As the canoes scattered, Arnold strained for the sound of a shout or a shot, but the rowing moved evenly out of hearing.

Wolfe's Cove emerged from the darkness. With an irregular clicking, the riflemen cocked their weapons, and, as birch bark groaned softly on sand, Arnold led his men over the side. Then rustling foliage made the only sound. The troops fanned out over

83

a dark field without encountering any pickets. The dim shape of a rifleman whispered to Arnold that the path which led up to the city was unguarded, and a minute later another shadow reported that the sentries on Quebec's ramparts were shouting, "All's well!" Clearly the enemy, convinced he could not pass the guarding warships, had taken no further precautions. Although Arnold had not intended to storm the strongly reinforced city, it suddenly seemed possible that on this quiet night America's greatest fortress might be taken by surprise.

The canoes had already returned to get another load. In continuing silence, there was a second shadowy landing and a third. Some 350 soldiers and Indians were gathered around their commander when the moon rode serenely into the heavens, making visible the hulls of the guarding warships, and even their spidery rigging. Several hundred men and the all important scaling ladders were still on the far side of the river; but for the night, ferrying was done.

Arnold had almost decided to attack anyway when alien oarlocks sounded. A British barge steered into the cove. Giving his voice as English a sound as he could manage, Arnold shouted to the sailors to come ashore. Instead, they backwatered. Arnold's riflemen fired, "a screaming and dismal lamentation" rose from the barge, but it disappeared around a bend to give the alarm. Arnold gave up all hope of surprising the city.

To attack would have been foolhardy to the point of madness; yet Quebec might have fallen. In their overconfidence, the British had left a huge gate open—the fastenings were out of order and no one knew where the keys were hung—and had neglected to lay out matches with which to fire the cannon. Or so Arnold's spies reported when it was too late. He may well have considered this an object lesson against military caution.

The next morning, Arnold advanced unopposed up the bluff to the Plains of Abraham. After the rest of his detachment had sneaked across the river, he blockaded Quebec, hoping that privation would make the citizens rebel or force the garrison to sally out, giving him a chance at battle. When redcoats finally issued from a portal, Arnold sprinted toward them at the head of his detachment, but the enemy were merely capturing a sentry. Arnold saw the great gate slam shut behind them.

His frustrated troops came to a ragged halt; he commanded them to line up in drill formation. On the parapets high above, citizens and soldiers yelled excitedly to see the ragged band march and countermarch behind their gamecock colonel. Finally, Arnold gave the order to fall out. Wriggling closer under whatever cover they could find, his men insulted high walls with musket and rifle shot. Then hatless, hairy figures jumped to their feet; they waved emaciated arms and dared the King's minions to come out and fight.

Governor Carleton had too little faith in the loyalty of the Quebeckers, too much respect for the haggard army at his gates, to risk an engagement that might lose the last British stronghold in Canada. His soldiers bustled not around the sally port but around the cannon. The first volley went over the heads of the Americans, the next churned the ground at their feet. "To these salutes," a private wrote, "we gave them all we could, another and another huzza." Arnold was amused when his men chased after the balls and picked them up with gestures of thanks.

Arnold, as he reported to Washington, perpetually defied the enemy "in the hope of drawing them out, but to no effect, though they kept a constant cannonading, and killed us one man." However, it was only when he was told that 200 soldiers who had escaped from Montreal were coming to join the defenders, that he ordered an examination "of our arms and ammunition, when, to my surprise, I found many of our cartridges unfit for use (which to appearance were very good) and that we had no more than five rounds to each man. It was judged prudent in our situation not to hazard a battle, but to retire to this place [Pointe aux Trembles] eight leagues from Quebec, which we did yesterday." He was waiting eagerly for Montgomery to arrive from Montreal with the ammunition and reinforcements that would justify a renewal of the siege.

Arnold's report to Washington is an amazing document. Instead of stating that he had for weeks courted battle before checking his ammunition, it would have seemed prudent to cite other valid reasons for the retreat: nakedness in freezing weather, increasing sickness, a greatly outnumbered force. Or he might have given some excuse for the belated discovery rather than emphasize, as Arnold did, "my surprise."

Since he was helpless unless reinforced by troops that had traversed the easier Lake Champlain route, all the rigors of the wilderness march had served no useful end; Arnold had reported the failure of his mission. Furthermore, Montgomery's arrival would reduce him to second in command; he had lost his chance to become famous as Quebec's captor. Yet to Washington he expressed no regret; and in other letters he grew lyrical over the achievements of his men. Their vain adventure was "not to be paralleled in history." He described how they had found themselves "short of provisions, part of the detachment disheartened and gone back, famine staring us in the face, an enemy's country and uncertainty ahead." Yet his force, "inspired and fired with the love of liberty and their country, pushed on with a fortitude superior to every obstacle." Once at Quebec, "my brave men were in want of everything but stout hearts, and would have gladly met the enemy, whom we endeavored in vain to draw out of the city, though we had not ten rounds of ammunition a man, and they double our numbers." As for the future, "My detachments are as ready as naked men can be to march wherever they may be required."

When Arnold had written home from mercantile voyages, his letters had been one long complaint against injustice and evil fortune; now, although buffeted by ill luck that made his business difficulties seem trifling, he did not complain. Leader of an exciting adventure, serving the same cause as his admiring companions, the perpetual misfit had at last found happiness. He felt neither lonely nor undervalued.

On December 1, Arnold stood at attention in front of his soldiers, as there alighted from a topsail schooner a tall and slender man, bald on the top of his head, who had a mild and dreamy look that seemed ill-suited to a soldier. But General Montgomery saluted with all the punctilio of his training in the British army and complimented Arnold's corps as "an exceedingly fine one. . . . There is a style and discipline among them superior to what I have been used to in this campaign."

Possessing in common physical courage and a thirst for military glory, Arnold and Montgomery complemented one another in other ways. Colonial-born and fresh from civilian life, Arnold was better at handling the militia, whose undisciplined vagaries Montgomery found endlessly irritating, but he respected in the former British officer the skill and judgment of the regular army. Montgomery, who was naturally apprehensive and melancholy, kept Arnold fascinated by the fine changing of his moods, and was glad to have his spirits buoyed by his subordinate's automatic optimism. Since he was consulted on all major decisions, Arnold could admire wholeheartedly the general's greater social position and breeding. Although he hated to be commanded by men he considered his inferiors, Arnold was no leveling democrat; under Montgomery, he played contentedly a subordinate role.

The general had brought clothes, ammunition, and a few of the cannon Arnold had completely lacked, but, since most of his militiamen had gone home after the capture of Montreal, he added only 300 men to Arnold's 675. That the combined force was strong enough to return to the Plains of Abraham did not solve the problem of how to take Quebec. Although Arnold cheerfully wrote Washington that the walls were "in a ruinous situation," they could withstand any artillery the Colonials possessed. Shells were lobbed over the ramparts, followed by arrows from which propaganda leaflets fluttered, but the shells were too small to do any real damage, and the propaganda did not persuade the inhabitants to throw open the gates.

Since trenches could not be dug in the frozen earth and the underlying rock forbade mining, a classical siege was out of the question. Even an effective blockade was barred by the fewness of troops and by the enemy cannon that kept sentries far from the walls. Nor was it expedient to wait for spring and reinforcements: as soon as the melting ice opened the river, regulars would probably arrive from England. Furthermore, until the fall of Quebec placed all Canada in American hands, no one would accept the only money Montgomery and Arnold had left—Continental paper—and supplies could not be requisitioned without the loss of essential good will. The troops were beginning to starve in the midst of plenty. To cap the climax, the enlistments of Arnold's soldiers ran out on December 31; and the men, who had not been paid, were determined to go home. The alternatives were to give up or attempt an escalade, an assault over unbroken walls.

Arnold had written that such an attack would require between 2,000 and 2,500 men; sickness had left the Colonials only 800 effectives. However, Montgomery and Arnold persuaded themselves that among the enemy troops, which greatly outnumbered their own, only the handful of Fusiliers from André's regiment were worth worrying about. Since Carleton had to protect two and a half miles of works for twenty-four hours a day, a sudden attack at an unexpected place would carry the Americans into the city. Then undoubtedly the Canadian militia would throw down their arms.

Montgomery and Arnold decided to try at night under the cover of the next blinding blizzard. However, the skies remained discouragingly fair. As sun and stars gleamed on long-fallen snow, as the smoke of Quebec's thousand chimneys hovered in windless air, smallpox broke out in the American camp, and a group of Arnold's officers announced that they would serve under him no longer.

Major John Brown, Arnold's old Ticonderoga enemy who had come with Montgomery from Montreal, had warned Captain Hanchet, the new enemy Arnold had made in the wilderness, that the unprincipled general was arranging to get him killed. Hanchet had thereupon refused to go on missions he considered dangerous. That others had gone gladly, and that Arnold had used "harsh language," did not heal the breach. Now that an admittedly perilous attack was planned, Hanchet joined two more of Arnold's captains in insisting that they would march their troops home unless they were placed in a separate corps under Brown. "This," Montgomery wrote, "is resentment against Arnold, and will hurt him so much I do not think I can consent to it," although the desertion "threatens to ruin our affairs." In the end, Arnold publicly apologized for overbearing actions—"I am a passionate man" —and the dissidents returned to his command.

On December 27, a snow storm blew in. At about midnight, the men were paraded, and ordered to put sprigs of hemlock in their hats so that, despite their lack of uniforms, they could recognize one another. A false attack was to draw the defenders to the business district by the river, while Montgomery and Arnold, with two-thirds of the army, clambered on ladders from the Plains of Abraham into the walled Upper Town. However, before the army could get in motion, stars appeared overhead. The only *Bostonnois* who entered Quebec that night were frightened deserters.

When movements in the city made it clear that the deserters had revealed their plan, Montgomery and Arnold decided to reverse it. After two detachments had decoyed the defenders to the walls which rose from the Plains of Abraham, the main attack would be made at the far side of the city, on the Lower Town which extended in an arc beneath the fortified cliffs and could be entered at each end by a narrow way along the river. Montgomery would come in from the southwest and Arnold from the northeast, hoping that no withering fire would pour from above while they were in the narrow lanes. Even if they could not fight their way up the heavily defended passages to the citadel, they would be in control of the business section; the merchants, whose wealth was endangered, might arrange a surrender. The remonstrances of subordinates, who pointed out that two British shots could leave the army commanderless, did not dissuade Montgomery and Arnold from their determination each to lead his own corps.

Everything now depended on the weather; it was a race between snow and the end of the year, when most of Arnold's men would go home. December 28 was "clear and mild"; the 29th "clear, fine weather"; the 30th dawned clear. But as Arnold looked angrily at the brightly rising sun, he felt a breath coming up river from the ocean. Soon a whistling wind brought clouds that joined to hide the sun, and then he heard a hiss of snow. When toward evening Arnold stepped from his headquarters, he could hardly see his outstretched hand. Rushing jubilantly back, he perfected his plans and gave peremptory orders.

About midnight, however, he looked up from his desk in consternation. The rattling on his windowpanes was abating. Outside, the snow fell with a light, lyrical gentleness. Arnold cursed and paced his floor. But gradually the rattling began again, louder and louder until it sounded like the distant drums beating to battle, like the fire of ten thousand muskets.

Now Arnold hurried into the blizzard and visited the houses

where his men were quartered; a quick examination of a rifle, an energetic word, and he was outside again, gleeful to see that the tight snow kernels rushed horizontally with the gale. At 2 A.M. flickering lights marked the opening of many doors; shadowy figures surrounded their commander. With tense efficiency, he lined them up in single file, first the forlorn hope of thirty men Arnold was himself to lead; then artillerymen holding ropes attached to a sled on which a cannon was mounted; then Morgan with a picked group of riflemen; and at last the long line of ordinary soldiers who held the lappets of their coats over the gunlocks that must not get wet. For identification each hat bore a paper on which was written "Liberty or death." Every head was bent forward since "it was impossible to keep our faces up against the imperious storm."

Stepping into the lead, Arnold advanced for some minutes and then halted, the snake of men coming to a stop behind him. Through the stinging darkness he stared toward the opposite side of the city where Montgomery's column was advancing. Suddenly high up in the snowy sky there appeared a light, then a second, then a third. The signal rockets! Arnold waved his sword and ran.

Instantly a wall loomed on his right. He had hardly passed the Palace Gate when a church bell clanged; a few more steps, and every bell in Quebec cried alarm. As he raced into a narrow passage between the river and the overhanging ramparts, the storm seemed to abate. The bastions against which he rubbed his shoulder remained silent, but cannon boomed on the other side of the Upper Town. A distant glow showed that fireballs were being shot out to illuminate the Plains of Abraham; some defenders, at least, were being drawn away by the feigned attacks.

When, with the rest of the forlorn hope crowding at his heels, Arnold ran out of the narrow way into the Lower Town, the storm struck again in full force. An uproar of musketry sounded behind him; his men had been discovered, and were being strafed from above. Although the walls near Arnold were still silent, he bore away from them, following the river. He found himself in a maze of wharfs and shops; he stumbled over an anchor half-buried in the snow; he ducked under a hawser. Ice thrown up by the river made an irregular wall at his left.

Now he came to a street with houses on both sides. He could not see them yet, but he knew that across this street there was a barricade and behind it two cannon, probably loaded with grape, that menaced the whole passage. To batter down this obstacle he had brought his own cannon on a sled. He paused for it to come up, but soon the artillerymen were around him with empty hands; the sled had foundered in a snowdrift. There was nothing to do but charge, and hope for the best. Arnold was still in the lead when an explosion rocked the alley and the houses rattled with a heavier hail. Men fell, but Arnold was not hit. He kept running, his nerves tense for the fire of the second cannon. Instead, he heard the smaller noise of musket shots "from the houses and other unexpected places." Arnold felt a sharp pain in his leg. The momentum of his run carried him almost to the barrier, but then he found himself leaning against a wall.

Morgan and his riflemen rushed by him and pushed their deadly weapons through the portholes of the barricade. Although the British artillerymen could no longer get at their cannon (one of which had misfired), the passage was still blocked. Musket shot continued to pour down from the houses. As more and more of his troops came to a halt in the murderous street, Arnold shouted orders and encouragement, but he was unable to drag himself from the wall. Pain and loss of blood made time move for him with great slowness: only a few minutes elapsed before the riflemen scaled the barricade, yet Arnold wrote it down as an hour. The obstacle captured, troops went over it in a stream.

Finally Arnold allowed Parson Spring and another man to help him toward the rear. He staggered with his arms over their shoulders, dragging his leg. Sometimes they stumbled over a body covered with snow. Arnold could see no enemy, but the ramparts overhead were alive with musket flashes; bullets sprayed everywhere. His troops were still advancing; "several," he wrote, "were shot down at my side." Seeing their commander being hustled by, the men paused irresolutely; Arnold cried in a cheering voice, "Rush on, brave boys! Rush on!" They resumed their running.

The wounded were being gathered in the Catholic *Hôpital Général*, some distance outside the walls. "Daylight," Dr. Isaac Senter remembered, "had scarce made its appearance" when Arnold was brought in. Two-thirds of a bullet, which seemed to have ricocheted from some hard object, had entered his leg halfway below the knee and traveled between the bones to lodge in the heel. Senter was extracting the fragment when a major appeared, wounded through the left shoulder, and "gave it as his opinion that we should not be successful. The fire and refire continued incessant. No news from the General [Montgomery] and his party yet, which gave us doubtful apprehension of their success."

Arnold lay helpless as messenger after messenger appeared, each recounting misfortune. Montgomery was dead, killed by the first cannon shot against his division; when their commander fell, his men had fled in disorder. Arnold's force had vanished into the city like a stone dropped into the ocean. An enemy sortie had captured one of the companies that was simulating an attack on the Upper Town. Then came the news that pulled Arnold upright; a British detachment was advancing on the hospital. Organizing stragglers and the healthiest invalids into a company, Arnold sent them off with some cannon.

The other invalids had risen waveringly from their beds and were tottering along the walls, gathering their possessions for flight. Shouting down a suggestion that he be carried to safety, Arnold ordered that the doors be locked: "The hospital must make the most vigorous defense possible." As the nuns who were tending the sick watched in terror, a weapon was forced into each shaking hand. His pistols and his sword on the bed beside him, Arnold intended personally "to kill as many as possible if they came in the room."

When the British failed to materialize—they had ducked back behind their ramparts—Arnold wrote Wooster, who was in command at Montreal, a brisk efficient letter in which he reported Montgomery's death, the defeat of the several columns, and that he was "exceedingly apprehensive" for his own corps. "They will either carry the Lower Town, be made prisoners, or cut to pieces. I thought proper to send an express to you to let you know the critical situation we are in, and make no doubt you will give us all the assistance in your power."

Canadians came in for news. Allowing none of the "excessive pain" he felt to show in his face, Arnold assured them that the

Lower Town had fallen and the citadel itself was cracking under siege. Since British power was almost at an end, his visitors, he assumed, would of course join his army.

However, his own officers refused to march out and reclaim some mortars left near the British walls; and almost a hundred of his few remaining troops made tracks for home. At last Arnold too gave in to nature. He resigned the command to a subordinate and lapsed into a coma from which he sometimes emerged to ask for news of the men he had last seen entering the Lower Town. There was no news. A soldier volunteered to find out; he vanished into the darkness toward Quebec, but never returned. While Arnold stirred in delirium, American morale sank so low that the army would have been helpless had the British marched out from behind their walls.

Three days after the attack, one of the great gates opened. From it there issued a drummer, a redcoat with a flag of truce, and Major Return Jonathan Meigs of Arnold's detachment. At the bedside of his commander, Meigs told of complete defeat; all the men Arnold had led into the Lower Town had been killed or captured. Full of hate for the conquerors, Arnold expressed amazement to hear that the prisoners were being treated "very humanely."

When Arnold was able to sit up in bed, the officers unanimously returned him to the command. Overwhelming Quebec was now out of the question; the primary need was to restore American prestige. Although in titular control of all Canada except Quebec, *Les Bostonnois* would be helpless before a change in civilian sentiment. The inhabitants, Arnold wrote, "having so long been habituated to slavery, and having, as yet, a faint sense of the value of liberty, are naturally timorous and diffident, and want every possible encouragement to take an active part." He was afraid to abandon the siege or even take precautions. However, smallpox led through the camp a procession of diseases that left him with less than 500 effectives. They were outnumbered three to one by an enemy who might at any moment sally from snug safety; if they showed their silhouettes against the snow, cannon roared; they were cold and hungry for there was now no way to buy supplies. Yet for week after discouraging week Arnold persuaded the usually unruly militia to sleep on their arms under Quebec's high walls in forts built of ice. This was, as Washington wrote, a truly amazing achievement. Indeed, it rivals Washington's own achievement at Valley Forge.

Arnold immobilized by a painful wound, his troops, staggering through blizzard, were the outposts of a convulsed cause. Back home, legislators were still arguing whether it was altogether politic to fight in Canada; militiamen who had done no more than parade on town greens dropped their arms when their enlistments were up; farmers by warm fires showed no interest in fighting or selling grain for the money Congress printed. Patriot leaders found it impossible to answer the requisitions Arnold sent southward for cash, supplies, and reinforcements.

Angry thoughts would have been justified, but Arnold expressed no angry thoughts. Indeed, many an officer on garrison duty complained more bitterly than the officer who that winter commanded the most exposed post of all. Arnold wrote Washington, "The repeated successes of our raw, undisciplined troops over the flower of the British army, the many unexpected and remarkable occurrences in our favor are plain proofs of the overruling hand of Providence, and justly demands our warmest gratitude to Heaven which I make no doubt will crown our virtuous efforts with success." He confided to his sister, "I have no thoughts of leaving this proud town until I first enter it in triumph. My wound has been exceedingly painful but is now easy, and the surgeons assure me will be well in eight weeks. I know you will be anxious for me. The Providence which has carried me through so many dangers is still my protection. I am in the way of my duty and know no fear."

Although Arnold looked forward to further battles, he was finding his administrative duties extremely irksome. His quarrel with John Brown had reached the point where he publicly accused that enemy of robbery. And the Catholic clergy, supported by the British Quebec Act, feared the low church propensities of *Les Bostonnois* and were creating grievous problems, even in the hospital where Arnold was confined. The nuns, it is true, nursed all sufferers, but their chaplain refused absolution to Canadians dying in the American cause. "I am now so much perplexed with a multiplicity of affairs," Arnold wrote Silas Deane, "that I can hardly form an assemblage of three ideas." He importuned Washington and Congress to send, along with the 5,000 men he believed necessary to capture Quebec, a "competent" general, preferably Charles Lee, who, like Montgomery, had served in the British army. "The service required a person of greater abilities than I can pretend to."

On January 10, 1776, Congress made Arnold a brigadier general. By mid-February, he was able to hobble around with a cane. Then, moving specks appeared on the frozen St. Lawrence: the long-awaited reinforcements! Their enlistments would run out on April 15, and so many came down with smallpox that by the end of March out of 2,505 men only 1,719 were fit for duty, yet Arnold's effectives had tripled. Able to ride again, he was full of renewed hopes for conquering Quebec. This was a task for which he felt perfectly fitted, yet Wooster—of all people—appeared to take the command.

As a New Haven official, Wooster had tried to stop Arnold's first military deed; because he had believed Montreal also in danger, he had refused Arnold assistance after the disastrous assault on Quebec. Arnold (and with justice) despised Wooster's military abilities, but Wooster, remembering Arnold as the aggressive nobody of his unhappy civilian days, "did not think proper to consult me in any of his matters." Perhaps it was perturbation of spirit that made Arnold ride so carelessly that his horse fell on his wounded leg. He was confined to his bed while orders were given around him. When he was well enough, he asked to be sent to Montreal as commandant there. Wooster "very readily" agreed, and Arnold saw shrinking over his shoulder the "proud town" he had intended to enter.

After months of pretending not to notice their army in Canada, Congress had finally appointed Benjamin Franklin chairman of a commission to bring the inhabitants into an official alliance. Arnold tried to impress the Montrealers by giving the emissaries a royal welcome. The cannon of the citadel shouted salutes as he led the committee to his headquarters where, so one of them wrote, "we were served with a glass of wine, while people were crowding in to pay compliments; which ceremony being over, we were shown into another apartment, and unexpectedly met in it a large number of ladies, most of them French. After drinking tea and sitting some time, we went to an elegant supper, which was followed with the singing of the ladies, which proved very agreeable, and would have been more so if we had not been so much fatigued with our journey."

However, neither the pomp with which Arnold tried to impress the inhabitants nor the commissioners' affability served any useful end; it was too late. Since the reinforcements that had been sent from the Colonies lacked both provisions and hard money, their presence had made supply officers outrage the Canadians by forcing Continental paper on them at bayonet point. Then many of the newcomers marched home because their enlistments had expired. The few and disease-ridden troops that remained would, it was clear to all, be helpless once British reinforcements sailed up the St. Lawrence that was rapidly becoming free of ice. In every town once-friendly citizens turned to enemies, and even Arnold's optimism cracked.

When, on May 6, a fleet transporting several thousand British regulars approached Quebec, the besiegers fled up the St. Lawrence, not stopping until they had retreated more than half the distance to Montreal. Almost instantly, a force of Canadians and Indians under English officers appeared from the north woods and captured at the Cedars many members of Arnold's command. He rushed to the rescue with a new detachment, but, when he reached the southern tip of the island of Montreal, saw the enemy "taking our unhappy prisoners" away in bateaux. "Words cannot express our anxiety as it was not in our power to relieve them." Arnold had no boats. As he waited for some to be found, he threatened the British commander with terrible vengeance if the savages harmed the prisoners. Word came back that the Indians threatened in turn to massacre the captives if Arnold dared to follow. He was, he remembered, "torn by the conflicting passions of rage and humanity. A sufficient force to take ample revenge, raging for action, urged me on one hand; and humanity for 500 unhappy wretches, who were on the point of being sacrificed if our vengeance was not delayed, plead equally strong on the other."

Finally, Arnold decided to push ahead whatever the consequences. In a birch-bark canoe paddled by four Indians, he led a flotilla of bateaux over glassy water under a brilliantly setting sun. One of his officers, James Wilkinson, wrote that when the force approached the enemy encampment, the British opened up with cannon, "every shot plunging beneath or passing over us, and the slightest touch of our fragile craft would have sent a crew to the bottom, as we were too deeply laden to furnish the smallest relief to each other." After Arnold had "darted about in his canoe, without apparent object or end," he reluctantly gave the order to retreat.

In a council held on the opposite shore, Arnold added to his growing band of enemies Colonel Moses Hazen, a Canadian landowner whose allegiance had teetered between the American and British causes until the capture of Montreal had made the Rebels seem the winning side. When Arnold insisted that it was necessary to destroy the enemy even if all the prisoners in their hands were murdered, Hazen objected so eloquently that most of the other officers sided with him. Outvoted, Arnold mounted to an Homeric fury. "The council," Wilkinson remembered, "broke up about midnight in discontent and disgust."

The next morning, the British commander sent word that he could not save the prisoners in case of an attack, but that he could persuade the Indians to release them if Arnold agreed to let his band retreat unmolested, and promised that Congress would release in exchange an equal number of British prisoners. When Arnold submitted to this unethical threat, he started a *cause célèbre* that was to have an important effect on André's fate.

Arnold had been careful of the rights of the Canadians while there remained a chance that they could be won to the American cause, but he now advocated that they be "coerced, as I am convinced that they are in general our bitter enemies." He expected soon to be forced to evacuate Montreal; if the citizens molested his withdrawal, he intended to burn the town. Meanwhile, he secured from the Congressional commissioners authority to seize all property that might be useful to the army, paying with almost valueless Continental paper. He was himself listing what had been requisitioned—as he complained to his superiors, he had no adequate commissary officers—when premature reports of a British advance made him bundle up the goods, place on each bundle the name of the owner, and send all to St. Johns for storage and more leisurely examination. Hazen, who commanded there, refused to receive the goods, perhaps because as a Canadian he disapproved of the whole proceeding. Not adequately guarded, the packages were rifled by persons unknown. Since there was no record of what was in them, the merchants could not be paid, even with useless notes. Arnold made public charges against Hazen.

Hazen replied that Arnold had made a handsome profit out of the plunder of the merchants. Years later, Wilkinson insisted that Arnold had purchased with his personal I O U goods which the owners had been forced to sell at a loss. When Wilkinson had objected, the general had told him he was "more nice than wise," and had ordered him from Montreal.

Hazen, who was defending himself, and Wilkinson, who was to be in his turn a traitor, were hardly reliable witnesses, yet when Arnold was in a similar situation as commandant of Philadelphia, he engaged in similar deals. Such behavior was not unusual; eighteenth-century army officers used their official power for private gain as commonly as municipal politicians do today. Furthermore, Arnold, habituated to being in business for himself, tended to confuse his private and public affairs; he had used his personal credit in Montreal to buy supplies for his soldiers. Perhaps he felt he had a right to pay himself back.

General John Sullivan, who had succeeded to the Canadian command, hoped to save Montreal by making a stand where the Sorel River joined the St. Lawrence, but Arnold warned him that the British would probably bypass his encampment, march directly to Chambly or St. Johns, and trap the entire American army by cutting their line of retreat. "Shall we," Arnold asked, "sacrifice the few men we have by endeavoring to keep possession of a small part of the country which can be of little or no service to us? The junction of the Canadians with the Colonies—an object which brought us into this country—is at an end. Let us quit then and secure our own country before it is too late. There will be more honor in making a safe retreat than hazarding a battle against such superiority, which will doubtless be attended with the loss of our men, artillery, etc., and the only pass to our country [Lake Champlain]. These arguments," Arnold felt it necessary to add, "are not urged by fear for my personal safety. I am content to be the last man who quits the country, and fall so that my country may rise. But let us not all fall together."

Sullivan's force finally retired to St. Johns. When English warships bore down on Montreal, Arnold was so ready for retreat that it took him only a few hours to ferry his men, with their sick and their supplies, across the St. Lawrence. His detachment marched efficiently to join the main army, which they found in utter disorder. More than half the troops had smallpox. Officers had no idea where their men were, and men well enough to walk thought only of walking home. Since no choice remained but to flee to the American end of Lake Champlain, Arnold volunteered to protect the embarkation and hold the rear.

Everything at St. Johns that was inflammable was set on fire. Lighted by flame, groaning bodies were lifted into boats, while invalids capable of motion hobbled into the forest. Finally, only Arnold's corps remained. They climbed into bateaux. He ordered all the boats except one cast off; he watched until they were out of sight. Then he called Wilkinson to his side and trotted toward the enemy.

The British advance guard had been moving through a countryside devoid of people when they saw two riders on the top of a hill. Recognizing the famous General Arnold, the enemy ran forward with a yell. Arnold and Wilkinson waited until they were almost within musket shot, and then vanished on their powerful mounts.

The fires at St. Johns had burned down to embers. Back at the riverside, Arnold shouted that nothing useful must fall to the enemy. The man who dearly loved fine horses pulled out his pistol and killed the mount which had served him so well. He forced the reluctant Wilkinson to shoot the other horse, and then ordered him to join the oarsmen in the bateau. With the sacrifices lying at his feet, Arnold waited alone on the shore.

The British column appeared at double-quick. He surveyed them haughtily for a moment; then pushed the boat into the stream and jumped on board. Benedict Arnold had led the first invasion of Canada; now he made good his boast that he would be the last to leave.

(The British commander, Lieutenant General John Burgoyne, reported home that he had almost captured his troublesome enemy. George Germain, Secretary of State for the Colonies, replied, "I am sorry Arnold escaped, not that I believe his military knowledge will distress you, though I think he has shown himself the most enterprising man among the Rebels.")

Arnold proceeded down the Sorel River, leaving behind the province which he had hoped to conquer but which seemed lost to the United Colonies forever. He could not blame himself. Washington had written him, "It is not in the power of any man to command success, but you have done more, you have deserved it." Washington had wished him "those laurels which your bravery and perseverance justly merit." He had won no laurels. His own men were not at fault; they had behaved heroically. He had seen them defy cannon with their fragile bodies; he had seen them march when almost too weak to stand; he had seen them die of bullets and disease and cold. And all in vain.

He was convinced that the cause had suffered for other men's faults: incompetent commanders like Brown and Wooster, who had opposed him; ill-trained militia whose craven behavior had almost made him ashamed of his countrymen; and above all, the politicians who sent men into battle but would not arm or feed or clothe them. "The want of a little attention in time," he wrote, "has lost us this fine country."

The high serenity that had carried Arnold through the first months of the invasion had vanished, yet he was not altogether discouraged. His mind had flown ahead: Lake Champlain must be held lest the British mount "an invasion that way. We have little to fear, but I am heartily chagrined." Fortune, he wrote, had long since deserted the American cause, "but as Miss, like most other Misses, is fickle and often changes, I still hope for her favors again, and that we shall have the pleasure of dying or living happily together."

CHAPTER NINE

Admiral Arnold

AFTER the Colonial army had tumbled out of Canada with Arnold bringing up the rear, the strategic situation became similar to what it had been when Arnold had commanded at Ticonderoga a year before. The British at the northern end of Lake Champlain were prevented from attacking the Americans at the southern by a little fleet of which the two sailboats he had captured were still the backbone. However, the vessels would not suffice for long to protect the army which was still so ill-supplied, so weakened by sickness and confusion that it could not be expected to stand up against British regulars.

The key American defense was behind the British lines: some ten miles of shallow water below St. Johns which prevented the enemy fleet on the St. Lawrence from sailing up the Sorel to Lake Champlain. However, boats were being taken apart at one end of the rapids and put together at the other. When this process was completed, the existing American fleet would be hopelessly outclassed. Frantically, the Colonials started to fashion from the green wood of the forest flat-bottomed gondolas and larger, keeled row galleys on which land guns could be mounted.

At this critical juncture, the top commanders all turned to one man. From his encampment in New York City, Washington wrote that if the fleet were "assigned to General Arnold, none will doubt of his exertions." Before he received Washington's advice, on July 29, 1776, Major General Horatio Gates reported to Congress,

"General Arnold, who is perfectly skilled in maritime affairs, has nobly undertaken to command our fleet upon the lake. With infinite satisfaction, I have committed the whole of that department to his care, convinced he will thereby add to that brilliant reputation he has so deservedly acquired." Schuyler was "extremely happy that General Arnold has undertaken to command the fleet. It has relieved me from very great anxiety under which I labored."

This unanimity reveals that Arnold had remained nonpartisan in the controversy that was rocking the northern army. When Schuyler had stayed in Albany while his troops were being defeated in Canada, criticism became so loud that Congress had appointed Gates to an autonomous command north of the border. However, Gates had hardly reached his army before it was forced to retreat into New York, which was Schuyler's territory. Then both generals claimed the command in a squabble that reflected not only personal rivalry but a deep cleavage in the patriot cause.

Used to unchallenged control of an estate that was in itself a little principality, Schuyler was restive under Congressional suggestion and scornful of lower-class militiamen. Gates, the son of an English servant, had resigned from the British army because his lack of social position had blocked his advancement. While the American-born Schuyler was trying to root deep a local aristocracy, Gates had crossed the ocean to find an equalitarian haven. Although far from handsome, Schuyler was tall and very much the gentleman; Gates's squat figure and red face, from which he peered through heavy glasses, proclaimed him a man of the people. Schuyler tried to handle military affairs with the gracious punctilio of a drawing room where class lines were sharply drawn. When others did not respond in kind, he was outraged. Gates was a scrapper: not expecting others to step aside to let him lead, he jostled ahead, elbowing his way with jokes and bluster. Each had his natural supporters. A hero to conservatives who regarded the war as a conflict between British and American gentlemen for hegemony over the American masses, Schuyler was politically powerful in those states where the right wing dominated, yet Yankee troops were loath to serve under him. In New England the leaders dreamed of social revolution: Gates was their man.

Gates was younger, in better health, and a trained professional soldier; Schuyler was a confused amateur—yet political considerations determined the outcome of their rivalry. The New York delegation forced Congress to back Schuyler. Gates accepted a subordinate role with surface politeness, yet bitterness remained like an unexploded land mine.

When Arnold finally took sides in the controversy, he was blown sky-high, but for the moment he got on equally well with both contenders: Schuyler represented what he hoped some day to be; Gates was closer to what he was. He treated the patrician with awed respect, and joked with the soldier man to man. Not politically minded, he hardly noticed the growing schism between the revolutionary left and right.

When Arnold disagreed with a fellow officer, it was certain to be in personal not abstract terms. As his fleet was building, he brought Hazen before a court martial, charging him with allowing the goods seized at Montreal to be plundered. When Hazen countered by accusing Arnold of stealing from the merchants in that city, Arnold objected that it was not he who was on trial, but the court refused to silence Hazen, and would not hear Arnold's key witness whom they believed prejudiced. Arnold thereupon showed what the court considered "marked disrespect and contempt"; they expressed "resentment" and demanded an apology. Accusing them of "indecent reflections on a superior officer," Arnold offered, "as soon as this disagreeable service is at an end," to give "any gentleman of the court the satisfaction his nice honor may require." The court then demanded that Arnold be arrested for trying to undermine military justice; Arnold answered that they were trying to "gloss over their private resentment in appearance of the greatest concern to keep up discipline, etc."

The squabble was thrown in the lap of Gates who, as combat general under Schuyler, was Arnold's immediate superior. "The warmth of General Arnold's temper," Gates wrote in sending the record on to Congress, "might possibly lead him a little further than is marked by the precise line of decorum," but, "if there was fault on one side there was too much acrimony on the other. Here again I was obliged to act dictatorially and dissolve the court martial the instant they demanded that General Arnold be put in arrest. The United States must not be deprived of that excellent officer's services at this important moment."

However, the charges against Arnold could not be so easily stilled. In August, Samuel Chase, who had been one of the Congressional commissioners in Canada, wrote him from Philadelphia that he was "distressed to hear so many reports injurious to your character about the goods seized. . . . Your best friends are not your countrymen" from Connecticut.

"I cannot but think it extremely cruel," Arnold commented, "when I have sacrificed my ease, health, and a great part of my private property in the cause of my country, to be calumniated as a robber and a thief, at a time too when it is not in my power [because he was on active service] to be heard in my own defense." At his request, Gates and Schuyler both wrote Congress expressing their faith in his integrity.

Arnold was engaged in an uneven race with the British shipbuilders. They could call on the stores and experienced personnel of the royal navy, while he was forced himself to draw plans for the boats, to show house carpenters how to fashion them from trees, and to wait for rigging to come by wagon from the Atlantic Coast 200 miles away. Since his calls for experienced seamen went perpetually unanswered, he had to make sailors out of clerks and dairymen. Having superintended the shipyard at Skenesboro until he feared the British fleet might be ready to sail, he proceeded up the lake with such boats as were finished, hoping the rest would follow him.

The orders Gates sent Arnold on August 7 show that he suspected his subordinate of rashness. Arnold was to stay near the American end of the lake, "incessantly reflecting that . . . it is a defensive war we are carrying on." He was to avoid "wanton risk or unnecessary display"; he was not to detach himself from the main fleet to go ahead with scouting parties; should an enemy force appear, he was to return to Ticonderoga unless there was a good chance that he could win a battle. "A resolute but judicious defense of the northern entrance into this side of the continent," Gates concluded, "is the monotonous part which is committed to your courage and abilities." That others shared Gates's fears is

Naval Engagement: Arnold and his navy on Valcour Bay. Although this watercolor by P. Randle bears the date of Arnold's desperate battle with a superior British force, there is no indication of the fight in this schematic drawing. Arnold stands aggressively in the center of the top section, with the "New England Vessels" shown behind him anchored in the bay. Below are portraits of sixteen ships, only half of which survived the battle. In the center of the upper rank was Arnold's flagship, the row galley *Congress* (left) and the schooner *Royal Savage*, both of which were destroyed. The vessels to the lower right were tiny, but some of them managed to escape. *Courtesy, Fort Ticonderoga.*

Horatio Gates, by Gilbert Stuart. A profound character study of the British-born and trained American general who commanded during the victory at Saratoga. First Arnold's close friend, Gates became Arnold's destructive enemy. *Courtesy, Mrs. Charles Pfeffer, Jr.*

revealed by Colonel Matthias Ogden's wish that Arnold "may be as prudent as he is brave."

The former skipper of diminutive merchantmen was at first happy walking the command-deck of a navy. He joked with Gates, writing him, for instance, for a surgeon "or someone who will answer to kill a man *secundum artem* [according to correct principles]." But he soon became anxious, for the water that stretched back to the American encampment was troubled only by small boats bringing dispatches; the warships he had left half-finished at Skenesboro remained as immovable in their stocks as if the green wood had rerooted in the ground. While his reinforcements failed to appear, disturbing advices came to him from British deserters and his own spies. He arrested the first bearer of the evil tidings that the enemy had put two heavily armed schooners together at St. Johns—the man had clearly been hired by the British to terrify him—but he was soon forced to admit that the enemy fleet might equal his own, even after all his vessels were completed. Despite vague rumors of a larger British boat, he seems to have remained ignorant of the ship-rigged *Inflexible* which, with its battery of eighteen twelve-pounders, could all by itself, under a favorable wind, sink the entire American fleet.

But the intelligence he did receive was terrifying enough to make his letters to Gates become increasingly shrill. "I beg that at least one hundred good seamen may be sent me as soon as possible. We have a wretched motley crew in the fleet; the marines the refuse of every regiment, and the seamen few of them ever wet with salt water." He made these amateurs practice aiming guns, but he could not let them fire as there was not enough powder.

He was momentarily cheered when one of the boats he most needed, the galley *Trumbull*, came sailing down the lake, but he soon discovered that she was "not half finished or rigged; her cannon are much too small." Furthermore, she had not brought the reinforcement of experienced sailors he had been promised. "I hope to be excused after the requisitions so often made, if with five hundred men, half-naked, I should not be able to beat the enemy with seven thousand men, well-clothed, and a naval force, by the best accounts, near equal to ours. . . . I wrote in July for cordage sufficient for eight galleys; I then supposed that number would be built. I am surprised at their strange economy or infatuation down below [in the States]. Saving and negligence, I am afraid, will ruin us at last." Gates could only pass the blame on to Congress.

The two more galleys that soon reached Arnold did not compensate for news they brought: the British army, which had been driven out of Boston by the cannon Arnold had helped to capture at Ticonderoga, had turned the tables by driving Washington from the city of New York. "It appears to me," Arnold wrote, "our troops or officers are panic-struck, or why does a hundred thousand men [*sic*] fly before one quarter of their numbers. Is it possible my countrymen can be callous to their wrongs, or hesitate one moment between slavery and death?" Arnold realized that the catastrophe made his mission doubly important. If the British from Canada could brush aside his fleet and then the ill-prepared northern army, they could march to Albany and beyond, making a junction with the British in New York City. The newly declared United States would be cut in half and the war brought, perhaps, to a disastrous end. Arnold was sure that if his opponents heard of Washington's defeat before the season was too far advanced, they would instantly advance against him with a flotilla "very formidable, if not equal to ours."

Despite his forebodings—and Gates's orders that he stay at the American end of the lake—Arnold had anchored his fleet in a narrow channel between Valcour Island and the west bank of Lake Champlain, twice as far from Ticonderoga as from the Canadian border. This position kept most of the waterway under American control and disrupted British communications, yet Arnold was hardly playing the "monotonous" defensive part which Gates had assigned him. If he were attacked by a superior force, he would be in serious trouble.

On the morning of October 11, Arnold discovered how woefully he had underestimated the British fleet. One after another, there appeared around a headland a long string of vessels: the ship-rigged *Inflexible* that could overpower everything on the lake; two schooners that were more than a match for the American boats of the same type; a cumbersome radeau (gun raft) floating the heaviest artillery on either side, twenty gunboats, four longboats, and twenty-four bateaux loaded with troops. Even in his most optimistic mood Arnold could not have denied that his own fleet was hopelessly outclassed.

After this terrifying array was sighted, the first movement among the American boats was the dash of a cutter from the flagship of Arnold's second in command, Brigadier General David Waterbury, Jr., to Arnold's flagship. Waterbury urged that "the fleet ought immediately to come to sail, and fight them on a retreat in the main lake, since they were so much superior to us in number and strength." Arnold, however, knew that his vessels were all slow and moved at different paces; the British would catch them one by one, chew up his force piecemeal. He preferred to keep his boats in their strong defensive position behind Valcour Island. Since the channel was only three-quarters of a mile wide, the British would be unable to bring all their vessels into action at the same time; and, furthermore, it was possible that before they saw the Americans behind the high bluffs of the island, they might sail past the northerly entrance, and be placed in the disadvantageous position of having to beat up from the south into a strong northwest blow.

Keeping the majority of his fleet at anchor, Arnold put in motion only the schooner *Royal Savage* and the four galleys that were propelled by oars and carried his heaviest guns. All stayed behind the bluffs, while the British proceeded rapidly before the wind along the opposite shore. Arnold's heart jumped when his lookouts reported that they had unconcernedly passed the northern channel. The strategic situation was now to his advantage; he ordered the schooner to the mouth of the southern channel, where it was in plain view of the British.

Instantly, the enemy flotilla came about into the wind. They had great difficulty advancing to the northwest, but so did the *Royal Savage*, which, Arnold wrote, "by some bad management fell to leeward" where she came within reach of the *Inflexible*'s big guns. Three hits by twelve-pound balls further confused the crew, and the schooner ran aground on the southern tip of the island, where she was abandoned.

The wind continued to dominate. As the enemy ships tacked in an effort to get closer, only the long-range guns of the *Inflexible* were fired, and they but occasionally, which showed, so writes the naval historian Admiral Mahan, "that Arnold was keeping his galleys in hand, at long bowls, as small vessels with one eighteen should be kept when confronted with a broadside of nine guns." The British vessels haltingly approached the mouth of the channel, but then their progress ceased for the waterway was too narrow to permit effective tacking, and the hills deflected the wind from northwest to north, making it blow directly on their bows. Before Arnold's fascinated eyes, the powerful British flotilla struggled like flies caught in flypaper.

The sails of the British schooner *Carleton*, shivering helplessly in the head wind, bellied suddenly with a flaw that had bounced off a nearby cliff; the vessel leaped forward "nearly into the middle of the Rebel half-moon." Before she could be blown back again, anchors were dropped that held her broadside. By this time, the British gunboats, which were amenable to oars, were coming up; seventeen pulled within point-blank range of the American flotilla. The narrow channel roared with gunshot.

It was now just a matter of slugging it out. Arnold was dashing about on the deck of the galley *Congress*. As soon as a cannon was fired, he aimed it for another shot, and then ran on to aim the next cannon, doing, as he believed, "good execution." He had to dodge falling rigging and keep his feet during thunderous shocks, for his vessel "received seven shots between wind and water, was hulled a dozen times, had her mainmast wounded in two places and her yard in one." Men were bleeding at the guns, and motionless figures lay in pools of blood, but Arnold was not scratched.

Hour after hour, the two groups of angry men faced each other across a hundred yards or so of choppy water that boiled with misdirected cannon balls. When rigging came away or missiles ground into hulls, a cheer would rise from the opposing line; sometimes a man fell backward with a cry. The vessels rode gradually lower in the water, but pumps spurted, and only a British artillery boat went under. In the background, the major vessels of the royal fleet still struggled vainly with the wind to get into the action. Despairing at last of advancing the cumbersome radeau, a lieutenant rowed with a boats' crew to the beached *Royal Savage*, and turned her guns upon her former friends. When he was driven away by American balls, he set fire to the schooner. Now the orange of flames reflected in the troubled water. Since England's Indian allies infested the woods, both shores rattled with gunfire.

The schooner *Carleton*, anchored broadside to the American line, received heavy damage, and then her anchor gave way; she swung bows-on to the Americans, her fire being thus silenced. The British commander signaled for her to withdraw. Despite the efforts of an intrepid officer, who clambered out on the bowsprit, under concerted American fire, to turn her jib to windward, she could not move. When she was finally towed away by two gunboats, a great shout went up from the Americans. The triumph was short-lived, for about nightfall the mighty *Inflexible*, which had been shooting ineffectually from the distance, caught a favorable gust and moved in to point-blank range. Five of her broadsides silenced the American line. Fortunately, darkness then stopped the battle.

Arnold summed up the American damage as follows: "The *Congress* and *Washington* [galleys] have suffered greatly; the latter lost her first lieutenant killed, captain and master wounded. The *New York* [gondola] lost all her officers except the captain. The *Philadelphia* [gondola] was hulled in so many places that she sank about one hour after the engagement was over. The whole killed and wounded amounted to about sixty." Since the British damage had been comparable, the day's battle had ended in a draw. However, the Americans were left in much the worse situation. Three-quarters of their ammunition had been expended; they had not yet met the true power of the British fleet; and the strong wind that had so far protected them was dropping to a breeze.

To hold the American boats for leisurely annihilation when day returned, the British anchored across the mouth of the channel and posted troops on both shores so that the crews could not escape by land. But Arnold remembered the night on which he had slipped an army past warships guarding Quebec; this night was equally dark. He ordered a lantern placed in the stern of each boat and masked to be visible only from directly in her wake; he ordered that no oars be dipped in the water, no more sails raised than were needed for steerageway. Anchors splashed gently from the flood, and then, in complete silence, the fleet uncoiled like a rattlesnake. Arnold watched as the boats, following each other at a distance of 100 yards, vanished one by one. He had kept for himself the most dangerous post; the anchorage was deserted when he put his *Congress* in motion. Moving through billows of mist, he could see nothing but the pinpoint of light under the stern of the *Washington*. Then he approached an irregular pattern of foggy glows, the vessels of the British fleet. An occasional sleepy voice sounded, but there was no alarm, and the glows shrank into the silent night.

Awakening the next morning eager for the day's carnage, the British officers waited happily for the fog that obscured their victims' anchorage to lift. The head of Valcour Island came in sight; then a hundred feet of empty channel; then another hundred. Finally, the sun broke through to reveal no American boats at all. "General Carleton," wrote a Hessian, "was in a rage. He at once had anchors weighed and sailed off in pursuit. But in his haste and excitement, he forgot to leave instructions for the army on the land, from whom, as a consequence, he became more and more separated. The wind, however, being averse, and nothing having been seen of the enemy, he returned and cast anchor in the bay in which he had passed the previous night."

Arnold was repairing his boats at Schuyler's Island, twelve miles away. Two gondolas proved so damaged that they had to be sunk; and wounded men groaned in every hold, yet he wrote, "On the whole, I think we have had a very fortunate escape and have great reason to return our humble and hearty thanks to God, for preserving and delivering so many of us from our more than savage enemies."

Both fleets began the next day a race to see whether the Americans could get behind the fortifications at Crown Point before the British caught them. Held back by the slow gondolas and a head wind, Arnold had by the following dawn made only six miles, while the British had gone thirteen to be only five miles behind; Crown Point was still twenty-eight miles away. The Americans continued to beat into a head wind, but "the enemy," so Arnold wrote, "took a fresh breeze from the northeast." Soon the *Inflexible* and the two British schooners bore triumphantly down on the galleys protecting the American rear: the *Washington* commanded by Waterbury and Arnold's flagship, the *Congress*.

Waterbury asked permission to beach and blow up his boats. Arnold denied it. He intended to gather the fleet together for a stand, to make the enemy pay heavily for their inevitable victory. However, those of his vessels that were out of range rowed away as fast as they could, and Waterbury, after receiving "a few broadsides," surrendered the *Washington*. Only four weakly-armed gondolas remained to support Arnold's *Congress* against a lakeful of British boats.

The *Congress* soon had two of the biggest enemy ships under her stern and one beside her, all within musket shot. The tremendous odds merely drove Arnold into a fiercer fighting frenzy, and the power of his emotion exalted his companions. The enemy, he wrote, "kept up an incessant fire on us for about five glasses [two and a half hours], with round and grapeshot, which we returned as briskly. The sails, rigging, and hull of the *Congress* were shattered and torn in pieces; the first lieutenant and three men killed." As the battle went on, more British vessels appeared, until "there were seven sail around me."

Finally, he ordered his sailors to row to windward, a direction in which the larger enemy ships, being dependent on sails, could not follow. The galley and four gondolas dashed up a creek; the vessels were set on fire. As a final gesture of defiance, Arnold commanded that the five flags be left flying. From the shore, the Americans held the British off with small arms until one after another, the little, battered ships exploded.

Then Admiral Arnold became woodsman Arnold. The British had sent their Indian allies into the forest to keep the crews from escaping by land. Yet Arnold and his blood-stained sailors moved so rapidly that they escaped ambush. "At four o'clock yesterday morning," he wrote from Ticonderoga on October 15, "I reached this place, extremely fatigued and unwell, having been without sleep or refreshment for near three days."

Then, as now, Arnold's deeds as a naval commander were a subject of controversy. Certainly, the presence of the American fleet on Lake Champlain kept the British from advancing until they had amassed a fleet of their own, and the summer was gone. Arnold's part in creating the guarding flotilla was incontrovertibly important. Admiral Mahan gives him credit for outsailing the royal navy when the two forces met, and can find nothing to criticize in his battle strategy. Yet the question remains whether he should have gone so far into the enemy end of the lake, and whether, when faced with a manifestly superior force, he should have engaged in a hopeless fight. On these matters too, Mahan supports Arnold, writing, "Admiration is due to his recognition of the fact—implicit in deed if unexpressed in word—that the one use of the navy was to contest the control of the water; to impose delay, even if it could not secure ultimate victory. . . . The navy was useless except as it contributed to this end, valueless if buried in port. Upon this rests the merit of his bold advance into the lower narrows; upon this, his choice of the strong defensive position of Valcour; upon this, his refusal to retreat as urged by Waterbury, when the full force of the enemy was disclosed."

Because of Arnold's advanced position, to which he had been encouraged by faulty intelligence concerning the enemy's power, he could not have avoided battle by retreat. His only practical alternatives were to fight on the spot or to surrender. That he fought may have been foolhardy, but its morale effect was incalculable. When Carleton started an invasion in October, he must have counted, as British professionals so often did, on a helter-skelter flight of his untrained opponents, since any prolonged campaign would leave his army in a "most howling wilderness" during a northern winter. He undoubtedly hoped to be snug in Albany before snow fell. Arnold's resistance did not upset his timetable much—only three or four days—yet it changed the complexion of the entire campaign. If the Colonials were going to resist like this at every step of the way, it was useless to go on. Carleton made no effort to besiege Ticonderoga. Explaining that the season was too far advanced, he returned with his fleet and men to Canada. Until spring, at least, the United States was safe from being cut in half.

In addition to discouraging the British, Arnold's adventure did much to inspirit the Americans. The tendency of individual militiamen to decide for themselves that a battle was hopeless and then run was one of the greatest weaknesses of our forces. Arnold had set them a shining example. The Rebels, a British observer wrote, "chiefly gloried in the dangerous attention which he paid to a nice point of honor in keeping his flag flying and not quitting his galley till she was in flames, lest the enemy should have boarded and struck it."

"It has pleased Providence," Gates wrote, "to preserve General Arnold. Few men have met with so many hairbreadth escapes in so short a space of time." Gates praised the "gallant defense" Arnold's force had made against great superiority, and added, "Such magnanimous behavior will establish the fame of the American arms throughout the world." (It may, indeed, have drawn the French further along the road to alliance.) Yet Gates must have noticed that Arnold had disobeyed the orders he had given him against rashness. Had Arnold stayed at the American end of the lake as he was told to do, he would have been able to honor Gates's specific command that, if faced with a superior force, he retire to Ticonderoga without fighting. Gates filed away in his mind that Arnold was not to be trusted with power unless aggressive, perhaps foolhardy, action were called for. Thus was laid another of the buried mines that were to explode into the disastrous climax of Arnold's career.

While Gates, conscious that morale would be served by praising Arnold's heroism, kept his doubts to himself, other critics were vocal. Arnold had long been glorious only in defeat, glory which it takes a friendly eye to see. Now he had lost ten of fifteen boats, let some eighty Americans be killed and wounded, some 200 be captured. His second in command, Waterbury, carefully disassociated himself from what he considered foolhardy behavior; and General William Maxwell wrote from Ticonderoga, "Arnold, our evil genius to the north, has with a good deal of industry got us clear of our fine fleet. . . . This was a pretty piece of admiralship, after going to their doors almost and bantering them for two months or more, contrary to the opinion of all the army."

Even before the battle, Arnold had been worried lest his swelling host of enemies block his military advancement. Some premonition made him feel a menace to his future when Congress raised Arthur St. Clair to brigadier. Having asked Gates to congratulate St. Clair for him, he added, "When the enemy drive us back to Ticonderoga, I have some thoughts of going to Congress and begging leave to resign. Do you think they will make me a major general?"

CHAPTER TEN

A Hero's Wages

WHEN the British returned to Canada, war came for Benedict Arnold to a temporary halt. He had often spoken during his perilous adventures of the time "when this disagreeable service is at an end," but as he walked Albany's silent streets, he was homesick for the crack of muskets from high walls, the roar of cannon over water. Then, he had struggled against adversaries he considered worthy; now a pack of curs was yapping at his heels.

Continuing his efforts to discredit Hazen, he had accused his hated enemy of selling public rum for private profit. Hazen dragged him before a military court on a charge of slander, and the judges decided for the querulous colonel. John Brown too was spitefully active. For months, he had been campaigning against Arnold—Schuyler had wished to prosecute him for "violent and ill-founded complaints"—and now he demanded that Gates arrest Arnold for a host of "crimes." Brown accused Arnold of slandering Brown, making a "treasonable attempt" to join the enemy when superseded at Ticonderoga, and "great misconduct" on the wilderness march. During Arnold's Canadian commands, Brown continued, he had suffered smallpox to spread and had promoted inoculation to the detriment of the service; had disobeyed his superiors; had willfully deprived the army of provisions; had made an unwarranted agreement with the enemy at the Cedars; had plundered the inhabitants of Montreal; and had directed "a whole village to be destroyed and the inhabitants thereof put to death by fire and sword." Brown made a clean sweep of Arnold's public record by adding that he had lost the Lake Champlain fleet through incompetence.

Although Gates indignantly refused to appoint a court martial, he was obliged to send Brown's charges to Congress, adding another to the many impeachments which, during the fighter's long stint of active service, had piled up against him there. The time had come, Arnold decided, to defend himself in Philadelphia.

But first he set out with Gates to deliver four regiments to Washington, who had long been encamped on the outskirts of British-held New York. At Kingston they learned that the Continental Army had suffered a major defeat and was last seen disappearing into New Jersey with the redcoats in hot pursuit. They led their lightly clad troops across the New Jersey mountains—they did not dare go further south—in a frozen search for Washington. Days passed before they discovered that their commander in chief had fled the entire width of the state while his soldiers deserted and the panic-struck inhabitants swore by the hundreds renewed allegiance to the Crown. A pitiful remnant of the army was on the far side of the Delaware, hoping that it could make a stand that would save Philadelphia from capture and the Revolution from complete collapse. Gates and Arnold led their regiments through the snow to the rescue.

Arnold saw one favorable circumstance—he could tell Washington how he had been maligned and secure the support of the general who had always been his partisan—but orders came that, while Gates advanced with the reinforcements, Arnold was to hurry to New England; a British fleet had appeared off Providence. Later dispatches revealed that New England was in no immediate danger; and Gates, seeing how disappointed his friend was, took on his own shoulders the onus of disobedience. He ordered Arnold to get "ample instructions" in a personal conference with the commander in chief.

During four days in the icy camp across the Delaware from Trenton—four of the blackest days the patriot cause was to know —Arnold revived his acquaintance with Washington, whom he had not seen since he had set out for the Kennebec. The commander in chief, just deserted by most of his own militia, could appreciate Arnold's achievement in inducing a few sick and wounded men to blockade Quebec throughout a frigid winter; he found comfort in this swarthy, hawk-nosed fighter who, it seemed, was willing to go to hell and back for the United States. And Arnold was so deeply reassured by the favor of his great leader that he agreed with alacrity to abandon his pilgrimage for vindication to Philadelphia. Whatever Congress did, he decided, Washington was on his side, and he was safe. He discussed with his friend the possibility of mounting a surprise attack across the Delaware, and departed four days before Washington's famous crossing that turned the tables of the war.

Arnold's orders still pointed him toward New England, yet, since the enemy were quiescent toward Rhode Island, Washington had agreed that he might first visit his family. Eighteen months before, he had sneaked out of Connecticut sick, discouraged, and under a cloud; despite the obstinacy of his enemies, his return was a triumphal progress. At Hartford, at Middletown, at New Haven, the hills reverberated with cannon fired to celebrate his approach, and he was met on the road by recently exchanged veterans whom he had last seen climbing over a barricade into Quebec's bloody Lower Town. Yellow still with prison fever, they wavered out to shake his hand; the artilleryman, John Lamb, wept at their reunion from the one good eye now left to him.

At New Haven, Hannah received her brother in the style befitting a homecoming hero. His three sons, now eight, seven, and four, crowded round their famous father in admiration; and neighbors, who had once avoided Arnold, dropped in to inquire about his health and listen to the story of his campaigns.

At last appreciated in his home town, Arnold organized an artillery regiment and put his friends in command: Lamb was colonel; Oswald, his former secretary, lieutenant colonel; one of his brothers-in-law a captain, another a subaltern. When Congress was slow in sending money, Arnold personally put up—he hoped as a loan—a thousand pounds. This was both generosity and recklessness. If he were not to become a pitiful bankrupt like his father, he would have in the end to find some way to be repaid.

After an expansive week at home, Arnold reported at Providence to the superannuated political general, Joseph ("Granny") Spencer, his titular commander, although Washington expected him to supply the initiative. He reported that the British were using Newport as a naval base and a winter encampment to relieve the pressure on New York. They had "no intention of penetrating the country"; but Arnold had every intention of attacking them. Having secured Washington's permission to ask Massachusetts and New Hampshire for the necessary reinforcements, he posted eagerly to Boston.

Now, after years of longing, he was received by the best society of a sophisticated city. To enhance the glamor of his uniform, he bought from Paul Revere a sword knot and sash, epaulets, and a dozen fine silk hose. Thus elegantly caparisoned, he attended a fateful party given by Mrs. Henry Knox, daughter of the former royal secretary of Massachusetts and wife of a patriot artillery colonel. Her double connection made her a social bridge between the army and those most polished charmers in the city, the Tory belles. In her drawing room, Arnold met a sixteen-year-old beauty, Elizabeth De Blois.

When Boston had been evacuated by the British, the girl had fled with her parents to Halifax. The city had remained unsafe for her rich Tory father, Gilbert De Blois—he sailed for England—but, after the occupation had proved peaceful, the girl returned with her mother to protect the family property. Watching Nature bring Betsy into perfect flower among the Rebels she considered weeds, Mrs. De Blois was in a frenzy lest her daughter be lured into marriage before eligible males recaptured the continent.

An irritated patriot lampooned the ladies in a farce called *The Motley Assembly*. Under the pseudonym of Mrs. Flourish, Mrs. De Blois is shown doing her best to be tactful to one of the Rebel officers who infest her drawing room: "I believe Mr. W[ashington], or General W——, if you please, is a very honest, good kind of man; and he has taken infinite pains to keep your army together; and I wish he may find his account in it. But doubtless there are his equals."

In the play, Mrs. De Blois, who refers to her daughter as "Miss Volubility," refuses to let her attend a Rebel dance, although Betsy loyally explains, "There is a set of us who agreed to go on purpose to make our remarks on the droll figures." Betsy weeps with rage and disappointment the entire night of the party, and the next morning asks a friend, "How did the he-bears behave? How did they handle their paws?"

Although Arnold's manners were courtly and he had worked hard to refine his speech, the ladies could not have been impressed with the social standing of the self-made general in a rascally army. Mrs. De Blois certainly found him painfully unintellectual, since the satirist shows her smiling contentedly when told that few women "are as accomplished as you are allowed to be." Here is her pronouncement on men: "I have found some capable of pleasing, but few, very few indeed, capable of informing me."

For her part, Betsy seems to have been flattered by the attentions of the hero, but more relaxed with Martin Brimmer, who could only match lace ruffles against Arnold's sword and epaulets. He was only a merchant apothecary such as Arnold had been before he became glorious through warfare, yet, when the general orated of battles, the unabashed civilian looked at Betsy with melting eyes—and suddenly the pair were no longer listening.

Clearly, Arnold was not using the right artillery. Although European finery was almost unavailable in blockaded America, he secured somehow a quantity of the silks for which beautiful women languished. "I have taken the liberty," he wrote Mrs. Knox, "of enclosing a letter to the heavenly Miss De Blois, which I beg the favor of your delivering with the trunk of gowns. . . . I hope she will make no objection to receiving them." Dilating on "the fond anxiety, the glowing hopes, and chilling fears that alternately possess my heart," he trusted that Mrs. Knox would "have it in your power to give me the favorable intelligence."

He wished he had a similar lever to use on the Massachusetts politicians who were disappointing his other "anxious expectation" by showing no interest in assigning him troops with which to storm Rhode Island. The soldier who had seen snow, grass, and angry water redden with blood could hardly believe the indifference that reigned not only in the De Blois living room, but in the legislative halls. He wrote Gates of his "great surprise" at finding Boston almost defenseless. "Some few works are indeed begun, but none of consequence completed. One fifty-gun ship might take, plunder, and burn the town, which is in the most perfect [psychological] security. The only contest they seem to have is with the farmers about eggs, butter, etc."

Arnold was still trying to kindle the sluggish civilians when the troops he wanted were ordered by Washington to Ticonderoga under command of the Massachusetts general, William Heath. This was a double blow. Not only was an attack on Rhode Island no longer possible, but Heath's appointment seemed to leave no place for Arnold in the northern army where he had so long played a conspicuous part. To Schuyler, with whom he felt on distantly respectful terms, he wrote only, "I am uncertain of my own destination in the ensuing campaign," but to Gates he confided that he had thought of a new sphere of usefulness. If "a command offers worth my acceptance, I should be fond of being in the navy, which to our disgrace is now rotting in port, when, if properly stationed, might greatly distress if not entirely ruin the enemy's army by taking their provisions ships." (Such service would be personally profitable since sea commanders kept a share of the prizes they captured.)

Having received no answer from Betsy nor any encouragement for his naval ambitions, Arnold rode sadly back to Providence. He was engaged in the purely defensive operations he found so galling, when he received from Washington news that seemed to strike all his hopes, all his ambitions to the ground. Washington wrote, "We have lately had several promotions to the rank of major general, and I am at a loss whether you have had a preceding appointment, as the newspapers announce, or whether you have been omitted through some mistake. Should the latter be the case, I beg you will not take any hasty steps in consequence of it; but allow time for recollection, which, I flatter myself, will remedy any error that may have been made. My endeavors to that end shall not be wanting."

According to the rules of seniority, Arnold should have received the next promotion to major general; but Congress had elevated five junior officers over his head. Washington wrote Richard Henry Lee to find out what had gone wrong. "Surely a more active, a more spirited and sensible officer [than Arnold] fills no department of the army." The vote "gives me much uneasiness, as it is not to be presumed (being the oldest brigadier) that he will continue in service under such a slight." It was common for officers to resign when passed over.

The *Pennsylvania Packet* tried to rationalize things by stating that Arnold had already received his promotion. When it became clear that this was not so, civilians and his own subordinates turned in the streets of Providence to stare at the general who appeared to have been publicly disgraced.

To Washington, Arnold wrote that he considered Congress's action "a very civil way of requesting my resignation as unqualified for the office I hold. My commission was conferred unsolicited, received with pleasure only as a means of serving my country. With equal pleasure I resign it when I can no longer serve my country with *honor*. The person who, void of nice feelings of honor, will tamely condescend to give up his rights and hold a commission at the expense of his reputation, I hold as a disgrace to the army, and unworthy of the glorious cause in which we are engaged.

"When I entered the service of my country, my character was unimpeached. I have sacrificed my interest, ease, and happiness in her cause. It is rather a misfortune than a fault that my exertions have not been crowned with success. I am conscious of the rectitude of my intentions. . . . I must request a court of inquiry into my conduct, and, although I sensibly feel the ingratitude of my countrymen, every personal interest shall be buried in my zeal for the safety and happiness of my country, in whose cause I have repeatedly fought and bled, and am ready at all times to resign my life. I shall cautiously avoid any hasty step, in consequence of the appointments that have taken place, that may tend to injure my country."

To his "crony" Gates, Arnold revealed his intimate thoughts. He was demanding a court of inquiry because "I know some villain has been busy with my fame, and basely slandering me." Yet his only crime was "to have sacrificed my interest, ease, and happiness in the public cause and to have stepped forth, at a time my health was impaired, on a hazardous and fatiguing command." Had he been content with barely doing his duty, "I might have remained at ease and in safety, and not have attracted the notice of the malicious or envious." He quoted from Otway's *The Orphan:* While soldiers bled, "selfish slaves" who pretended to fawn on them, "like deadly locusts, eat the honey up, which these industrious bees so hardly toiled for . . .

> *But who will rest in safety that has done me wrong?*
> *By heaven, I will have justice,*
> *And I'm a villain if I see not*
> *A brave revenge for injured honor.*

In his own voice, he continued, "When I received a commission as brigadier, I did not expect Congress had made me, for their sport or pastime, to displace or disgrace whenever they thought proper, without a sufficient reason, and giving me an opportunity of being heard in my defense. I think it betrays want of judgment and weakness to appoint officers, and break or displace them on trifling occasions. If this plan is pursued, no gentleman who has any regard for his reputation will risk it with a body of men who seem to be governed by *whim and caprice*. . . . I sensibly feel the unmerited injury my countrymen have done me. . . . I cannot think of drawing my sword until my reputation, which is dearer than life, is cleared up, when I am willing to bleed for my country if necessary."

Historians, reasoning back from the treason, have agreed with Arnold's assumption that he had been passed over because Congress distrusted him; but the Massachusetts delegate, Elbridge Gerry, noted that he was "considered by Congress as a brave and deserving officer, and, had it been possible to have proceeded in the line of succession in appointing officers, would undoubtedly have been promoted." Although his character had been impeached, so had the character of every conspicuous soldier, and it was impossible for Congress, an unsolidified government dealing with a new army in the middle of a combined foreign and civil war, to separate justifiable charges from slander. He did not, it is true, have a personal following among the delegates, yet their decision did not reflect on him personally. It turned on the most basic problems that perplexed the emerging nation: apportioning power between the civil authorities and the army, between national and state interests, between the upper classes and the people. Although

Arnold had ignored the controversy between conservative and radical revolutionaries, the issues in which he happened to be involved were such that the right supported his interests, the left opposed them. The political forces which were to drive Arnold over the line into treason were beginning to impinge on him now.

Arnold's fellow officers agreed with him that promotion should be by seniority, but radical congressmen, who feared that the Revolution might end in a dictatorship, objected that this would make the army independent of legislatures. That Washington placed his prestige behind the military point of view, did not impress delegates who were worried by Washington's rising power. "I have been distressed to see," said John Adams, "some members of this house disposed to idolize an image which their own hands have molded. I speak here of the superstitious veneration that is sometimes paid to General Washington. . . . It becomes us to attend early to the restraining the army." Honoring seniority had already made major generals of antique veterans of the French and Indian War. "Schuyler, Putnam, Spencer [who was at that moment Arnold's commander], Heath," Adams continued, "are thought by very few to be capable of the great commands they hold. . . . I wish they would all resign. For my part, I will vote, upon the general principles of a republic, for a new election of general officers annually."

The conservatives argued that the new crop of generals, of whom Arnold was a conspicuous example, were able and worthy of trust. Propertied delegates, terrified of "mobocracy," were glad to support seniority as a method of according power not based on popular vote.

A further source of debate was whether commanders should be selected on a national basis—which would have been to Arnold's benefit since Connecticut was already over-represented—or apportioned among the states according to the number of troops each furnished. The issue was a ticklish one for the shaky federation. Union between the mutually suspicious states was necessary if the war were to be won, but union could not be forced too far lest the alliance break up in internecine rage. On this issue, too, disagreement was grounded on broad political preconceptions. Radicals, with their unhappy memory of kings, were more in favor of states' rights than the conservatives, who felt that a single strong power would help protect the property of the fortunate.

After days of angry talk, Congress achieved a compromise. It was decided that promotion would be determined by three criteria: seniority of service, state quotas, and merit as it was seen by Congress. When it was pointed out that so vague a rule would make it seem as if "the officers of the army held their honor at the pleasure of a precarious majority," the majority was not impressed. "I have no fears," wrote Adams, "from the resignation of officers if junior officers are preferred to them. If they have virtue, they will continue with us. If not, their resignation will not hurt us."

In the polling for specific candidates, the Congressmen, "notwithstanding many declarations to the contrary," showed their weak sense of national unity by placing their principal emphasis on state quotas. Although, ever since the Ticonderoga affair, Connecticut delegates had been critical of Arnold, they voted for him as a native son. However, he was defeated because Connecticut had supplied few troops and already had two major generals. New Jersey secured the election of William Alexander (Lord Sterling); Pennsylvania of Thomas Mifflin and Arthur St. Clair; Virginia of Adam Stephen; and Massachusetts of Benjamin Lincoln. Stephen was so far down the list that he was promoted over eleven brigadiers, and Lincoln, as a militia officer, was brought into the Continental Army from the outside. Congress had succeeded triumphantly in tweaking the army on the nose.

Since Arnold was the senior brigadier, and a celebrated officer, his plight attracted the most attention. Completely oblivious of the broad issues involved, he was convinced that, after a trial had enabled him "to acquit myself of every charge malice or envy can bring against me," Congress would automatically restore his rank. He cursed the fate that had a few months before kept him from visiting Philadelphia to answer his enemies, and resolved now to launch on a campaign of vindication.

But first he would have to establish the defenses at Providence on a solid basis. To his intense irritation, "Granny" Spencer wanted to attack Rhode Island. Although Arnold's whole being screamed out for a battle that would quiet his nerves and restore his reputation, he was sure that the 4,000 "raw militia" would be defeated; he was forced to give advice that made him seem afraid of the enemy. Ezra Stiles, who knew perhaps as much about military affairs as most presidents of Yale, criticized him for "obstructing" the plans of the local armchair generals. Then, to top everything, bad news came from Boston. As Mrs. Knox wrote her husband, "Miss De Blois has positively refused to listen to the general, which, with his other mortifications, will come very hard upon him." The charmer had not only spurned the trunk of gowns, but was planning to marry Arnold's rival, Martin Brimmer.

When, in early April, he was released from his duties, Arnold did not seek vindication at Philadelphia or Washington's headquarters; he fled home. His career had come a complete circle since he had lain, racked with gout, in his New Haven house after the Ticonderoga campaign. Once more he had been denied by a legislature what he considered his rights; once more he had taken as a personal insult a piece of broad political policy he did not understand. Washington tried to straighten things out for him in a letter which explained that "as Connecticut had already two major generals, it was their full share. I confess this is a strange mode of reasoning, but it may serve to show you that the promotion that was due to your seniority was not overlooked for want of merit in you. . . .

"As no particular charge is alleged against you, I do not see upon what ground you can demand a court of inquiry. Besides, public bodies are not amenable for their actions. They place and displace at pleasure, and all the satisfaction that an individual can obtain, when he is overlooked, is, if innocent, a consciousness that he has not deserved such treatment for his honest exertion." After thanking Arnold for sticking at his Providence command as long as there was any danger, Washington made it clear that he had only asked Arnold to hold off his resignation until it could be determined whether Congress had really passed him over. "The point does not now admit of a doubt, and is of so delicate a nature that I would not even undertake to advise; your own feelings must be your guide."

Arnold could hardly have found this letter comforting. He was supposed, it seemed, to regard Congress as his mother had wished him to regard God, as a superior power to which you submitted in a mood of abject praise. To be abject had not suited his temperament as a boy and it did not suit him as a man. The only alternative, and he could read between the lines that it was the one Washington expected him to follow, was to resign from the army.

To resign from the army! To strip off his uniform, to renounce battle, the joy of leading men in a common cause; to return to the lonely struggles of commerce! A month ago, he had looked back on civilian life as at a long illness. He had recovered to happiness, to power, to fame. He only needed, or so it had then seemed, a few more battles to catapult him to the greatest heights his ambition could envision. But now—he was again undervalued for no fault of his own.

Certainly, he could never again trust politicians. That Washington and his fellow officers shared his sense of outrage was some comfort, yet their very indignation made them believe that his honor, that most precious of all possessions, required that he resign. And if he resigned—

So his mind whirled round and round. He tried to occupy himself by joining his crony Oswald in a violent hunt for subversive activities among the New Haven Tories, which resulted in one man being hanged as a spy. But he could not forget his own plight. He might well have succumbed to the illness that normally accompanied his depressions had he not been waked about 3 A.M. on April 25, 1777, by a heavy pounding at his door.

Told by a breathless militiaman that 2,000 enemy soldiers had landed on Compo Point, near Norwalk, Connecticut, and disappeared inland, Arnold sprang into the uniform that he had feared he would never wear again. He was soon galloping over muddy roads in a heavy rain. Beside him, sagging a little in the saddle, was the elderly General Wooster, now commander of the Connecticut militia. Although not friends, the two had seen much action together; both had been affronted by Congress. Silently, they spurred their horses, each eager to achieve a bold stroke that would refurbish his tarnished reputation.

When they reached Fairfield, they learned that the British were heading for the major army depot at Danbury; local militia units were trailing them. With a few followers, Arnold and Wooster pushed on. Rain thundered down and cascaded up again from plunging hooves; farm boys joined them from lanes, with fowling pieces in trembling hands. At Redding, the generals found an excited turmoil of militia, but when the force lined up it was unimpressive: only some 500 amateur soldiers to attack 2,000 experienced enemy armed with cannon.

Down a road cut by multitudinous British feet, Arnold and Wooster led the advance toward a flickering glow which indicated that Danbury was in flames. At Bethel, they halted. Too few to attack, their drenched guns incapable of firing, they resolved to wait for day, and then prevent the enemy from returning to their ships. The red in the sky faded out, but about 3 A.M. sprang up once more. More militiamen gathered, and, as dawn filtered through a heavy fog, word came that the enemy were marching for the shore. Wooster agreed to fall on the British rear with 200 men, while Arnold blocked their path with a force that had now swelled to 500. The two old campaigners saluted each other formally; they were not to meet again in this world.

As Arnold led his troops on a forced march, no rooster crowed, for all were hidden in cellars; the houses that loomed through the mist were blind with shutters. Just before Ridgefield, the road tightened between a rocky ledge and a massive farmhouse. Here Arnold ordered his men to build a barricade. They were piling up logs, wagons, chairs, anything they could get their hands on, when the sound of firing revealed that Wooster had engaged the enemy. To this overture, the mist rolled back revealing low, peaceful hills and an empty road. The firing ceased, and then there arose an indefinite rustle which indicated the nearness of a large body of men.

Arnold ordered 300 troops to fan out on his flanks, 200 behind the barrier. He posted himself in the very center, and, looking out from horseback over the jumbled rampart, he saw come around the bend royal officers with drawn swords, followed by an unending column of soldiers, three abreast. A shout of orders, and the British stood still. Cannon were brought forward. After grape had rattled against the logs and overturned wagons, the British infantry advanced. Firing became general. As Arnold rode from side to side in the narrow pass, encouraging the farm boys, the noise of battle spread to the flanks. Hessians appeared on a cliff that overlooked the American left.

Seeing the enemy above them, Arnold's men abandoned the barricade. When, conspicuous on his tall mount, he lingered to keep the retreat orderly, thirty Hessians raised their guns, aimed, and fired. Eight bullets struck his horse, which fell so precipitously that Arnold, although unhurt, could not disentangle his foot from the stirrup. He landed face downward in the bloody grime. As he lifted his face, he saw a soldier in the hated uniform of a Tory regiment leaning over him with a naked bayonet. "You are my prisoner!"

Arnold's pistol hand came free. "Not yet!" he cried and pulled the trigger. Dodging the falling body, he sprang to his feet and sprinted for a nearby swamp through a hail of musket shot and grape. As he stood there panting, still unharmed although his hat was full of bullet holes, he learned that Wooster had walked boldly into cannon fire and fallen with a mortal wound.

The rest of the day, Arnold rode "from place to place in order to stir up the people, to collect them and make a stand." Although the British gave him time by proceeding cautiously and halting for the night at Litchfield, he was unable to enlist enough new men to make up for those he had lost through wounds or fear. His force was reduced to 250, but his friend Oswald had arrived from New Haven with three cannon. Arnold marched his little army to within sight of the British ships in Norwalk harbor, and ranged the men along the Saugatuck River which the enemy troops would have to cross in order to reach their transports.

Again he watched as a precise column advanced briskly, led by royal officers. Arnold "ordered a shot to be thrown among them, which halted the whole first division," so Hugh Hughes, an American commissary, wrote, "and a second [shot] put them into some disorder, as it overset some of them." The British wheeled, and forded the river higher up. As the Americans also crossed, they were providentially joined by the militiamen who had been with Wooster. "A constant skirmish ensued." Trying to inspire his raw troops, Arnold "exposed himself almost to a fault. . . . We drove them several times into a smart pace till they gained Compo Hill, which is a fine, commanding eminence, joining the beach where their shipping lay."

Rowboats filled the harbor as the British landed a fresh force; artillery appeared on the hill. Arnold's own cannon had either broken down or run out of ammunition, but he tried to lead his troops on a charge. They allowed him to advance alone. Then, to Hughes's horror, Arnold turned his back on "the full force of the enemy's fire of musketry and grapeshot . . . the enemy advancing just toward him, and our men retreating." He conjured his men, "by the love of themselves, posterity, and all that is sacred, not to desert him, but it was all to no purpose. Their nerves were unstrung."

Had any citizens of Norwich been among the wavering militia, they might have had visions of a child posturing on the roof of a burning house. On this occasion, too, Arnold escaped unhurt.

His unsupported heroism did not prevent the British from reaching their ships, yet it improved his personal fortunes. His exploit forced the legislators' hands; on May 2, Congress commissioned him major general. Yet, adhering to their determination to flaunt the traditional procedures of armies, they failed to restore Arnold's seniority in relation to the five officers they had promoted over his head. Washington wrote Congress, "General Arnold's promotion gives me much pleasure. . . . But what will be done about his rank? He will not act most probably under those he commanded but a few weeks ago."

Now Arnold began an all-out campaign for vindication. Washington gave him the necessary leave, and in a letter to the legislators explained Arnold's point of view. "These considerations," Washington wrote, "are not without weight, though I pretend not to judge what motives may have influenced the conduct of Congress upon this occasion. It is needless to say anything of this gentleman's military character. It is universally known that he has always distinguished himself as a judicious, brave officer of great activity, enterprise and perseverance."

Washington could not have put his support more strongly without risking the charge that he himself was being insubordinate. As Arnold advanced on Philadelphia, he was not unjustified in believing himself the representative of the entire army, for his had become the test case in the soldiers' efforts to force their criteria of promotion on the civil authorities.

The conflict was personified in Arnold's lodgings, where he stayed with Congressman Benjamin Rush. The Philadelphia physician was a brilliant and overserious intellectual; an amateur general quite unconscious of his military incompetence; a moralist who disapproved of flirting, drinking, and inhaling snuff. Rush considered that Arnold's "conversation was uninteresting and sometimes indelicate."

Yet, even if they did not approve of swashbucklers, Congress had to make use of them. Anxious to placate Arnold without abandoning their stand on promotion, they voted him "a horse properly caparisoned," in "approbation of his gallant conduct" during the Danbury invasion. The warrior was not satisfied.

Discounting all other explanations, he still suspected that the cause of his troubles was slander and that were he tried and vindicated, his rank would be restored to him. His old enemy, John Brown, inadvertently came to his rescue by publishing the thirteen charges in which he had impeached every aspect of Arnold's career—marvelous charges to have investigated, since they were so extreme that, had Arnold been guilty of one in five, no one would have entrusted him with a corporal's guard. He called them to the attention of Congress, who referred them to the Board of War.

Shocked by what they considered "wicked lies" subversively aimed at undermining army morale, the board did not honor them with serious investigation. Brown was not summoned nor any of the witnesses he had indicated, although Arnold was allowed to speak in his own defense, and Samuel Chase, who had left Canada before Arnold was supposed to have robbed the merchants, testified to his good behavior at Montreal. When the board resolved that Brown had "cruelly and groundlessly aspersed" Arnold's character and Congress accepted their report, Arnold confidently expected the restoration of his rank.

In the meantime, he wrangled with a Congressional committee to secure large sums which he insisted he was owed. During the Canadian campaign he had acted as commander, quartermaster, and paymaster rolled into one. Bedeviled by such multiple duties, even the most cautious man would have had difficulty keeping proper vouchers; Arnold was far from cautious. As he had done in the earlier argument about Ticonderoga expenses, he demanded that, in the absence of documents, accountants take his word of honor. Accountants are not thus constructed. Furthermore, when he did try to pin expenditures down, some of the people to whom he said he had given money denied that they had received it. And Arnold demanded that he be paid £1,000 for his financial activities, this being, he argued, a modest commission for handling £25,000. Further large claims were based on Arnold's brigantine, which he had been unable to call back from Canada in 1775. The boat had been burned by the Americans. Although at that time she had ostensibly belonged to a Canadian, Arnold stated that this had been no more than a ruse to keep her from being seized by the British. He wished to be paid for the vessel and also for the cargo of horses, which he asserted had been requisitioned by Wooster. But Wooster was dead, and other proof was lacking.

It all added up to a tangle which even Solomon on one of his best days could not have unraveled. The Congressional committee suggested a compromise—they would pay more than Arnold could prove though less than he demanded—but he shouted that if they denied him a single cent, they would be impeaching his honor. Congress remained in debt, though no one knew how great a debt, to Benedict Arnold.

The more Arnold fell out with the civil authorities, the more he turned to his fellow officers for reassurance. Schuyler was in Philadelphia continuing his endless battle to keep himself from being superseded by Gates; Arnold was enchanted that the patrician received him cordially. When Gates appeared, eager to undermine Schuyler, Arnold spent many a convivial evening with the professional soldier. Admired by both, he still saw no reason to choose between them.

After the date had been set for the heavenly Miss De Blois's marriage to Brimmer, Knox came to Arnold on a somewhat embarrassing embassy. The girls in Boston were eying the trunk of gowns which Betsy had refused. "Mrs. General Greene" was yearning for one special dress, and Lucy Knox wanted various pieces. "At any rate, I must not relinquish the scarf," she had written her husband, "as I cannot get anything to make me one." Arnold knew that a defeated soldier saves his ammunition for another campaign; he insisted on keeping the clothes.

When ladies asked him for permission to go through the American lines to British-held New York, he did not inquire into their politics or their motives. He gave so many passes that Washington asked him to stop, but he did not take this order too seriously. If more than gallantry lay behind his actions, if he sent any of the ladies on illegal business errands to smuggling merchants in New York, there is no record of it. The month-long pass he signed for Thomas Riché's family may have been commerce or flirtation or both. Riché was a business connection dating back to his New Haven years; Miss Polly, a blushing twenty-one, was seen on his arm at balls.

During June, the British mounted another attack across New Jersey and Arnold was ordered to command the militia that guarded the crossings of the Delaware. Washington, instead of allowing himself to be drawn into battle, won a strategic victory by staying in his strong encampment among the Jersey hills, which so menaced the British rear that they could not advance on Philadelphia. Thus frustrated in his need to impress Congress with further heroic deeds, Arnold planned a move so foolhardy that it implied hysteria even in a general not famous for caution; he dreamed of crossing the Delaware and fighting the main British army himself at the head of his raw militia. "Fight them we must . . . ," he wrote. "We cannot avoid it with honor." Washington vetoed Arnold's plans, and the British, having failed to lure anyone into a fight, returned ignominiously to New York.

Riding back to Philadelphia, Arnold found that Congress had taken no action to restore his seniority. His friends made a new effort to explain the issues to him. If he were told, what one congressman wrote, that his promotion was blocked because it raised "a question of monarchical or republican principles at a most crucial time," he could have wondered whether an ambitious soldier might not be better off under a king.

At last, the uniform which had been so great a pleasure to him became a burden. When people turned to stare in the streets, he no longer assumed that they admired; certainly they were despising the man whose sense of honor was so weak that he allowed his inferiors to be raised above him. On July 11, he took the action he had dreaded for so long; he presented his resignation from the army. However, he wrote Congress that, were his rank restored, he would gladly shed his blood again in the glorious cause. He hoped that, when faced with the actual loss of his services, the legislators would meet his terms.

Even as Arnold was writing out his resignation, a post rider bore toward Philadelphia news of disaster in the north. The British army, which had returned to Canada after being battered by Arnold's navy, had reappeared with the warm weather. Since the boats that had impeded them were mostly on the bottom of Lake Champlain, they sailed unopposed to Ticonderoga. The professional eye of the enemy commander, Lieutenant General John Burgoyne, noted an unfortified hill that commanded the fortress. When deadly ordnance frowned down upon them from the eminence, the American garrison, under the command of St. Clair, only waited for darkness before they fled. Thus were abandoned without a battle the works on which the safety of the northern states was believed to depend.

Washington was horrified. "The most disagreeable consequences," he wrote Congress, "are to be apprehended." Remembering how different things had been the year before, he urged that Arnold, if he had "settled his affairs and can be spared from Philadelphia," be sent to the rescue. "I am persuaded his presence and activity will animate the militia greatly, and spur them on to a becoming conduct. I could wish him to be engaged in a more agreeable service, to be with better troops, but circumstances call for his exertion in this way, and I have no doubt of his adding much to the honors he has already acquired." Meanwhile, Washington would dash for the Hudson, hoping it was not too late to keep Howe from sailing up the river, joining Burgoyne, and cutting the Colonies in half.

Arnold was mooning in his lodgings, trying to find the resolution to face a return to New Haven and civilian life, when a missive came from Congress. It made no mention of the restoration of his rank, and it ignored his resignation. However, Washington's flattering paragraph was copied out for him to see, and followed by a Congressional order that he hurry northward. To accept would be to lose his only bargaining point, and make it seem that he held his honor lightly. But he was needed, as he wanted desperately to be, and how can a war horse ignore the shrilling of the bugle? Asking Congress to table his resignation until the crisis was over, he galloped off to battle.

Book Three

TRIUMPHS
AND
TRIBULATIONS

CHAPTER ELEVEN

Prison Without Walls

IN EARLY November 1775, John André left behind him the ruined fortress at St. Johns, which had been the graveyard of his hopes, and began his long journey to internment in the wilderness city of Lancaster, Pennsylvania. On the banks of Lake George, he was immobilized by blizzard and forced to spend the night in a miserable log cabin that served as an inn. He was dismayed to see that the floor was already covered with sleepers, but the landlord pointed out that there was room for a slim man under the same blanket with a stocky stranger. Kept awake by the roar of wind and snow, the blanket-mates fell into conversation, and after the talk had turned to literature, they enchanted each other till morning. It was an odd sensation to find, when they both arose and put on their uniforms, that they were enemies dedicated to killing each other. André's companion introduced himself as Colonel Henry Knox, and explained that he was on his way to Ticonderoga to fetch back to Cambridge, now at long last, the cannon Arnold had helped capture seven months before.

Stopping for some weeks in Albany, André was invited to the house of General Schuyler. The top commander of the rabble that had captured him lived in a mansion suitable to a British aristocrat, and greeted the prisoner as gentleman to·gentleman. He was delighted, he explained, to repay the courtesy which had been shown him by British officers when he had traveled in Europe. Schuyler's powerful, ugly features contained the mingling of eccentricity

137

with the habit of command which André had seen on many upper-class English faces, and the sentiments he expressed were unbelievably correct for a man who had loosed on officers of the Crown an ill-clad and ill-educated mob. André was later to suggest to the British high command that Schuyler could easily be persuaded to rectify his mistake. Yet if the prisoner brought his smooth chatter around to politics, Schuyler's small eyes hardened, and he turned at once into an aggressive enemy commander.

Abraham Cuyler, the royal mayor of Albany, tried to explain the situation to the puzzled lieutenant: the Revolution had been incited by a few "sinister" men eager to make their fortunes by rigging the currency; "if twelve or fourteen of the ringleaders were hanged," Albany would return to its rightful allegiance. André listened with interest, yet he could not fail to recognize that, compared to the aristocratic Schuyler, Cuyler was a pushing member of the middle class.

Better to forget it all and concentrate on his art. While among the Canadian snows Montgomery and Arnold planned their desperate assault on Quebec, André sat in Cuyler's warm parlor, drawing pencil profiles of his host and hostess. He made Mrs. Cuyler a pert little thing in a mob cap, comically grave as she posed for her portrait; while all the mayor's stubborn aggressiveness was revealed in the likeness which André focused on his sitter's sharp and angry nose. The little ovals have an urbanity almost unknown in American art; they might have been drawn in some European city far from the social upheaval that was rocking a wild new land.

On January 2, 1776, André set out for Lancaster with the soldiers' baggage. His voyage down the Hudson was, as he wrote his mother, "often retarded by adverse winds and hard frosts." When he was forced to go ashore, he could not guess what his reception would be: some Rebels stared at him with hatred, but at Haverstraw a militia colonel asked him to dinner. Among the guests was a local landowner, Joshua Hett Smith. André was uninterested in the foolish-faced young dandy, for he could not know that Smith was to be his companion and nemesis on a disastrous journey that would end his career.

The road to Lancaster went through Philadelphia, and, once in that civilized city, André could hardly bear to leave it. He was nervously gay in the company of dazzling belles who were suspected by Pennsylvania patriots of having Tory hearts. Drawing a miniature of the female wit of the Revolution, the darkly statuesque Becky Franks, he presented it to her "accompanied by a few beautiful lines of poetry." He also flirted with an intense blonde of fifteen, the moody Peggy Shippen.

When, unable to delay any longer, André finally reached Lancaster, where he might be confined for years, he found the prisoners he was joining were on thoroughly bad terms with the fire-eaters of the town. Congress, strapped for funds and unused to such problems, had failed to make adequate provision for the British enlisted men who were crowded into dilapidated barracks. The officers were supposed to take care of themselves, but they lacked cash and had refused to draw bills of exchange on England, partly because they feared the bills would not be honored and partly because, as they asserted, being billeted in taverns forced them to live "in a more expensive manner than they would otherwise have done." They "had frequently made application for private lodgings, but without effect." Whigs did not want royal officers in their houses; Tories were afraid to have them for fear of the Whigs; and the officers refused to pay the tavernkeepers. Everyone became angry, and in the end, the citizens had to bear the expense of subsisting a whole pack of hated foes.

While ignoring the prisoners' physical needs, Congress hoped that "by mixing and working with the inhabitants" they would "be convinced of the justness of our cause, and become rather the friends than the enemies of America." A local official, however, reported that by "mixing with the people they have done much mischief. They adhere with an extraordinary firmness to their tyrannical master and his cause." On February 20, 1776—three days before André signalized his arrival in Lancaster by signing his parole there—the Pennsylvania Committee of Safety added, "We learn that the kind treatment given them meets with very improper and indecent return; that they often express themselves in most disrespectful and offensive terms; and openly threaten revenge whenever opportunity shall present." The committee, fearing that a British force might land on Chesapeake Bay and the prisoners make a break to join them, urged that the officers be separated from the men and dispersed in different towns or "among the farmers in the country where their opportunities of doing mischief will less correspond with their inclinations."

André did not join his fellow soldiers in their sullen anger; he labored to charm the civilians, and soon he made friends both among the German and the English settlers. Yet he was conscious of a strangeness in this westernmost of American cities that he could not drown out with civilized conversation or the notes of his flute playing minuets. His new companions were interested in his music, in his talk of poets and painters and the great European centers; their responses showed they were not ignorant of such things, and some, indeed, already knew by heart the tunes he played, had seen the same monuments he had seen; yet somehow—it was hard to explain—their minds seemed to be away somewhere: in the forest surveying land for cities that were a dream, but a different kind of dream; in the workshop creating not with paint, or words, or deeds of honor, but with metal coming red hot from a hideous forge.

All the places André had previously visited in America had seemed outposts of European culture in a raw land that would eventually be refined; but here in Lancaster it seemed as if the land were stronger than the culture, as if man himself were to be changed. Gentlemen, in costumes that would not have been too out of place in London, walked the streets with hunters in fringed leather who had seen the mighty flow of the Mississippi; and a new world seemed to be shaping between them. Typical of Lancaster was the Kentucky rifle, which had proved so deadly against the English in Canada. Its ancestor was a German hunting gun, but in Lancaster's workshops it had been transmuted into an unbelievably quick and accurate firearm that already presaged the end of warfare as André had learned it in London and Göttingen. Against such weapons, British regulars would not long wear red coats or stand in close files, swords would become decorative appendages. The hero on horseback—André's vision—made too good a target; he fell dead before an ordinary man holding a machine.

André, of course, foresaw these things only dimly, yet he felt powerfully the need for escape. Physical flight was impossible—he had given his word of honor—and he did not wish to join his fellow

officers in their unpopularity, their sullen resentment. He decided
that childish drawings by the twelve-year-old son of a prosperous
Quaker, Caleb Cope, proved the lad a genius. John Cope would
become "my disciple"; they would paint together; he would defeat his hostile environment by implanting in the bosom of this
New World child the great and traditional beauties of the Old.

Wandering in other parts of America, André had depicted with
his brush wild landscapes and wild men, but he sought that kind
of picturesqueness no longer. As a sample of his art, he drew for
his disciple a cottage with a thatched roof behind an ancient carved
stone fence and surrounded with the well-ordered foliage of England. This, he explained, was a place where he had once been
happy.

Far from encouraging John Cope to seize a coach painter's brush
and, in the manner of most American limners, slap down a likeness before he knew how to draw, André urged him to copy "whatever good models he can meet with . . . and never to think of fin-
ishing his work or imitating the fine flowing lines of his copy, till
every limb, feature, house, tree, or whatever he is drawing is in its
proper place." He urged the boy, when he sketched from life, to
correct the result by comparing it with prints after established
masters. Above all, he must obey the "rules" which André had
learned in Europe and now repeated to him. Other children may
have sat in on the lessons: ten-year-old Benjamin Smith Barton was
supposed to have caught from André the interest in drawing that
made him years later illustrate his own books on natural history.
A legend that cannot be proved says that Robert Fulton, who was
a professional painter before he turned to invention, received his
first instruction at the age of ten from André.

When André returned from his infant academy to his lodgings,
he was received with black looks. The tavernkeeper, who had not
been paid, finally ordered the officers out of his establishment.
They took "great pains" to find private houses where they would
be received, but without success. Not mollified, the tavernkeeper
insisted that "no more provisions would be dressed for them." The
Lancaster Committee of Safety was made up of men of property:
Peggy Shippen's grandfather had been chairman and the office was
now held by her cousin, Jasper Yeates, who wrote, "To gentle-

men in that delicate situation, though enemies, we could not avoid rendering every service in our power. We made interest with some of the inhabitants to afford them private lodgings . . . where they lodged and breakfasted attended by their own servants." They dined at a common mess. Caleb Cope, who was suspected of being a Tory, had been afraid to take his son's instructor in, but when officially appealed to, he did so.

André was so outraged at having been evicted that, although he seems to have had funds, he joined with another officer in refusing to pay the tavernkeeper, Michael Bartgis, the £6.10.0 they owed. Then he threw himself with enthusiasm into the Copes' family group. John's younger brother was to remember him "sporting with us children as if one of us. . . . I often played marbles and other boyish games with the major."

If tradition in the Cope family is to be believed, André abandoned the military ambitions which had brought him not glory but ignominious defeat and the first unpopularity he had ever known. "On more than one occasion," he said he would "sell his commission" if Caleb Cope would allow his young disciple to accompany him to England where "he would educate him at his own expense for the profession of painter." Certainly André did not plan to take up again the despised profession of merchant; he probably intended to occupy himself, as an amateur or a professional, with the arts. Although Cope suspected that André was less interested in educating the boy than in an honorable excuse for escaping from his unhappy situation by going home, he promised to think the proposition over.

At that moment, the Rebel authorities decided to carry out the recommendation that the enemy officers be scattered over the wilderness frontier. André was one of ten who, with their servants, were ordered to the hamlet of Carlisle, forty miles deeper in the forest. He importuned Cope to let his disciple go with him, but the father insisted that he should first find out how he would be received.

Only thirteen years earlier, during the Indian troubles known as Pontiac's War, a backwoods mob from around Carlisle had descended on Lancaster, broken into a jail where twenty peaceful Indians had been placed for protection, and scalped the defenseless basket-weavers. Now that a new set of defenseless enemies was being thrown to the frontiersmen, the Lancaster Committee were worried. They admonished their Carlisle counterpart to protect the prisoners: "As men, they have a right to all the claims of humanity; as countrymen, though enemies, they claim something more."

Probably on March 22, André and his companions plunged into the wilderness. Through swarms of insects, their "stage wagon" moved in a perpetual shadow. Occasionally, the silence was broken by the groan of wood turning on metal, and an ocean liner of the forest, a Conestoga wagon, churned majestically along; the driver looked over his shoulder and cursed. The dark men who lounged by on strange-shaped horses, the ragged broods at the doors of isolated cabins, stared angrily at the redcoated gentlemen bouncing together in the stage.

Carlisle had been destroyed during Pontiac's War, but now some 200 houses, all built in the previous eleven years, disputed the ground with the forest. They were inhabited by lovers of physical action, men who hated the established civilizations to which often they had failed to adjust. André sought lodgings with some "quiet, honest" Quakers of whom Cope would approve, but none wished to draw "great odium and much invective upon themselves" by showing sympathy for an English officer. André was forced to room in a tavern. His eagerness was such that he tried to persuade the father to send little John on anyway. He would "give all my attention" to the boy's morals and keep him "the greatest part of the day . . . employed in the few things I am able to instruct him in." He would pay all the expenses expecting in return only "a little assiduity and friendship."

To Eberhart Michael, a Lancaster brewer with whom he had struck up a musical friendship, André wrote in German "because I am happy to express myself in a language in which I have had intercourse with so many honest and sensible men. Though I should prefer to be with you, I must say this is a fine country, and the inhabitants show considerable respect toward me. We seldom have conversation with them, because generally no good results from it: nothing but uncivil and hostile answers. We pass our time in making music, reading books, and await humbly our liberation and upon more peaceful times. Myself and Mr. Despard are much engaged in playing duets."

Late in June, the British army sailed into New York Harbor and Congress called on Pennsylvania to establish a defensive "flying camp" in New Jersey. The Carlisle authorities reported that "the spirit of marching to the defense of our country is so prevalent in this town" that soon no one would be left to watch the Englishmen. Although the prisoners could not be charged "with such behavior as would warrant us to confine them, yet we have reason to believe that their conversation has influenced many weak and ignorant persons." A special guard of twelve men was hired.

When, with fine fowling pieces and hunting dogs, André and his roommate, Captain John Despard,[1] set out for the woods that were within the six-mile limit of their paroles, from across the street a dour, Scotch-Presbyterian face watched with great suspicion. Seeing them in conversation with two suspected Tories, Mrs. Ramsay sneaked out of her back door, and soon a posse came running down the street. The Tories took to their heels but were "arrested somewhere between town and South Mountain." In their pockets were found letters, signed John André, that seemed to be in code. Finally, someone recognized the writing as French, but no one could actually read that outlandish tongue. To be on the safe side, the authorities imprisoned the Tories, and ordered André and Despard to stay within the streets of the town.

André had in common with his roommate a love of music but Despard was no sensitive poet who believed in turning the other cheek. Although only five years André's senior, the Irishman was a professional fighter of long experience; when an ensign at the age of fifteen, he had "had the standard of his regiment shot out of his hand." Now André joined his companion in smashing their fowling pieces. "No damn Rebel," they explained, "should ever burn powder in them."

With the speed of galloping post riders, word came down from Canada of the negotiations at the Cedars in which Arnold, under the threat of Indian massacre, had agreed to an exchange of British prisoners for Americans whom he could have rescued in battle. André anticipated his own release, but Congress refused to honor an agreement thus illegally extorted, and a committee recommended that, should the British punish some hostages they had kept, "the progress of human butchery" should be stopped by punishing enemy officers in American hands. André remembered that he gave way to "wrath." He considered the congressmen "perfidious dastards who have worked the ruin and spilled the blood of so many credulous wretches. . . . After receiving 500 of their own men out of the hands of the Indians on condition of delivering up the garrison of St. Johns, they treacherously withheld us, inventing a falsehood."

Slower than the post riders, yet too fast for comfort, some Americans who had been captured at the Cedars returned to Carlisle with accounts of Indian cruelties: some of their companions, they insisted, had been roasted alive. The frontiersmen, who a few years before had retaliated for similar atrocities on unarmed old men and boys, had only to raise their eyes to see British officers, resplendent in red coats and powdered hair. André's cosmopolitan graces grated particularly on the woodsmen; he became the butt of popular wrath. A rumor rose that, while at liberty in Canada, he had encouraged the maltreatment of American captives.

From far-flung clearings in the wilderness that has become Perry County, militiamen hurried angrily to a tavern; a few hours later, they staggered out and formed a wavy line. Marching to Carlisle, they surrounded André's house and "swore lustily" that they would have his blood. André and Despard, their fowling pieces broken, could only draw their swords and resolve to sell their lives dearly. But from across the street there came running a nightcapped figure brandishing a broom. Mrs. Ramsay had recognized the militia captain as her husband's former apprentice; Captain Thompson recognized the broom, paled, and ordered a retreat. "As he countermarched his company," writes a Carlisle chronicler, "with a menacing nod of his head he hollered to the objects of his wrath, 'You may thank my old mistress for your lives!'" André and Despard sent Mrs. Ramsay a box of spermaceti candles, which she indignantly returned.

The situation had become very tense. Rumor raced down forest roads that a militia company, passing through Carlisle on the way to Lancaster, had "wantonly fired upon and wounded some of the prisoners . . . and had particularly attacked the house wherein Lieutenant André resided, fired several shot through the window, and had wounded him." The Lancaster authorities called out their own militia, determined to defend the captives in their charge "to the utmost of their power."

Although this particular report proved false, André drew up a blistering protest to the Carlisle authorities: "We should not have deigned to complain of defamatory papers spread about the town to render us odious to the people, or of insults from infant zealots just let loose from school, but the late attacks upon our persons have been too serious."

André had concluded, so he later confided to his mother, that Carlisle was "inhabited by a stubborn, illiberal crew called the Scotch-Irish, sticklers for the Covenant, and utter enemies to the abomination of curled hair, regal government, minced pies, and other heathenish vanities. A greasy committee of worsted-stocking knaves had us here under their ferule, and pestered us with re-solves and ordinances meant to humiliate us and exalt themselves. Sometimes they enacted penal statutes binding us to be at home at such and such hours on pain of imprisonment, at other times they broke open our letters and withheld them, or, finding us guilty of some misdemeanors, attempted to extort confessions before their tribunal." Jail was constantly threatened, although André only went there to visit some of his less fortunate friends.

"We were every day pelted and reviled in the streets, and have been oftentimes invited to smell a brandished hatchet and reminded of its agreeable effects on the skull, receiving at the same time promises that we should be murdered before the next day. Several of us have been fired at, and we have more than once been waylaid by men determined to assassinate us, and escaped by being warned to take different roads. Such is the brotherly love they in our capitulation promised us."

The rough inhabitants of the extreme frontier were, of course, not typical of all America, yet they profoundly affected André's attitude toward the war, for he was forced to live with them month after angry month. No man could have been more out of place. A peacetime camping trip in the snow had seemed to him to "take humanity a peg lower"; and his reaction against his business background had made him, even for a well-bred Englishman, unusually concerned with aristocratic graces. The woodsmen's rough hardihood, the equalitarianism nurtured by the wilderness, could have no virtues in his eyes. And the accomplishments that had brought him admiration in every other part of the world, opened him here to treatment unsuited, as he put it, "to a civilized country." The constant danger was bad enough, but the humiliation was worse. Greasy worsted-stocking knaves used brute force to exalt themselves over him and his fellow gentlemen. He felt terrifying forces at work, forces which, if they were not halted, would destroy all that he considered elegant and fine, everything that for him made life worth living. That cultivated men like Montgomery and Schuyler lent their talents to the rabble, only made the menace seem more grave. Dimly, he envisioned the excesses of the French Revolution; the head of a beautiful queen leaping bloody into a basket while washerwomen cheered.

Although Lancaster had seemed alien, he had not sensed there a force strong enough to destroy the aristocratic world: he had felt justified in fleeing from unpleasantness to missionary work with one talented convert to art. But as the dreadful months at Carlisle lagged by, he lost his belief that he was justified in seeking so personal an escape; his letters to Caleb Cope came to express only perfunctory interest in "your son, my disciple."

An inhabitant of Carlisle remembered André as "a very handsome young man" who, after the streets had become no longer safe, "confined himself to his own room, reading constantly. . . . He used to sit and read with his feet on the wainscot of the window, where two beautiful pointer dogs laid their heads on his feet." His body was quiet, but his mind was spinning with an emotion which was new to him, with hate. He no longer wondered why two sets of men killed each other. The poet had been made over into a dedicated soldier.

CHAPTER TWELVE

The Killer and His Aide

EXCITING rumors penetrated into John André's wilderness prison at Carlisle. The Americans and the British, the word ran, had agreed on a general exchange of captives: a colonel for a colonel and a private for a private as long as the supply held out. Nurturing visions of freedom, André laid down his flute, closed his books, and set out to confirm the reports. But the knaves who had threatened to split his skull with tomahawks would give him no information. On the same day that Arnold fought the British fleet at Valcour Island, André managed to send a letter to Caleb Cope at Lancaster in which he wondered what "likelihood there is of an exchange of prisoners."

The British officers were ordered to be ready to move on November 28, 1776. As he stood in line with his companions, André waited for some indication whether he was to march into the further wilderness or toward the British lines. His heart leaped when the column moved eastward.

From Reading, André wrote Cope, "We are on our road, as we believe, to be exchanged." In this letter, the word "happy" appeared in almost every sentence. Concerning that young genius, Cope's son and his disciple, he wrote, "Desire him, if you please, to commit my name and my friendship to his memory."

As he moved through the Rebel country, André found an excuse to stare at everything; in his mind's eye he saw the icy fields filled with British regulars. If infantry commanded this eminence, that village would fall automatically; engineers could easily transport cannon across that brook. When a heavy snowfall marooned the prisoners at Crooked Hill, on the road to Pottstown, André, so his host's daughter remembered, "spent most of his time in examining and drawing charts and maps of the country."

This was the grievous moment for the American cause when Washington was in full flight across New Jersey. That the Rebels were being driven "from a labyrinth of citadels by a much inferior number" confirmed André in his conclusion that the enemy were "dastards," yet he had no intention of drying up sources of information by publicly admitting such sentiments. Working hard to please the more civilized Americans he now met, he "did not, like the majority of his brother officers, engage in vituperation against the Colonists. . . . Of a light, agile frame, active in his movements, and of sprightly conversation," he proved himself "a fine performer on the flute" and "an excellent vocalist." The landlord's daughter added that "his polished manner, and the grace and charm of his conversation" made him "popular with his fellow officers."

A few days before Arnold and Gates led their regiments across the mountains of northern New Jersey in a frozen search for the Continental Army, André traversed the state further south and in the opposite direction. The American troops through which he advanced were retiring in disorganized discouragement, and the British prisoners, so Washington complained bitterly, took advantage of confusion to gather intelligence: "A lieutenant of the Seventh Regiment went through our whole army, and was at last discovered by a mere accident; he had a pass from the Council of Safety, and that was all." This semilegal spy may well have been André, who joined the royal forces at Brunswick about December 10.

He proceeded to New York whence he wrote his mother, "My situation is so new to me that, free as I am, I scarcely dare trust my pen to its former license, but ever imagine suspicious committees may intercept my letter, and make me suffer for my indiscretion." What a relief it was to be back in British-held territory, in such a gracious European world as had sometimes seemed a mirage in the overhanging wilderness! "I am in perfect health, am in a good house by a good fire." Not knowing that Washington planned to cross the Delaware, he considered that "the campaign is over. . . . You may conclude my carcass to be very safe for this winter, and, as I have some regard for myself, you may depend upon it I shall do my utmost to make myself as happy and comfortable as I can. . . . Nothing but good can befall me for some time, having had in this year and a half a considerable dose of evil in advance."

The honorable excuse to return to London he had longed for in Lancaster now offered, since the officers of his regiment were being sent home to recruit. But he had learned to hate: "I am now putting irons in the fire to obtain a plea for remaining in America."

During his captivity there had been additions to the army which promised him advantage. Down the streets of New York walked mustachioed Germans in heavy boots and high metal helmets. When the Hessians jabbered at most British officers, they could only shrug, but André jabbered back. "My wishes," he continued to his mother, "are to be attached as aide-de-camp to the person of some one of our commanders, for which post my understanding of German qualifies me—if I were equal in other respects—in preference to most others. I believe my name has in this hour been mentioned to General Howe."

André had combined the military tactics he had learned in Göttingen, the maps he had drawn and copied behind the Rebel lines, and what he had been able to observe there into a letter which he sent to his commander in chief. Howe found it "exceedingly able and intelligent," and when he met the young lieutenant, he was charmed. He promised him a staff appointment should one fall vacant and approved his purchase of a captaincy in the Twenty-sixth Foot, which was staying in America.

André spent a quiet winter on Staten Island, where legend remembers him as "a gentlemanly and agreeable companion." The farming community crawled with British soldiers. Like a prisoner escaped from a subterranean dungeon, André felt his cramped spirit expand in a society where common men knew their place, where officers were gentlemen, and the sunlight of the British Crown shone over all. Back home, the business which he scorned, but on which his prosperity depended, throve under the care of an uncle; he did not have to worry about spending-money. On his finger, as a will he made at this time reveals, there flashed a ring worth £50. He left, apart from his residuary estate, cash bequests of £32,000, in modern currency perhaps half a million dollars. Still concerned with his literary reputation, he provided that a friend have "the first inspection" of his "papers, letters, and manuscript . . . with liberty to destroy or retain whatever he thinks proper."

The opportunity for which he was waiting sailed into New York Harbor on June 5, 1777, in the person of Major General Charles Grey. Howe "begged to recommend to him a young officer of great abilities, whom for some time he had wished to provide for." André became aide-de-camp to a forty-eight-year-old professional soldier who had seen many violent engagements and been scarred by many wounds. Grey was genial, but his tiny eyes stared from under a low forehead with an unabashed hunger for blood. Although personally friendly with Howe, he considered his commander in chief too soft to be a general. A Whig who deeply regretted the American war, Howe nurtured the hope that, if he could make their cause look ridiculous, the Rebels would give up of their own accord, and believed that the less damage the British inflicted, the easier it would be to achieve peace without bitterness. He was inclined to call back his troops when the Colonials, by fleeing, admitted that they had lost a battle. Grey considered it the function of a soldier to burn and kill, to inflict as much suffering as possible. He made it clear that any engagement committed to him would be carried out with the maximum cruelty permitted by the rules of war.

Here was just such a ruthless soldier as André had sometimes dreamed himself to be when menaced by the ignoble citizens of Carlisle. Faced with the reality, the companion of poets was repelled; yet he was determined to admire and please his new commander. Again, as during the siege of St. Johns, he would drive from his mind everything but war. This time it was easier. In the journal that he kept as a souvenir for Grey of their campaigns together, there is little of the strain that was evident in his earlier diary; he never shows sympathy for the enemy or any soft emotion. Even his letters to his mother are now, for the most part, phrased as if she were a fellow officer interested in the minutiae of campaigns.

André began his journal with the British march into New Jersey that drove a spearhead between Washington to the northeast and Arnold on the far side of the Delaware. His style is laconic and businesslike: "The Rebel light-horse were frequently seen hovering around Lord Cornwallis' camp, and the avenues to both camps were infested by ambuscades which fired on our patrols and out sentries." We must imagine for ourselves the sound of hooves in the darkness, the crack of a sharpshooter's rifle; the sentry swept from somnolence to death.

When the outmaneuvered British failed to lure any American force into battle, Howe gave up hope of reaching Philadelphia through New Jersey; André returned to his comfortable lodgings on Staten Island. Grey, he had found, "improves upon acquaintance." He was soon to write, "I am in the most happy situation with my general . . . whom I esteem and am attached to more and more every day. I believe that I am fortunate enough to meet with his good will in return."

His brief experience as a staff officer had so confirmed André's enthusiasm for the military life that he acted dictatorially as his family's eldest living male. A few months before, he had written his mother about his younger brother, "I am glad to find William is employed *en grand garçon* and emancipated from Mr. Moritz's school. I hope he is still busied in polishing and accomplishing himself as, whatever is his vocation, a good education is the most valuable present you can make him." Now he knew exactly what his brother's vocation should be; he secured him a lieutenant's commission in his own former regiment, the Royal Fusiliers. Since the boy or his mother would be informed in due time by the proper authorities, he did not even bother to notify them.

Early in July, André marched with most of the army into transports. As the boats rocked day after day in New York Harbor, he sent Major Preston, his old commander at St. Johns, a detailed account of the Twenty-sixth Regiment. "I am determined," he wrote the possibly influential officer, "to call myself back to your memory before we start for regions unknown."

Everyone expected Howe to navigate the Hudson in support of

Burgoyne's invasion from Canada, and then, by holding the river line, to cut the Colonies in half. But Howe was unimpressed with the Rebel army that was retreating before his fellow commander. That a former apothecary named Arnold was rushing to the rescue seemed no more than comic. Certain that in a few weeks Burgoyne would be safe in Albany, Howe set sail on July 20 for Philadelphia. His fleet reconnoitered the mouth of the Delaware, but, finding the river fortifications strong, moved on to Chesapeake Bay where, after more than a month on the ocean, they finally landed.

Now André experienced the pleasures of his first major campaign as a staff officer. "Health," he wrote home, "attends my labors, all my work being on horseback, and having so much of this exercise that three horses hardly suffice me." His time being "very much taken up," he was forced to lay aside his more literary writings. "I hope, however, to retain pretty satisfactory memoirs of our campaign unless some unlucky ball stumbles against me."

In three existing accounts of the march—his detailed journal for Grey, a summary he kept for himself, and a letter to his mother— André expressed disdain for the Rebels. He called Washington not "General," but "Mr." or at best "Major," the last rank the renegade held in the British army. The Americans, he explained, would only fight if under the influence of "an extraordinary quantity of strong liquor"; and, in describing a clumsy English maneuver, he commented, "It is fortunate we had not an enterprising, well-informed enemy near us." Although he objected to his own army's tendency to plunder, he explained that "no method was as yet fixed upon for supplying the troops with fresh provisions."

The countryside was deserted except for "a few affrighted people who probably had not time to make their escape." As the British marched between walls of Indian corn sometimes fifteen feet high, Rebel horsemen "retired before us and stopped at every rising ground to see if the troops continued advancing. Some had arms, but they did not appear accoutered as Light Dragoons." No effective opposition appeared until they reached the Brandywine River, where Washington's army awaited them.

"Mr. Washington," André continued sarcastically, "in an involved rhapsody had persuaded them they were to exterminate us, had generously given up to his troops his own share of our baggage, and had committed the fate of America, on which the world was intent, to battle. Part of the [British] army marched the straight road to the ford and took post opposite the Rebel army, which they cannonaded without attempting to pass the water. This made them imagine we were staggered by the strength of their position, and so perfectly answered the purpose of amusing them that they were vain enough to send express to Philadelphia that they had stopped the British army."

However, the main force crossed the river further up, and fell on the Rebel right. "With astonishment they received this news; time enough, however, to drag their unwilling myrmidons to several commanding heights rising amphitheatrically one above the other." Although "jaded with a long march, loaded with knapsacks, unrefreshed by any halt," the British drove their rested opponents "from wood to wood on every side." Then the other royal force swept across the Brandywine and also "drove all before them." Washington's army, André insisted, would have been annihilated had not Howe called off his weary troops as darkness fell. However, on surveying the battlefield, André noticed something ominous: the cannon the Rebels had left behind were made in France.

In the Battle of the Brandywine, the staff officer did not play as heroic a role as he would have wished; Grey's corps, held in reserve, only moved "centrifugally in the rear of the whole, and inclined successively to the parts most engaged." But a few days later Howe slipped the leash on Grey, ordering him to get rid of a force under General Anthony Wayne that was hanging on the British flank. Instantly, André carried grim orders. The American squirrel-hunters were expert with firearms but helpless at close range before the swords and bayonets of trained European man-killers; André rode from company to company, making sure that his men took the flints out of their muskets. Grey intended to demonstrate how the war could be won. The British regulars would attack with cold steel from complete silence; for once there would be no shilly-shallying with Rebels who were better dead.

After dark, André set out with Grey's division. Every house they passed was searched and all the inhabitants kidnapped so that no one could give an alarm. American advanced pickets made only small noises under the blows of sword and bayonet. Alerted a moment before the British appeared, Wayne shouted orders, but in their haste his files of farm boys marched into each other. As they tried to disentangle themselves, they were silhouetted against their own fires when the British line tiptoed invisibly from the dark forest. André heard steel piercing flesh, strangled death cries. In a few minutes, several hundred men who were trying to flee were skewered, many of them, so patriots charged, after they had fallen on their knees to implore mercy. The wounded were given a second jab. André notes that about 200 were killed, forty seriously wounded, and only thirty-one captured not grievously hurt.

The Americans called the engagement the "Paoli Massacre," and even British participants dwelt on its "horror"; one regular considered it "altogether the most dreadful I ever beheld." André wrote impassively that the infantry put "to the bayonet all they came up with and, overtaking the main herd of the fugitives, stabbed great numbers and pressed on their rear till it was thought prudent to order them to desist." He was so pleased with this passage from his journal that he had it published in the New York *Gazette.*

In the less official version among his papers, he indulges in mirth at the thought that the dead men's commander had been a tanner, and describes what a nice party the victors had staged with "some good gin" that had been intended for now insensate throats. To his mother, he commented, "It was a most bloody piece of work and, I believe, will alarm them very much." Grey was "much respected in the army, and this last coup has gained him much credit. I must be vain enough to tell you that he seemed satisfied with my assistance on that occasion, and that he thanked me in the warmest terms." André was now "most satisfactorily situated" with his general, "upon the most friendly footing," gaining prestige from the association as well as improvement in military knowledge.

Wayne's defeat so upset Washington's strategy that Howe reached Philadelphia unopposed. While a detachment occupied the city, the main force remained in Germantown, facing toward the Rebel army. It was a countryside of rich estates. With Grey, André occupied Carleton, which had recently been Washington's headquarters. In this "most sumptuous house," he wrote his mother, he was in danger of being "spoiled as a soldier." Of an evening, he rode to an even more elegant mansion, Clivedon, the seat of the former Chief Justice of Pennsylvania, Benjamin Chew. Chew himself had been interned as a Tory in the New Jersey mountains, but his family was in residence, and one of them drew André to the ornamental gardens. Peggy Chew was at seventeen a slim brunette, gentle, very feminine, her long, fine-boned face almost too delicately made. When at rest, her dark eyes seemed melancholy, but they grew gay at the sight of the handsome young aide, who dashed off for her amusement such poems as:

The Hebrews write (and those who can,
Believe) an apple tempted man
To touch the tree exempt:
Tho' tasted at a vast expense,
'Twas too delicious to the sense,
Not mortally to tempt.

But had the tree of knowledge bloomed,
Its branches by such fruit perfumed
As here enchants my view—
What mortal Adam's taste could blame
Who would not die to eat the same
When God's might wish a Chew?

Now that he had leisure, André got around to writing his mother, "You will long ere this have learned the step I took with regard to William [buying him a commission], and, although perhaps it may have given you a momentary dissatisfaction, I am confident you will not blame me, but perhaps be glad you have been in some measure forced into complying with a thing which you must feel the expediency of, although your affection kept you in suspense. I hope to see him here before the winter sets in, and, if in the same place, I doubt not but he will meet with great civility from General Grey."

Before he mailed his letter, he received one from his mother. Her statement that she wished his brother to go into the family business, drew from André an angry postscript: "My step with regard to my brother no longer gives me any anxiety after what you tell. I rejoice at having taken it. As to your reflections concerning an essay in a countinghouse, I cannot agree with you." He admitted that familiarity with "pen and ink matters" might be useful, "but consider the lost time, the danger of falling into bad company, the expense, and the dissatisfaction it would have given him." André was sure his brother's reactions would be the same as his own.

He interfered less in the affairs of the ladies. "Your tour to France is a very good scheme, setting aside that it withdraws my sisters from all chance of preferments. You can judge of those matters best *en famille*. What think you of William and I coming to see you in some retreat of that kind? *Il ne coûte rien de faire des châteaux en Espagne*."

André thanked her for the affection she sent him, but returned none of his own, and manifested no further concern for her than that she should not be worried about him. Her "fears" had undoubtedly represented him "in too precarious a situation," particularly since she remembered his "having been burnt in Amsterdam," but, he assured her, "I am safe and ungrazed."

André's private notes reveal that he considered the war as good as won. "I believe our success to be decisive, in its consequences, but it is not immediately so. . . . We shall probably make a very short stay here, but whither our course is to be directed is not as yet known. . . . Moving and pushing distracts and demolishes these people. When we lay still, their treacherous engines go to work; they get intelligence; they harass us and retrieve their own losses." He adds that, although numerous inhabitants received the British in Philadelphia, "a great many desperadoes have withdrawn themselves."

About daybreak on October 4, André was awakened by heavy firing. He and Grey jumped into their clothes, mounted their horses. As they led their hastily grouped soldiers into a line with other advancing divisions, several broken regiments fled into their midst, creating such confusion that it looked as if the whole army might be swept into a desperate retreat. But the pursuing Rebels did not materialize. Washington's army, which had surprised the British outposts to the north, had been stopped by a small group of regulars who had darted into Peggy Chew's house and were holding it as a fort, which if bypassed, would menace the American rear.

Given a breathing spell in which to achieve their formations, the British advanced in the deadly line for which they had been trained. Grey's division cleaned out the village of Germantown. From horseback, André helped command the troops that were "rushing up the streets, scrambling through the gardens and orchards under a pretty heavy fire, and not without some loss." As the enemy fell back, he saw looming through fog and powder-smoke, his young lady's once peaceful mansion. The avenue where he had walked with the sensitive girl was now, he remembered, strewn with "a prodigious number of Rebel dead. . . . The house pierced with hundreds of shot (both cannon and musketry), the dead and wounded, within and without, told its own story without the necessity of comment." The Rebels ran on, and the British pursued until once more Howe called back his army.

More than any other he had experienced, the Battle of Germantown fitted André's romantic conception of his role as a soldier. On horseback, flourishing his sword, he had led a triumphant advance through resounding fire. His mount, he wrote, had been struck with four or five buckshot "that hurt him so little that I wish I had received them myself to make people stare with the story of five wounds in one day." As the Rebels fled like rats, he exulted to see how feeble, after all, were the forces that menaced his world. Their plan of attack, he wrote, was "too complicated, nor do their troops appear to have been sufficiently animated for the execution of it in every part, although the power of strong liquors had been employed."

It had been a glorious victory over despicable foes, yet the stupid enemy would not stay beaten. American fortifications on the Delaware kept the British navy out in the ocean, far separated from the army. According to all rules, the unprofessional mud forts should have vanished at once under professional siege; but week after week, although the British suffered heavy losses, the fortresses held. Philadelphia had fallen, yet the captors were pinned in a small triangle between rivers, unable to secure supplies.

Every few nights, as André noted, irritating displays of fireworks rose from the American encampments; deserters reported that the Rebels were celebrating triumphs in the north over Burgoyne. That a British general had been checked by amateurs—had even surrendered, as the wildest rumors said—seemed impossible, yet Howe's army had no way of finding out for sure.

The enemy were staging daily raids on the outposts near Germantown. Sentries disappeared or were found dead. As Grey, probably with André at his side, was engaged in a routine inspection, a clump of trees rustled and out galloped a detachment of light-horse. The British officers could only turn tail in ignominious flight.

Finally, Howe had enough: he withdrew his entire army behind the entrenchments that had been thrown up around the city. The British had captured the Rebel capital, and that was all they controlled. A few miles from the city, men with impunity hissed George III. Instead of describing, as he had hoped, the mounting triumphs of a rapidly moving army, André recorded, "The system became totally defensive."

"Affairs," he now admitted, "are not yet at an end. Washington will quit the field [for the winter] with a more respectable army than last year. Will he appear again in the spring recruited in the same proportion?" André trusted not, for he believed that the Rebel army was made up largely from English and Irish settlers, and "the immigration is now stopped which furnished these subjects." He feared that the enemy might receive further assistance from France, but hoped they could find no other "center of business, seat of government, harbor, quarters" to substitute for Philadelphia. "Will they continue unanimous? Does not famine threaten? . . .

"We have reason to fear great scarcity of provision in Philadelphia this winter, unless by driving off Mr. Washington the country people can be emboldened to bring in their products. Immediate death is the fate of whomsoever found guilty of bringing any provisions to the British. . . . Their light-horse have overspread the country to enforce these mandates." The royal forces should retaliate, he argued, by executing farmers who refused to sell to them. "I think were men reduced to the agreeable alternative of choosing by whom they would be hanged, principle alone must turn the scale, so that by threatening at the same rate as the enemy, we should render a whole continent conscientious, a thing devoutly to be wished for."

André agreed with Grey that the British command was fighting the war without adequate ferocity. "Have we not," he asked, "fire as well as the sword, a horrid means yet untried?"

CHAPTER THIRTEEN

Who Is My Enemy?

O N HIS way north to strengthen the army fleeing from Burgoyne, Arnold stopped off at Washington's head-quarters. The commander in chief was deeply moved, since Arnold would have to serve under St. Clair, one of the generals who had been promoted over his head and a soldier who, so Washington was convinced, had proved complete incompetence when he had abandoned Ticonderoga without a fight. To Schuyler, Washington dilated on the "generosity" with which Arnold "upon this occasion lays aside his claim and will create no dispute should the good of the service require them to act in concert."

Gossiping with General Nathanael Greene, Arnold took one of those seemingly trivial steps which alter a man's destiny. At Greene's recommendation, he invited a nineteen-year-old boy to be his aide. Well-educated in the classics, French, and dancing, Matthew Clarkson had cast himself as a warrior, but had been unable to secure a commission commensurate with his social position. He had served occasionally as a volunteer and was now eating his heart out as the guest of his uncle, Governor William Livingston of New Jersey. Glad to add so well-bred a young patrician to his military family, Arnold did not realize that, since Clarkson's background and family were intertwined with Schuyler's, he seemed to be deserting the impartiality he had always maintained in the continuing controversy over the northern command. Schuyler was still in the saddle, but the ignominious retreat of his subordinate,

St. Clair, gave new ammunition to the faction that wanted to displace him with Gates.

As he posted northward, Arnold was determined to stiffen the resistance, but, when he joined Schuyler at Fort Edward about July 24, 1777, he found the fortification so dilapidated, the troops so dispirited, ill-supplied, and outnumbered by the enemy, that he was forced to agree to a further retreat. Two weeks later, he wrote Gates that the army was still retiring down the upper Hudson, unable to make a stand unless they were reinforced "of which there seems little possibility. I expect we shall be obliged to return to the other side of the Mohawk River, whose passage we shall dispute at all events." The picture was black, "yet we have one advantage over the enemy: it is in our power to be free, or nobly die in defense of liberty." The possibility of a more tangible gain, Arnold noted, was supplied by the rumor that Howe's fleet had appeared in the Delaware. If this were not "a feint to draw General Washington," it meant that a second army would not sail up the Hudson to support Burgoyne and fall on Schuyler's rear.

Arnold had expected the civil authorities to reward his magnanimity, but instead, so Schuyler reported to Washington, he "received a letter from a member of Congress [maybe George Walton of Georgia] advising him that it is not probable that he will be returned to his rank." He asked Schuyler's "leave to retire," but when the shortage of general officers was pointed out to him, he gladly agreed to stay on.

Arnold confided to Gates—in a manner he was later to curse as indiscreet—that he had heard a rumor "that Congress had accepted my resignation. I have had no advice of it from the president. . . . No public or private injury shall prevail on me to forsake the cause of my injured and oppressed country, unless I see peace and liberty restored to her, or nobly die in the attempt."

Arnold's hatred for the enemy was increasing. "Infernal savages," he wrote, "of whom they have about 500, joined by a number of more savage and infernal Tories, painted like furies, are continually harassing and scalping our people. . . . The miserable defenseless inhabitants" were being "inhumanly butchered, without distinction of age or sex, and some, I am credibly informed, have been roasted alive in the presence of the *polite and humane British army,* and no doubt contributed greatly to their pleasure and satisfaction."

Despite Burgoyne's pleading, his Indian allies refused to abandon their own methods of fighting. Finally they brought to the British camp a scalp from which dangled more than a yard of blonde hair: they had murdered Jane McCrae, the fiancée of a royal officer. That she was described as a great beauty, made her fate seem doubly horrible; that she had been a Tory engaged to a Briton, made it clear that no one was safe. Hundreds of farmers who had been dreaming of neutrality took down their muskets and joined the American army.

Arnold heard the word "traitor" echoing on every side, since the New England troops, who had never trusted Schuyler, were sure that he and his general officers had sold them out when Ticonderoga had been abandoned. The subsequent retreats, to which Arnold had agreed, increased the clamor and suspicion, and on August 10 the news came that Congress had discharged Schuyler. Washington was empowered to appoint a successor, but from him there was no word. Like Arnold, who wore a sword and epaulets but did not know whether or not his resignation had been accepted, Schuyler was forced to continue giving orders because there was no one else to give them. The similarity of their troubles broke the reserve that had separated the two men; and Arnold achieved his first aristocratic friend. Together they damned the civilians who ruled the United States. As soon as he was vindicated, Schuyler swore, "I shall put it out of the power of anybody on earth, however respectable, to offer me further indignities, and shall . . . resign every office I hold under Congress." With such sentiments, Arnold could only concur.

As Burgoyne advanced with cautious slowness, a second British invasion reached the stage of crisis. About 875 white troops and a thousand Indians had penetrated through the north woods to the Mohawk River, but had been blocked in their march on Albany by 550 backwoodsmen in a star-shaped wilderness stockade, on the present location of Utica. Although dilapidated, Fort Stanwix (also called Fort Schuyler) could withstand the few small cannon the British possessed; and the enemy commander, Lieutenant Colonel Barry St. Leger, was no Arnold who attempted to scale unbroken walls. He waited for an uprising of local Tories which he had been led to expect.

Members of the baronial Johnson family, who had title to thousands of acres on the Mohawk, had accompanied St. Leger from Canada, in the conviction that the freeholders of the region—mostly German immigrants—would follow them to the royal side. Instead, the settlers gathered around an almost illiterate farmer, Nicholas Herkimer, and marched to the rescue of Fort Stanwix. St. Leger ordered his Indians to ambush them. In the bloody battle of Oriskany, the patriots were turned back with such heavy losses that the power of the Mohawk Valley to defend itself was shattered.

As far east as Albany, the inhabitants gave way to panic; only Fort Stanwix now shielded them from the scalping knife. Schuyler could ill spare any of the troops facing Burgoyne, but he had no choice. Despite a whispering that they were weakening the army to help the British, his general officers voted unanimously to relieve the fort. Washington had already suggested that Arnold should be sent to Stanwix "if anything formidable should appear on that quarter"; now Arnold volunteered to go.

The area for which he started on August 13 was still in uneasy equilibrium between the whites and the Indians. The seventy houses of its metropolis, German Flats, clustered around two stockades behind which the settlers were in the habit of fleeing, with their horses and cattle, at the rumor of savage raids. Realizing that the Indians were the real power on the frontier, Arnold called for help from the friendly Oneidas and Tuscaroras; they promised but did not come. Since the local militia were so cowed that, "notwithstanding my most earnest entreaties, I was not able to collect one hundred," Arnold failed to reinforce the 900 Continentals Schuyler had sent. Outnumbered two to one, informed that Fort Stanwix was in no immediate danger, he curbed his impatience and waited at German Flats for the situation to change.

He soon received good news. A major British foraging expedition had been chewed to bits at Bennington, and Arnold's new commander was his old friend, Gates. Rushing off his congratulations, he asked, as a dutiful subordinate, for positive orders to advance or retire.

Arnold was chafing at inaction when two Tories, who had been sentenced to death for holding a royal recruiting rally behind the American lines, were brought to headquarters. Walter Butler was a gentleman well known to Arnold's officers; they pleaded for his life and Arnold gave him a reprieve. The other prisoner sat on a bench, his dirty face twitching and his body, in bedraggled Indian costume, weaving through strange contortions. No one seemed to care whether Hon Yost Schuyler lived or died. Then there rushed into the room a woman who could not have combed or washed for months; her costume was half-gypsy, half-squaw. She threw herself on the ground and grasped Arnold's knees in a Herculean grip. Tears rolled from her eyes as she expostulated in unintelligible English. Behind her stood a stolid young man in the fringed buckskin of a hunter.

These were Hon Yost's mother and brother. They were well-connected—related to General Schuyler and the mother a sister to General Herkimer—but they had lived in the Upper Mohawk Castle so long that they had forgotten white ways. Hon Yost was venerated there, because he was considered crazy and all Indians knew that madmen were in direct communication with the Great Spirit. How crazy? Arnold wondered, for he had been struck with an inspiration.

Having shouted the three savage Schuylers into silence, Arnold addressed himself to the madman. Could Hon Yost use his special powers to frighten St. Leger's Indian allies into flight? At the question, the face stopped twitching, and the eyes fixed with cunning. Nothing easier, said Hon Yost. The Indians knew he had been captured; he would fire through his clothes to make it look as if he had escaped perilously, and then he would tell stories—what stories!—of the invincible might of Arnold's arms. The brother agreed to be locked up as a hostage for Hon Yost's behavior, and the madman set out for the enemy encampment at a tireless lope.

Since Arnold was engaged in ruses, he amused himself in writing to the commander at Stanwix a letter obviously intended to fall into British hands. The militia were flocking to his banner, giving him an irresistible force. "Howe with his shattered remnants of his army are on board ship. The last account was the 4th instant. He was in the Gulf Stream becalmed. Burgoyne, I hear, this minute is retreating to Ty [Ticonderoga]. I have no doubt our army, which is near 15,000, will cut off his retreat."

But tricks were less Arnold's trade than fighting. When word came that the enemy were digging a trench toward Fort Stanwix that threatened a disastrous break in the works, he "determined at all events to hazard a battle rather than suffer the garrison to fall a sacrifice. . . . You will," he continued to Gates, "hear of my being victorious or no more." The need for haste did not make him forget that a long column traversing "excessive bad roads" through "a thick wood" was vulnerable to ambush. He proceeded with such caution that the army had only covered ten miles when, as darkness fell, a messenger appeared. Fort Stanwix had been miraculously relieved. Inexplicably and "with the utmost precipitation" the British had vanished into the forest. Then Hon Yost Schuyler had sauntered up to the fort to shout that Arnold was on his way.

When the madman had first reached the British camp, he had peered from the forest to see the Indians round a council fire. The powwow was proceeding angrily for, in urging the tribes to join the expedition, the British had promised them that they could smoke their pipes and watch the fun while the shattered Americans fled before the royal soldiers. Instead, they had borne the brunt of the fighting at Oriskany, and, while they were away on this bloody errand, the Americans had sallied from the fort and captured all their possessions. Now St. Leger wanted them to ambush Arnold's force, which sounded dangerous since Arnold was known as "the heap fighting chief."

The orators had fallen silent, and prayers for guidance were winging upward when Hon Yost ran into the firelight, screaming with the madness that showed him in close contact with the Great Spirit. For a long time, the anxiously listening braves could make no sense of his gibberish, but it gradually became clear that his references to the leaves on the trees referred to the number of Arnold's men. At this moment, an Oneida who had accompanied Hon Yost from Arnold's camp appeared with a belt of wampum and Arnold's assurance that his quarrel was with the British, not the Indians. Then a second Oneida rushed in to tell of a talking bird whose croak had urged the Indians to flee before it was too late.

The chiefs stalked to St. Leger and insisted "that I should retreat." When he objected, they grew "furious and abandoned," seized the officers' liquor, and "became more formidable than the enemy." The British thought it prudent to obey orders; they fled, leaving their tents standing and their cannon in place. However, their former allies galloped around them in the forest, giving the war whoop, massacring stragglers. A brave would shout to a British platoon that Arnold was only a few feet behind. Taking off at a run, the soldiers jettisoned their packs, which the Indians plundered at their leisure. As the stampede continued, the royal officers exchanged reproaches and would have skewered each other on swords had not the Iroquois chiefs intervened.

Word went through the patriot army that Arnold's very name was enough to make the British flee. As he rode back in triumph, he passed for hour after hour through fertile wilderness, part of the Johnson estate, Kingsborough. His officers growled that this royal grant typified the inequalities against which the Revolution was being fought, but Arnold could not help thinking how wonderful it would be to control so large a piece of the world. An aggressive proprietor, with the ability to lead men—and here he looked back at the troops docilely following him—could people the area with happy and loyal dependents, becoming powerful as the Old World noblemen who had once seemed to the Connecticut scapegrace another order of being. Kingsborough, he knew, had been confiscated because the Johnsons were Tories. Perhaps when the war was won a grateful government would reward a heroic general, who had made independence possible, by granting him this estate. Then no one could any longer undervalue Benedict Arnold.

Congress, however, was less concerned with rewarding Arnold than with keeping their authority over military promotions; a motion that his seniority be restored was voted down. The South Carolina planter, Henry Laurens, considered the reasoning of his colleagues "disgusting." Arnold, he stated, "was refused not because he was deficient in merit, or that his demand was not well-founded, but because he asked for it, and that granting at such insistence would be derogatory to the honor of Congress." However, the schoolmaster and Massachusetts representative, James Lovell, regarded the vote as a triumph of "republican" principles. He was not worried lest Arnold insist on his resignation (concerning which Congress had taken no action): the general was "at liberty to quit . . . a patriotic exertion" because his "self-love was injured in a fanciful right incompatible with the general interest of the Union."

Congress's action increased Arnold's allegiance to the army. The soldiers who had been promoted over his head had publicly stated their willingness to take their rightful place behind him; it was the civilians who were doing him dishonor. To renew his resignation would be to separate himself from his supporters, place himself completely in the power of men who were, he could no longer doubt, misgoverning the nation. Better to continue service under Gates, his "affectionate friend," whom he trusted to give him appreciation and power.

When Arnold joined Gates's army, it outnumbered Burgoyne's, which had been weakened by the defeats at Bennington and Stanwix. Since Howe was in Maryland, Burgoyne could expect no reinforcements, but more militiamen were daily joining Gates. The British, who could not spend the winter in the wilderness, had to capture Albany before snow fell. This meant cutting their line of supply by crossing the Hudson. Burgoyne was now waiting for enough provisions to come from Canada to support his men until they could fight their way to populous areas.

Gates put Arnold in command of his left wing and began an advance to the woody defiles of the upper Hudson where the British regulars would be unable to fight European style. When some new militia units arrived, he asked Arnold to assign them to brigades, but, after Arnold had done so, his general orders disposed of them differently. Feeling he had been placed in a "ridiculous light," Arnold complained; Gates said it had been a mistake, as he would make clear in ensuing orders. Day after day, Arnold scanned the orders that came from headquarters with increasing irritation; Gates never publicly admitted the error.

The general who had achieved the northern command after years of struggle could not help noticing that Arnold's quarters were becoming a rendezvous for the partisans of his displaced rival,

Schuyler. Arnold's aide, Clarkson, had invited in his friends. There was Clarkson's first cousin, Henry Brockholst Livingston, son of the governor of New Jersey. As Schuyler's beloved aide, Livingston had accompanied the deposed general to retirement. Bored with waiting for Schuyler to have him commissioned, at nineteen, a lieutenant colonel of the line, he had returned to the army for a visit. "General Arnold," he wrote, "having given me an invitation to spend a few weeks in his [military] family, I did myself the pleasure to join him on the ninth instant." This was the day before Gates contradicted Arnold's orders.

As Arnold relaxed with Clarkson and Livingston, Richard Varick was their perpetual guest. Formerly Schuyler's military secretary, this twenty-four-year-old lieutenant colonel still held the position as muster master to which Schuyler had appointed him. He complained that service under Gates was "hell on earth"; saw insults in every one of his commander's actions toward him, and was delighted to insult Gates back. As the army passed through land belonging to Schuyler, Varick wrote his patron, "By good fortune, I have laid my hands on one of Mrs. Schuyler's cows yesterday. General Gates's family claimed her. However, I have established my right and shall keep her, one, for milk, and two, lest Gates take her again."

Varick wrote Schuyler two letters a day, repeating every bit of gossip he could collect to the detriment of Gates, and Livingston often added a third letter. Certainly, Arnold should have realized that his public patronage of these two trouble-makers would irritate his old crony Gates, but, in his strange blindness when it came to human relations, he seems to have failed to do so. He considered his friendships strictly his own business. The youngsters were all patricians, the kind of men whom the socially ambitious Arnold could never, a few years before, have lured to his table. They delighted him by being as angry with Congress for Schuyler's sake as he was for his own. He was so in agreement when they denounced the "insidious acts" of that body, its "iniquitous conduct such as no officer should submit to," that he did not question their motives when they encouraged him to take mounting offense at Gates's contradiction of his orders. He did not know how gleefully Varick reported to Schuyler that "a little spirit" had broken out between the two generals.

Gates decided to await Burgoyne where the road along the Hudson ran narrowly under a continuous bluff; Arnold is said to have helped the Polish engineer Kosciuszko select the exact site. As the patriots dug trenches and used the earth to wall in cannon, the British crossed the river twelve miles above. Carrying only thirty days' provisions, they had only that long to brush the Americans aside and reach Albany.

Arnold's young friends were all eagerness for bloody action. When their general led a reconnoiter in force, Varick galloped up to him and shouted that he had seen some redcoats on a hill. He was "in hopes of the General's ordering a party to attack them, but, it being near evening, the General thought it prudent to retire." Livingston complained to Schuyler that there was not more skirmishing. The truth was that the mornings were so misty, the hills so steep, and the woods so thick that the information necessary for orderly military operations was unobtainable. With only the dimmest conception of the American position, Burgoyne, in particular, could only thrust ahead blindly and hope for the best.

On the morning of the 19th, the British were moving in three widely separated columns: Hessians guarding the baggage on the river road; some 1,200 regulars under Burgoyne himself a small distance inland on the hills; and, further inland, the strongest division. Burgoyne's own force traversed a wagon track between sweet-smelling pines and came at last to Freeman's farm, a deserted log cabin in a field which opened up for about 350 yards the blue sky of a crisp autumn morning. Here they halted, most of the detachment hidden by the woods, but some pickets in the field visible to American scouts.

The report that the enemy had appeared at Freeman's farm touched off a debate between Gates and Arnold. The commander insisted that time was on the patriot side, since Burgoyne's provisions were limited and his numbers static, while the Americans were continually supplied with food and reinforcements. To emerge from his fortifications for an engagement between raw militiamen and experienced regulars would, he argued, be foolhardy; better to let Burgoyne storm the prepared works at his disadvantage.

Arnold believed "we ought to march out and attack them." If the Americans waited, he argued, the British would bring up their cannon for a classic siege, a method at which they were expert, while in a battle fought among the woods, the patriots, who were naturally guerrilla fighters, would have the advantage. Furthermore, if a defense of the works were unsuccessful, the Americans would have no place to flee, while they could retire from a defeat in the forest to prepared positions.[1]

Neither general convinced the other, but Gates agreed that Morgan's riflemen and some light infantry might march out to reconnoiter. Coming to the southern end of Freeman's field, they saw the British pickets sitting at ease among the weeds. A volley put the pickets to flight. The patriots chased after them into the pine woods, ran into Burgoyne's large force, and tumbled back through the clearing to their own forest. Burgoyne then marched into the field and lined up his regiments for battle. Around his grim array, the autumn woods were a tight and gaudy wall. The British forces to the left and right heard the firing, as did the Americans in their encampment, but no one knew what had happened. Even Morgan temporarily lost his men in the thick forest.

When Gates and Arnold finally learned that their invaluable riflemen were in trouble, two New Hampshire regiments were sent out to "support them." The reinforcements, finding that the riflemen had regathered at the American edge of the field, took a position to their left. Standing motionless in files, the British made perfect targets. A volley made them break for their own woods, leaving behind their cannon. The Americans ran into the clearing and tried to turn the guns on the enemy, but, before they had succeeded, the British reappeared, wielding the bayonets with which they were so deadly. The Americans fled for their woods.

The engagement adhered to this pattern. Since the right was blocked—and, they believed, protected—by a steep ravine, the American regiments that arrived one after another extended the line inland. This pulled the British flank increasingly to the west, but, the woods being too thick for battle, had little effect on the active fighting, which was limited to Freeman's field. Over and over again, the Americans drove the British from the clearing, advanced, and were driven back in turn. Only the mounting piles of bodies, thrashing or motionless in the weeds, marked the passing of the hours. Meanwhile, the Hessians by the river and the strong British detachment a considerable distance to the west were standing on their arms, while a majority of the American troops remained behind their breastworks, a mile and a half away.

Finally Burgoyne, outnumbered and in danger of being outflanked by the extending American line, ordered the Hessians to support him, although this left the supply train on the river open to attack. As they appeared from the ravine that the Americans had believed protected their right, they threw the patriot line into confusion. General Learned's whole brigade was thereupon ordered from the American camp, but they became lost in the forest, and, before they could be brought to bear, darkness ended the slaughter.

Neither Burgoyne nor Gates—so Gates's aide, Wilkinson, pointed out—wanted the battle. Each believed the other was attacking, and "only took what steps were necessary for defense. Thus neither general engaged in any maneuvers or used more than a fraction of his troops." In the end, the Americans retired behind their fortifications, leaving Burgoyne in possession of the field, but the British losses had been almost 600 to the patriot 320. That the Colonials had again demonstrated their ability to stand up against European regulars raised American morale and lowered the enemy's. Although both sides claimed victory, the fact was that Burgoyne had received a terrible mauling and was not appreciably closer to Albany.

The majority of American history books show Arnold personally leading our forces at the Battle of Freeman's Farm, but overwhelming evidence indicates that they are wrong.[2] As Gates listened to his passionate demands for a "complete and general victory over the enemy," he must have remembered how, when naval commander on Lake Champlain, this man had ignored his orders to play a defensive role, and had thereby, however heroically, lost the American fleet. Gates kept his rash subordinate under his own eyes at headquarters; and there, Wilkinson remembers, the orders were "worked out by both commanders." It was not an amicable process.

The American units that were successively engaged were almost all from the left wing, which was under Arnold's specific orders, and he tried to make use of this to force Gates's hand. Varick reported to Schuyler that, while the top commander "was in Dr. Potts's hut backbiting his neighbors (for which words are likely to ensue between him and me)" Arnold was "ordering out the troops. . . . And this I further know, that he [Gates] asked where the troops were going when Scammell's battalion marched, and, upon being answered, he declared no more should go; he would not suffer the camp to be exposed." Arnold dispatched more troops than Gates thought wise, but not enough to achieve the victory he desired.

Above all, he was eager to gallop onto the field of battle, to experience again the joys of warfare, to achieve the personal triumph he needed to make Congress acknowledge his worth. Wilkinson remembered that "Gates and Arnold were in front of the center of the camp, listening to the peal of small arms," when a messenger "reported the indecisive progress of the action. At which Arnold exclaimed, 'By God, I will soon put an end to it!' and, clapping his spurs to his horse, galloped off at full speed." Gates shouted an order to Wilkinson, who caught up with Arnold and remanded him to camp, where he was again tied to the apron strings of the old woman he had once admired as a soldier and loved as a friend.

That evening Varick dined at Gates's table. Taking offense at "words which dropped from Gates," he sprang to his feet and screamed out his resignation as muster master; he would rather see Gates "drawn and quartered" than serve under him any longer. Then he hurried to the room where Arnold was brooding on the frustrations of the day. Raising his angry, hawklike head, Arnold publicly insulted Gates by appointing Varick to his personal staff.

CHAPTER FOURTEEN

A Modern Achilles

ON THE morning after the Battle of Freeman's Farm light filtered into the American encampment through fog thick as cotton. Arnold's troops had slept uneasily with their fatigues and memories; their commander had paced most of the night thinking of the great victory he could have achieved had Gates not been a pusillanimous fool. Then a British deserter appeared, his face still black with yesterday's powder, to say that the British were on their way to attack the American left, which Arnold's men held. Wilkinson reports consternation at the discovery that the troops' exhausted ammunition had not been replaced, but Arnold and his aides report only hunger for battle. Staring into the fog, the general's heart leaped to see between shadowy stumps and dead trees the approach of battalions, but the visions disappeared in swirls of mist.

After the fog had lifted, revealing empty forest, Arnold hurried over to Gates's headquarters, brusquely demanded permission to attack "while the enemy were in confusion." On this occasion, as on others when his subordinate demanded aggressive action, Gates paid "little or no attention. . . . I have been received with the greatest coolness at headquarters," Arnold complained, "and often huffed in such a manner as must mortify a person with less pride than I have in my station in the army."

Gates was more than ever determined to deny the British a pitched battle. Burgoyne could expect no effective assistance, while

General Lincoln was on his way to the American camp with 2,000 men. The foe, Gates believed, must either flee or "by one violent push endeavor to recover the almost ruined state of their affairs." If they retreated, they would get into trouble, for Arnold's personal enemy John Brown had retaken Ticonderoga; if they attacked, Gates intended to meet them behind his fortifications.

In this situation, Arnold seemed as dangerous as a blowtorch would be in mending a watch; Gates decided it would be safer to detach the riflemen, who were the most mobile force in the army, from Arnold's command and add them to his own. Livingston and Varick stoked Arnold's resentment. Gates, they explained, was treating him with "disrespect" and being "insufferably rude" because he was piqued that "Arnold's division had the honor of beating the enemy."

Arnold, who needed above all prestige in Philadelphia, was now told that, in reporting to Congress on the battle, Gates had not mentioned his name, referring to his division merely as "a detachment of the army." He rushed to Gates's quarters where, so Livingston wrote Schuyler, "matters were altercated on a very high strain. Both were warm. The latter [Gates] passionate and very assuming."

First Arnold recounted all the "wrongs" which he believed Gates had done him since he had returned from Stanwix; then the two fought over credit for the victory. Gates argued that even if the troops had belonged to Arnold's division, he personally had sent them out. A major general, Arnold replied, should be censured if his division did badly and was "justly entitled to applause" if it "behaved with spirit and firmness in action." Gates then reminded Arnold of the resignation he had sent Congress, adding that he did not know Arnold "was a major general or had any command in the army."

Arnold threatened to return to Philadelphia and leave Gates in the lurch. Gates replied that, when General Lincoln arrived, Arnold would not be needed, and added, so Arnold remembered, that "you thought me of little consequence in the army, and that you would with all your heart give me a pass to leave it, whenever I thought proper." This so surprised Arnold that he could think

175

of nothing to do except cry that he would not "brook such usage," and slam the door behind him.

At least he had until Lincoln came to think out some course of action. But he had hardly emerged from the terrible interview when he heard cheering, and there was the corpulent Lincoln, trotting in on a granny's horse Arnold would have disdained to ride. He found Varick and Livingston waiting excitedly at his own headquarters. Having pumped him, each rushed off a report to Schuyler. Varick's letter shows that he saw the whole matter in terms of his patron: "The reason for this disagreement between *two cronies* is simply this, *Arnold is your friend!* . . . I have the fullest assurance Arnold will quit the department in a day or two."

Comforted by the memory of an influential man who had always supported him, Arnold wrote Gates for a pass to Philadelphia (which had not yet fallen) "where I propose to join General Washington, and may possibly have it in my power to serve my country, although I am thought of no consequence in this department." Then he rehearsed all his grievances, obviously hoping that he could still persuade his only crony to admit himself in the wrong. However, no contrite commander appeared on his doorstep that night, and in the morning a courier handed him a letter from Gates to the president of Congress stating that Arnold, at his own request, had been given permission to go to Philadelphia. "His reasons for asking to leave the army at this time shall be, with my answers, transmitted to Your Excellency."

Arnold instantly wrote Gates that he himself had been "entitled to an answer." Gates might "at least have condescended to acquaint me with the reasons which have induced you to treat me with affront and indignity." As always when he was in trouble, he was certain that "I have been traduced by some designing *villain*"; he wanted to know what "crimes" were charged against him so that he could vindicate himself. He then objected to Gates's letter to Congress, saying that he had asked for a simple pass to leave the army.

Gates replied, "You wrote me nothing last night but what had been sufficiently altercated between us in the evening. I then gave you such answers to all your objections as I think were satisfactory." The letter to Congress "not being so agreeable to you as a common pass, I send you one enclosed."

But Arnold could not bear to go. "As the enemy are hourly expected," Livingston wrote Schuyler, "General Arnold cannot think of leaving camp." Varick's explanation was that a "determination to thwart Gates's wish to have none but such as will crouch before him" made Arnold stay. But he was "so much offended" that he would undoubtedly challenge Gates to a duel as soon as the service permitted. Then Varick wrote ominously, "Arnold is determined not to suffer anyone to interfere with his division and says it will be certain death to any officer who does in action, if it be not settled before."

Arnold happened on Lincoln giving orders in his division; he demanded to know whether this was according to Gates's direction. When Lincoln admitted it was not, Arnold told him to return to the right wing where he belonged; he himself continued to command the left and Gates "ought to be in the center." He told Lincoln to tell Gates this. Gates ignored him. He did not officially remove Arnold from command, but began giving orders himself to the troops Arnold had formerly led.

"General Arnold's intention to quit this department," wrote Livingston, "is made public and has caused great uneasiness among the soldiers." A petition was drawn up, probably by Varick and Livingston, giving Arnold great credit for the recent victory and begging him to stay on. Livingston blamed the refusal of many officers to sign it on their fear of Gates. "Some, indeed, were weak enough to suggest that Arnold should make concessions and thus bring about a compromise. His spirit disdains anything of that kind. He seems more determined than ever."

The trouble-makers were rocked back on their heels to receive a letter from Schuyler expressing not pleasure at the squabble between the generals, but concern for what might happen if the army were left altogether in Gates's hated hands by the departure of "that gallant officer" Arnold. The youngsters thereupon agreed to a mild petition, which did not mention Arnold's role in the battle, merely asking him to stay with the army at so critical a time. This was signed by all the general officers except Lincoln and, of course, Gates.

Gates, however, was not happy about the rift. "He has thrown out in an unmannerly manner that Arnold's mind was poisoned by those about him," Varick wrote Schuyler. "It seems to be a heart-sore to your successor that our major [Livingston] should live with Arnold." Although Varick had returned to his post as muster master, he realized that his relationship with Arnold was also involved.

Major Chester—Livingston considered him "an impertinent pedant"—was encouraged to tell Arnold that overtures were necessary on his side, and that, "the first step toward an accommodation would be to get rid of Livingston." Varick wrote that Arnold "disdained so ignoble an act"; and Livingston amplified the scene: "When this was said to Arnold, he could scarcely contain himself, and desired Chester to return for an answer that his judgment had never been influenced by any man, and that he would not sacrifice a friend to please The Face of Clay. . . . Arnold told me what had passed and insisted on my remaining with him."

But the young men, who suddenly had been brought to realize what a tragic role they were playing, determined to return to Albany. Arnold begged Livingston to wait over a day "lest it should appear like concession on his part," and found other ways to make certain that the departure of the two trouble-makers did not lead to conciliation. When Gates, obeying an act of Congress, refused to honor a certificate for "the pitiful sum of fifty dollars" with which Arnold had rewarded a soldier for special services, Arnold wrote his commander that no other person would have suspected him "of deceit sooner than they would have done General Gates."

Arnold was so wound up that he could not stop, although the controversy was for him a disaster. He was alienating his most intimate friend among his superiors and shattering the unanimity with which the high command had supported his pretentions to rank. Above all, he needed to return to active service so that he might electrify the nation with another feat of bravery. Gates held the opportunity open. He allowed Arnold to remain in the camp, "murmuring discontent and scattering sedition"; he made no other appointment to the command of the left wing. Yet Arnold insisted that all concessions would have to come from his opponent. If Gates would not publicly admit himself in the wrong, Arnold could see no solution except, once the campaign had ended, to shoot Gates down.

When Arnold, disgusted by the way the two armies were settling ever deeper behind their fortifications, wished to win Gates to an opposite strategy, he began his letter of persuasion as follows: "Notwithstanding the repeated ill treatment I have met with and continue daily to receive, treated only as a cipher in the army, and never consulted or acquainted with one occurrence in the army, which I know only by accident. . . . Notwithstanding I have reason to think your treatment proceeds from a spirit of jealousy, and that I have everything to fear from the malice of my enemies; conscious of my own innocence and integrity, I am determined to sacrifice my feelings, present peace and quiet to the public good, and continue in the army at this critical juncture, when my country needs my support." Having stated that when Congress sent him north at the request of Washington "they thought me of some consequence," and expected that Gates would consult him, he came to the point:

"I think it my duty, which nothing shall deter me from doing, to acquaint you that the army are clamoring for action. The militia, who compose a great part of the army, are already threatening to go home." A fortnight's inactivity would reduce Gates's force by at least 4,000 desertions, while Burgoyne might get reinforcements and make good his retreat. Gates had missed the opportunity to annihilate the enemy when he had refused Arnold's advice to attack on the day after Freeman's Farm, but "that is past. Let me intreat of you to improve the present time. I hope you will not impute this hint to a wish to command the army and outshine you, when I assure you it proceeds from my zeal for the cause of my country, by which I expect to rise or fall."

As a matter of fact, farmers were still joining the American forces while Burgoyne's auxiliaries were deserting. Although both sides were short of food, the Americans were in a better position to procure it. Gates's strategy was working out as he had intended.

Miserable but unable to make himself leave, Arnold sulked about the camp. Not even in his New Haven years, not since he was a small child, had he felt so helpless under unfair treatment. What a mockery were his epaulets and his sword and his general's uniform! He watched lesser officers streaming to Gates's headquarters for councils of war. Brigades marched; skirmishers fired; but he did not know what was going on. And always he felt himself in a ridiculous position before the whole army.

Indian summer brought warm, gentle days, but the trees turned flame yellow or flame red, as if the forest were lighting campfires against approaching winter. The nights were cold, and deserters from the British camp told that the enemy shivered on short rations, while their horses drooped for lack of forage. Gates speculated that Burgoyne's "despair may dictate to him to risk all upon one throw; he is an old gambler and in his time has seen all chances." Tension mounted until shortly after noon on October 7, when from the advance guard in the American center there rose a resonance of drums.

Arnold saw Gates's aide, Wilkinson, gallop in the direction of the alarm. Wilkinson returned, riding hell for leather, and dashed into Gates's quarters. Morgan's riflemen lined up. They disappeared at a lope into the forest, to be followed by Poor's and Learned's brigades. Although ignorant of their destination, Arnold considered all these troops to be under his command.

The heavy voice of cannon spoke thrillingly from the woods, and then came a multitudinous roar which Arnold recognized as the mass firing of a British line; he concluded that the enemy were drawn up in an open field. Between the great bursts of British sound there was audible the irregular shooting typical of Americans shielded behind trees. Arnold saw more troops leave the camp, and soon a second battle developed a little way to the left of the first.

No longer able to stand still, Arnold leaped on a huge black stallion and "rode about the camp, betraying great agitation and wrath." He saw Gates, at ease before his headquarters, chatting with his aides. When soldiers arrived from the battle with reports Arnold ached to hear, Gates seemed hardly to listen. Finally, the commander looked in Arnold's direction. Arnold grew faint with anticipation—surely he was needed—but Gates looked through him.

Arnold rode to where ranks of troops stood nervously at arms. They cheered, and waited for him to give them some news, some orders. He could only wave his sword and ride on. Now he was at the ramparts, staring at two dark mushrooms of smoke, lighted from below by multitudinous flashes, which had appeared above the forest. Wounded men were being dragged back. When they saw Arnold sitting idly on his great horse, reproach, or so it seemed, appeared in their pain-clouded eyes. He opened his mouth to explain—but how could he explain? A courier came panting from the woods, with a look of importance on his features. Arnold tried to intercept him, but he dodged and hurried on to Gates.

As the noise of battle augmented, there came to Arnold's nostrils the acrid smell of burned powder. He shouted, "Victory or death"; he dug his spurs into his horse's sides. The powerful animal leaped out the sally port, into the woods, toward the lovely sounds of battle.

Gates was horrified to see Arnold disappear, certain that the unleashed warrior would upset his strategy. When Burgoyne had repeated the folly of Freeman's Farm by drawing up some 1,500 men—less than a third of his army—in an open field surrounded with forest, Gates had taken advantage of the situation, but he did not wish a major battle. The majority of the opposing forces were still in their fortifications, and the action was limited to the two flanks of the exposed British division on which the Americans could fire from the protecting forest. This was the way Gates wished the battle to remain. He commissioned Major John Armstrong to order Arnold back to his quarters. Mounting a fast horse, the major set out in pursuit.

Arnold was far ahead. On a wagon road between high trees, he met some retreating stragglers; they cheered and followed him back toward the enemy. Soon he was surrounded with the familiar faces of Learned's brigade, drawn up along a stream that marked a break in the forest. In the clearing beyond, Arnold saw a gentle rise and on the top, tight-packed Hessians knee-deep in wheat, their guns at rest but all their faces turned toward him. The grain rippled in a breeze and the sun glistened on helmets. This was the center of the British line. Since the Hessians stood in open ground suited to mass firing, they had not been attacked.

Hardly pausing in his gallop, Arnold urged his horse over the stream and up the exposed slope; he shouted, "Come on, brave boys, come on!" The troops had been hesitating before the deadly task, but they followed him. When the Hessian line fired, Arnold hardly noticed in his exultation. Then he realized that he was advancing alone: the charge had broken.

Wheeling, Arnold returned to the stream. While bullets richocheted around him, he called to the men. They followed him once more, firing desperately, and this time it was the Hessians who broke. Those who had not fallen, fled for the further woods, leaving Arnold in possession of the field. "In a square space of ten or fifteen yards," Wilkinson remembered, "lay eighteen grenadiers in the agonies of death, and three officers propped up against the stumps of trees, two of them mortally wounded, bleeding and almost speechless. . . . I found the courageous Colonel Cilley astraddle on a brass twelve-pounder and exulting in the capture, while a surgeon, a man of great worth, who was dressing one of the officers, raising his blood-smeared hands in a frenzy of patriotism, exclaimed, 'Wilkinson, I have dipped my hands in British blood!' "

The enemy were in full flight, but Brigadier General Simon Fraser managed to halt enough regiments to form a new line. Their unexpected fire threw the celebrating Americans into panic. Major Armstrong had almost caught up with Arnold when the insubordinate general galloped to the rescue. As in Homeric times, the battle turned on individual champions: Fraser, a highborn Scotch professional who had learned war on many European battlefields; and Arnold, a merchant-apothecary who had raised himself to general in two years. On an iron-gray horse, Fraser exposed himself recklessly as he rallied his men; Arnold, on his own huge stallion, shouted and raged his sword. Then Morgan's riflemen, children of an un-Homeric age, intervened. Their deadly long barrels aimed at Fraser, and, in an instant, the British champion pitched forward from his horse. The enemy, as the Trojans had done when Hector fell, broke and ran.

One of Morgan's officers was preparing to follow when Arnold galloped down upon him, raised his sword, and "in a state of furious distraction," struck his own rifleman on the head. Then, unconscious of what he had done, he "darted off to another part of the field."

Arnold was now riding everywhere, commanding everybody. As he came up to one group of men, he asked, "What regiment is this?"

"Colonel Latimer's, sir."

"Ah, my old Norwich and New London friends. God bless you! I am glad to see you. Now come on, boys; if the day is long enough, we'll have them all in hell before night."

On a slower horse, more cautious when bullets flew, Major Armstrong was still trying to get near enough to Arnold to order him back to his quarters. There was now more than ever reason, for the British were retiring behind their fortifications. According to Gates's strategy, the engagement was won and should be terminated; but his commission as commander in chief was only current in the camp where he still held most of his forces. On the battlefield, his defrocked subordinate was commander in fact.

Leading the troops like a pied piper, Arnold galloped through forest and out onto Freeman's field. The further end was now protected by a hollow square of logs from which the British fired cannon and small arms at the Americans who were "entirely exposed or only partially sheltered by trees, stumps, or hollows." Arnold's men followed him in a charge that captured a line of felled trees laid with sharpened branches sticking outward. Finding shelter where they were supposed to find danger, they fired hectically with rifles and muskets, but to little effect. The walls were sturdy and manned by most of the enemy who had escaped from the earlier engagement.

Arnold decided to shift the attack to a pair of fortified log cabins that occupied the gap between the strong point before him and another which constituted the western tip of the British position. Too excited to skirt through the woods, he spurred into the open space that separated the two armies. While everyone on both sides held their breaths and Major Armstrong decided it would be wiser not to follow, the hero on his foam-flecked mount passed by, exposed to the fire of both forces. Coming on Learned's brigade, he led them in a wild surge that silenced the log cabins.

The left and rear of the redoubt on the extreme British right were now exposed. Shouting to the troops nearest him, Arnold galloped into a clearing that rose toward the ramparts of logs.

The troops answered his shout and followed him. Some cannon rattled grape around them, but musket fire from the ramparts was slack, since most of the garrison had gone out to the battle and none had returned. Arnold led his men to the rear, where the walls were less high. As he reined in, the foot soldiers went over the walls. The portal shook as if it were about to be opened, but before Arnold could reach it his horse gave a convulsive leap and fell dead. He was thrown at full length, and when he started to rise, his leg which had been wounded at Quebec crumpled beneath him. As he writhed on the ground, fighting the pain and the helplessness, a shadow fell upon him. Major Armstrong delivered Gates's order that he return to his quarters.

Darkness now brought an end to the battle. Since the capture of the redoubt had outflanked the entire British position, Burgoyne would have to withdraw; he was soon to surrender. Arnold had struck a tremendous blow for the American cause, but now he was surrounded with a knot of doctors. Medical opinion was unanimous; they would have to amputate his leg. The hero held on to consciousness long enough to refuse them permission and then sank into a coma. He was never again to bear arms for the United States.

Book Four

LOVE

CHAPTER FIFTEEN

Peggy

THE AMERICAN forts on the Delaware, that were keeping the British fleet from their army in Philadelphia, fell at long last. As a seventeen-year-old girl watched, the river came alive with boats; on the morning of November 26, 1777, sixty-three vessels, seemingly a whole new world, were drawn toward her by white sails. Each anchor that dropped presaged an infusion into the city streets: fine gentlemen in laces, naval officers in cocked hats, pigtailed sailors trained to be respectful to young ladies carrying parasols. The stores, which had so long displayed repulsive homespun, filled with luscious stuffs that revealed the latest fashions being worn at the Court of George III. The soldiers already in the city put on fresh uniforms. Into Peggy Shippen's parlor flooded such elegant, graceful, and accomplished youths as she had glimpsed only in adolescent reveries. Although the days were getting colder and wet snow spattered down, in Peggy's life it was spring, glorious spring that brought an end to what had seemed an eternal winter of discontent.

Margaret Shippen had been born on June 11, 1760. That evening her father sat down to write his own father. After he had completed a business discussion, he mentioned that his wife had "made me a present of a fine baby which, though of the worst sex, is yet entirely welcome. You see, my family increases apace. I am, however, in no fear, by the blessings of God, but I shall be able to do them all tolerable justice. It is but staying a few years longer before

I ride in my coach." Thus grudgingly was heralded the entrance on the world stage of a beautiful lady.

Edward Shippen, Jr.'s, disappointment was understandable: he already had three daughters and only one son. Two more boys were born to him, but both died in infancy. At the age of nine, Peggy became the permanent baby of the family.

She belonged to one of a leading dynasty of what had become the British empire's second largest city. During the seventeenth century, one of her ancestors had kept a deer park within a few miles of the primeval forest. Shippens of every generation had read the ancients in the original tongues, founded learned institutions, dabbled in astronomy, made money, and helped rule Pennsylvania as hereditary allies of the Penns. When Peggy's grandfather, Edward Shippen, Sr., had deviated from the family norm by moving to Lancaster—a handier place for the fur trade that fed his imaginings—her father stayed behind. In their correspondence, roles are reversed: Edward, Sr., bubbles with childish enthusiasm; Edward, Jr., tries to soothe him down.

When studying law in London, Peggy's father had felt that "the reputation of his country [Pennsylvania] was tied up with his own," and had struggled to "rank with the most accomplished . . . in exterior polish." He considered amateur theatricals "an amusement the most useful of any to young people . . . for I think there is no method so proper to teach them grace of speech." As "men of letters are everywhere respected," it paid "to pursue learning with great assiduity"; but one must be careful, since "two-thirds of the books in the world . . . only serve to fill the minds of young people with wrong prejudices." However, Edward Shippen, who deserted his own father's Presbyterianism for the Church of England, was no prude. Noting that "painting, sculpture, and all the polite arts flourish greatly," he decided that Paris, a Babylon of iniquities to the Puritans, was "the metropolis of the polite world."

When Edward became engaged to the daughter of Tench Francis, Philadelphia's leading lawyer, a tussle between the two families over the marriage settlement almost broke off the match, but in the end Francis gave £500—part of which the groom instantly invested in a fine library—and the elder Shippen supplied the house in which Peggy was raised. Built of red and black brick, with classic pediments over the doors and windows, it contained "commodious" quarters where slaves and indentured servants labored so that the masters might live in great style. The Shippens' formal garden and orchard filled much of the interior of the block.

From babyhood, Peggy was acclimated to a great movement of gracious people. The other rich allies of the Penns lived within a block or two, and visiting was the order of each day. The great Benjamin Chew, attorney general and soon to be chief justice, was often accompanied by his own Peggy, who was Peggy Shippen's age. The two girls sometimes squabbled over dolls as they were to vie for a British officer who was now writing verses in Göttingen.

When "all the little cousins" went to the house of their uncle, Joseph Shippen, to celebrate their grandfather's birthday, Peggy saw hanging round her a greatly admired collection of copies of old masters; she was not interested. Nor did she disturb in her father's library the fine sets of English and classical authors. Her brother, who should by rights have been her father's business disciple, proved so incompetent that Edward finally resolved never "to put it again in his power to trade or make any improper use of money"; it was Peggy who had the business head. Although she seemed a toy with her light hair, her dainty features and figure, when her father talked of affairs, her gray-blue eyes fixed on him with interest and intelligence. In the letters she wrote as a woman, she never mentioned art, literature, or any cultural matters; her words were of society and business. After completing a most difficult financial settlement, she boasted, "Few women could have affected what I have done. And to you, dear parent, I am indebted for the ability to perform what I have done, as you bestowed upon me the most useful and best education that America at that time afforded."

Peggy became the favorite of a man who lacked the dash necessary for trial lawyer, but filled successfully his hereditary role as an officer of government. Edward Shippen was simultaneously Judge of the Vice-Admiralty Court, town clerk, member and clerk of the Common Council, and protonotary of the Supreme Court. He was remembered as a judge who lacked originality, but re-

vealed "some talent," much "common sense," and a mind "of eminently practical cast." Adding to his official fees by cautious operations in real estate, he was well off, but he never ventured into the
type of speculation that might have made him a really rich man.
At his knee, Peggy learned a political sophistication unknown to
Benedict Arnold, and business methods exactly opposite to those
her future husband was employing in New Haven.

From the elevation of her father's confidence, Peggy looked
down on her mother. In later years, she wrote perpetually to
Edward, but never to Mrs. Shippen; when she referred to that lady
—which was rarely—it was usually to express concern lest the
weakling collapse under some blow. As Edward was inclined to
treat his father like a son, so Peggy treated her mother as an
incompetent and exasperating daughter.

Only after Peggy reached maturity, did people comment on her
unusual strength of mind—and then they commented on it continually. Feminine and delightfully young, she seemed to her relations "so gentle and timorous a girl." The family connections noted
her devotion to her father which caused her to make "his comfort
her leading thought."

Peggy was a shy child. The wild fits of hysteria to which she
was prone, probably from the first, reveal that her association with
her father did not ground her temperament on security. He was
one of the most apprehensive of men, and the times did not soothe
his nerves. When Peggy was five, Parliament passed the Stamp Act.
As her father read that "great riots and disturbances are going forward in New England," his hands trembled. "I think the act an
oppressive one," yet he opposed plans to destroy the stamp paper.
"What will be the consequences of such a step, I tremble to think.
. . . We may call ourselves the slaves of England," he wrote and
wrung his hands. "Poor America! It has seen its best days."

An attempt to use stamps would open him to local persecution;
if he transacted business without them, the royal government might
make him an example. Shippen decided to abandon the activities
from which most of his income came, and economy became the
watchword in his household. He gloomed around the house and
complained to his little daughter.

Finally word came that the Stamp Act had been repealed; Edward wrote his own father, "I wish you and all America joy!" But the next day he was more worried than ever; a boat that had left London only five weeks before brought news that if the act were negated, which seemed improbable, it would be "on such terms as will be grievous for America." After a harrowing week, the original good news was confirmed. Toasts were drunk everywhere, and it may be that little Peggy, standing with her family in the dining room, was allowed to touch wine to her lips as all shouted the name of George III.

However, new trade restrictions soon appeared, and Edward, as an admiralty judge, was in the center of the resulting controversies: he confided his terror and self-doubt to his favorite daughter. When Peggy was ten, the Vice-Admiralty Courts, which the British did not consider adequately zealous, were abolished; but almost at once the governor appointed Shippen to the Provincial Council. As a member of Pennsylvania's highest governing body, it was more than ever his duty to enforce British laws.

Shippen admitted that the Colonies were being unjustly treated, but the whole cast of his mind repudiated disobedience: the remedy for evil statutes was to have them repealed. When American petitions of grievances met increasingly deaf ears in London, he could see no way out. He explained over and over again to Peggy how the doctrine that "natural law" superseded the enactments of the proper authorities opened the way to anarchy; the battle against prerogative abroad might extend to prerogative at home. The Shippens had valuable offices to lose. In 1765, for instance, 2,650 German immigrants had paid $2.00 apiece to be naturalized; three-quarters of this sum enriched Edward, the remaining quarter his brother Joseph. Peggy's grandfather, who was willing to take risks, became chairman of the Lancaster Committee of Safety, but her father could not decide whether he had more to lose by British intervention or American resistance. He was certain of only one thing: it would be unwise to take any public stand. He behaved as cautiously as he knew how, yet he feared that, because of his position and connections, street mobs might attack his house. No wonder Peggy saw the world as a frightening place!

During the First Continental Congress, Edward carefully invited the delegates to dinner. Thus Peggy met George Washington. He was probably more interested in the charming fourteen-year-old than she was in the ungainly planter who usually failed to make a great impression on the ladies.

When actual war broke out, Shippen wanted all his family to stay neutral; but Edward Burd, his nephew who had been his apprentice and was now a suitor for his eldest daughter's hand, accepted a lieutenancy in a Lancaster rifle company. "I wrote him my sentiments . . . that, having not been used to the woods, nor to hunting, nor to the use of rifles, he would be deemed a very unfit person for that service, and that it would appear to all the world a ridiculous thing for a young man bred in an office to command riflemen, who are expected to be men bred in the woods and inured to hardships." How Arnold would have despised such old-womanish advice coming from a man only twelve years his senior!

Since the war was officially not a revolution but a loyal protest, the Provincial Council continued to meet; Shippen sat with his peers at the very table from which they had recently exerted great power, but Pennsylvania was ruled by an illegal Committee of Safety, and the Council passed only enough innocuous motions to demonstrate that they still claimed authority. For the most part, they exchanged intelligence. Arnold had hardly set out on his supposedly secret march to Quebec before Shippen brought home the news. Two months later he hurried in to report that Montgomery had been killed and Arnold wounded. As the fifteen-year-old beauty heard her father, whose whole life was dedicated to avoiding risks, describe the desperate midwinter assault on a great fortress city, she must have wondered what manner of man it was who did such things. What could this Arnold, who lay wounded in the northern snows, look like? Was he a brute like the drunken sailors she had seen fighting on the water front; was he a knight from ancient chivalry?

Her father's nerves were increasingly strained. A sudden knock on the door would make him clutch his newspaper convulsively, since rabid patriots believed that all who were not actively for the revolution were against it; some of his friends were already in jail. With a black face, he showed Peggy "a book called *Common Sense*, wrote [*sic*] in favor of total separation from England, [which] seems to gain ground with the common people. It is artfully wrote, yet might be easily refuted. This idea of independence, though some time ago abhorred, may possibly by degrees become so familiar as to be cherished." If only his brother-in-law could promote at Lancaster a resolution "that would strengthen the hands of the advocates of reconciliation in the Congress."

After Shippen had conferred with James Drummond, who called himself Earl of Perth, the household was almost gay, for the elegant Scot, a close friend of "Lord North and others in the administration," said that England would make peace on the most favorable terms if Congress sent representatives to London. But the smiles soon faded: Congress did not show "any disposition for sending over persons to negotiate." Now Edward repeated in a trembling voice Drummond's threat that, should the Americans remain obdurate, so powerful an army would be mounted against them that "every exertion is to be dreaded."

Shippen expressed desperate concern for Pennsylvania's "tottering constitution." A representative of the proprietary party, he had fought the Assembly as hopelessly radical; now it seemed delightfully conservative, for the members were, at least, gentlemen, and they represented an electorate limited to persons of property. The plan to allow common men to vote for a legislature unchecked by any appointive body of the best people would create "so great a state of anarchy as will put us on a level with some of the Colonies to the eastward."

As Peggy ripened toward young womanhood, nature directed her thoughts toward other men than her father, toward pleasures beyond the domestic circle. She had long known what to expect, for she had watched her elder sisters one by one put on grown-up clothes and step out into gaiety. How she had thrilled when the local swains, having drunk "as hard as we can, to keep out the cold," set out about midnight "with a band, which consists of ten musicians, horns, clarinets, hautboys, and bassoons," to play under the windows of the ladies they "chose to distinguish." Whirling privately in her nightgown to her sisters' serenade, Peggy resolved that there would be bigger, louder bands for her. No woman ever manifested a greater hunger than Peggy was to do for the pleasures of the great world. As a child, she certainly counted the years, the months, the days that intervened before she could burst forth as the great belle everyone agreed she promised to be.

During the first year of the war, she was fifteen. Already her sisters' beaux looked at her in a new manner; she had some suitors of her own; and, on the way to internment at Lancaster, the handsome Englishman John André had smiled into her eyes. Then her world collapsed to the sound of guns.

When British warships were reported in the Delaware, militiamen rushed by the Shippens' door to man the tiny navy—including the gun-raft *Arnold*—which had been prepared for such a crisis; Edward expressed apprehension that the defenses would not hold. After more than a day of anxious silence, a distant booming of cannon came through the closed windows of the room where Peggy sat. The night was quiet, but with the hush of terror, and at dawn the firing resumed. Shippen excused himself from attending court at Reading: "You may be sure my family are too much alarmed to make it eligible for me to be absent till I can fix them at some little distance from the town."

Although the British were driven off, Shippen remained frightened. Peggy had been looking forward to her sixteenth birthday as a time of jubilation—it was spent in anguished packing. The plate, which had graced so many parties at which her sisters had presided, disappeared into barrels. After furniture was loaded on carts, the Shippens emigrated to Amwell, New Jersey, where Edward had bought a farm. They spent their first night with a neighbor, and, in a kitchen that smelled of stale grease, Peggy heard her father plan to abandon the way of life that had made her family great and their household elegant. He decided to become a rural storekeeper.

The farm Edward had found "is very pretty: a fine house" and "a clever tract of land with a good deal of meadows." However, they would have to share it, when winter came, with another family. "After a pleasant journey," Shippen reported bravely, "we arrived yesterday at our place of retirement, all pleased with our situation, though as yet indifferently provided."

To escape from daily anxiety was a relief, but the Shippens could not have remained for long calm or happy. The mother, it is true, enjoyed hiking over the fields—Peggy later commented with distaste on her passion for exercise—but the father, as he tried to look with an appreciative eye at a fine stand of wheat, must have mourned the King's bench and the Provincial Council. As for his four daughters, they were sophisticated city belles, and they might be trapped on the farm indefinitely. In later years, Peggy found the idea of living in the country "extremely painful. . . . A country town would be still worse, very few affording that society I could tolerate, it being chiefly composed of card-playing, tattling old maids, and people wholly unaccustomed to genteel life."

Every day they stayed at Amwell damaged, as Peggy realized, the Shippens' economic and social status. They were spending money but making none—Edward's dreams of a country store came to nothing—and in her father's absence the institutions on which their family eminence had been grounded were being blasted by more determined men who had stayed in Philadelphia. The rural church bells that pealed to celebrate the Declaration of Independence rang out remorselessly all Edward's royal offices. And soon the proprietary government of Pennsylvania, that cornerstone of Shippen prosperity, was abolished to make way for such a radical constitution as Edward had dreaded, written, he was sure, by "a certain brawling New England man called Dr. [Thomas] Young, of noisy fame." As the aristocratic Philadelphians mooned in melancholy exile, uncouth farm boys jigged beside their cows, whistling "Yankee Doodle." Were such oafs to rule a land formerly guided by gentlemen?

So Peggy wondered, as her family, no longer able to hope that compromise would end the war, wrangled nervously among themselves. Brother Edward would love, if only his father would let him, to shoot some Rebels. Such remarks brought tears to sister Elizabeth's eyes, for her lover, Edward Burd, was with Washington. Their father agreed with both and with neither: he referred to the patriot forces as "our army," but dreaded the political results if they won.

Word came that Burd had been killed at the Battle of Long Island. To the sound of her sister's weeping and her own sympathetic tears, Peggy sought desperately to understand. Why had Neddy died; why was her own life suspended in rural meaninglessness; was there no way to escape from suffering and waiting? Her spirit, more like Benedict Arnold's than her father's, hated the wringing of hands; her spirit called for action. But the only action open to her was to scream with hysterics or stare out over empty fields. When they learned that Neddy had been captured, not killed, it eased the immediate crisis but in no way altered their basic plight. Mourning in isolation a world that was dying, the Shippens could think of nothing to hope for.

The New Jersey Legislature filled up, after the Declaration of Independence, with ardent Rebels, and in October they passed "an act to punish traitors and other disaffected persons," which placed men who had not renounced allegiance to the Crown in an intolerable position. Shippen could be jailed if—to take one possibility among many—yokels turned rural justices of the peace disapproved of his conversation. It was unpleasant to have her father menaced as a traitor, but Peggy was not altogether sorry, for Edward now decided the family would be safer in Philadelphia. Away with potatoes and cows; hurray for new dresses and beaux!

The city house was opened and aired, but young men had hardly begun to line up on the doorstep when Washington's flight across New Jersey placed Philadelphia in danger of capture. Arnold, marching with Gates through the Jersey mountains, hoped the inhabitants would burn their city rather than surrender it; rumors of contemplated arson reached the Shippens. Then the Committee of Safety urged all who wished to protect their women from "a licentious soldiery" to rush them from town. As the girls stared at each other in terror, Edward sprang on horseback to seek a new burrow.

It was freezing winter when the family bundled into their coach. Wheels slithered on ice; and then they found themselves in a farmhouse far enough from the fashionable suburb at the Falls of the Schuylkill to be regarded by Shippen as "a very clever, retired place." The plebeian building, sagging under the weight of snow, was desolation exemplified. It was lonely, lonely. But if a dark figure moved across the frozen landscape, Peggy's heart contracted with fear.

In the absence of the militia, who had marched to Philadelphia's defense, the authorities feared a Loyalist uprising. "A persecution of Tories (under which name is included everyone disinclined to independence, though ever so warm a friend to constitutional liberty and the old cause) began," so wrote one of Peggy's cousins. "Houses were broken open; persons imprisoned without any color of authority by private persons; and, as was said, a list of 200 disaffected persons made out, who were to be seized, imprisoned, and sent off to North Carolina. In which list, it was said, our whole family was set down." At any moment, armed men might come for Edward Shippen, leaving Peggy, her mother and sisters, unprotected among hostile revolutionaries.

Washington's victory at Trenton, which removed all pressure on Philadelphia, reduced the Shippens' anxiety; but when details of the action came in, they discovered that they had been thrown into new difficulties. Edward had for once trusted his son, allowing him to ride on business into New Jersey. Instead of attending to his tasks, he had joined three older cousins, sons of former Chief Justice William Allen, in a gallop to the British lines and renewed oaths of allegiance to the Crown. (Arnold and Gates heard of this desertion as they marched to join Washington, and spread the word along their route.) The Allens had gone on to New York, but Peggy's brother was fascinated by the vision of himself marching into Philadelphia with the first British battalion to enter the city. He stayed with the advanced guard at Trenton; caroused with the Hessians on Christmas Eve, and was captured at dawn. Pennsylvania militiamen, noting that the prisoners included "one of Edward Shipeng [*sic*] sons," considered that their suspicions of his family had been proved correct.

As Peggy was to be at her moment of greatest crisis, Edward Shippen III was examined by Washington. All the starch had gone out of his loyalism; he begged that he might return to the neutrality of his father's house. Deciding to treat the disaffection of the eighteen-year-old boy as a childish prank, Washington sent him home. The elder Shippen received him sternly, but blamed everything on outside agitators: "I highly disapprove of what he has done, yet I could not condemn him as much as I should have done, if he had not been enticed to it by those who were much older." Peggy's reactions are not recorded. Certainly, her brother's attempt to join the British had been unsuccessful; but she may well have blamed that on his celebrated incompetence. If the fool had only gone on to New York with the Allens he would at that very moment be having a gay time with sophisticated Englishmen in a brightly lit city, instead of staring with the rest of them at a frozen cow pasture. And she must have noticed that, despite the failure of his desertion, her brother had got into no serious trouble with either her father or Washington.

If Peggy foresaw, now that the British had been beaten back, a return to the gaieties her expanding spirit required, she was disappointed; her father's thoughts were running not to a normal life but to even deeper exile. He was sure that with the reappearance of warm weather, Philadelphia would fall. Washington would then try to recapture the city, "and the country will be laid waste by the two contending parties. In this dreadful situation, I am at a loss to know how to dispose of my family."

Where they went, as long as it was not back home, could not have made too much difference to the girl, since she was even prevented from visiting friends who were only a few miles away. Edward considered the roads no longer safe. He pointed out that one of his cousins, paying calls with her children beside her, had been attacked by a Pennsylvania militia company who resented the elegance of her carriage. "They pushed their bayonets into the chariot" and endeavored to upset it, the lady the whole time "begging to be let out and the children screaming."

The times had deteriorated until even Peggy's Lancaster relations, though once ardent patriots, suffered "the blue devils." Her cousin, Jasper Yeates, wrote that the new Pennsylvania Legislature had "infringed the *inviolable* frame of government" through acts that gave "infinite dissatisfaction to men of property and understanding." The old aristocracy, who had long used governmental power to further their own prosperity, were not pleased to see their lowborn successors do the same. Peggy's father believed that, if the war continued beyond that summer, "we are all ruined as to our estates, whatever may be the state of our liberties. The scarcity and advanced price of every necessity of life makes it extremely difficult for those who have large families and no share in the present measures to carry them through."

On June 13, 1777, the Pennsylvania Assembly passed a law very similar to that which had driven the Shippens from New Jersey. Called the "Test Act," it provided that all who did not renounce the King and swear allegiance to Pennsylvania "as a free and independent state," should be incapable of holding office, voting, or suing for debts; if they traveled without a permit, they could be arrested as spies. New Jersey's statute had in effect called Peggy's mild father a traitor; now Pennsylvania was eager to consider him a spy. It would not be surprising if the words traitor and spy should cease for Peggy to carry much reproach.

Shippen had no intention of renouncing the King, nor, it seems, did his more radical father. "I presume," the younger Edward wrote the elder, "your [governmental] office will get into other hands. . . . In these times, I shall consider a private station a post of honor, and if I cannot raise my fortune as high as my desires, I can bring down my desires to my fortune. 'The wants of our nature,'" he quoted, "'are easily supplied, and the rest is but folly and care.'"

This quotation undoubtedly did not impress his daughters, who needed a little "folly" as an antidote for the deadly quiet of their lives. Edward protested even the most reasonable expenditures. Certainly Peggy was not extravagant when she wanted to occupy her hands and augment her wardrobe by knitting, yet she had to plead hard before her father would release "four silver dollars to be laid out in wool."

Having no profitable business to attend to, Edward occupied himself with elaborate ruses to keep his town house from being considered empty and therefore seized as a barracks. "Almost every day" he left his daughters freckling their noses in their cow pasture and journeyed to the city "that I may be seen in and about my house." If he noticed coming down the street the celebrated Arnold, who was in Philadelphia seeking restoration of his seniority, Shippen undoubtedly banged open a window to attract his attention and then bowed respectfully, for it was just such wild and unaccountable Rebels whom he most needed to convince that the house was occupied.

When in midsummer Howe's army, instead of going up the Hudson to support Burgoyne, sailed into the ocean, the Shippens' aching hearts told them that Philadelphia was the objective. When the fleet appeared off the Delaware, they were convinced that the enemy would avoid the forts on the river by marching overland, crossing the Schuylkill above the Falls, and bringing to their farm "all the calamities of war."

Suddenly, the hot air vibrated to distant fifes and drums. It seemed unbelievable—Howe could not have traveled so fast—and, indeed, the troops who appeared around Peggy's house proved to be the Continental Army. Sharing Shippen's guess on the British strategy, Washington had resolved to encamp at the Falls of the Schuylkill.

Now Peggy saw for the first time the crack troops of America, the mainstay of the new nation. They were, Lafayette wrote, "ill-armed and worse clothed. . . . Many of them were almost naked, the best-clad wore hunting shirts." They waved and shouted in an ill-bred manner at the pretty girl; she lifted her nose in disdain. Shippens did not associate with such people; yet such people now had the power to force themselves on the Shippens.

There came a knock on the door, and a pompous commoner, surrounded by militiamen, presented a warrant for Edward Shippen's arrest; the Pennsylvania authorities were afraid to leave suspected Tories at large. While the sound of drums filled the countryside and Peggy wept, Edward argued with his captors. Although her father was finally allowed to stay with his family, on the promise he would not leave the farm or express political opinions to anyone, Peggy had no reason to remember the appearance of Washington's army as the arrival of friends.

The next day, word came that the British had again disappeared into the ocean. Having no idea where they were going, Washington allowed his troops to collapse with the heat. The soldiers were orderly, and some of the better-bred officers enlivened the Shippens' parlor, but even Peggy must have sighed with relief when the martial array marched off again toward New York, convinced that Howe's gesture at Philadelphia had been a ruse. The enemy, Washington reasoned, was sailing back to the Hudson to support Burgoyne.

Relief was short-lived, for the British landed in Maryland and moved on Philadelphia. How pivotal the Falls of the Schuylkill was likely to be in the subsequent campaign was revealed when

Washington's army reappeared near the Shippen farm, this time to lick their wounds after the defeat at Brandywine.

They marched off almost instantly for another effort to save the city, but were thrown off balance by the massacre of Wayne's force in which André participated. Howe crossed the Schuylkill above the Shippens' farm and advanced down upon it. Since the State Council had rewarded Edward for his neutrality by enlarging his parole to include all Pennsylvania, he was in a position to flee, yet he feared that this would make him seem on the side of the patriots. His Philadelphia real estate might be confiscated when the city fell, and if the British won the war, which now seemed likely, he would face jail. He would have to let his family be captured—but it was a dreadful choice. Anything might happen when they were being engulfed by the victorious army. Even Tory leaders complained that at such a time "wives and daughters were violently polluted by lustful brutality of the lowest of mankind, and friends and foes indiscriminately met with the same barbarian treatment."

Moving from the farm, where they were helpless in isolation, to their town house offered Peggy and her family no assurance of safety, for new rumors had arisen that, rather than let it fall to the British, the Rebels would set the city on fire. And even if the Shippens survived the fury of the retreating patriots, they would still have to bear the onrush of the violent conquerors.

Whether Peggy received the invasion in the country or in Philadelphia, her experiences were basically the same. She was like a swimmer watching helplessly the advance of a tremendous wave. Nearer and nearer it rolled, rising ever more dreadful as her heart beat with terror; there was the awful moment when it broke over her: she was stifled, engulfed, in indescribable danger.

But after the crest had passed by without harming her and she was safe on the other side, she found herself in a changed universe. She was back in Philadelphia, her exile ended; the city was suddenly gay; and the Shippen parlor was full of accomplished British aristocrats, vying for smiles from the belle who like Cinderella had magically come into her own.

CHAPTER SIXTEEN

Indian Summer of an Invasion

O N DECEMBER 30, 1777, André closed his military journal with the words, "The army came into winter quarters in Philadelphia." To his mother, he explained, "I believe I shall be in a very quiet station henceforth. Mr. Washington, it is said, has divided his army, and means to seize outposts and attack small detachments. You know, *we generals* have nothing to do with retail fighting."

Beginning with the occupation of Boston, the officers had produced amateur theatricals wherever they went; and now André signalized his rise to the gay inner group about the commander in chief by becoming a leading member of "Howe's Thespians." Although he was remembered as "a poor actor," he was assigned important parts; he wrote rhymed prologues (but not all those ascribed to him); he painted scenery. He was kept busy, since in five months thirteen plays were produced.

One of his sets revealed "a landscape presenting a distant champagne country, and a winding rivulet, extending from the front of the picture to the extreme distance. In the foreground and center, a gentle cascade—the water exquisitely executed—was overshadowed by a group of majestic forest trees. The perspective was excellently preserved; the foliage, verdure, and general coloring artistically toned and glazed." The mood was "calm and harmonious." (This set, which remained in the theater, was later used as the backdrop for a scene in which a player representing André was captured by three low-comedy yokels.)

Peggy Shippen, Arnold's future wife. A drawing
made by André during the British occupation of
Philadelphia, when Peggy was one of the high-
flying belles with whom he flirted. *Courtesy, Yale
University Art Gallery.*

Two British officers accoutered for a mock tournament. A souvenir of the Revolution's most famous ball, the Meshianza in Philadelphia, drawn by André for the beauty he escorted—Peggy Chew, not Peggy Shippen. For the future Mrs. Arnold, the evening was one of intense frustration. A reproduction published in the *Century Illustrated Monthly Magazine. Courtesy of the New-York Historical Society, New York City.*

Howe's Thespians boasted at least one professional actress, Miss Hyde, who "sang 'Tally Ho' between the play and the farce." Wives of enlisted men helped out. "They were generally," according to the doorkeeper of the theater, "of no character. They and the officers were about the theater all day. When any piece was to be rehearsed, they would all flock around the back door or the side lot."

It may all have been sordid—soldiers selling their wives to their officers; the officers boasting in the prologues about the sufferings of the Rebel prisoners; the Old Southwark Theater far from elegant, with square columns interrupting the view from the boxes and the stage lighted by plain lamps without glasses; the military actors mouthing their lines—but to Peggy Shippen, it was all Paradise.

Lord Rawdon considered her the handsomest woman he had seen in America, and Captain A. S. Hammond of the *Roebuck* remembered, "We were all in love with her." Combine this testimony with a Hessian officer's report that "assemblies, concerts, comedies, clubs, and the like make us forget there is any war, save it is a capital joke"—and you have the scenario of an exciting winter. The pleasures Peggy's "constellation of beauties" enjoyed were described by Becky Franks to Mrs. William Paca who, because she was a congressman's wife, was exiled in the country: "You can have no idea of the life of continued amusement I live in. I can scarce have a moment to myself. I have stole this while everybody is retired to dress for dinner. . . . Most elegantly am I dressed for a ball this evening at Smith's, where we have one every Thursday. You would not know the room, 'tis so much improved. . . .

"The dress is more ridiculous and pretty than anything that ever I saw: great quantity of different colored feathers on the head at a time, besides a thousand other things. The hair dressed very high. . . . I have an afternoon cap with one wing, though I assure you I go less in the fashion than most of the ladies. [There's] no being dressed without a hoop."

At Rebel balls, girls had been supposed to dance only with the men who brought them—all that was antiquated. "No loss for partners. Even I am engaged to seven different gentlemen, for you must know 'tis a fixed rule never to dance but two dances with the same person. Oh, how I wish Mr. P. would let you come in for a week or two—tell him I'll answer for your being let return. I know you are as fond of a gay life as myself—you'd have an opportunity of raking as much as you choose either at plays, balls, concerts, or assemblies. I've been but three evenings alone since we moved to town. I begin now to be almost tired. . . . I must go finish dressing as I'm engaged out to tea."

Peggy's admirer, Captain Hammond, gave "a splendid dinner and dance" on board the *Roebuck;* she was piped on board with great ceremony. Rocking gently on the dark water, with the city in the background, the warship was illuminated by lanterns. One hundred and seventy-two people sat down to dinner, and then Peggy danced with one charming Englishman after another. They whispered in her ears that such beauties as she belonged at the Court of George III. Everywhere she looked, neat sailors with tarred pigtails bowed as if she were a countess. If this were a dream, how she prayed not to waken!

Sometimes, when the moon was high, she set out with a shadowy officer—André or another—in a sleigh behind swift cavalry horses. The town would soon be behind them and they would dash through a world of white. But after they had gone only a few miles, their way was blocked by fortifications that marked the limit of British glory. On the other side, men in homespun were fingering plebeian but deadly rifles. Her officer would boast that the ramparts would soon come down and the whole country be theirs. Peggy clapped her hands, for then she could sail on forever behind these swift horses.

When she got home, she found pacing the hall the father who was no longer her beloved companion. As determined to be neutral under British rule as he had been under American, he refused to hold offices and did little business; no money was coming in. His little store of gold—no one would accept paper—seemed hardly sufficient to buy plain food for his family, since "every kind of provision [is] treble in price. . . . There is no remedy for any of us," he explained, "but abridging every article of expense that does not actually supply us with some real comfort of life. Our clothes we can wear over again, we can lessen our number of horses, and we can perhaps do very well without adding to our furniture."

Such speeches threw Peggy into a terrified fury. Not only did the imported silks and laces, which were now purchasable in any quantity, make her image in the mirror glow, but, since all the other girls had them, they were an absolute necessity in the magic world she had just discovered. How could she entertain without new furniture, or go abroad when there were no horses in the stable for the chariot? By frequent bouts of hysterics Peggy secured the minimum necessities for gay living, but she feared that at any moment her father's stubbornness might congeal.

His lectures on economy had a disturbing way of slipping over into moral indignation; he was afraid that the British officers would corrupt his daughters. Did not their commander flaunt his affair with Mrs. Joshua Loring, and did not Loring, the grafting commissioner of prisoners, show no displeasure: as long as "he fingered the cash," he was enchanted that "the general enjoyed madam." At a public review, Major Williams's doxy rode down the whole line in an open carriage, her horses, servants, and her own person embellished in the colors of her lover's regiment. "The woman," commented a horrified Philadelphian, "was singularly beautiful." Officers stated that rather than depopulate America, they were careful to father a bastard for every Rebel they had killed, nor was this altogether an idle boast; André's friend, Oliver De Lancey, created two nameless children during the war.

Despite Shippen's fears, Peggy was probably no more than a spectator to immorality. Philadelphia girls enjoyed "a liberty which to French manners would seem disorderly," the Duc de la Rochefoucauld wrote a few years later, yet their desire to make good marriages kept them circumspect. That it was unsafe to compromise a well-connected American girl, André's companion, Major Lord Cathcart, discovered when Howe forced him to wed the daughter of a New York Tory. Peggy and her friends were charming playthings for a courtly evening, but not objects for lust unless you wished to get married. Although Becky Franks did carry off a colonel, few Britons wanted to get seriously involved.

Dazzled by the brilliantly uniformed denizens of the great world, many Colonial maidens dreamed of marrying British officers. Peggy Chew's wounded heart bled for André even after her wedding to that leading Baltimorean John Eager Howard. Whether Peggy

Shippen was also overwhelmed it is impossible to be certain, since her family soon had compelling reasons to destroy all evidence that linked the girl who married Benedict Arnold with the Englishman most responsible for his treason. Yet she turned naturally to André when the moment came for getting in touch with the enemy; and to her dying day she kept, hidden among her effects, a lock of his hair.

Too ambitious to weigh himself down with a provincial beauty, André moved from one well-furnished parlor to another. How Peggy and her friends, the girls he called "the little society of Third and Fourth Street," admired him! Sometimes he played the flute to Captain Ridsdale's violin, while "the sisterhood of both streets" sat in rapt attention; or he would dance more beautifully than the girls themselves without losing his masculine air. As the snow fell, he talked of European cities, fabulous places that his audience had experienced only in books, and was very knowing about the relative virtues of Raphael and Corregio. With expressive gestures slightly exotic for an English officer, he quoted poetry by authors he had actually met, or even by himself. He was glad to oblige when Becky Redman asked him to compose verses to her favorite German tune:

Return enraptured hours
When Delia's heart was mine. . . .

André's acquaintance from his Swiss school days, Du Simitière, who wished to found a museum in Philadelphia, was "extremely desirous of obtaining a miniature by his hand." André promised to prepare something, but, so he said, could not find the leisure, and in the end gave Du Simitière "a few drawings of no other value but that they were done by him, and gave some idea of his superior talents, which were fully displayed in the curious journal he kept of his travels." While too busy to make a picture for a museum, he sketched as a parlor game likenesses of the charmers with whom he was surrounded. His gaily urbane portrait of Peggy Shippen reveals a pretty girl, with high forehead, regular features, and full cheeks—but is more concerned with her elaborate costume than her character. Sometimes he cut silhouettes of everyone at a party, the quick-clipping scissors communicating a powerful sense of form.

He took more trouble with artistic activities that furthered his career: scenery painted for the delectation of his superiors, the military maps that abound in his papers. Showing sometimes campaigns at which he had not been present, the maps were undoubtedly based on official surveys; they are neat, clear, and carefully lettered, with trees and hills indicated by conventional symbols, the whole pleasing to the eye although he practically never added any decorative frills. When he made freehand sketches in the field, they were rough notations of natural features he wished to emphasize.

As André, preparing himself for future high commands, thought out the war as a whole, he could not escape the conclusion that it was going badly. The capture of Philadelphia had done no more than inconvenience the Rebels, while Burgoyne's surrender had caused repercussions on the Continent which the half-French officer could hardly believe. Only a few months before, he had not opposed his mother's plan of moving with his sisters to France; now the French, convinced that the Americans were worthy allies, were planning to join the war against hated England. André's tribulations at Carlisle had opened his eyes to what Louis XVI could not see. Conscious that the forces being loosed menaced all aristocracy, he dimly foresaw the guillotine. More immediate was the danger to his own status as a gentleman of property, which was vulnerable to the French fleet since it was based on holdings at Gibraltar and the West Indian island of Grenada.

In London, Parliament, not prepared to fight all over the world, hurried through an act which offered America everything except independence. A peace commission rushed across the midwinter ocean as fast as sails could carry them, but they were beaten to these shores by news that the French had entered the war. The Philadelphia Tories, who had staked their all on a British victory, were in despair. They could only hope that, before a Gallic force arrived from Europe, Howe would crush Washington's army which, they assumed, was too sick and frozen to defend Valley Forge. When the British did not march they blamed it on the unwillingness of the officers to rise from beside their mistresses.

The officers, in turn, blamed the home government for not sending enough troops to subdue a nation at arms. Even André's sanguinary general, Grey, considered that an attack on Washington's well-entrenched encampment would be foolhardy. In disgust, Howe sent home his resignation. Everyone believed that sooner or later Philadelphia would have to be abandoned, and all its American inhabitants given the choice between exile and the outraged fury of their returning countrymen.

The city was like a rich vessel foundering in a stormy ocean. As Edward Shippen trembled, his daughters floated downstairs in new dresses that had not been paid for, and disappeared with British officers as fine in their red coats as if they were winning the war. All night the military bands played with increasing frenzy, all night the girls pirouetted faster and faster. At dawn, her sleepless father heard Peggy come home, giggling ecstatically. Outside the walls the Rebel pickets came ever closer like sharks waiting for the ocean to lap over luxurious decks.

When Howe was called home to defend the actions of his army, his playmates felt, as André put it, "dejection, regret, and disappointment." André was among the twenty-one officers who subscribed £3,312 to say farewell with such a pageant as America had never seen.

For the marriage of the Earl of Derby, brother of one of the subscribers, General Burgoyne had staged, a few years before, a fete in which English lords and ladies had dressed up as shepherds and shepherdesses, but this conceit did not appeal to gallants who were beleaguered in a provincial city by revolting peasants. Preferring to remember the happy days when armored knights were invincible to the commoners who were not even mentioned in their chronicles, the officers determined to joust, as André put it, for the favor of "ladies selected from the foremost in youth, beauty, and fashion" in a "tilt and tournament according to the customs and ordinances of ancient chivalry." Since it would be difficult to dance in armor, they selected for themselves court costumes from the reign of Henry IV. But to dress American girls as matching aristocrats seemed unsuitable. Remembering that Henry IV had lived in the age of crusades they cast their partners as Turkish maidens. The parallel was fascinating: as knights who fought infidels in a holy cause entertained pretty heathens, so would the British invaders entertain America's Tory belles.

The fourteen jousters divided themselves into teams: Knights of the Blended Rose (device: roses entwined; motto: "We droop when separated") and the Knights of the Burning Mountain (device: a volcano; motto: "I burn forever"). In the crests painted on their individual shields, all but André mingled love and war. A typical device showed "a heart aimed at by several arrows and struck by one"; the motto: "One only pierces me." But André had "two gamecocks fighting," and the boast, "No rival."

Selected seemingly on dynastic grounds, the Turkish girls came from a few leading families. André took Peggy Chew. The three Shippen sisters who were invited represented, because of Edward's long neutrality, one of the poorer and less powerful families; Peggy, their youngest, drew the youngest of the knights, a boy of her own age. She could not help being jealous of her rival, yet to be one of the fourteen girls chosen from all Philadelphia was tremendous fun.

Edward Shippen did not share the enthusiasm of his household; dressing three daughters *à la* Turk would drain away most of his remaining hard money. But it is difficult for a man to stand out against the united pleas of his women. What each girl bought was thus described by André: "They wore gauze turbans spangled and edged with gold or silver, on the right side a veil of the same kind hung as low as the waist, and the left side of the turban was enriched with pearl and tassels of gold or silver and crested with a feather. The dress was of the Polonaise kind and of white silk with long sleeves. The sashes which were worn around the waist and were tied with a large bow on the left side hung very low, and were trimmed, spangled, and fringed according to the colors of the knight." A Hessian observer commented, "The great English shop of Coffin and Anderson took in £12,000 sterling for silk goods and other fine materials, which shows how much money was lavished on this affair, and how elegantly the ladies were dressed."

The ball was called the Meshianza (so spelled on the ticket, variously spelled by André and everyone else) because "it was made up of a variety of entertainments." The managers were all older officers, but André had charge of the ladies' heads: "The Mesquinza [*sic*]," he wrote, "made me a complete milliner." In addition, he painted much of the elegant *décor*, a labor he considered worthy of his best talents, since it furthered his military glory and he was propagandizing in the New World for the artistic glories of the Old.

There were the interior of a confiscated Rebel mansion to redecorate; a pavilion, 180 feet long, to paint from top to bottom; two triumphal arches in "the Doric order" to be covered with emblems and devices. Regiments had to be scanned for enlisted men with classic proportions to stand in niches as statues; classic texts had to be examined for mottoes that were lettered everywhere; and all the time more amphitheaters and pavilions were building. The British army had not been so busy for months.

Some twenty-five miles away, the same spring that warmed the tournament ground warmed Valley Forge. Shoeless feet, lately cut and frozen, had become whole again as they pressed on grass. There had already been a celebration in the American camp. Generals, who recently were tradesmen or minor provincial officers of the British army, stood on a little rise, surrounded by unfashionably dressed women. Before them there marched not exactly in step and to fifes too rusty to be in tune, some thousands of men in ragged clothes, among whom a complete uniform seemed ostentatious. Yet the troops walked with a springy stride, and on their faces were marks of pure joy. When they had paraded enough to please their hearts, they drew up before the tall campaigner André called "Mr." Washington. A chaplain stepped in front of each brigade, read the treaty of alliance with France, and called for a minute of silent prayer. This over, the soldiers cheered, threw their hats (if they had any) in the air, and wasted a little scarce ammunition by rattling out salutes. Then they all went back to animal-like huts, and drank raw rum to the anticipation of a glorious campaign.

As the day of the ball approached, Peggy was in an ever-mounting fever of excitement. There were anguished sessions with her dressmaker; hours under the ministrations of a hairdresser almost out of his mind with his responsibilities; rehearsals before the mirror. How she prayed that it would not rain on the glorious 18th of May; how happily, rising from the bed where she had hardly slept, she saw the sun's first rays slide clear and warm into a cloudless sky! She fondled her beautiful Turkish costume, and soon the whole household was awake, the women circling around Peggy and her two equally bright-eyed sisters.

No one noticed when a somberly clad deputation of Quakers came to see Edward Shippen. After the Friends had departed, Edward rang for servants and sent them on errands. Then he called his women. They came down the stairs with much giggling, but were silenced by the sternest look they had ever seen on the face of the head of the house. The Quakers, Edward announced, had confirmed his own doubts; they had "persuaded him that it would be by no means seemly that his daughters should appear in the Turkish costumes designed for the occasion." He had already notified their escorts that they would stay home. The girls were "in a dancing fury," but for once Edward could not be moved.

How Peggy must have hated the father who had once been her dearest friend when a British orderly appeared to carry off the dress she had so lovingly prepared; lest the pageant be ruined, some other woman would wear it. Her face not handsomely powdered but streaked with tears under unbecomingly puffy eyes, the belle lay in a darkened room. Even closed windows and pulled blinds did not keep her from being taunted by the revelers' music, so sweet, so very sweet.

As Peggy wept, André glittered. His vest, he wrote, "was of white satin, the upper part of the sleeves made very full, but of pink, confined with a row of straps of white satin laced with silver upon a black edging. The trunk hose were exceedingly wide. . . . A large pink scarf fastened on the right shoulder with a white bow crossed the breast and back, and hung, in an ample loose knot with silver fringes, very low under the left hip. A pink and white sword belt laced with black and silver girded the waist. Pink bows with fringe were fastened to the knees, and a wide buff leather boot hung carelessly round the ankles. The hat of white satin, with a narrow brim and high crown, was turned up in front and enlivened by red, white, and black plumes; and the hair, tied with contrasted colors of the dress, hung in flowing curls upon the back."

In an account he prepared as a souvenir for Peggy Chew, André reverted to a style that would have pleased the Swan of Lichfield: "The gaudy fleet, freighted with all that was distinguished by Rank, Beauty, and Gallantry, was conveyed down the River, along the whole length of the City, whilst every ship at the wharfs or in the stream was decked in all her maritime ornaments. . . . The music, the number of spectators, and the brilliancy of the gay tribe which peopled the river made the whole uncommonly solemn and striking."

Disembarking at Joseph Wharton's mansion—the owner was dying in exile—the gay tribe advanced, "with all the bands of the army massed in front," under the triumphant arches to the amphitheater, where the Turkish maidens were escorted to conspicuously placed sofas. "The colors of the army waving at different intervals framed in the ground with martial uniformity and splendor."

André and his six companions paraded in on horses caparisoned with pink, black, and silver, the "trimmings and bows hanging very low from either ham and tied round their chest." Before each knight walked his esquire, carrying a silvered shield and a lance "fluted pink and white." Then a herald appeared with three braying trumpeters. "The Knights of the Blended Rose," he intoned to murmurs of delight, "by me their herald proclaim and assert that the ladies of the Blended Rose excel in wit, beauty, and every accomplishment, those of the whole world, and should any knight or knights be so hardy as to dispute or deny it, they are ready to enter the lists with them and maintain their assertions by deeds of arms, according to the laws of ancient chivalry."

Now there appeared with slow ceremony seven knights "in black satin contrasted with orange and laced with gold." Their herald answered, "The Knights of the Burning Mountain enter these lists not to contend with words, but to disprove by deeds of arms the vainglorious assertion of the Knights of the Blended Rose and to show that the ladies of the Burning Mountain as far excel all others in charms as the Knights themselves surpass all others in prowess."

Having made "a general salute to each other with a very graceful movement of their lances," the knights, so André continues, executed "with great rapidity and dexterity," a martial dance on horseback. At full gallop, each shivered a spear against his opponent's shield; turning rapidly, they twice fired pistols as they passed. Then they paired off and, circling around each other, appeared to fight hand to hand with swords, until "they were parted by the interposition of the judges of the field, who doubtless deemed the ladies so fair and the knights so brave that it would have been impious to decide in favor of either."

As the jousters, "thus reconciled by a happy compromise," received as rewards for their prowess favors which the Turkish maidens unpinned from their turbans, a few miles away in a rural tavern Rebel light-horsemen were joking with the barmaid. They had already made sure that their guns and sabers were in order, that their camp kettles were full of whale oil. They were only waiting for it to become dark.

At twilight, the festive tribe in formal procession entered Wharton's house which, according to André, "was lighted and ornamented with much brilliancy and taste. A great number of looking-glasses multiplied every object. They were festooned over with flowers, knots, and scarves of pink and green silk; and the walls were decorated with ornamental paintings in fresco in a very elegant style." Tea was served and the young people danced.

As, in the deepening twilight, the Rebel horsemen mounted, the revelers crowded to the windows to watch a display of fireworks which, so André wrote condescendingly, "besides its real merit, had that of novelty to recommend it to the greatest number." At the climax, a triumphal arch burst into light, revealing, on the very apex, Fame, from whose trumpet issued in letters of fire, "*Tes Lauriers Sont Immortels.*"

Supper was announced. "There was," André wrote, "some appearance of enchantment on entering the room, when such a perspective of ornament and illumination caught the eye unexpectedly; when at the upper end were discovered twenty-four Negroes in blue and white turbans and sashes, with bright bracelets and collars, bowing profoundly together, as the company journeyed through the prodigious length of the Saloon; and when the most pathetic music was performed by a concealed band. Everyone seemed to hesitate as if they should proceed—whether [because] the objects before them appeared sacred, or whether they involuntarily stopped to gratify their surprise." Our more materialistic Hessian informed his government that the 330 covers were "loaded with 1,040 plates," and that the British fleet had rushed rare fruits up from the West Indies.

Suddenly, the British fortifications in the direction of Germantown went up in flames. Having tethered their mounts in a thicket, the Rebel light-horse had sneaked up, poured out their kettles of whale oil, and clicked their flints. English drummers pounded the alarm, cannon boomed, frightened sailors on the river tore down the pennants that covered their ordnance. As Howe assured the ladies that this was merely more fireworks, officers slipped away to meet the alarm. The damage done, the Rebels had vanished. Fresh from their tournament, the Britons tried to follow, but were forced to turn tail by Kentucky rifles in unchivalrous hands.

Instead of mentioning this disturbance, André told how trumpets were blown and toasts were drunk: the King and Queen; "the founders of the feast"; General Howe and his brother, the admiral, on whose faces "a generous emotion answer[ed] the undissembled testimony of our love and admiration. Freighted now with new strength and spirits, the whole repaired to the ballroom and daylight overtook them in all the festive mirth with which a youthful band can be animated."

The girls who went to the party considered, as one wrote, that "we never had, and perhaps never shall have so elegant an entertainment in America again." (Poor Peggy!) However, many Loyalists were outraged: "This day," commented Mrs. Henry Drinker, "may be remembered by many for the scenes of folly and vanity. . . . How insensible do these people appear, while our land is so greatly desolated, and death and sore destruction has overtaken and impends over so many." And when the news got back to England, the newspapers expressed indignation at this triumph given to a commander who had almost lost a war.

André's own conviction, manifest in the manuscript he gave Peggy Chew, was that the British officers had set a wonderful example to the provincial Americans. He drew for her his most attractive watercolor, which showed a Knight of the Blended Rose accompanied by esquire and page. With taste and subtlety, he muted all other tones to give emphasis to the prevailing light pink of the costumes, and washed a little pink into the shadows.

Even before the Meshianza, Philadelphia Tories had noted disturbing "movements in the army which we do not understand: the heavy cannon are ordered on board the ships, and some other things look very mysterious." However, fears that the British were preparing to retire were lightened by good news: a large force under Lafayette had emerged from the Rebel camp and was vulnerable. With Grey's division, André rode out to cut all escape routes, while Howe's main army moved to crush the enemy from the front. The country glowed in early spring, and Lafayette sat like a hare too deaf to hear the hounds. Inexorably, exactly according to plan, the trap closed—it was empty. At the last minute, in a brilliant maneuver, Lafayette had slipped away.

This was the end. Ordered to reinforce the Indies against French attack, Howe's successor, Sir Henry Clinton, felt obliged to consolidate in New York the weak forces that would be left in the Colonies. When Du Simitière called at Benjamin Franklin's house, where André was quartered with Grey, he found the aide putting in packing cases books taken from the shelves of the devilish philosopher who had negotiated the French alliance. Du Simitière remonstrated, but to no purpose. Various witnesses report that André took a valuable set on China, and the epoch-making *Encyclopédie*, both the property of American institutions, as well as music and musical instruments, electrical apparatus, and one of Franklin's personal account books. His most splashy booty, a portrait of the philosopher painted by Benjamin Wilson, he gave to Grey. (Returned generations later by one of Grey's descendants, it now hangs in the White House.)

Clinton offered to take with him into exile any Philadelphians who were afraid to be captured by the Americans, but the Shippens and the Chew ladies resolved to stay with their property. André pressed a poem into Peggy Chew's hand:

> *If at the close of war and strife*
> *My destiny once more*
> *Should in the varied paths of life*
> *Conduct me to this shore;*

Should British banners guard the land
And factions be restrained;
And Cliveden's mansion peaceful stand,
No more with blood be stained—

Say! Wilt thou then receive again,
And welcome to thy sight,
The youth who bids with stifled pain
His sad farewell tonight?

If André gave Peggy Shippen a similar effusion, it has been destroyed with other records of their friendship.

Although her father no longer yearned for rural hide-aways—"I find," he wrote, "almost every person who has removed from home repented it"—Peggy's eighteenth birthday was as dreary as her sixteenth had been. Then, she had been pulled away from life; now, life was leaving her. Philadelphia, our Hessian wrote, "greatly resembled a fair on the last day of business." All the laces and silks Peggy admired—and sometimes delightedly secured for her own—were being packed up by the British storekeepers. The theater was shut. The officers with whom she had sleighed and danced were busy preparing for a retreat that would take them from her, perhaps forever. How could Colonial yokels ever take their place in her eyes and heart?

CHAPTER SEVENTEEN

A Wounded Body Wounds a Mind

AFTER the triumph over Burgoyne, the road back to Albany had been full of wounded. Under flaming autumn trees, they groaned in carts, leaned faintly over the necks of horses, or staggered on foot: Englishmen, Hessians, riflemen, Yorkers, farm boys from the deep South; and among them Benedict Arnold, in a carriage attended by doctors who still insisted that they must cut off his leg. But he adhered grimly to his statement that he would rather be dead than crippled.

The hero whose bravery had won the battle proved in the Albany hospital the most troublesome of all the wounded. "Last night," wrote Dr. James Thacher, "I watched with the celebrated General Arnold. . . . He is very peevish and impatient under his misfortunes, and required all my attention during the night." However, he seemed to recover "very fast": in two days there was no more talk of amputation.

Arnold was soon "in good spirits although he has a touch of gout." News of the desperate plight of the British army, and then of Burgoyne's surrender, convinced him that his political troubles were over. Gates, it is true, continued to give him little credit, but he was sure that Congress could no longer be fooled. They would restore his rank, and then, when his leg got well again, he would proceed down the highroad to glory. He counted the days it would take a messenger to reach Philadelphia and return with proofs of gratitude.

Congress ordered a gold medal struck in honor of Gates, but made no move to restore Arnold's rank. After this news had reached the hospital, visitors found him "much weakened," "full of pain," "low-spirited" and "very ill." He denounced endlessly the "ungenerous, scandalous manner" in which Gates had deprived him of credit for a great victory.

General Lincoln, one of the officers who had been promoted over his head and who still outranked him, was suffering in a nearby room. The doctors annoyed Arnold by pointing out that, although more dangerously wounded, his rival was mending faster because of a calm mind. Lincoln revealed "the politeness of the gentleman, the patient philosopher and pious Christian. Not so the gallant Arnold. His peevishness would degrade the most capricious of fair sex. . . . He abuses us as a set of ignorant pretenders and empirics." Having lost faith in his doctors, Arnold sent Oswald on a midwinter quest through Connecticut for "old Dr. Jones"—but no one could help.

The fighter was deep in pain and discouragement when he learned that Congress had at long last (November 29, 1777) given in to popular pressure and empowered Washington to restore his rank. Daily and perhaps hourly, Arnold asked for the dispatch box that would bring him his commission written out in his dear friend's hand, but weeks passed with no word from headquarters.

Arnold's leg and shattered hip were fastened to a wooden fracture box. Although the feverish soldier, held eternally on his back, seems a less significant figure than the same man braving cannon, Arnold's months in the Albany hospital were among the most important in his career. Except when he excoriated his doctors or orated to a caller against Gates, he was trapped with his mind. Only in our own imaginations can we follow the grievous campaigns fought inside his skull: the ambuscades from which there was no escape because the attacker was also the attacked, the redoubts that once stormed had to be stormed again, over and over, till dawn blanched the windows. In these feverish maneuvers, punctuated with nausea and pain, defeat was certain, for Arnold's mental arsenal was devoid of the one weapon that would have helped—dispassionate reason.

His vision embraced no more than his personal situation; the fate of other men was dim to him unless it closely resembled his own; explanations, if they were complex, faded or formed themselves into irrational bugaboos. All his life, he had been able to escape from mental troubles only into physical action. His joys, his mystical flights had been a plunge into cool water on a summer's day, the speed of a galloping horse, the firmness of a pistol raised in the exhilaration of battle. These were behind him. A strong man crippled is like a beautiful woman disfigured: he loses not only his opportunities for ecstasy but his defense against the world.

A revolutionary soldier, Arnold had fought for "freedom" as he understood it: for motion without hindrance, for the right of the individual will—his will—to answer, light and jocund, the call of individual destiny. Where was his freedom now? Strapped to a wooden box, he was imprisoned as he had never been.

Late in January, the long-awaited letter came from Washington enclosing a commission restoring him "to the rank you claim in the army." The busy commander in chief, unconscious of the anguish his eight weeks' delay had caused his subordinate, made no further apology than that "the situation of my papers and the want of blank commissions prevented me doing it before." Arnold waited almost to a day as long as Washington had kept him waiting before he answered the question whether he would be well enough to serve in the ensuing campaign. The answer was no. He was mending, but not fast enough.

When, after three and a half months in the hospital, he was finally released to go home, he was far from well. At Kinderhook, New York, tradition tells us, a jamb had to be ripped out of Dr. John Quilhot's door so that he could be carried in on a stretcher. A day's ride from New Haven, his journey was halted. He spent two months in Middletown, where his children were at school.

Engaging in the type of speculation that appealed to him—a fortune or nothing—he bought a share in the privateer *General McDougall*. To see this ship, so much bigger than any in which he had shared during his New Haven years, sail down the river with her ten guns bristling and her crew of thirty lined up on deck, made him feel better: he bought some gold buttons and a new mounting for his small sword. How glad he was that he had refused to let Lucy Knox get possession of the trunk of gowns he had left in Boston! The time had come to put them on the back of the "heavenly Miss De Blois." His charmer was still available; although she had gone to church to marry his rival, her mother had risen from a pew to "forbid" the match.

"Dear Madam," he wrote out in a more elegant hand than he used even to Washington, "Twenty times have I taken my pen to write you, and as often has my trembling hand refused to obey the dictates of my heart. A heart which has often been calm and serene amidst the clashing of arms, and all the din and horrors of war, trembles with diffidence and the fear of giving offense when it attempts to address you on a subject so important to its happiness. Long have I struggled to efface your heavenly image from it. Neither time, absence, misfortunes, nor your cruel indifference have been able to efface the deep impression your charms have made; and will you doom a heart so true, so faithful, to languish in despair? Shall I expect no returns to the most sincere, ardent, and disinterested passion? Dear Betsy, suffer that heavenly bosom (which surely cannot know itself the cause of misfortune without a sympathetic pang) to expand with friendship at last, and let me know my fate. If a happy one, no man will strive more to deserve it; if, on the contrary, I am doomed to despair, my latest breath will be to implore the blessing of heaven on the idol and only wish of my soul."

After Betsy had answered with conventional coyness, Arnold wrote that he would never have forgiven himself had he realized his letter "would have occasioned you a moment's uneasiness." However, "you might as well wish me to exist without breathing as to cease to love you." He pointed out that in "romantic passion . . . fancy governs more than judgment," while a union grounded on "friendship and esteem" is more certain of lasting happiness. "The heart must be callous to every tender sentiment, if love is not lighted up at the flame. . . .

"If fame allows me any share of merit, I am in a great measure indebted for it to the pure and exalted passion your charms have inspired me with, which cannot admit of an unworthy thought or action. . . . Pardon me, dear Betsy, if I called you cruel. If the eyes are an index to the heart, love and harmony must banish every irregular passion from your heavenly bosom." He enclosed a letter to her parents; stated that he would rather perish than "give you one moment's pain to procure the greatest felicity to myself"; and added primly (perhaps remembering how she had been offended by his frank, soldierly offer of the gowns), "I hope a line in answer will not be deemed the least infringement on the decorum due to your sex, which I wish you strictly to observe."

Betsy was at loose ends. Although she had lacked the courage to elope with Brimmer, her father, furious that she had even considered such a match, struck her from his will. Arnold must have seemed a way out, for among the heirlooms that descended in her family was a ring of rose-colored gold set with four irregular diamonds and bearing the inscription "E. D. from Benedict Arnold 1778."

On May 1, Arnold moved on to New Haven, where for the second time he was given a hero's welcome. He was met on the road by the cadet corps and "a number of respectable inhabitants"; thirteen cannon were fired. Again he could not resist impressing his old neighbors by behaving in a grand manner. That Congress had made no provision for the children of General Joseph Warren, who had died at Bunker Hill, reminded him of how he himself had been mistreated. He offered to bring the two youngest Warrens up in "a manner suitable to their birth," until he could persuade the government to do its duty, or could raise a private subscription.

Arnold joined Washington at Valley Forge two days before André danced at the Meshianza. Moved to see that the warrior still could not "stand upon his leg," Washington promised him that, after the British evacuated Philadelphia, he would be made military governor there.

As his aides, Arnold appointed Clarkson, the young patrician who had been at the bottom of his trouble with Gates, and also a dandy named David Salisbury (Solebury) Franks. Perhaps a cousin of Philadelphia's rich David Franks, he had emigrated from England to Montreal where, during a political argument, he had punched an equally belaced seigneur in the nose, landing in a British jail. Franks had lent the Americans what money he had, fled with them, served as a volunteer against Burgoyne, assisted Arnold in writing letters from the Albany hospital; and now he was in Washington's camp, expounding the glories of freedom when not too busy powdering his hair. Jefferson characterized him as "light, indiscreet, active, honest, affectionate," with "a good enough heart and understanding somewhat better than common, but too little guard over his lips." Silas Deane was more severe; he considered Franks "volatile and trifling . . . mere wax, and never either too hot or too cold to receive the impression of the last application."

That neither of his aides had any experience in administering civilian affairs did not worry Arnold, for he expected to command Philadelphia as if it were an army camp. When the painter Charles Willson Peale stated that he had been appointed by the Pennsylvania government to seize the effects of Tories fleeing with the British army, Arnold replied that he would keep Peale and all other civilians out of the city until he had commandeered all attainted goods for the army. Peale complained at Washington's headquarters, and Arnold did not carry out his threat.

The issue was an important one, for the city was crammed with European goods which would bring a tremendous price in the patriot-held territory that had so long been starved for imports. Arnold had already arranged to get some across the lines for his personal advantage. When officer of the day at Valley Forge, he gave Robert Shewell a pass permitting the schooner *Charming Nancy*, loading at Philadelphia, to land unmolested in any Rebel port. Shewell was suspected of Tory leanings, as were his partners, James Seagrove and William Constable, since all had traded in British-held territory. Arnold, who was often to make a fourth in their deals, probably joined their partnership at this time. If so, he gave passes for two additional ships, which Constable sailed from Philadelphia to Wilmington; and protection, after the city fell, to a quantity of European goods and £500 worth of medicine which Constable had hidden to keep the British army from carrying them away or the Americans from seizing them. The profits must have been tremendous.

Franks talked of leaving the army to recoup the fortunes he had damaged in the cause of liberty, and Arnold instructed him to purchase in Philadelphia European and East Indian goods "to any amount" for which Arnold would furnish the money. Since the commandant should not be caught speculating, Arnold added to the agreement "a strict charge" that Franks hide even from "his most intimate acquaintance that the writer was concerned in the proposed purchase." Although Arnold drew up the paper in his own handwriting, he considered it wiser not to sign it. He would have been even wiser not to have written it, for Franks was, as Deane noted, "of a communicative turn."

The day the British withdrew, Franks galloped into the city. Had Peggy, as she observed distastefully the raggedness of the Rebel conquerors, seen Franks pass by, she would have been reassured, as he had dressed with special attention for his mission of finding General Arnold a suitably elegant house.

That night Franks had to be satisfied with crowded lodgings, and the next morning Colonel John Fitzgerald, an aide to Washington, saw "lying on the window two open papers"; one was Arnold's secret agreement with Franks. Fitzgerald recognized the handwriting. Since Arnold had been ordered to prevent the sale of all goods until it was determined what should be seized as enemy property, Fitzgerald was puzzled, but for the moment he said nothing. The wounded hero still bore "a good character" when he rode into Philadelphia through cheering crowds in a procession led by town notables and a regiment of Massachusetts militia.

Arnold was soon "much crowded with business," and, a caller observed, "in a state of health which I thought rendered him unequal to the fatigues of his then station." The lank, radical Pennsylvania leader, Joseph Reed, inserting himself into the situation, drew up a proclamation which he persuaded Arnold to sign. It closed all shops, and ordered all merchants to report their holdings so that the "quartermaster, clothier, and commissary generals may contract for such goods as are wanted for the use of the army."

This made Arnold's agreement with Franks out of date, but he was in no mood to give up speculation, especially as his privateer, *General McDougall*, had been captured. With Clothier General James Mease and his deputy, William West, Jr., the commandant executed a secret paper: "Whereas by the purchasing goods and necessaries for the use of the public, sundry articles not wanted for that purpose may be obtained, it is agreed by the subscribers that all such goods and merchandise which are or may be bought by the clothier general, or persons appointed by him, shall be sold for the joint, equal benefit of the subscribers, and be purchased at their risk." The Supreme Executive Council of Pennsylvania soon complained that while the shops were closed the clothier general had bought "large quantities" of merchandise "at a price deemed to be equivalent to the cost of the same," and that Arnold subsequently permitted "persons possessed of such goods" to sell them. The Council considered this unfair to the original owners, but did not charge Arnold with dishonesty, although a doubt may have entered their minds.

The cavalryman Allan McLane insisted years later that he had had more active suspicions. After Arnold had tried to hustle him out of the city because he knew too much, he had, he stated, told Washington of the illegal purchases, but had been so snubbed that he had kept quiet thereafter. This could have happened. Washington trusted Arnold, and knew that McLane was always brawling with someone.

Buying foreign goods for what they had cost during the British occupation and selling them to the long-blockaded patriots, yielded tremendous profits. The maneuver was illegal, yet typical of the shenanigans in which many profiteers were engaged. Arnold could see no reason why civilians who had contributed nothing to the patriot cause should make more money than he; had he not sacrificed health and most of his fortune? After all, he was only paying himself back a little.

Lest the Philadelphia Whigs, who had so recently been persecuted by the Tories, retaliate with violence, Arnold was ordered to "give security to individuals of every class and description." This placed him in the center of a controversy between the radicals, who wished to be severe, and the conservatives, who had sympathy with their erring brethren. A test case developed over Mrs. Joseph Galloway, wife of the apostate patriot who had been Howe's chief of police. Her husband had absconded, leaving her behind to hold the family property. The day Philadelphia was recaptured, Peale notified her that the Pennsylvania Council had empowered him to seize her house. She refused to move out, and soon received a call from Franks "with General Arnold's compliments and assurances of protection." Emboldened by this, she asked Arnold for active help, but "he told me he could do nothing in the case. I thought I was received rather coolly, but civilly."

After the Pennsylvania Assembly had in a special act confiscated her mansion, officials tried to dislodge her by locking her out of her front parlor, which was thus exposed to deprivations from the street. She sneaked to Arnold, who "kindly sent a guard. . . . He treated me with great politeness, and I went to bed in better spirits." Peale, thereupon, prepared to evict her bodily, but, wishing to make it as easy for her as possible, asked Arnold to lend him his "chariot." If the military commandant had agreed, he would have been co-operating with the civil government; instead, he sent his housekeeper to Mrs. Galloway to say that he would lend the carriage to her personally, but "would not let it come till I wanted it." She sent for it at last, and one of the richest women in Philadelphia rode off to live miserably on the charity of friends.

Mrs. Galloway was only one of the ladies about whom contention raged. After the Battle of Monmouth, General Wayne asked a friend to tell the girls who had stayed in Philadelphia and flirted with the British invaders "that the heavenly, sweet, pretty red coats . . . the Knights of the Blended Rose and Burning Mount have resigned their laurels to the Rebel officers, who will lay them at the feet of those virtuous daughters of America who cheerfully gave up ease and affluence in a city, for liberty and peace of mind in a cottage."

Peggy Shippen was bored by cottages; she had no intention of discarding the costumes that made her kinship with the Meshianza ladies clear. The "virtuous daughters of America," wearing homespun over shoes nailed together by rural cobblers, stared with resentment as she tripped by in imported finery bought during the British occupation; Peggy replied with the haughty air of a lady ignoring her social inferiors. Becky Franks spoke for the fashionable set when she wrote of an effort to snub Tory girls: "Oh! the ball. Not a lady there. The committee of real Whigs met in the afternoon and frightened the beaux so much that they went to all the ladies that meant to go to desire they'd stay home. . . . I'm delighted that it came to nothing, as they had the impudence to laugh at US."

When the French alliance was signalized by the arrival of an ambassador from the Court of Louis XVI, Count Conrad Alexandre Gérard, the infant nation was presented with a major social problem. Adequately elegant accommodations were secured for the titled visitor by quartering him with General Arnold, who had taken over the Penn mansion so recently occupied by Howe. But what about a party to repay the sumptuous entertainment Gérard had given on board his warship? Although some patriots insisted Republican principles were being tarnished, the French officers had to be feted at a ball, and there was no way to secure enough accomplished partners without inviting Tories.

On the dance floor, the high coiffures André had designed for the Meshianza made the Loyalist maidens tower over their Republican rivals; there was no doubt which group was the more elegantly dressed, the more polished in the dance. Some patriots agreed with Wayne that the ladies who had associated with English officers "have really in a great measure lost that native innocence, which was their former characteristic, and supplied its place with what they call an easy behavior." But Arnold knew great belles when he saw them.

The Tory girls clustered around the wounded warrior, moueing and giggling and rattling irresponsibly in the manner of their sex and time; putting on little pomposities, and then laughing at themselves; gay, sweet-smelling and brightly colored; desirable; and never, never serious. It amused the girls to pet a hero and imagine what desperate deeds had been accomplished by the heavy hands that now patted their little fingers. The harassed soldier basked in their warmth; he joked and was gayer than he felt. But sometimes, when a bitter thought pushed into his mind, he noticed especially a face as handsome as the others, but graver; gray eyes that stared even as they smiled; a full, shapely mouth which never lost its angry petulance. Under Peggy Shippen's gentle-seeming femininity, a fierce dissatisfaction echoed Arnold's own.

CHAPTER EIGHTEEN

Venus Ascendant

SILAS DEANE, Arnold's earliest political supporter,[1] had helped negotiate the French alliance. When he returned to the United States with Ambassador Gérard, Joseph Reed advised him not to stay in Arnold's Philadelphia mansion lest his reputation as faithful patriot be damaged.

Just elected president of the Supreme Executive Council of Pennsylvania, Reed was in effect governor of the state; indeed more, for he often thought of Pennsylvania as an independent nation allied with the other states for purposes of war. He was bound to hate Arnold, for their convictions and temperaments were opposite. To Reed, people were not human beings but Whigs or Tories. The charms of a woman, the talents of a man only made them seem more dangerous if they disagreed with Reed. Disgrace, or exile, or death, he felt, should be the fate of all who blocked America from evolving in the radical directions he considered right. He could have been one of the Jacobins who, during the French Revolution, gleefully counted the heads that rolled from the guillotine. Arnold was more like the Hessian officers who fought for personal advancement and the love of battle. Uninterested in political philosophies, he could not believe that a man who was not bearing arms against the United States was a dangerous enemy. And as for women, the softer sex should be completely immune to the rigors and hatreds of war.

Without any conscious intention, Arnold was carried by his

personal tastes into the opposite camp from Reed's. He loved luxury and display, he loved wealth; and he felt that a wounded hero had a right to indulge himself. Lesser men galloped gaily on spirited horses; he needed four attendants to help him into his carriage. Others fought campaigns; his military activity was limited, as he teetered on crutches, to instructing a few militiamen in military etiquette. He issued a broadside ordering sentries to stand with shouldered arms, and added a list of "the proper compliments with a drum" to various dignitaries. Such considerations annoyed the soldiers, who considered them only suited to the hired mercenaries of kings, and did not really interest Arnold. No wonder he was afflicted, in addition to his wound, with "a violent oppression" in his stomach.

Memories of battle remained with him, poisoning pleasures that surpassed the wildest dreams of his young manhood. In the Penn mansion, he set up an establishment as grand as that which his British predecessor, Sir William Howe, had kept. He employed a housekeeper, coachman, groom, and seven lesser servants; he rode in a fine chariot behind four horses; he would pay £1,000 for two pipes of wine. The most important people graced his table: the Pennsylvania Council came in a body, and he usually had a congressman or two. Great merchants like Robert Morris, who would once have hardly permitted him their anterooms, joked with him as an equal.

Yet he wished to escape. Since a crippled man can command a navy, he told Gérard, in a sudden burst of hopefulness, that he was to be entrusted with creating a strong sea force; and he asked Washington to back him for the post of admiral. Washington replied that he was "no competent judge in marine matters"; and nothing came of his hopes.

Gérard suspected that his naval schemes were not unconnected with the desire "to carry off European merchandise." As Schuyler's partisan against Gates, Arnold had become a special favorite of the most conservative ruling group still in power, the patroons of New York. One of their congressmen, William Duer, lived in his house, while three others, John Jay, Gouverneur Morris, and Robert R. Livingston, were perpetually in his company. They took Arnold into their business deals and introduced him to their Philadelphia connections.

These men had been well-to-do when the war broke out, and had never felt that patriotism required the sacrifice of property. Since (as Edward Shippen had demonstrated) financial inactivity walks a descending path, they traded, taking advantage with all the acumen they possessed, of the special conditions created by the times. Robert Morris was to defend himself from the charge of profiteering on other people's misery by asserting that, although profits of wartime operations were great, so were the losses, and that at the end of the Revolution his assets had been about the same as at the beginning. The wealthy opposed any governmental regulation of business and felt tolerant about trading with the enemy. Realizing that their position was shaky, they were glad to welcome to their standard so famous a hero as Arnold, even if he were not born to their class.

Since Arnold, who had not entered the war as a rich man, lacked capital, his asset was official position. He prepared to get possession of foreign goods in the territory that the British would abandon if, as many believed, the French menace to their holdings elsewhere in the world forced them to withdraw all troops from the states. Pooling his power with the social rank of Robert R. Livingston's brother John, he smuggled offers to four leading New York merchants: unless protected, the merchants would "suffer greatly in their property" when the city changed hands. If, however, they would each hide goods worth ten to thirty thousand pounds sterling, giving Arnold and Livingston, on credit, a two-thirds share, Arnold would guarantee to protect all their possessions when the Americans took over, and also give them a share in a quantity of Virginia tobacco which he and his partner hoped to have convoyed to Europe in their own ships by the French fleet. The commandant of Philadelphia offered "a great reward" to anyone who would bring an illegal answer through the lines, and agreed with Livingston that they would support each other in "whatever misfortune both or either of our characters may suffer from this correspondence."

Although Arnold recognized the need for discretion, he did not consider the scheme disgraceful. When he tried to interest

General Sullivan, who was besieging Rhode Island, in what seems to have been a similar plan to profit from the expected fall of Newport, he wrote, "This may be of service to the public as well as to our private interest." Was it not a patriotic act to make scarce goods available to the patriots? Sullivan's reaction is unrecorded, but of the four New York merchants only one replied, and he wanted cash not promises.

In partnership with his aide, Clarkson, and the suspected Tories Seagrove and Constable, Arnold induced Captain James Duncan, an officer who had legitimate business in New York, to serve them on the side. If Duncan thought the city was about to be evacuated, he was to hide valuable goods; otherwise he was to smuggle them out. For this he was to use his own credit; in return Arnold's partnership would give him a share in any "rice and vessels which we shall purchase in Carolina and Georgia."

Arnold now had a half-interest in the *Charming Nancy* which he had enabled Seagrove and Constable to get out of British-held Philadelphia. When the vessel was menaced by a British raid on the smuggling center, Egg Harbor, he was eager to salvage the cargo, and asked the army wagon-master for twelve teams. Since he intended to pay hire, he considered the request both legitimate and safe, forgetting that Reed's Pennsylvania Council, outraged by the perpetual drafting of wagons, had protested the very levy which Arnold now wished to use for his personal ends. The wagon-master was nervous. Although he gave in to repeated demands, he hid from the teamsters that they were being sent on private business. After twelve days on the road, they delivered in Philadelphia a quantity of loaf sugar, tea, wool, linen, glass, and nails, the sails of a schooner, and five or six swivel guns; from the sale of which Arnold seems to have got £7,500. However, the teamsters discovered the truth, and returned to western Pennsylvania complaining loudly of injustice.

Trade with New York involved the movement of persons back and forth, as did humanity when many families were separated. Abuses became so frequent that Congress limited the power of giving passes to Reed's council, and specifically ordered Arnold to recall any he had granted. Washington soon scolded Reed for sending through women who, "under pretense of visiting their friends, have, in fact, no other business but that of bringing out goods to trade with"—but when Arnold asked for a pass for Miss Hannah Levy, he was denied because she was related to the rich merchant, David Franks, of whom the council disapproved. Arnold later claimed that she was engaged on military business so secret he could not disclose it even to the patriot authorities; for whatever reason, he would not take no for an answer. He sent an illegal personal request to the officers commanding on the lines, and when this failed, turned again to the council. They were so irritated by his second appeal that they had to redraft their refusal to make it even reasonably polite.

Arnold was rapidly becoming the storm center of a rift in the patriot party that rose to the brink of a war within the war. Although the recent British offer, which granted almost all American demands except independence, was spurned by Congress, it appealed strongly to Edward Shippen's circle, the proponents of "the old cause" who had resented injustices but had always opposed separation. Since Arnold was soon to write Shippen about their "differences of political sentiment," we need not believe his statement, made years later when he was suing for the favor of the Crown, that he had urged acceptance of the peace offer; yet he was in daily association with persons who would have been glad to call off the fight.

These lukewarm patriots formed partnerships with men whom Reed's followers suspected of wishing to crown an American king. They made vast sums in mysterious ways and spent them in a manner that was only too clear. Never had property differences been as obvious on Philadelphia's streets. Although inflation was so great that a soldier's salary would hardly buy patches for his worn-out uniform, men who did nothing but buy and sell—even Tories who had stayed in the city during the British occupation—wallowed in luxury. Enlisted men watching their families starve were not pleased to hear of grand parties where "160 dishes" were served to a select company, nor was their appreciation increased by the realization that the sumptuous hosts were often the same individuals who had supplied the army camps with inferior and inadequate provisions. It seemed as if the Revolution, which poor men had regarded as a struggle against all aristocrats, was spawning a new aristocracy even worse than the old.

Washington thundered against the general feeling that the war was won, the "lax public virtue" which made him "feel more distress on account of the present appearance of things than I have done at any time since the commencement of the dispute"—yet many of his top subordinates were caught up in the riot. As commandant of the city, Arnold seemed the master of the Tory revels, but Generals Cadwalader and Mifflin were also criticized. In the very act of attacking the profiteers, a colonel wrote that fighting men could not let civilians have all the fun: " 'Tis really flattering to the officers of the army the attention paid them by the people." Word reached Greene on the battlefront that "Arnold has rendered himself not a little unpopular" with the officers in Philadelphia, "by not giving them an invitation to a ball he gave the civilians." This, Greene feared, would raise "a clamor and cabal of those who conceive themselves injured."

Franklin's niece, Mrs. Bache, wrote that her baby daughter gave "such old-fashioned smacks, General Arnold says he would give a good deal to have her for a schoolmistress to teach the young ladies how to kiss." He felt relaxed about such matters, but the radicals, most of whom belonged to strict religious sects, feared that America was becoming as immoral as the royal courts of Europe. When angry men looked into the ballrooms from outside, they seemed to see hellish centers of debauchery. It was the last straw when officers, by staging amateur theatricals, imitated the British fops who had so recently occupied the city. John Adams was shocked that Arnold countenanced such goings on, and Congress resolved firmly that "any person holding an office under the United States" should be dismissed if he "shall act, promote, encourage, or attend such plays."

If the war were almost over, Reed's followers reasoned that only made the situation more dangerous, since peace might permit the present inequalities to harden into a permanent class structure. Eager to strike a heavy blow "against a crafty and designing set of men," the Pennsylvania Council sentenced to death two Quakers who had been convicted of collaboration during the British occupation of Philadelphia. In urging "a speedy execution for both animals," Reed wrote that compassion for the enemies of the state, "though not in our treason laws, is a species of treason of not the least dangerous kind."

The death sentence touched off a tremendous controversy. Conservatives were horrified by what they considered an act of terrorism which menaced all men of property; while Reed complained that the executions were opposed because the culprits were "rich." Arnold injected himself in the situation by giving, the night before the Quakers were hanged, "a public entertainment" in which "not only Tory ladies but the wives and daughters of persons proscribed by the state and now with the enemy in New York formed a very considerable part. The fact," Reed continued incredulously, "is literally true." Arnold had nominated himself as the next individual whom the Executive Council would try to make into an example.

Peggy, whose father complained endlessly at home about the executions but kept his mouth shut abroad, was thrilled by Arnold's public gesture. Edward Shippen still pursued the cautious path which, since it kept him from earning money, menaced all her pleasures. While daring men raked in inflated dollars for their daughters to spend on ribbons, Edward stated that far from being able to afford Madeira wine, he could not afford sugar syrup. And when Peggy played her trump card, pointing out that she could not be seen in grubby old clothes without disgracing the family, he had a terrible answer. He threatened to move from "this scene of expense" to Lancaster, where he could abolish "the style of life my fashionable daughters have introduced into my family; and their dress."

Peggy had suffered too much from her father's expedient withdrawals to regard this as an empty threat. She hardly dared protest when rubbed places appeared on the Shippen chairs; she hardly dared invite friends to dinner lest they be lightly fed. What a pleasure it was to go to Arnold's house where all the furniture was fresh, and where, after everyone had eaten heartily, the platters went back to the kitchen almost as full as they had appeared.

Although Arnold had never shown interest in the "virtuous" Republican girls, Peggy had watched him flirt, as André had done, with a whole garland of Tory belles. He is said to have courted Miss Christian Amile, who expressed to another of his girls, Polly

Riché, disgust with Rebel suitors: "But what are we girls to do? You know, bad as the currency is, there is no other passing just now." Miss Amile could not understand preferring "an American soldier to a British one."

When Arnold began to single Peggy out, she was enchanted. How her heart beat as the commandant's chariot, the most conspicuous in Philadelphia, drew up with a great clatter of hooves at her door! The wounded lion banged in on his crutches and was received with distant courtesy by her father. Seated in the parlor, Peggy compared the two men. Both were handsome: Shippen with quiet distinction, Arnold because of the vitality that irradiated his light-blue eyes and his high-cheekboned face. The parent communicated breeding without movement; the lover was flamboyant in his courtesy. When the discussion turned to politics, Arnold raised his voice and would certainly, were his leg not stretched out before him on the chair, have paced the floor; Shippen replied without audible excitement. Although old enough to be her father, the general had, in many a murderous encounter—the thought made Peggy shiver deliciously—proved his courage. Although crippled and from an obscure background, he made more money than Shippen with all his connections—and he spent money like a gentleman, in fine confidence that the sums exhausted today would be replaced tomorrow.

When Peggy sat silent, the men addressed their remarks to her; and when she joined in the discussion, making trenchant points in her sweet girl's voice, their four eyes fixed in admiration. Shippen wanted to win back the daughter who had been closest to him of all living things; Arnold had never before seen so many desirable qualities combined in one person.

Although he had always been lonely, Arnold had rarely, in his pride, made close friendships with men who were his equals; more rarely could he brook, as in the case of General Montgomery, intimacy with his superiors. Keeping inferiors in their place, he could only relax with men much younger than he: Oswald until he had risen above Oswald; then the New York patricians who had deflected his entire career. But even with these youngsters there were moments of unfortunate comparison: Arnold accepted most easily dependence on women. Hannah had been a great strength to him, but there are limits to what a sister can do, and she was turning into an old maid. His wife, Peggy Mansfield, had failed him completely, and as for Betsy De Blois, he had not seen her for more than a year.

Peggy Shippen was soft and appealing as a daughter, bright and sexual as a wife; she was strong and intelligent. Since she possessed by birthright the social position and assurance he was working to achieve, it did not bother him that she was no longer wealthy. With her help, he would make enough money for a dozen. She was gay; she loved luxury; she had found the world a hard place, even as he had done, and like him she intended to bring it to heel.

No document reveals how Arnold's engagement with Betsy was ended. We only know that she was reconciled with her Tory family at about this time, and that she never married. Meeting her a decade later, John Quincy Adams wrote that she "has been much celebrated as a beauty, and she may still be called very handsome, though she be as much as twenty-seven. She is sociable and agreeable, though she is not yet wholly destitute of that kind of vanity which is so naturally the companion of beauty. She puckers her mouth a little, and contracts her eyelids a little to look very pretty, and is not wholly unsuccessful."

Miss De Blois's charms faded so rapidly from Arnold's mind that he found nothing strange in rewording his two letters of proposal to her into a single letter to Peggy.[2] He had begged Betsy to let her "heavenly bosom . . . expand with friendship," but to Peggy he stated "friendship and esteem you acknowledge," and implored that she let her "heavenly bosom . . . expand with a sensation, more soft, more tender." Where he had complained to Betsy of absence, misfortune, and "your cruel indifference," he substituted an entirely new passage: "My passion is not founded on personal charms only. That sweetness of disposition and goodness of heart, that sentiment and sensibility which so strongly mark the lovely Miss P. Shippen renders her amiable beyond expression, and will ever retain the heart she has once captivated." Although he begged both ladies to forget him rather than suffer "one moment's inquietude," Peggy's letter ends with a new phrase: "My latest breath will be to implore the blessings of heaven on the idol and only wish of my soul."

Arnold wrote Shippen for his approval. Stating, "my fortune is not large, though sufficient," he asked for no dowry and offered to make any settlement on Peggy that was "consistent with the duty I owe to three lovely children. . . . My public character is well known, my private one is, I hope, irreproachable. . . . Our difference in political sentiments will, I hope, be no bar to my happiness."

Peggy's sisters are quoted as saying that their father never liked Arnold. Why should he? The general was one of the people from nowhere who had been whirled high by war and now wished to be aristocrats like the Shippens. Policy urged the old order to accept such allies against the leveling republicans, but it was bitter policy. Furthermore, Edward distrusted and feared individuals ungoverned by reason; it was a tragic proof of his separation from his favorite daughter that she should encourage such a man. Yet, as a celebrated hero who seemed to be translating his military eminence into wealth, Arnold was a good match, and Shippen realized that he himself could not support his "fashionable daughters" to their satisfaction. Perhaps it would be better to let Peggy marry Arnold than to force her into exile at Lancaster. Edward mourned and bothered and worried. Finally, he decided to put up a fight for his beloved Peggy; the proposal was refused.

The girl herself agreed to this refusal, but there was something in her manner that did not discourage Arnold too much. He pressed his suit all the harder, and concentrated on changing himself from a cripple to a healthy man worthy of a young and attractive bride. By October 15, "with the assistance of a high heeled shoe and cane he begins to hop about the floor and in great measure dispense with his crutches." Peggy found both fear and fascination in the energy with which her middle-aged lover now propelled himself into her house.

"We are very gay . . . ," wrote Mrs. Robert Morris. "We have a great many balls and entertainments, and soon the Assemblies will begin. . . . Even our military gentlemen here are too liberal to make any distinctions between Whig and Tory ladies. If they make any, it's in favor of the latter. . . . It originates at headquarters, and that I may make some apology for such strange conduct, I must tell you that Cupid has given our little general a more mortal wound than all the host of Britons could. . . . Miss **Peggy Shippen** is the fair one."

In increasing numbers, letter writers called Arnold a Tory and blamed this on Peggy's influence. The girls of her set were flying too high to hide their pro-British sentiments, however much they got their menfolk into trouble. While David Franks was fighting to keep from being deported, his daughter, Becky, got into the newspapers for mocking the poor attire poverty forced on American soldiers. Peggy Chew and her sisters boasted to Mrs. Galloway "of the kindness of English officers"; or burst into her parlor "full of the news that the officers send their compliments to them." The lady who had lost her fortune because those same officers were losing the war replied that they should all be broken to privates. The Chew girls went home in a huff.

The fashionable set even went out of their way to laugh at the wife of the powerful and violent ruler of Pennsylvania; Mrs. Reed gritted her teeth all the harder because she had an old grievance against the Shippens. Before she was married, she had written her fiancé that Peggy's cousin, Mrs. William Shippen, Jr., "has behaved extremely unhandsomely to our family and particularly to me. . . . She has endeavored to make me appear not only ridiculous in saying that I was deeply in love with Dr. [John] Morgan, but really hinted that I have been very ill, that I was sly, and that religion is often a cloak to hide bad actions." Watching Peggy and her suitor with angry eyes, the Reeds saw much to horrify them.

That, despite Reed's warning, Deane was staying with Arnold had increasing repercussions: a fellow purchasing agent in France accused Deane of cheating Congress on a monumental scale. Rumor had it that Robert Morris and others of Arnold's rich friends had been Deane's confederates. When the radical pamphleteer, Tom Paine, carried the attack to the newspapers, the Deane faction attributed their reply to Arnold's aide Clarkson. Duer, another resident at headquarters, was active in Deane's support, and Gouverneur Morris expressed the attitude of the group who met there when he dismissed Paine as "a mere adventurer . . . without fortune, fame, or connections." Radicals came to regard Arnold's house as the nexus of a plot to rob the United States.

Deane appealed to Congress for vindication. However, the matter was so complicated (it has never been completely cleared up) and so involved with dangerous national and international issues, that the legislators could only procrastinate. All day, Arnold heard Deane and his friends excoriate Congress for "deepest ingratitude."

Nearly everyone Arnold knew, so it sometimes seemed, was squabbling with the authorities. Lamb, Oswald, and his brother-in-law Mansfield, the three old companions for whom he had once organized an artillery regiment, were in Philadelphia bickering over their ranks. Lamb achieved, in the end, a satisfactory settlement; but Mansfield and Oswald resigned because their service as volunteers under Arnold was ignored in the dating of their commissions. Mansfield went to South Carolina on business, perhaps as Arnold's representative; and Oswald set up a newspaper at Baltimore in which he attacked Washington, called the local officials "scoundrels in power" and the Maryland patriots "an execrable junto."

Arnold was in no passive mood when Gideon Olmstead, a seaman from Connecticut, "with whose connections I was acquainted," appeared in his parlor to tell a tale of heroism rewarded with injustice. As he was fishing with three companions, Olmstead had been captured and impressed on the British sloop *Active*. The four patriots overpowered the enemy crew of nine, locked them in the hold, and steered for New Jersey. Melting pewter spoons into bullets, and forcing up the hatches, the British swept the deck with their fire. Although severely wounded, Olmstead succeeded in turning a swivel gun which drove the enemy again below. Now the British captain cut a hole in the stern and wedged the rudder so that the Americans could not steer. The boat drifted helplessly, until hunger and thirst forced the enemy to release the rudder. The Yankees continued their course to New Jersey, but just as they came in sight of land they were overhauled by an armed brig belonging to the State of Pennsylvania. The brig carried the *Active* to Philadelphia where a Pennsylvania court, brushing aside the Connecticut sailors' claim that they had been in control of the boat, awarded three-quarters of the prize money to their own state and its sailors.

Since Arnold loved fighting men and hated politicians, this tale made his blood boil—and he saw a chance for profits. In return for a half interest in the four sailors' prospects, he "agreed to advance them money to carry on the suit and for their own support, clothing, etc." Since they wished his support of their cause to seem disinterested, the sailors promised to keep his financial involvement secret.

When Arnold engineered an appeal to Congress, Reed was outraged. Fearing centralization of power as the first step toward conservative tyranny, the radicals meant it when they called the Executive Council of Pennsylvania "Supreme"; and now Congress had claimed the right to review the decision of a Pennsylvania court! Arnold had inserted himself into so important a test case on state *vs.* federal prerogative that it was not to be settled for thirty years, and was, we are told, the only issue over which Pennsylvania resisted the United States by force of arms. Arnold's secret financial interest was soon suspected and hinted in a newspaper paragraph written under an assumed name by Timothy Matlack, secretary to the council.

As luck would have it, Matlack's nineteen-year-old son was on militia duty at Arnold's headquarters when Franks discovered that the powder on his hair was uneven. A lesser man might have given way to panic in such a crisis, but Franks took effective action. He called a serving maid. She ran to young Matlack and told him to fetch the barber. Although the lad considered the errand demeaning, he set out, and, finding the barber not at home, left a message. Soon after his return, Franks rushed up to him with a tense face "and asked me if I had been for his barber." The lad replied he had left instructions, at which Franks shook his disarranged head and remarked piteously that "he did not believe he would come." Time passed, and then Franks reappeared in even greater agitation to say "he believed I had better go again." Making no reply, Matlack went into the entry and asked a colored man whom he found there whether it was usual to send orderly sergeants on such errands. When the Negro said it was, Matlack exclaimed angrily, "The militia could not be expected to do such duty."

Enter Franks. "Sergeant," he said, "I thought I had ordered you to go for my barber."

"I told him," the boy remembered, "I had received no such order. He then asked me why I did not go. I told him I waited his orders. He then told me to go, and I told him, with his orders, I would go, and did go. Major Franks, on my return, asked me if I had been. I told him I had, and left the same orders as before.

"The next morning, I made complaint to the general." Arnold "gave me to understand, not in an abrupt manner, that if I did not like such duty, I should not have come there"; and added, "If Major Franks had insulted me at the time he gave me the order, it was wrong, and he did not approve of that." Not mollified, Matlack ran home to his father who, from his official eminence on Reed's council, sent Arnold a lecture about the nobility of the militia: "Freemen will hardly be brought to submit to such indignities."

Arnold replied, "No man has a higher sense of the rights of a citizen and freeman than myself," yet when necessity made a citizen a soldier, "the former is entirely lost in the latter, and the respect due to a citizen is by no means to be paid to the soldier, any further than his rank entitled him to it." Arnold pointed out that he personally had served a whole campaign under Lincoln, "who was not known as a soldier until after I had been some time a brigadier." He had sacrificed his feelings to the interests of his country. As for Matlack's threat that the militia would not enlist unless treated respectfully, "self-preservation is the first principle of the human race; theirs will induce them to turn out and defend their property."

Arnold had stepped into another hornets' nest: freemen, who feared that the higher officers would try to perpetuate themselves as an American aristocracy, resented being forced into subservience by their very efforts to abolish it. Arnold's service under Lincoln, Matlack wrote, had been dictated by "the essential interests of your country" and "a regard to your own fame"; Arnold would have refused to obey "commands dictated by pride and insolence." An officer might send a citizen to certain death but not order him to clean his shoes. Unless Arnold recanted, Matlack would withdraw his son from the militia, and publish his reasons for doing so.

If Matlack intended to threaten him, Arnold replied, "you have mistaken your object; I am not to be intimidated by a newspaper." However, he wished to close the correspondence since "disputes as to the rights of soldiers and citizens . . . may be fatal to both." Franks and young Matlack should settle their argument between

them; if the aide had "behaved amiss, it is his duty to make repara-
tion. I trust I never shall countenance pride or insolence to inferiors." This was as conciliatory a letter as Arnold was capable
of writing, but it was too late. He had opposed the Pennsylvania
government on almost every matter which they considered essential to the creation of a virtuous and democratic nation.

During December, Peggy's oldest sister finally married Edward
Burd. Although the groom was a cousin and old friend, the bride
suffered "the quakes, tremblings, and a thousand other quirks."
Peggy, who was besieged by a wild, strong, crippled stranger, was
frightened into "a solemn oath never to change her state." However, she was used to hysterics, and she soon made light of the
whole matter, betting General Cadwalader a dozen pair of gloves
that there would be "twelve marriages among her acquaintance
before next Christmas."

Shippen was trying to view what might be inevitable from the
pleasant financial side: "I gave my daughter Betsy to Neddy Burd
last Thursday evening, and all is jollity and mirth. My youngest
daughter is much solicited by a certain general on the same subject. Whether this will take place or not depends on circumstances.
If it should, I think it will not be till spring. What other changes
in my family may take place to forward or prevent my removal
from Philadelphia is still uncertain.

Peggy's grandfather foresaw "another match in the family"; he
considered Arnold "a fine gentleman." And letters smuggled to
Joseph Galloway in London expressed gratitude to Peggy for making the commandant show "leniency to the Tories."

Perhaps as the church bells dramatically rang in the year 1779,
Peggy softened her refusal. "My expectations," her new brother-
in-law wrote, "have been answered . . . a lame leg is at present
the only obstacle. But a lady who makes that the only objection,
and is firmly persuaded it will soon be well, can never retract, however expressly conditional an engagement may have been made.
However, we have every reason to hope it will be well again,
though I am not so sanguine as he is in respect to the time; but the
leg will be a couple of inches shorter than the other, and disfigured. He appears from the slight knowledge I have of him to be a
well-dispositioned man, and one who will use his best endeavors to

make P. happy, and I doubt not will succeed. He has acquired something handsome, and a settlement will be previously made."

"The gentlemen of the State of New York" had offered through Schuyler to give Arnold some mark of their approbation. He would like, he replied, "a tract of forfeited or unlocated lands" on the frontier, say the 130,000 acres on the Mohawk which had been confiscated from the Johnsons and through which he had marched when he relieved Fort Stanwix. Or Skenesboro, about 40,000 acres at the base of Lake Champlain which, although considered unhealthy, were suited to "iron works, mills, etc." (Skene, the attainted owner, was an acquaintance, but business is business.) He hoped the legislature would sell him the land very cheaply, since he would promise to increase the relative power of their state by settling, directly the war was won, a large number of families from "the neighboring states." [3]

The New York congressmen endorsed the scheme in two letters to Governor George Clinton. New York's constitution, they pointed out, was attractive not only to Arnold, but to other military leaders, since it offered a "stability and vigor . . . loose and less guarded kinds of government cannot provide." (In other words, it was more favorable than that of the radical states to men who wanted to make fortunes.) Since New York also had its radicals to keep down, it was to the advantage of the leaders to bring in such allies. Furthermore, "the necessity of strengthening our frontiers is obvious." To counter Virginia, which was already offering land to veterans, Arnold would bring "the officers and soldiers who have served with him." (Significantly, the New Yorkers did not wish, like the Virginians, to make grants directly to small holders, a move that encouraged democracy.) Several of the congressmen endorsing Arnold's scheme owned disputed New York titles in Vermont; they may have wanted Arnold up north so that he could lead, when the main war was won, a campaign against his old enemies, the Green Mountain Boys.

As the conservative New York government offered to enrich Arnold, the radical Pennsylvania authorities acted to impoverish him. The council responded to the action of a Congressional committee, which reversed their court on the *Active* case, by seizing the prize money before it could be given to Arnold's partners. He complained to Congress, but Reed insisted that Congress had over-stepped its powers.

Then the council learned of Arnold's private use of public wagons, and of his attempt to get Hannah Levy illegally to New York despite their opposition. They summoned Arnold and Clarkson to testify before them, but the soldiers replied, in hardly civil terms, that they were accountable only to Congress and General Washington. Reed instantly complained to Congress that Arnold had offered "indignity" to the freemen of Pennsylvania; the miscreant should be removed from his command in their state "until the charges against him are examined." Congress appointed a special committee to consider the matter.

This put the council in a quandary. If they presented evidence to a federal body, they admitted that congressional authority superseded theirs; if they withheld evidence, Arnold would certainly be acquitted. Reed compromised by offering to supply evidence on the misuse of wagons, but added that the council, "while thus we act upon motives superior to the gratification of our feelings," had not forgotten that they were competent to vindicate their own honor. If Congress should permit its officers "to affront us without feeling any marks of your displeasure," Pennsylvania would think long before trusting Congress again. The council was using a threat to force a decision against the enemy they now so hated that, to strike him on his most sensitive point, they tried to reopen the matter of his rank. Since Pennsylvania had supplied more troops than Connecticut, Reed argued, Armstrong and St. Clair, although junior officers, should be elevated above Arnold.

The general was equally intransigent. When Reed sent Jesse Jordan, the chief of the teamsters who had gone on Arnold's business, to get the pay for which the teamsters had never asked, Arnold added to a sticky situation by protesting the bill, because he suspected Reed of having upped it. He had no intention of letting his enemy, who had seized the *Active* prize money, pick his pocket any further.

In general, Arnold's speculations had gone badly. Since the British had not abandoned Newport or New York, all his plans for hiding goods in those cities had come to nothing; and his smuggling operations through the lines had failed to bring in enough money to support his elaborate establishment. He was obliged to relinquish his share in a privateer building at New London, and to borrow £12,000.

His New York land scheme now presented his best hope for reviving his fortunes. Although he knew that the Pennsylvania authorities were trying by every legal means to keep him from evading their fury by leaving the state, on February 3 he set out for the New York Legislature at Kingston. Reed's council instantly prepared a proclamation containing eight charges: 1. Arnold had granted persons of "disaffected character" an unjustified pass to enable them to get a vessel (the *Charming Nancy*) from British-held Philadelphia into a port of the United States. 2. He had closed the shops on his arrival at Philadelphia while he privately made considerable purchases "as is alleged and believed." 3. He had imposed menial services on militiamen and defended his right to do so. 4. He had interposed in a prize case (the *Active*) by illegal purchase at an inadequate price, "as has been publicly charged by a reputable citizen." 5. He had used public wagons to transport private property. 6. He had tried illegally to slip an "improper" person (Hannah Levy) into New York. 7. When "requested" by the council to explain about the wagons, he had returned "an indecent and disrespectful refusal." 8. His "discouragement and neglect" of patriotic persons and his "different conduct toward those of another character are too notorious to need proof or illustration." The council closed by stating that while Arnold remained in the Pennsylvania command, they would pay none of its costs, and would call out the militia only under "the most urgent and pressing necessity."

Since the proclamation was sent to all governmental bodies and published in the newspapers, the charges were soon on every tongue. How far gossip foreshadowed the future is revealed by a note in a Philadelphia merchant's diary: "News of the day is that General Arnold has left Philadelphia and gone over to the enemy."

The proclamation caught up with Arnold while he was on the road to Washington's encampment at Middlebrook, New Jersey. Eager to be comforted by his friend and commander, he ordered his coachman to hurry on. The chariot slithered queasily on ice

Benedict Arnold, engraved in Paris from a drawing made, probably in Philadelphia during 1779, by Pierre Eugène du Simitière. As Arnold became famous and then infamous, other prints of him were published, but this alone is authentic.
Courtesy of the New-York Historical Society, New York City.

Joseph Reed, by Charles Willson Peale. The Pennsylvania political leader who pushed Arnold toward treason by hating and hounding him when the crippled fighter was military commandant of Philadelphia. *Courtesy, Independence Hall National Historic Park.*

and stuck in snowdrifts, but he could not get out to push; he could not even ride one of the horses to get to headquarters more quickly. He had crippled himself in the patriot cause, and this was how he was being repaid!

Although Arnold's report to Peggy that Washington and his officers "bitterly excoriate Mr. Reed and the council for their villainous attempt to injure me," was later contradicted by Washington himself, the hero, who had been injured by the enemy and now again by the politicians, was undoubtedly, as he claimed, "treated with the greatest politeness." Washington urged him to have Congress hear the charges, but Arnold felt safer in the hands of his fellow soldiers. In a letter he sent back to the *Pennsylvania Packet* he stated that he would seek a court martial, which would prove the council's proclamation "as gross a prostitution of power as ever disgraced a weak and wicked administration."

Washington saw no reason why he should abandon his trip to Kingston, but in moments of anguish Arnold always fled home. "My dearest life," he wrote Peggy, "never did I so ardently long to see or hear from you as at this instant. I am all impatience and anxiety to know how you do. Six days' absence without hearing from my dear Peggy is intolerable. Heavens! what must I have suffered had I continued my journey: the loss of happiness for a few *dirty acres*. I can almost bless the villainous roads and the more *villainous men* who oblige me to return. I am heartily tired with my journey and almost so with human nature. I daily discover so much baseness and ingratitude among mankind that I almost blush at being of the same species, and could quit the stage without regret were it not for some few gentle, generous souls like my dear Peggy who still retain the lively impression of their Maker's image, and who with smiles of benignity and goodness make all happy around them. Let me beg of you not to suffer the rude attacks on me to give one moment's uneasiness. . . . The day after tomorrow I leave this and hope to be made happy by your smiles on Friday evening; till then, all nature smiles in vain, for you alone, heard, felt, and seen, possess my every thought, fill every sense, and pant in every vein."

Lovers who have not been encouraged do not write in such

physical terms. The true meaning of this letter has been obscured because the first historian to quote it copied it inaccurately, and the rest have trotted at his heels. The general, we have been told, sent his best regards to "your mama"; actually, he wrote "*Our Mama*" and underlined the phrase. Benedict Arnold and Peggy Shippen were engaged.

CHAPTER NINETEEN

Jumping-off Place

SINCE the council's charges against Arnold involved almost every major issue that plagued the infant republic, Congress was thrown into an uproar. A motion that he be given the court martial he demanded was tabled lest radicals accuse Congress of putting the people at the mercy of the military. A motion on the opposite side that Arnold be removed from his command was defeated, after "great debates," to the outrage of a Pennsylvania member who demanded a roll call so that freemen could see which legislators "manifest a disposition to support the authority of civil government." Only Pennsylvania had a majority for suspending Arnold, and even that delegation was divided: William Shippen, Jr., backed his cousin's fiancé. In the end, Congress referred all charges to the committee already considering some of them.

When William Paca, the chairman, called for evidence, the council was upset. They could not prove, since Arnold's contract with the clothiers general had not been discovered, that he had bought goods when the shops were closed. The charge that he owned a share in the *Active* was based on a guess—and even if he did, it was hardly a crime. Whether Arnold had encouraged disaffected persons, depended on who was considered disaffected, a ticklish question since the council suspected conservative congressmen, and even Paca, a rich Maryland planter whose wife belonged to Peggy Shippen's circle.

The charges for which the council had evidence were not very grave. Arnold's pass to the *Charming Nancy* violated no specific statute and could be considered an error in judgment. His claim that he had tried to smuggle Hannah Levy through the lines on secret government business justified him in answering no questions. Although he had disagreed with Matlack about militiamen's duties, the question was one on which disagreement was legitimate; and whether he had been disrespectful to the council rested on a definition of good manners. Arnold's use of the wagons was the most damaging matter that could be proved, yet he had never concealed that he wanted them for private business. Perhaps it was the wagon-master's fault for letting him have them on those terms.

A long established government would have included agencies—detectives, prosecutors, grand juries—to collect the information the executive needed, but the members of the council were forced to do their own investigating in whatever time they could rescue from the multiple duties of ruling the commonwealth. Reed wrote many letters seeking evidence, but received few effective replies.

He blamed his difficulties on "the parties dividing the state." It had not been proved that Arnold had displayed anything more than bad judgment, and most capitalists engaged in deals which radicals would criticize; the business community was afraid that, if such "highly colored" charges were encouraged, no man's private affairs would be safe from unsympathetic scrutiny. Without fear that they would give him away, Arnold told his friends that he needed £5,000 to enable the *Active* claimants to leave Pennsylvania before poverty forced them to reveal his own financial involvement. (In the end, he bought out "two or three" of the four Connecticut sailors.)

Although Arnold knew that he was guilty of several of the council's charges, he believed that many respected citizens were similarly vulnerable; and he was widely encouraged to feel that he was being made the goat by violent men out to destroy the fabric of sound society.

Able to substantiate no more than Arnold's misuse of the wagons, the council insisted that in the other charges they had merely expressed "their sense of his conduct . . . an opinion operative only as the world shall give it weight, drawing with it no civil or military punishment." Arnold could defend himself by appealing, as they had done, to "the public judgment."

But the council did not fight Arnold man to man. Dismissing the militia at Lebanon and Lancaster, they announced that they would not call out replacements until he was removed from command in the state. Reed warned politicians that if they sided with Arnold they would incur the undying enmity of Pennsylvania, and tried to frighten them with outright lies, whispering that "the council had evidence about Arnold which the gentlemen of Congress little dreamed of, and that those who supported him will be injured by it."

In the newspaper war which now arose, the soldier was no match for the lawyers on the council. Matlack dug up Brown's outrageous outdated attack, which he published in an anonymous letter worded to imply much more than it said: "How far these charges can *all of them* be supported it is unnecessary to say" since the publication was merely intended to refute a statement by Arnold that his character had never been impeached. However, footnotes were added which assumed the charges were true. Concerning the most extreme of all, that Arnold had massacred an entire Canadian village, Matlack wrote, "General Arnold's *humanity* would naturally induce him to forget, as soon as possible, such orders and their horrid consequences."

After Arnold wrote that it would have been "candid" to tell the public that he had been acquitted of Brown's charges, Matlack replied that Arnold had brought the publication on himself by his "pride and folly" in insisting he was above reproach. Then, with seeming generosity, Arnold's tormentor admitted "the improbability that one man was ever guilty of so many crimes and of so black a die"—however, Arnold's acquittal had been meaningless, for Brown had not been asked to testify. "When I meet your carriage on the street and think of the splendor in which you live and revel . . . and compare these things with the decent frugality necessarily used by other officers in the army, it is impossible to avoid the question: from whence have these riches flowed if you *did not plunder Montreal?*"

The Congressional committee believed "common justice required that a trial and conviction should precede every judgment of condemnation," and were "repeatedly pressed by General Arnold for a hearing, with all the sensibility of a soldier injured in his honor." After two weeks, during which the council objected to technicalities and submitted no evidence, Paca notified them that his committee would hear Arnold on March 5, 1779. The council refused to send a representative but complained that the committee was meeting privately with the accused; Pennsylvania was being insulted. Should the committee consider any of the charges Congress wished them to try, except the matter of the wagons, their action would be "derogatory to the rights and interests of the state and the honor of this council. . . . If any misstep should be taken . . . you shall be accountable for it."

Paca replied, "Vehement declarations and violent protestations are sometimes the result of passions. . . . As to the honor of the council, we shall report the truth, and therefore, if you yourselves have done nothing derogatory to the honor of the council, you have nothing to fear from our report."

In forwarding evidence to the committee, Arnold argued that the council's failure to do the same proved them inspired by no more than personal malice. He defended his right to give passes to the *Charming Nancy* and to Hannah Levy; presented affidavits from the *Active* sailors but made no mention of his financial concern; sent without comment his correspondence with Matlack on militia duty; and noted that he had already given Congress papers about the wagons. He declared "upon my honor" that he had made no purchases when the shops were closed, a statement he may have justified on the flimsy grounds that the actual buying from which he profited was done by the clothiers general. His letters to the council, he continued, were as respectful as that body "had any right to expect or were entitled to." He had been courteous to all patriots "who have put it in my power to take notice of them"; and as for the Tories, "The president and council of the state will excuse me if I cannot divest myself of humanity to my enemies and common civility to all mankind in general, merely out of compliance to them."

Early March was for Arnold a period of triumph. If state courts made independent decisions concerning boats captured on the high seas, they could embroil the United States in war; Congress reiterated its right to override Pennsylvania by awarding all the *Active* prize money to Arnold's partners. And Paca's committee sent in a report exonerating the general of the six charges they considered civilians capable of trying. Arnold had no fear of what Washington would do about those dealing with militia service and the wagons which the committee wished forwarded to him. Sure that he was about to be completely vindicated, he resigned his command which he had long found more of an irritation than a source of pleasure or profit. He became a major general without assignment.

He urged Congress to accept at once the committee's report, thus silencing "a set of wretches beneath the notice of a gentleman and a man of honor." As a public servant attacked by public officers, he was forced, he explained, to rely on a public body to defend him, although "as an individual I trust I shall ever have the spirit to be the guardian of my own honor."

Politically acute observers realized, however, that far from calming the storm, the Paca committee's report would only make it blow harder. The "animosities" between Arnold and the council, a congressman wrote, "may form parties in Congress and thereby injure the public weal"; while the rumor circulated that the federal and Pennsylvania governments were at such loggerheads that Congress might move to some other city or the state authorities to Lancaster.

Reed's fury was increased by a local movement that endangered his power and the principles in which he so uncompromisingly believed: Pennsylvania conservatives had organized the Republican Society, aimed at overthrowing the constitution which made the Supreme Executive Council supreme. Reed accused congressmen from other states, and particularly the New York delegation who were Arnold's principal supporters, of secret assistance to the Republican Society. His own group, the Constitutional Society, linked the two controversies in a resolution denouncing Arnold.

That the extreme right and the extreme left seemed about to spring at each other's throats, causing a war within a war, forced the majority of Congress to regard personal justice for Arnold as a secondary consideration. They empowered a new committee to reach a compromise with Reed's council. The resulting negotiation was stormy. After an all-night session, Henry Laurens wrote, "I feel this morning as if my life was breaking." It was finally agreed to ignore the Paca committee's report and, although it was hardly fair to put an acquitted man in renewed jeopardy, to try Arnold all over again, this time by court martial.

When Congress was notified, they resolved that only four of the charges were amenable to such action: the *Charming Nancy* pass; speculating when the shops were closed; assigning menial duties to the militia; and misusing public wagons. No method was fixed on for settling the other issues. Congressman Burke of North Carolina was officially rebuked for saying that the council had acted in a "waspish, peevish, and childish manner," but his comment must have seemed ridiculously mild to Arnold. That he knew he was guilty of some of the charges from which he had been so fortunately exonerated, only increased his outrage at being placed again in danger.

Peggy's grandfather had become extremely nervous about "a number of things laid to the charge of G——l A——d," and her father, if family tradition is to be believed, was only prevented from forbidding the match by his fear that the hysteria with which she greeted any opposition would damage her health. Her fashionable friends encouraged her determination by damning as "ungrateful monsters" Arnold's enemies. "Poor Peggy," wrote Betty Tilghman. "How I pity her! At any rate, her situation must be extremely disagreeable. She has great sensibility, and I think it must often be put to trial."

As a wedding gift, Arnold, who had no intention of trimming his sails to please his enemies, bought Mount Pleasant, the mansion on the Schuylkill which John Adams considered "the most elegant seat in Pennsylvania." This was little more than a bold speculation, a grandiloquent gesture, since the house was rented—he was never to live there—and he kept a mortgage said to be £70,000 Pennsylvania currency. However, Arnold's acquisition of this famous mansion started a new crop of rumors as to dishonest ways he had got the money.[1]

His sister and his three sons had been living with him for some time. He now sent the two older boys to a school in Maryland kept by an Anglican clergyman who had been driven from his pulpit because he would not renounce allegiance to the Crown.

"They have been," Arnold wrote of his children, "for some time in this city, which is a bad school, and my situation has prevented me paying that attention to them that I should otherwise have done." With many misgivings, Hannah relinquished her charges to a stranger and prepared to share the house with her brother's bride.

On April 8, 1779, Arnold and Peggy were married. Although their courtship, paid for by the general, had been resplendent, their wedding, paid for by Shippen, was so quiet that gossip reports only that it was held in the evening, and that "Arnold, during the wedding ceremony, was supported by a soldier, and, when seated, his disabled limb was propped upon a campstool." Edward undoubtedly did for Peggy what he had done for her sister when she married Burd: "We had none who lived out of the family except Aunt Willing, Mr. Tilghman, and the bride's man and maids present at the ceremony. . . . We saw company for three days, and on Friday evening had a little hope for our unmarried acquaintances. This, with punch drinking, etc., is all the entertainment that was given."

Now that Benedict Arnold and Peggy Shippen were together, treason flowered almost instantly; the bride was in the plot from the first. Since they whispered behind closed doors, we must reconstruct, from scattered writings and our knowledge of their characters, the steps by which they reached in unison their dreadful decision.

Arnold's full-dress explanation, his *To the Inhabitants of America*, published after he had joined the British army, explains little, for it puts forward the favorite ideas of William Smith, the head of the Loyalist propaganda machine. Such sentences as "in the plainness of common sense, for I pretend to no casuistry, did the pretended treaty with the court of Versailles amount to more than an overture to America?" bear no resemblance to Arnold's style. Smith's diary discloses that Arnold made only a few changes in the prepared draft: they are easily recognizable, as when he writes of those who criticized his acts, "I shall treat their malice and calumnies with contempt and neglect."

The arguments Smith put in Arnold's mouth associated him with what Shippen's circle called "the old cause." He had entered the war to redress grievances; he had considered the Declaration of

Independence "precipitate," but had gone along until his eyes were opened by the horror of an alliance with "the enemy of the Protestant faith," France. This, coupled with the generosity of the British peace offers made at the same time, had opened his eyes to the fact that the Revolutionary leaders were "criminally protracting the war from sinister views at the expense of the public interest." He could never forget that the patriots were wallowing in the blood of their brothers.

Far from considering the Declaration of Independence "precipitate," Arnold had thought it too long delayed, since fear of a complete break had kept his Ticonderoga and Quebec campaigns from being adequately supported. If he favored the peace offers of 1778, the secret was so well kept that Edward Shippen, whom he had every reason to please, considered him in opposition. As for the French alliance: in 1776, he had expressed disappointment to Schuyler that French aid seemed unlikely, and in 1777, he referred with pleasure to the increasing possibility that Louis XVI would enter the war. Although, as we shall see, he developed personal irritation with French diplomats who refused to give him money, he had no ideological objections to alliance with a Catholic power. The trouble which priests had made for him in Canada had only impressed him with the importance of having them on his side. Years later, in suggesting a British expedition "to liberate Chile, Peru, and both Mexicos," he had commented that the clergy "must be particularly attended to and supported in their consequence; they are the machines by which the common people must be in a great measure governed." Among the motives Smith attributed to Arnold, we need only believe that the general hated the aspects of the civil war which made beautiful girls like his bride objects of patriot suspicion.

Although the Revolution was now causing Arnold unhappiness, it had made possible his greatest opportunities and pleasures. But to Peggy it had brought only exile, disillusionment with the father she had once adored, social and economic down-grading. She had begun to live when the British captured Philadelphia; and accomplished officers like André had taught her to love the royal army. Since she was a convinced Tory, the first serious suggestion that they change sides probably came from her lips.

Arnold was characterized by team spirit; he must have found the idea shocking. However, he was deeply in love, and, as his conflict with Gates had shown, easily led by youthful advisers. The soft femininity of his nineteen-year-old bride hid the power of her intellect and encouraged him to believe that the ideas she expressed were his own, as indeed they almost were, for every argument found an answering chord in his resentments and fears. He may even have harbored the same thoughts, but been frightened to acknowledge them.

"Self-preservation is the first principle of the human race," he had written Matlack, scoffing at the idea that ideological considerations made the militia fight. How narrowly the man who despised philosophers thought in terms of personal advancement is revealed in a letter he sent his sons' schoolmaster: "I wish their education to be useful rather than learned. Life is too uncertain to throw away in speculation on subjects that perhaps one man in ten thousand has a genius to make a figure in."

Although Arnold would never admit to himself that in the long-established army of a stable nation he could not possibly have risen from obscurity as rapidly as he had done, it was plain to him that the confusions attendant on an experimental government were now working to his disadvantage. When he had been a merchant menaced by British legislation, he had adhered to the Revolutionary cause as automatically as a trout floats in the river where fate has thrown it. Now his personal stream seemed to have turned and to be flowing in the opposite direction.

Taken up by a conservative group who feared that the conflict would open up a Pandora's box of levelers, Arnold was surrounded by disgruntled men. Yet his companions were not meditating treason. Possessed of a vision which saw beyond their own interests of the moment, they tried to guide the emerging nation by expedients open to politically minded men: propaganda, legislation, stubborn adherence to basic philosophies of business and society. These expedients meant nothing to Arnold. In asking Congress to protect him from opponents in public office, he had regretted that he could not fight such enemies in duels. Since Congress had not protected him, perhaps he should try to vanquish the entire United States in personal combat.

As Peggy's arguments and his own anger inclined him increasingly toward the royal cause, Arnold, who never thought of consequences, may well have visualized one of the daring and dramatic acts with which he had so often met his troubles: mounted on a fine horse, he would gallop to the British lines under the fire of both armies. Certainly a flood of unhappy patriots would follow him, joining the great Tory force which he would lead on a triumphant crusade. All through the conflict which had altered its official direction as the crisis deepened, a trickle of leaders had thus openly changed sides. Peggy, who as a Shippen always thought of consequences, had observed the results. Take her kinsman, Joseph Galloway, for example: he had made no important dent in the Rebel cause and all his property had been confiscated. His wife was now splashed with mud by the carriage in which she had once ridden in splendor. A shared love of luxury had brought Arnold and Peggy together; fear that luxury would be driven from America was one of their reasons for dreaming of a British victory; they would be fools to impoverish themselves.

After the consummation of the treason, Arnold was to advise the royal government that the back pay and premiums of land which American soldiers would receive should independence be established were "the strongest motive that induces them to continue in the service"; they would quickly give up if the British promised to indemnify them for what they would lose. Arnold believed that Congress owed him £2,500, of which he hoped to get £2,000 paid in specie (about £100,000 in inflated Continental currency). He owned his house in New Haven and the Philadelphia mansion, Mount Pleasant. Although his New York scheme was under the same cloud as the rest of his affairs, it was still possible to hope that, should the war be won, a grateful nation would allot him a huge slice of some frontier.

The Arnolds agreed that, before they took any drastic step, the British would have to promise them the equivalent of all they held and hoped for. Perhaps they would be granted something even more exciting. Arnold was to sign some of his treasonous correspondence "Monk," identifying himself with Cromwell's general who brought about the restoration of Charles II and was constituted Duke of Albemarle. "A *title* offered to General Washington,"

Arnold was to write Lord Germain, "might not prove unaccept-able." How agreeably the phrase "Lord and Lady Arnold" tripped from the tongue! But for such rewards, something more devious and more deadly than an honest change of sides would probably be required.

Although Arnold had never been scrupulously honest, the idea of selling out the "brave boys" he had once loved and led must have been a second shock. Before he could seriously consider such action, he would have to convince himself that, as a superman who saw further than his companions, he was doing what was best for the benighted souls who would hang him if they knew. Peggy argued, and his own bitternesses urged him to agree, that when faction-torn America was returned to a firm class structure under the equitable rule of a chastened Crown, everyone would be grate-ful to him as the creator of peace and prosperity. Arnold had al-ways felt within himself stirrings of greatness which his meteoric rise to world fame seemed to justify. Would this be his mightiest accomplishment of all, the great mission for which he was born?

When the patriots treated him with what he considered injustice, he was inclined to think so; but sometimes things went right. Three days before his marriage, a jury of Pennsylvania freemen resisted, as Arnold put it, "all the arts made use of to poison the fountains of justice"; and dismissed the council's charge that Arnold had "by force and arms" interfered in the *Active* case. At that moment, Arnold could not "but congratulate my countrymen upon the glorious effects of the exertions we have made to establish the liberties of ourselves and our posterity upon the firm basis of equal laws. . . . When I reflect on this circumstance, I contemplate, with a grateful pleasure, the scars I have received in the defense of a system of government the excellence of which, though fre-quently before the subject of my speculation, is now brought home to my *feelings*."

Less than a week after this triumph, Arnold made a renewed effort with Congress, appealing to them in most conciliatory terms. If his being tried again for charges of which he had been acquitted was "for the public good and to avoid a breach with the state . . . I will suffer with pleasure." However, "as a piece of justice due to a faithful and honest servant," Congress should accept their committee's dismissal of the four charges held not amenable to a military court. Although this seemed reasonable, fear of arousing Pennsylvania made the legislature vote—over the opposition of New York, North and South Carolina, and Rhode Island—to table Arnold's request.

This was a severe blow, but Arnold had never trusted Congress. It was to the army that he owed allegiance, and the commander in chief was his friend. "Mr. Reed," he wrote Washington, "has by his address kept the affair in suspense for near two months . . . and will, I make no doubt, use every artifice to delay the proceeding of a court martial, as it is to his interest that the affair should remain in the dark." Begging that an early date be fixed, Arnold warned that the council would seek a delay "for want of their evidence. Mine will be ready on the shortest notice." He was confident, he continued, of obtaining justice if the trial took place, "as every officer in the army must feel himself injured" by the way their fellow soldier had been maligned.

On receipt of this plea, Washington wrote both Arnold and Reed that he had called the trial for May 1. Arnold was reassured; Reed was irritated.

The President of Pennsylvania had accepted the court martial as a compromise, but was not pleased with it, for he still lacked proofs, and he did not believe that civilians could get justice from the army. He wrote Washington a threat—if the military considered Arnold's misuse of wagons trivial, Pennsylvania would never again supply them with transport—and demanded postponement so that he could collect witnesses.

Ignorant of the letter that left Washington no choice but to put off the trial, Arnold felt so encouraged that he again asked Congress to dismiss the charges which the court martial would not consider. A strong movement rose among the legislators to do the wounded hero this act of justice. But Reed was notified by his own representatives, and he dashed off a letter insisting that Pennsylvania had expressed "confidence, veneration, and respect for Congress" on the understanding that the Paca committee's exoneration of Arnold be completely forgotten. If action favorable to Arnold were now taken, the American people faced "a melancholy prospect of perpetuated disunion between this and the other United States." Such a threat could only be regarded as "a very serious matter indeed"; Congress buried Arnold's appeal in a committee.

At almost the same moment, Arnold received a letter from headquarters. "Dear Sir," it read in full. "I find myself under a necessity of postponing your trial to a later period than that for which I notified your attendance. I send you this information in a hurry, lest you set out before it might arrive, if delayed to an hour of more leisure. In a future letter, I shall communicate my reasons, and inform you of the time which shall be finally appointed." Across the bottom ran the signature of the man Arnold had most relied on—George Washington.

The letter that trembled in his hand left him, he believed, no resource within the United States: the army as well as Congress had failed him. Assisted by his triumphant bride, he began his search for a safe way to offer his services to the enemy.

CHAPTER TWENTY

A Career Soldier

WHEN the British government recalled Sir William Howe, a major check was offered André's ambitions. It was only a matter of time until General Grey would follow his friend back to England, and at that moment the aide would recede to the minor role of junior captain in his regiment unless he could find himself another general. But the new commander in chief, Sir Henry Clinton, disliked Howe and was so cold to Howe's favorites that no one was inclined to befriend them. André's only hope was to charm the new commander, a difficult task since Clinton was "haughty, morose, churlish, stupid, and scarcely ever to be spoken with." This characterization by the Loyalist chronicler, Judge Thomas Jones, was seconded by William Franklin, the philosopher's illegitimate Tory son, who wrote that "the commander in chief is gallant to a proverb, and possesses great military knowledge in the field, but he is weak, irresolute, unsteady, vain, incapable of forming any plan himself, and too weak, or rather too proud and conceited to follow that of another." The necessary object of André's ambitions was short and stout, with a full face, prominent nose, and tight nervous mouth. He squabbled with his equals, kept his inferiors at a distance, and achieved a sense of unity with his fellow humans only in liquor or the arms of light women.

André's lack of pleasure in his first campaign under this new commander is evinced by the sketchiness of the description, in the diary he was still keeping for Grey, of the successful retreat from

260

Philadelphia across New Jersey to New York City. At Monmouth, as they had been at Brandywine, Grey's brigade was held in reserve. Concerning the earlier battle, André had written a long description laudatory to Howe; he dismissed the second with a brief notation of positions.

Grey's troops were quartered at Bedford, Long Island (now engulfed in East Brooklyn). As the barracks were gable roofs over long trenches, the encampment resembled a village which had sunk almost out of sight in quicksand; André's residence, a one-and-a-half-story farmhouse, seemed by comparison to rise to a tremendous height. The daughters of his involuntary host, Leffert Lefferts, had long made fun of the British officers to their faces in Dutch, but André, so we are told, flabbergasted them by answering them in the same language, and then cautioning them not to gossip about their guests.

When an American army attacking the garrison at Newport was stranded in Rhode Island because the French fleet fled into Boston harbor to refit after a storm, the Rebel soldiers seemed ripe to be cut off. Grey's troops—4,333 men according to André's count—marched onto transports under Clinton's top command. While the British were becalmed or moved cautiously for fear of the French, André experienced his first close association with the new commander in chief. Eager to provide for his aide, Grey pushed them together, and, during long, idle days on the frigate *Carisfort*, André discovered that by proceeding with cautious tact he could whittle away Clinton's reserve. Like all shy, morose men, His Excellency was lonely; although he rebuffed friendship, he desperately needed a friend. André had made considerable progress before Clinton, finding that the Rebel army had escaped from the trap, sailed back to New York.

He left Grey's division behind to harass the coast. However, Clinton agreed with his predecessor, General Howe, that magnanimity would win back the Colonies more effectively than terror; he insisted that only military installations be damaged. When André and Grey raided New Bedford, they did their best to carry out their instructions, but André expressed irritation that they had to be mortified because flames spread from the warehouses they were burning to "a few houses of committee[men] and colonels of militia."

Clinton's policy, André argued, was ridiculous, as the Rebels had, on their reconquest of Philadelphia, exercised "very great rigor . . . against all persons who have befriended us." He believed that the only effective British action of the year had been the raids on the Mohawk Valley, which was "desolated by Indians under Colonel Butler, who has driven the advanced inhabitants back into the country with terror." André hoped that this campaign would make the Colonials fear that Clinton too "may begin devastation," yet he suspected that the commander in chief would remain quiescent "at or about New York this winter." This was unfortunate since the Rebels, although plagued by inflation, shortages, and "their aversion to the French . . . stand fast for independence," and the peace commissioners "have done nothing of late. Such," André concluded to his uncle, "is the state of affairs here. I am tired of forming erroneous opinions, and therefore shall leave it to you to reason."

Eager to encourage his aide's budding friendship with the commander in chief, Grey sent him back to New York with a note: "I write in haste and am not a little tired. Therefore, beg leave to refer you for the late plan of operations [at New Bedford] and particulars to Captain André." The young officer continued to cultivate Clinton, but hoped that he could remain with his present general: "We talk of an expedition under Major General Grey to the West Indies. I imagine, from the confidence with which people assert, that it is true." It was not true.

After raiding Martha's Vineyard, Grey returned to the encampment in New York, where André was awaiting him. Entrusted with a foraging expedition up the Hudson, they resolved to repeat the demonstration he had given at Paoli on how the enemy could be exterminated. Again ordering the troops to use only bayonet and sword, he surprised Baylor's Virginian light-horse near Tappan. The murderous blades plunged into the Americans before they could rise from their sleep. Even that convinced Tory, Judge Jones, was shocked: "The whole corps (a few who concealed themselves excepted) were massacred in cold blood, and, to the disgrace of Britons, many of them were stabbed while upon their knees humbly imploring and submissively begging for mercy . . . an act inconsistent with the dignity or honor of a British general and disgraceful to the name of a soldier." In his *Journal*, André notes without emotion, "The whole corps within six or eight men were killed or taken prisoner." There were six or seven prisoners. "The rest," he repeats, "were killed."

Red leaves still hung in the warm autumn air when the British army went into winter quarters, having accomplished practically nothing. Grey sailed back to England, but André was not stranded. He became one of Clinton's aides.

Thus he joined a corrupt administration ruling a convulsed city. The only metropolis left to the British, New York was crowded not only with soldiers, but with Loyalists from all thirteen Colonies. Fire had destroyed many blocks of residences. In the ruins, girls who in normal times would have been respectable housewives were receiving one redcoat every fifteen minutes; poor refugees had no legitimate means of livelihood. Even leading Tories, their estates confiscated by the Rebels, subsisted on tiny pensions grudgingly allowed by the military. All appeals for an effective civil government were brushed aside: Clinton, who regarded civilians as an encumbrance, granted only a pretense. The situation which had set off the Revolution in the first place was being repeated in New York: the Americans were calling for autonomy, the British denying it.

As provisions grew scarcer and prices skyrocketed, as Americans grew thinner and more despairing, royal officials fattened. Quartermasters charged the government for goods requisitioned from Loyalists, but refused to pass the money on; it was almost impossible to get redress even in cases of outright looting. And Clinton did nothing to stop the grafters. Jones describes him and his favorites "regaling themselves in routs, dinners, little concerts, and small parties, over good, warm, comfortable fires, and enjoying all the ease and luxury in life, while the poor soldiers (for whom the wood was provided) were, with their wives and children, perishing in the barracks in the severity of winter for want of that fuel . . . lavished away and distributed among strumpets, panderers, favorites, and pretty little misses."

The corruption and inefficiency that surrounded the new aide enabled him to shine like a single candle in a dark room. When anyone wanted to get anything done at headquarters, André was the man to see. Far from growling from the depths of a hangover, he would tell petitioners at once "whether it would be proper for him to undertake their business. If he did not, he gave his reasons, which were always satisfactory; if he did, they were almost sure of an answer in twenty-four hours." His manner was "affable and attractive."

André possessed all the money he wished to spend, and his hatred for the countinghouse that had darkened his youth made him look on financial deals with ill-favor. To his family he confessed that he gave "so little attention to my prosperity" that his only concern was "in general not to be extravagant." His lack of interest in graft enabled him to prepare for Clinton a strong memorandum on plundering. "The stripping and insulting of inhabitants" merely for "the wanton pleasure of spoil," was, he wrote, shocking because it served no public or private good. He described eloquently the "horrors" inflicted on "a harmless peasant, a decrepit father of a family, a widow or other person as little an object of severity." When victims were Loyalists, the matter was even more grave: "conduct so atrocious . . . involves our friends in ruin, and falsifies the word of the general." However, the most serious effect of all was on military discipline, since plundering involved "disobedience of orders, desertion, and the falling into the enemy's hands." He pointed out that during Howe's march on Philadelphia, such causes had lost the army 200 men in a few days.

Stealing "cattle and other articles of food wears," he found, "a softer aspect." Since the interest of the army was furthered, André no longer mourned for decrepit fathers and widows. If they were Rebels, they should in no way be reimbursed for supplies the Crown needed; yet a board of safeguard should be set up to see that Tories were paid. Another officer, a commissioner of captured cattle, should handle those aspects of the matter that involved military discipline, making sure that "licentious regiments" turned in their plunder, that soldiers receive at least a token recompense for what they captured, and that the fresh meat be equitably distributed. This is an able document, and, had André's suggestions been carried out, the Loyalists would have been given much protection.

In penning emotional passages about the sufferings of civilians, André had taken into consideration Clinton's aversion to total warfare—but he had not abandoned his own belief that widespread burning of Rebel property was "a horrid means" well worth trying. The Tories agreed with André; for they hated the former neighbors who had impoverished and exiled them. When Loyalist militia under General William Tryon were permitted to raid Connecticut, they put Fairfield and Norwalk to the torch. Clinton "confessed himself shocked by the news" and resolved to suppress the defense Tryon inserted in his official report. André managed, however, in some subtle way that did not infuriate his commander, to smuggle this argument for a scorched earth policy off to the ministry at London.

In England and New York, Loyalists were screaming that, if they were given a free hand, they themselves could overwhelm the Rebels. The home government, writing Clinton that their "spirits in general with regard to your prospects are not very high," urged him to make more use of the Tories both within and without the Rebel lines. During the summer and autumn of 1779, the issue turned on proposals which William Franklin made to Clinton, using André as the intermediary. Franklin urged a board of intelligence, consisting of leading Loyalist refugees from each state, who would be empowered to gather information and foment unrest by subpoenaing witnesses, granting passes, and employing their own spies. Secondly, the Loyalists wished to be land privateers. Banded together as the Associated Refugees they would, at their own discretion, raid enemy territory, and pay themselves back with plunder for their own property which the miscreants had confiscated. Although untrained generals like Washington and Arnold could make good use of skittish agents and militia, the British commander, despite his great shortage of manpower, could see no effective way to employ men who lacked conventional military training and discipline. He feared that the board of intelligence would undermine his own adjutant general's office, that the Associated Refugees would tangle his military operations and practice brutalities at variance with his policies. Neither proposal was encouraged. That

André urged on his commander a more conciliatory attitude is shown by Franklin's praise of his judgment.

Since the Loyalists considered André "the only man of abilities" on Clinton's staff, they regretted time he took from headquarters by acting "on the stage all winter." When the theater opened on January 9, 1779, André delivered—and probably wrote—one of the prologues. In elaborate metaphor, he compared the house to a battlefield on which the actors faced the public: the boxes were "flanks," the pit "a ravine," the orchestra "a palisade." Having asked the critics to show charity "ere the catcall sounds the dread alarm," he launched into a passage praising the rape of the Sabine women which could hardly have pleased Americans with pretty wives:

> *Lest bloodshed should ensue, each* gentle *woman*
> *With condescension took her fav'rite* Roman.
> *No less compliant, to appease the strife,*
> *Each* Sabine, *on* true ton, *gave up his wife.* . . .
> *Give but the fair: the treaty shall prevail;*
> *We will, like* Romans, *use the* Lady *well.*

André used his literary gifts to amuse his fellow officers and their women. At a private party, a diarist reports, he "read an extempore on love and fashion, and a characteristic *Dream* about the Rebels, for which he gained much applause from the fair and bold." In the *Dream*, which the *Royal Gazette* published, André imagined himself in "a spacious apartment" where "the infernal judges administered justice" through the transmigration of souls. Arnold's friend, Silas Deane, appeared dressed up like "a French marquis with all the *external frippery* that so eminently distinguishes the most *trifling* characters of that *trifling* nation," and "slipped off with very little change, in the character of *'the monkey who had seen the world.'*" General Lee became an adder; John Jay a rattlesnake; and the members of the Continental Army "were ordered to put on the shape of the *timid hare,* whose disposition they already possessed. With *ears erect,* they seemed to be watching the first approach of danger, and ready to fly even upon the appearance of it."

André combined his literary and dramatic activities with the robust masculine pleasures of Clinton's entourage. A handball court in the red-light district was "made notorious, not to say famous," as their daily resort. After his morning business was concluded, the commander would gallop "from headquarters, near the fort, up Broadway to this five-alley, and, after exercising there, he again mounted and galloped, like a sportsman at a fox chase, out of town and in again, followed at full speed by his aides and favorites."

Close association had made André and his general extremely good friends. When the aide penetrated beneath "the roughness of a bear" which Clinton revealed to strangers, he found a personality of great gentleness, delicacy, and diffidence. Clinton could show in battle "the bravery of a lion," but in less obvious situations, he was the perpetual victim of self-doubt. He fled from confusion into dissipation. That he permitted common soldiers and civilians to be mistreated stemmed not from innate brutality but from his carelessness and lack of self-identification with less well-born mortals. His letters make one wonder whether he was not so unenterprising as a general because there dwelt deep down in his nature a repugnance for violence which he could not overcome until the cannon actually began to bellow. André was a stronger man than he, and also more accomplished. Coming to identify himself with this brilliant youngster, Clinton allowed himself to be led in a way that amazed observers who had found him impervious to other human influences.

In the twentieth century, a rumor has arisen that André advanced himself in Clinton's esteem as a homosexual, but this seems to reflect no more than the morbidity of our own times. Although the aide had been considered, when a very young man at Göttingen, to display almost feminine gentleness, no equivalent comment was recorded during all his American years. In the eighteenth century, to paint scenery and design ladies' coiffures did not make a man suspect; his enemies' worst charge about his relationship with Clinton was that he had wormed his way into favor by being "a cringing, insidious sycophant." And Clinton cherished among his papers a poem written in André's hand that gloats most explicitly over the particular characteristics of heterosexual love:

THE FRANTIC LOVER

And shall then another embrace thee my Fair!
Must envy still add to the pangs of Despair!
Shall I live to behold the reciprocal bliss!
Death, death is a refuge, Elysium to this!
    The star of the evening now bids thee retire
Accurs'd be its Orb and extinguished its fire!
For it shows me my rival prepared to invade
Those charms which at once I admired and obey'd.
Far off each forbidding Incumbrance is thrown
And Sally thy beauties no more are thy own.
Thy coyness too flies as love brings to thy View
A Frame more ecstatic than Saint ever knew!
And yet I behold thee 'tho longing to die
Approach the new Heaven with a tear and a sigh!
For oh! the fond sigh midst Enjoyment will stray,
And a Tear is the Tribute which Rapture must pay.
Still, still dost thou tremble that pleasure to seek,
Which pants in thy Bosom and glows in thy cheek;
Confusion and shame thy soft wishes destroy
And Terror cuts off the weak blossom of Joy.
Ah! had I been blest with thy Beauty, my fair,
With fondest attention, with delicate care
My heart would have tried all thy fears to remove
And pluck'd every thorn from the Roses of love.
My Insolent Rival, more proud of his right,
Condemns the sweet office, that soul of delight.
Less tender he seizes thy lips as his prey
And all thy dear Limbs the rough Summons obey.
E'en now more licentious—Rash Mortal forbear
Restrain him, O Venus! Let him too despair!
Freeze, freeze the swift streams which now hurry to join
And curse him with passions unsated like mine!
    How weak is my rage his fierce Joy to control.
A Kiss from thy body shoots Life to his Soul.
Thy frost too dissolv'd in one Current is run
And all thy keen feelings are blended in one.

Thy limbs from his Limbs a new Warmth shall acquire;
His passions from thine shall redouble their Fire
'Til wreck'd and o'erwhelmed in the Storm of delight
Thine ears lose their hearing, thine eyes lose their Sight.
Here Conquest must pause tho' it ne'er can be cloy'd
To view the rich plunder of beauty enjoy'd,
The Tresses dishevelled, the Bosom display'd,
And the Wishes of Years in a moment repaid.
A Thousand soft thoughts in thy fancy combine
A Thousand wild horrors assemble in Mine;
Relieve me kind death, shut the Scene from my View,
And Save me, oh save me, ere madness ensue!

When André was taken ill with what he described as "a treacherous complaint," Clinton sent him for the summer air to Oyster Bay, the extreme British strong point on Long Island. He stayed in the mansion of Samuel Townsend, a Quaker who had shown such rebellious tendencies that it took all the charms of two beautiful daughters, Audrey and Sarah, to keep him out of trouble with the English soldiers. Still visible on the windows are inscriptions said to have been cut with diamonds by royal officers: "The Adorable Miss Sarah" and "Miss A. T. The most Accoml [*sic*] young lady in Oyster Bay." A fellow guest was the local commandant, Major John Graves Simcoe, an Englishman whose full cheeks and double chin maligned the energy of his spirit. As commander of the Queen's Rangers, a corps of Tory hussars, he was a dashing partisan officer; and he could rival André as a poet. The two flirted with Sally Townsend. Simcoe sent her a perfervid valentine in verse, and André, having surreptitiously sketched her "as a beautiful girl in a riding habit," slipped the drawing under a plate for her to find. When Sally was giving a tea party, André hid the doughnuts and cakes in a cupboard; she was "in a state of frantic excitement and perplexity" before, in pretended innocence, he found them for her.

Tradition tells that Sally's love for Simcoe was responsible for her never marrying; but the two officers did not take the provincial girl seriously enough to let her come between them. Absorbed, as André wrote, "in sober and various occupations," they made

269

sketching excursions together with "two or three books, ink and pencils"; they talked far into the night "concerning Prologues and twenty other things"; they awoke early the next morning to hunt small animals "in a grove of laurel." After André departed, they remained fast friends. On one occasion Simcoe wrote him, "I send you a very intelligent Negro boy within the circle of his knowledge. When you dismiss him, I will be obliged to you to pass him to the Quaker house, as I mean to keep him."

By April, André had returned to what he called "the Sisyphean labors of headquarters." However, his health collapsed once more; "I have been so chagrined and full of ailings that I have scarce had any other than selfish cares." Clinton kindly lent "one of his country houses, where I am repairing [recuperating] for the Jersey tour."

The Jersey tour was André's first important mission, a negotiation to arrange for such a general exchange of prisoners as had freed him in 1776. Washington's only motive in agreeing to discuss the matter was humanitarian—American captives were being disgracefully treated by the British—but Clinton had a military advantage to gain. Since he could no longer expect reinforcements from England, the return of Burgoyne's professional army would be much more valuable to him than Washington would find the return of amateur soldiers, many of whose enlistments had already expired. Clinton instructed André and his fellow negotiator, Colonel West Hyde, to get the existing British prisoners back at once, and to arrange a cartel for continuing monthly exchanges.

At Perth Amboy, André and Hyde met with two Rebels from the South, Colonels William Davies and Robert H. Harrison. These men belonged to the class whom it always perturbed André to find on the Rebel side; they were, he wrote, "personally such as we could have wished to confer with" and they "urge their arguments with good temper and politeness." They even admitted the lower-class foibles of the American militia—yet they gave not an inch. Indeed, by questioning Clinton's authority to sign a cartel, they tried to trick Hyde and André into urging an act of Parliament that would strengthen the Congress in "their usurped dignities." When the Britons discovered that the Americans would agree to no more than a limited exchange that might work to their own advantage, André decided that their purpose was "to amuse the clamorous prisoners in our hands" by pretending to make an effort at freeing them. The only issue left was which side could make a better appearance in the newspapers. To keep the enemy from publicly justifying their action, Hyde and André demanded a plain yes or no when they sent a proposal they knew would be refused. The answer was no, and André returned to New York "with the utmost disappointment and frustration."

The youthful enthusiast had hoped for a great coup, but Clinton was not surprised by the failure; he continued to advance his favorite. Late in April 1779, André was put in direct charge of British intelligence and of encouraging disaffection among the Rebels. As he ran over in his mind the names of important Americans who might possibly be seduced to the royal cause, he did not include the violent fighter, Benedict Arnold, who had just married Peggy Shippen. However, André's name was already on the traitorous couple's lips.

Book Five

TREASON

CHAPTER TWENTY-ONE

The Devil Can Bargain

NOW THAT the Arnolds contemplated changing sides, one false step would dangle him—and possibly his bride as well—from the gallows. Hesitating to trust anyone, "ashamed," as Benedict wrote, "of the human race," they realized that every person they confided in would be an added danger. Yet they could not by themselves get word to the British commander of their treasonous desires.

Although Sir Henry Clinton was notoriously unapproachable, Peggy could suggest a safe road through his headquarters to his ear. Captain André was in daily conversation with the chief, and she could vouch for André's discretion and ability. Arnold, whose psychological insecurity seems never to have manifested itself in sexual jealousy, was reassured by his wife's description of her former swain, and agreed to include him in the conspiracy.

In addition to Clinton and André, one more collaborator was needed: a go-between who would, without implicating the Arnolds, arrange for the movement of messages through the lines. The search for such a man must have caused much anguished discussion, since anyone in Philadelphia could gain money and celebrity more safely by carrying Arnold's message not to Clinton but to Washington. They settled at last on a crockery dealer, Joseph Stansbury. The suggestion was probably again Peggy's, since Arnold was hardly a man to whom a suspected person would express pro-British sentiments. However, Peggy, as she had moved on the arms of British officers, had been in a position to hear Loyalists talk and judge of the sincerity of the speakers. She knew that when Stansbury had taken an oath of allegiance to Pennsylvania, this had been merely to keep from being driven into exile; his heart was with the England where he had been born and educated.

The tradesman was, at thirty-three, a social climber who dressed as fashionably as a gentleman and fawned on the best society. Sitting behind his counter, he giggled to himself as he wrote comic verses, and sometimes raised his voice in song to see whether the lines fitted the air. But, if a shadow fell on the door, with a single practiced gesture he hid his poems; jail would encompass him on the very day that the patriot leaders discovered that he was the author of lampoons they found so annoying. When a servant in Arnold's livery ordered him to wait on the general, he probably sensed nothing more momentous than another order of china for his old customer's sumptuous table. He later remembered the date as early June, but it was about the first of May 1779.

"General Arnold sent for me," Stansbury wrote, "and, after some general conversation, opened his political sentiments respecting the war carrying on between Great Britain and America, declaring his abhorrence of a separation of the latter from the former as a measure that would be ruinous to both. . . . General Arnold then communicated to me, under a solemn obligation of secrecy, his intention of offering his services to the commander in chief of the British forces in any way that would most effectually restore the former government and destroy the then usurped authority of Congress, either by immediately joining the British army or cooperating on some concerted plan with Sir Henry Clinton."

Peggy's complicity in the plot was not hidden from Stansbury. We can imagine her looking very handsome, flushed with excitement and purpose. After years of being buffeted by every wave, she was at last taking arms against a sea of troubles.

Stansbury knew that the deliverer of such a message would not only strike a blow for Britain, but could expect a large reward. Assuring Arnold a dozen times that he would put nothing in writing and would pretend, if captured, to be on a simple business mission, he agreed to slip through the American and British lines, to call on Captain André.

No sooner had Stansbury disappeared along whatever devious route would carry him to New York without a pass than Arnold received a letter from Washington. The court martial, it was explained, had been held up by the council's desire to summon witnesses from distant states; it should be convened by June 1 or, at the latest, the first of July. "Though the delay in your situation must be irksome," Washington continued, "I am persuaded you will be of opinion with me that it is best on every principle to submit to it rather than that there should be the least appearance of precipitancy in the affair."

Arnold's reply was hysterical. The misdeeds of which he was accused were hardly capital, yet he wrote, "If Your Excellency thinks me a criminal, for Heaven's sake let me be immediately tried, and, if found guilty, executed. I want no favor; I ask only justice. . . . Let me beg of you, sir, to consider that a set of artful, unprincipled men in office may misrepresent the most innocent actions, and, by raising the public clamor against Your Excellency, place you in the same disagreeable situation I am in. Having made every sacrifice of fortune and blood, and become a cripple in the service of my country, I little expected to meet the ungrateful returns I have received from my countrymen; but, as Congress has stamped ingratitude as a current coin, I must take it. I wish Your Excellency, for your long and eminent services, may not be paid in the same coin. I have nothing left but the little reputation I have gained in the army. Delay in the present case is worse than death."

The man who had summoned up the devil still hoped to be rescued before he signed the contract with his blood.

Stansbury arrived safely in New York. However, his nerves were so shattered that he needed the comfort of a friend. Disobeying Arnold, he widened the plot to include another poet, the Reverend Jonathan Odell, who had been an officer in the British army before becoming an Episcopal minister. A rabid Tory, he had been forced to flee from his parish in New Jersey, and he was now active in British intelligence. Where Stansbury's talent ran naturally to comic songs, Odell called on his muse to grant him

Some deleterious powers of acrid rhyme,
Some ars'nic verse, to poison with the pen
These rats who nestle in the lion's den.

We can see André, who was himself a poet, rising with relaxed good humor to receive his two colleagues, but in a moment the door was shut and locked. Since, in all their speculations on what patriots could be induced to change sides, the British had never even considered Arnold, the poets' story dumbfounded André. Asking them to wait, he rushed off to Clinton. Finally he returned with a reply which Stansbury translated into "mysterious notes." After the two poets had departed, André felt so ill that he was forced to flee to the country house which Clinton had placed at his disposal.

Stansbury boarded a British sloop that beat out through the Narrows and followed the wooded shore of Staten Island. Some three miles from the tip, it came to anchor next to a warship in Prince's Bay which was the limit of effective British control. Waiting until dark had fallen, Stansbury climbed into a whaleboat. A "confidential person" steered as he was rowed in secret silence the eight long miles to a deserted cove in Rebel-held New Jersey. He probably spent the rest of the night in the house of a British agent, "our slender friend" John Rattoon.

As Stansbury threaded his way toward Philadelphia, terrified lest he be recognized, Arnold received two more communications from Washington. The first stated that the court martial had been definitely set for June 1; the second expressed concern at Arnold's violent letter, but less because of the state of mind it revealed than because Washington feared that Arnold doubted his own impartiality: "I feel my situation truly delicate and embarrassing, on one side your anxiety, very natural in such circumstances . . . on the other, the pointed representations of the state on the subject of witnesses, and the impropriety of precipitating a trial so important in itself left me no choice." He was not prejudiced against Arnold, he insisted, but neither did he soothe him as a friend. "I cautiously suspend my judgment 'til the result of a full and fair trial shall determine the merits of the prosecution."

In his replies to Washington, Arnold expressed regret that "my cruel situation should cause Your Excellency the least embarrassment or uneasiness"; and added that he desired vindication only so he could take a command in the army "and render my country every service in my power at this critical time. . . . The interest I have in the welfare and happiness of my country, which I have ever evinced when in my power, will, I hope, always overcome my personal resentment." The interjection of "I hope" made this sentence mirror Arnold's thoughts exactly. Was it a slip of the pen, indicating that he was not yet an accomplished conspirator; or was he warning Washington that he could not be pushed too far?

Perhaps a commander who had the seeds of disloyalty in his own heart, to whom treason was a personal possibility, might have noticed the telltale words; but Washington was so firm in his own constancy that he could not doubt the constancy of a man he believed worthy of trust. His suspicions were not aroused. If he sensed Arnold's peculiar state of mind, he thought only of the brave fighter's wounds and discouragements.

When a man feels driven to murder or treason, and yet hopes that in some miraculous way he will be stopped, time does not pass tranquilly. Gout tortured Arnold's undamaged leg; he became unable to walk a step, sicker than he had been since the first anguished months of his wound. The inevitable moment was not long delayed when there came through the front door, meek and smooth, the crockery dealer Stansbury, bearing perhaps a saleable bowl as an excuse for his visit. While the servants are still in hearing, he extols the bowl in unctuous tones; locked with Arnold in a back room, he changes his manner. The serpent is now speaking to an excited Eve and Adam.

Slowly deciphering his "mysterious notes," Stansbury delivers André's message. Arnold wanted to be assured that the British would not give up the war; this assurance is given. In reply to Arnold's demand that he be promised suitable pay for his treason, André agrees in general terms but refuses to name such a specific sum as Arnold had desired; the amount must depend on the services rendered. Although Arnold had asked whether he should openly join the British or serve them secretly while an American general, André did not consider the first possibility worth discussing. Pretending still to be a patriot, Arnold should make possible "the seizing an obnoxious body of men" by "enabling us to attack to advantage." If this were impossible, he should send information on the contents of dispatches, on discussions in Congress, on the plans of "foreign abettors," on military organizations. He should induce other generals to betray their commands and encourage any party that was fomenting civil unrest. If Arnold could further the return of Burgoyne's army through an exchange of prisoners, that would raise "the *honor* of America."

As to means of communication: Stansbury had brought with him a dictionary of which there was an identical copy in New York; words were to be indicated by numbers referring to page and line. However, Stansbury did not wish to handle papers that, even if undecipherable, were on the face of them strange. For a man already under suspicion this would be, he pointed out, extremely hazardous. He was glad that the ingenious Captain André had thought of a safer mode for sending messages.

"The Lady," André had suggested, "might write to me at the same time with one of her intimates. She will guess who I mean, the latter remaining ignorant of interlining [writing in invisible ink between the lines], and sending the letter. I will myself write to the friend to give occasion for a reply. This will come by a flag of truce, exchanged officer, etc., every messenger remaining ignorant of what they are charged with. The letters may talk of the Meschianza [*sic*] and other nonsense."

"The Lady," they all knew, was Peggy Arnold; the friend, who was to be innocently involved in treason, was the girl who so loved André, Peggy Chew. Arnold seems to have burst out at this point. Unlike the Meshianza knight, he believed in protecting women. "He depends on me," Stansbury mourned, "for conveying, which is dangerous."

Poor Peggy Chew! How unhappy she would have been had she known what was being planned for her by the British officer of whom she dreamed. Earlier that month, Mrs. Galloway had written sourly in her diary: "Nancy and Pegg Chew drank tea with me. All their discourse was of the officers, and said And[ré] and Cumble [Campbell] and Riddle [Ridsdale] with many others sent them cards and messages, and that they kept the birthdays of six of them by meeting together and drinking their healths in a glass of wine, and that the gentlemen kept theirs in the same manner. . . . They bragged so much of their intimacy that I was quite sick of it."

Peggy Chew must have been bragging without much basis, for when André sat down to involve her in the treason, he began: "I hardly dare write to you after having neglected your commissions and not apologized for my transgressions. I would with pleasure have sent you drawings of headdresses had I been as much a milliner here as I was at Philadelphia in Meschianza times, but from occupation, as well as ill health, I have been obliged to abandon the pleasing study of what relates to the ladies. I should however be happy to resume it had I the same inducements as when I had the pleasure of frequenting yours and the Shippen family. . . . I trust I am yet in the memory of the little society of Third and Fourth Street, and even of the *other Peggy*, now Mrs. Arnold, who will, I am sure, accept of my best respects and, with the rest of the sisterhoods of both streets, peruse not disdainfully this page meant as an assurance of my unabated esteem for them." The letter then went off into gossip about various English officers, and stated, in connection with his negotiations for the exchange of prisoners, "I intended in case of agreement to have subjoined a clause that all hearts on either side should be restored or others sent in exchange. This would have afforded considerable relief to many swains who still magnetically turn to the banks of the Delaware."

A draft of this letter was placed with the other treason correspondence in Clinton's files, but there is no evidence that the efforts to involve the gentle Peggy Chew went any further. Presumably, Arnold put a stop to it.

André's communication to Arnold had not pleased the general and his bride. The British, it seemed, were so unimpressed with his personal prestige that they had not the slightest interest in having him publicly change sides. They considered that he would be really valuable to them only if he did what his wound made impossible: secured a command that he could betray. Although they would be happy to receive intelligence if he cared to send it, for this—indeed for everything—they refused to name specific payment. After Arnold had risked the gallows by helping them, they would, in their majestic superiority, dole out to him whatever they pleased. André's message seemed more suited to some tradesman, say Stansbury himself, than to the man who was in his own and his wife's eyes the greatest American warrior.

Two heads, the soldier's black now touched with gray and Peggy's young blonde, bent together over the dictionary Stansbury had left, preparing in code a reply from Arnold to André.[1] They protested that no definite price had been offered—"as life and everything is at stake, I will expect some certainty"—and, with unconscious irony, paraphrased the congratulation Washington had sent Arnold in Canada. "It is not in the power of any man to command success, but you have done more, you have deserved it," Washington had written. The conspirators wrote Clinton, "I cannot promise success; I will deserve it." They added that Arnold could be more useful if he knew in advance of Clinton's secret plans.

Then they sent some intelligence, no item detailed, and none hard to get. They reported that Washington was going to the Hudson and some gossip about the French alliance. Most interesting was the statement, "C[ongress] have given up Charleston if attempted; they are in want of arms, ammunition, and men to defend it." This was a taste to whet André's appetite, nothing more. "Madam A.," the letter ended, "presents you her particular compliments."

In New York, Odell could hardly wait for the fruition of the plot that would make his fortune. Every knock on the door brought him bounding in search of a message. At last one came, an innocuous letter from Stansbury and a sheet of paper marked "F" for fire. He had no right to examine it, but, so he wrote André, "my joy on getting the letter was such that, before I had made the reflection, I had already flown to the fire with my paper." The writing had been so spread by dampness that it was illegible. André assumed that the message had been from Arnold, but the evidence indicates that it was only a report from Stansbury.

Arnold's own letter was mysteriously held up. While it lurked in some unimaginable hiding place, the two poets corresponded in what seemed, despite the danger of sending messages, largely nervous eagerness. They wrote in code or stated things obliquely to make them sound like ordinary business matters; they had Rattoon rowing between South Amboy and Prince's Bay on many an inky night; they gave papers to ladies moving through the lines on passes. Some letters got lost, creating confusion. Stansbury had to flee Philadelphia for a while—the Whigs were too active in hunting down suspected Tories—and thus lost touch with his code book and Arnold. Finally André poked up Odell, and Odell poked up Stansbury, writing, "Lothario is impatient. Convince him of your sincerity, and you may rely upon it that your most sanguine hopes will be surpassed." Otherwise, "both your credit and mine will suffer greatly."

The date set for Arnold's court martial approached, and he set out for Washington's headquarters in the New Jersey highlands. His pain-racked body had to be lifted into a carriage; his mind seethed. Perhaps it was lucky that the British had received his offer coldly. The moment had come when he would be vindicated in patriot eyes and his enemies disgraced; then Peggy would be convinced; then he himself would be convinced; then his wound would heal and he would rejoin the cause for which he had bled. He would win back to the sense of unity with his fellow man which had made his months on turbulent rivers and in frozen Canada the happiest in his life.

Arnold carried with him a letter from Deane to General Greene that reveals with what sentimental adulation he was regarded by his intimates. Having described Arnold's wounded state in the most piteous terms, Deane exclaimed, "Great God! is it possible that after the bold and perilous enterprises which this man has undertaken for the service and defense of his country, the loss of his fortune, and the cruel and lingering pains he has suffered from the wound received fighting their battles, there can be found among us men so abandoned to the base and infernal passions of envy and malice as to persecute him with the most unrelenting fury, and wish to destroy what alone he had the prospect of saving out of the dreadful wreck of his health, fortune, and life: his character?" And so on for four pages.

Greene commented, "A sly letter." He invited Matlack, who was to present the council's case, to stay with him, but feeling was so intense that the Pennsylvanian thought it wise to refuse, since Greene's quarters were near to Arnold's.

In the armed camp, surrounded with the shouts of soldiers, Arnold felt at home and expected his fellow officers to take his part. Washington, whose position required complete neutrality, complained that he "self-invited some civilities I never meant to show him, or any officer in arrest, and he received a rebuke before I could convince him of the impropriety of his entering upon a justification of his conduct in my presence." Himself incapable of the judiciousness that was one of Washington's great strengths, Arnold misinterpreted it. More and more he found reason to believe that the commander, whom he had relied on to support him against all comers, was a false friend.

The trial started on June 1, but Arnold hardly had time to protest the inclusion in the court of Pennsylvania officers before it was indefinitely postponed; the British were advancing up the Hudson. As Washington hurried to the defense, Arnold made his way painfully back to Philadelphia.

Clinton's army had already appeared, in boats and on foot, before the two American outposts guarding King's Ferry. After a good look at the vast array facing them, the Americans skedaddled from the unfinished fort at Stony Point. On the other side of the river, at Verplanck's Point a garrison of seventy-four men, who were outnumbered fifty to one, tried to flee from a blockhouse called Fort La Fayette, but found themselves surrounded, and were forced to return to their pitiful fortification. André used all his histrionic powers to demand and receive the surrender of the tiny works with as much ceremony as if they had been a great city.

"On the Glacis of Fort Fayette, June 1st, 1779," he wrote. "His Excellency Sir Henry Clinton and Commodore Sir George Collier grant to the garrison of Fort La Fayette terms of safety to the persons and property (contained in the fort) of the garrison; they surrender themselves prisoners of war. The officers shall be permitted to wear their side arms. John André, Aide-de-Camp." He enjoyed posturing there in the eyes of both armies: it helped blot from his memory the bitter surrender at St. Johns, when it had been he who laid down his arms. However, he was also serving affairs of state.

An American paragrapher asked, "What excuse will a person

of Mr. André's reputed sense make for this parade?" and answered that Clinton wished "to astonish all Europe" by pretending he had achieved a great victory. The paragrapher had guessed right. Clinton flattered the ministry in London by writing "to you I need not describe Verplanck's Point"; and then made the capture of the outpost sound like a major triumph. In the same dispatch, he called the government's attention to his favorite: "I refer you to André [who enclosed a paper] for foreign intelligence."

His army weakened by expeditions sent southward, Clinton returned to New York, where André engaged during the summer in the routine activities of gathering intelligence. He received from outposts reports of enemy movements, and correlated them for his commander. More exciting were his dealings with actual spies. Men came through the lines bringing samples of information and offering, for money or favor, to return and gather more. They boasted of having generals or congressmen in their pockets; of secret lines of information which discretion prevented them from communicating. They claimed they could raise armies of saboteurs as soon as they fingered British cash. Usually such stories could not be checked without violating the necessary secrecy. André had to judge the men who sat beside his desk, squirming nervously or speaking with Olympian confidence, only by what he saw and heard.

Alexander Brink appeared on the lines at Kingsbridge shouting his loyalty to the Crown and bringing some intelligence. When he was searched, papers were found calling him "Lieutenant" Brink. Yes, he said, he had joined the militia, but only better to serve the King. He had connections in Canada and would take messages to the British general there; but first he would like to rest for a day or two on Long Island. Ignoring this request, André gave him dispatches to carry north and bundled him to Paulus Hook for nighttime transportation to New Jersey. Brink made excuses for not starting and finally returned to New York with new reasons for going to Long Island. André threw him in jail.

Edward Fox, a captured government clerk, presented letters of recommendation from important Loyalists. He claimed, so André noted, to be "in partnership with C—— [Samuel Chase], a member of Congress, and on the information derived from their stations they speculate." Although André wrote Fox's sponsors that he could not "show petulant solicitude" for the services of a man about whom he knew so little, he agreed to let the presumptive spy return to Philadelphia. Fox promised to give intelligence to a messenger who was to "make a cross in chalk on the pit door of the playhouse at night, and on the next day to find an hour and address marked over it when to call for a parcel." Whether the cross was ever drawn at André's old haunt is not clear, but certainly Fox carried Washington valuable information concerning military movements he had seen in New York.

The most grandiose plot of all Clinton and André inherited from their predecessors. Led by Colonel William Rankin, a group of militia officers near Carlisle—how well André remembered that hateful town—said they were recruiting a secret Loyalist army. When André took over the negotiation in June 1779, they claimed more than a thousand men and offered to arm themselves by capturing the major Rebel magazine at Carlisle; they wanted Clinton to send a force by water to support them. When Clinton did not move, they increased their estimates of their army—by 1780 to 6,000 men—and insisted that they needed immediate help since their leaders were on the verge of being recognized. William Franklin offered to lead a Loyalist force from New York to meet Rankin's secret army "on the frontiers of Pennsylvania." The proposers of these schemes believed André to be sympathetic, but Clinton always vetoed action. The very size of the claims made him suspicious—many thousand men could hardly be organized without leaks to the Rebel authorities—and anyway he did not trust the Tory militia.

That André was more sanguine than his general about operations behind the Rebel lines is further revealed by his reaction to Arnold's letter, which finally reached him after about three weeks in transit. In drafting a reply, André gave away Clinton's designs on Charleston by urging Arnold to take the command in Carolina so he could deliver the troops stationed there. Other glorious possibilities occurred to the young aide: the British could march into New England drawing Washington after them. Arnold would lead and betray the advance corps and also give Clinton the information he needed to cut the American supply lines, making the Continental

Army unable to defend itself, forcing it to disperse from hunger. "At such an hour, when the most boisterous spirits were with the army and everyone intent on its fate, the seizing of Congress would decide the business."

This vision so excited André that he continued it in a memorandum for Clinton. Arnold's friend, General Mifflin, would be the proper man to seize Congress, although André wondered whether he was "enterprising." As Washington's army disintegrated, Schuyler, the patrician whose adherence to the Rebel cause had always puzzled André, would certainly see the error of his ways; he would lead an insurrection in Albany and perhaps hand over the forts at West Point. Maybe Generals Maxwell and St. Clair would join the rising Loyalist wave. After an expedition from Canada had destroyed General Sullivan's frontier force and captured Fort Pitt, "there could remain no resource." André ended by wondering whether Arnold could be "promised provincial major general's rank; he asks his own rank in the British army."

Clinton was more amused than impressed with his young favorite's castles in the air; and he thought his letter indiscreet. The cautious commander was not certain who they were communicating with: Stansbury might be a Rebel agent trying to gather intelligence by using Arnold's name. And in any case, Clinton was far from "sanguine in my ideas of General Arnold's consequence, as he was said to be in a sort of disgrace . . . and not likely to be employed," which "made him less an object of my attention."

Under Clinton's instructions, André wrote Arnold that, since the British could not reveal their plans, he should himself suggest an effective stroke. Intelligence so definite that it led to a specific victory "shall be rewarded beyond your warmest expectations." Better yet, Arnold should "join the army, accept a command, be surprised, cut off—these things may happen in the course of maneuver, nor you be censured or suspected. A complete service of this nature, involving a corps of five or six thousand men, would be rewarded with twice as many thousand guineas."

Eager to make certain he was really in touch with Arnold and to discuss methods for damaging the Rebels, André suggested fatefully "my meeting you as a flag of truce or otherwise as soon as you come near us."

After his return from the frustrations of Washington's headquarters, Arnold indicated his continuing interest in treason by sending André some intelligence, none of it important. Then he could only wait for an answer to his previous letter. Forty-five days dragged by before Stansbury appeared with the expected sheet from André. Peggy received it and told the go-between to return for her husband's answer.

Even before they started to decode, the Arnolds were horrified, for the handwriting was strange; although they did not know it was Odell's, they realized that the British had taken an unauthorized person into the plot. And as the words came clear, their gloom and rage deepened. When Stansbury reappeared, he was informed that "a multiplicity of business prevented" Arnold from giving the business the requisite attention. Three days passed and then the agent called again. Arnold, he was told, "had made some progress with an answer" which he intended to send to the crockery shop that evening. A servant in Arnold's livery appeared on schedule, but the note he handed Stansbury stated that Arnold "had carefully examined the letter, and found by the laconic style, and little attention paid to his request, that the gentlemen appeared very indifferent respecting the matter. He therefore omitted sending me the memo he intended in the morning, and wished to see me."

Behind locked doors a heated discussion went on between the agent, the beauty, and the general. Stansbury lied, assuring the terrified conspirators that Odell had not known to whom the letter he had coded was addressed. Then Arnold insisted that he was not satisfied to be offered payment only if his treasonous activities produced concrete, valuable results. "He expects," Stansbury wrote André, "to have your promise that he shall be indemnified for any loss he may sustain in case of detection, and, whether this contest is finished by sword or treaty, that ten thousand pounds shall be engaged him for his services." Arnold sent some information, most of it discouraging to the British—"plenty of everything at camp supplied from everywhere"—and none of it specific enough to produce a definite coup. Peggy added a list of goods she would like André to procure for her in New York: material for a pale pink dress of mantua decorated with broad ribbon of the same color, satin for shoes, diaper for napkins, and "one pr. neat spurs. . . . She will pay for the whole with thanks."

In the same packet to André, Stansbury offered the services of another spy, Samuel Wallis, whose plans for defeating Sullivan's expedition against Detroit included a false map that would lose the army in the wilderness where the British could surround them. Also enclosed was a sealed letter from the Arnolds to Major Aquilla Giles, an American prisoner at Flatbush whose friendship with Peggy's circle is attested to by a jealous note from the Tory girl he was currently courting: "Your correspondents in the other lines, you tell me, are all of the male kind. Now that is a fib. I beg you will not conceive I profess your ceasing to correspond with the *fair Philadelphians*." She mentions Becky Franks and "the other ladies."

Stansbury's "Mercury"—probably Rattoon—set out with the thick packet which, if discovered, might well cost his life. What flight, what terrified hiding lies beneath Odell's statement that he was "detained by some embarrassments on the way"?

In the meantime, Arnold wrote Washington pleading for an early court martial that would rescue him from his "cruel situation. . . . My wounds are so far recovered that I can walk with ease, and I expect soon to be able to ride on horseback." To restore his slipping fortunes by effective service either to the patriot or the British cause, Arnold needed to be acquitted. Only then could he secure a command which he could lead, as circumstances dictated, to glorious victory or prearranged defeat. Washington replied that the trial could only take place after the end of the campaign.

When Stansbury's packet finally reached New York, Odell was afraid that André would throw up the whole negotiation in disgust, particularly as "the late unfortunate event [Wayne, taking a leaf from Grey's book, had recaptured Stony Point using only the bayonet] may . . . render it difficult for you to find time at present to attend to a *seemingly* fruitless correspondence." He urged André to write "once more at least, as it cannot do any harm, and *may* possibly be still worthwhile."

André tossed Peggy's shopping list in a drawer and wrote Arnold that he would get no money until he had procured "real advantage" or made "a generous effort. . . . Permit me to prescribe a little exertion." Rather than limiting himself to "general intelligence," Arnold should send "an accurate plan of West Point" (now first mentioned) and specific information concerning the boats guarding the Hudson River. The "order of battle" of the American army would also be welcome.

"Would you assume a command and enable me to see you, I am convinced a conversation of a few minutes would satisfy you entirely, and I trust would give us equal cause to be pleased." Although André looked forward eagerly to this interview, Clinton could not help wondering whether an older and more experienced soldier would not be more suited to so dangerous and complicated a mission. He forced his aide to suggest an alternate plan: General William Phillips, who had been captured with Burgoyne and was interned in Virginia, could be brought to New York on parole and pass through Philadelphia where he would confer with Arnold. Either stratagem was a violation of the rules of honorable war. If André met Arnold, he intended to do so under a flag of truce; flags did not legally cover suborning treason. If Phillips met Arnold, he would violate the word of honor he gave when he signed his parole.

André's letter did not budge Arnold, who replied verbally through Stansbury, "However sincerely he wished to serve his country in accelerating the settlement of this unhappy conflict," he would be unjust to his family to "hazard his all . . . and part with a certainty (potentially at least) for an uncertainty." He refused to write himself or send any more information until he was guaranteed payment, but he would be glad to talk to Phillips or, as he planned to "join the army in about three weeks," arrange a rendezvous with André.

That Arnold did not get off to camp when he said he would may have increased British suspicion that they were not really in touch with the general. In any case, Major Giles was allowed to return to Philadelphia on parole and entrusted with a letter, seemingly innocuous, which he was certain to deliver to Peggy. "It would make me very happy," André wrote, "to become useful to you here" as her milliner by entering "into the whole detail of cap wire, needles, gauze, etc., and, to the best of my abilities, render you in these trifling services from which I hope you would infer a zeal to be further employed." Peggy's reaction was to ask Stansbury why her earlier request for dress materials had not been filled. The question moved secretly in code across New Jersey and elicited Odell's reply that he had been stopped by being unable to secure a suitable means of conveyance. However, even now the goods were not bought. Late in October, a note was handed to André:

"Mrs. Arnold presents her best respects to Captain André, is much obliged to him for his very polite and friendly offer of being serviceable to her. Major Giles was so obliging as to promise to procure what trifles Mrs. Arnold wanted in the millinery way, or she would with pleasure have accepted it."

Thus Peggy brought the treason negotiations to a close. Since the devil would not meet her husband's price, Arnold would keep his soul, and—for the time being at least—try to achieve wealth and new glory as a patriot.

CHAPTER TWENTY-TWO

Interlude for Drums

WHEN a general tries to sell his honor it is hardly pleasant to lack for takers, or to be lectured by an enemy subaltern. "Permit me," André had written, "to prescribe a little exertion." During the summer and fall of 1779, Arnold seems to have been incapable of exertion. His health went up and down, but vigor did not return to him. General Lincoln, who had been wounded at the same time as Arnold but more severely, had been on active duty for a year; there were still weeks when Arnold could not walk. The difference, as the doctors pointed out, was in the two men's mental attitudes.

Arnold was as defeated as it is possible for a man with a beautiful wife to be. As her tender young body swelled into pregnancy, Peggy was a joy, but around her shining image everything was black. Even if he became well enough, he could not secure a command until he was cleared by a court which he could not induce to convene. All sense of common purpose with his fellow men was shattered; except when he spoke to his wife or Stansbury, he spoke as a hypocrite. If any other person he met found out what he had done, he would be hanged by the neck until he was dead.

His prosperity, too, was falling apart. Since most deals profitable in those war-torn days were considered by zealots like Reed unpatriotic or illegal, merchants considered secrecy essential. Perpetually under Reed's scrutiny, Arnold was a dangerous man to do business with. Furthermore, he had lost what had been his greatest trading assets, influence and official position. The owners of privateers,[1] we are told, at one time cut him into their profits "in return for his countenance and protection"; now they tried to "exact his proportion" of all losses, and the knowledge of his difficulties only served to make them more urgent.

It became essential for Arnold to collect the money which he insisted Congress owed him. On top of the bills running back to his expedition up the Kennebec, which he had never been able to substantiate to Congress's satisfaction, were new bills resulting from the elaborate establishment he had kept as commandant of Philadelphia, of which many congressmen had disapproved. His charge for £5,000 for nine months, Arnold insisted, was reasonable considering the high cost of everything and how much his position had forced him to entertain. When the Treasury Board pointed out that he had taken endless supplies from the public stores, he replied that he had a right to twenty-eight rations—fifteen for himself and one for each of his aides and servants—because he was a major general. He made concession difficult by insisting that the payments given him for expenses would be a precedent and asking General Heath to discuss the matter with his fellow generals: "I do not think myself at liberty to agree to any settlement which will involve them without their approbation."

For nine months Arnold had wrangled intermittently with the Treasury Board. He "relied on his military character rather than the accuracy of his vouchers" and insisted that the commissioners, activated by personal malice, purposely mislaid papers that were to his advantage. When the board finally gave up in despair, Congress appointed a special committee, but the committee could get nowhere, and, at last, Congress again referred Arnold's claims to the board which had already denied them. Despite Arnold's shrill protests, the board stuck to their guns, offering him 2,328 Continental dollars. This came to $485 in gold, hardly enough to keep up his establishment for a few days.

Congress also refused to take a stand on their dispute with Pennsylvania over the *Active;* they sat idly by while the state paid Arnold's partners only £12,570 of the £51,000 they had resolved was due them. When Jay nominated Arnold for the Board of War, his fellow legislators persuaded him to withdraw the name that would loose a storm of controversy.

This was no moment to take any action that would encourage disunion, for civil war was already brewing on the streets of Philadelphia. When the Republican Society, that organ of merchants sympathetic to Arnold, tried to hold a mass meeting, club-swinging bullies had silenced General Cadwalader. Mobs broke shop windows and then the militia marched into town determined to arrest the speculators they accused of creating high prices. A group of merchants, barricaded in James Wilson's mansion, were soon besieged; muskets cracked and bleeding men fell to the ground. In his own house nearby, Arnold heard the shots and remembered how the militia had always obeyed him, even when he led them to death. He resolved to stop the battle.

His feet did not carry him quickly as of old; he limped down the street on his high heel. When the militiamen saw him approach, a cry came from their throats. It was not a cheer, but a shout of rage. They threw stones, forcing Arnold into a hobbling retreat. Two men dashed at him. He threatened them with his pistols and was able to gain the safety of his own house. He barricaded the doors and windows, waited grimly for an attack. Then word came that the militia which no longer listened to his voice had been quieted by his archenemy, Joseph Reed.

Arnold complained to Congress that "an honest man" could expect no protection from the Pennsylvania authorities; he wanted "a guard of Continental troops." Congress referred the letter to Reed, who supplied Arnold with a Pennsylvania guard. While such militiamen as he had once led paced outside his house, hating the man they were protecting, Arnold played at being a philosopher. He had a microscope and an electrical machine; he tried some experiments—but the instruments blurred as there sounded in his mind's ear water cascading down the Kennebec, shots from high walls, the yells of men applauding a great leader.

André, too, was having his troubles. For some time he had "bent all my views toward the rank of major." Although he was only a young captain, Clinton would undoubtedly approve the promotion if the necessary commission could be bought from a retiring officer. The cost would be " £2,100 or more." André "was offering the sums of money then in my power to obtain it, when it pleased M. D'Estaing to interfere, and all my golden dreams vanished."

The French admiral had captured the West Indian island of Grenada on which the Andrés' prosperity was based. Assuming that his family would have to alter "their mode of life," John offered to give his pay as aide-de-camp to his mother, living on his salary as captain. He had kept no records, he wrote, but he assumed that he must have some savings in England. Far from being "very lavish," he had in the previous year drawn only £300, of which he still had £80. Upwards of £100 had been given to "friend William," his brother.

When André had forced the youngster into the army, he had taken it for granted that their tastes were alike—but William had shown no interest in his military duties, run over his income, and forced André to pay his debts. He was, the ambitious staff officer complained, "rather indolent and negligent as to his person. He reads, though at present only books of amusement; they will lead him to others giving more instruction." André lectured the youngster on the necessity of living within his pay, as he himself now had to do.

"While I was lamenting my disappointment," André wrote home, "the post of adjutant general became vacant by the resignation of Lord Rawdon, and the deputy adjutant general, Colonel Kemble, became desirous for private reasons to withdraw himself likewise. [Kemble's private reasons were that he feared André, a much junior officer, would be put over his head.] . . . Here then was the first office in a large army vacant. The discharge of its functions, though not the office itself, I conceived to be within my reach, and I saw the opportunity of getting the wished-for rank [major] at small expense. My wishes were gratified. I saw myself selected by the commander in chief to fill the station of deputy adjutant general in the room of Colonel Kemble, with the rank of major, and with all the duties of the principal of the department [Clinton appointed no full adjutant general]." André's commission was dated October 23, 1779.

"You may well conceive how much I am flattered at being called in the space of three years from a subaltern in the Fusiliers to the employment I hold, and the favor in which I live with the commander in chief." However, his eyes were fixed even higher. "Should I continue to deserve the general's favor and he continue many months more in command; should success attend the present expedition and cheerfulness prevail, perhaps it is not unreasonable to hope to be vested with the honors of the office I shall virtually have discharged, and to be appointed adjutant general."

Since André's regiment was going home, he had been forced to exchange his regimental commission (which, despite his staff appointment, remained his basic rank in the army) with his brother's; William was glad to leave. A second exchange was also required. The result lowered André's seniority, placing him "at the bottom of the captains" in the Fifty-fourth. He realized that, should he lose Clinton's favor or his commander be recalled, he might well "stagnate" in that regiment "with the rank of major doing captain's duty, and with the retrospect of my disappointment for the amusement of my leisure hours; and I keep this in view, both to be prepared for the event as well as for a spur to deserve that it should not happen."

Many officers would have enjoyed his predicament had André fallen. Although he had bought off his predecessor, Kemble, with various financial promises, that disgruntled functionary insisted that Clinton was "despised and detested by the army for his un-heard-of promotion to the first department of boys not three years in the service, his neglect of old officers, and his wavering, strange, mad behavior." Others whispered that "Major André had the ad-dress to insinuate himself so much into the favor of the commander in chief" that he "gained absolute ascendancy over that officer. The consequence was that he disposed of all favors and offices, and drove out of Sir Henry Clinton's family all his former friends and favorites, who possessed too much independence of soul to accept anything through the medium of Mr. André, and were too honest to stoop to use those means by which this pattern of virtue suc-ceeded." André's methods had been those of "a cringing, insidious sycophant."

Highborn officers found pleasure in taking a fall out of the up-start. When Lord Cathcart expressed rage at receiving orders signed by André, the adjutant replied, "I imagined, perhaps improperly, that a signature in an official capacity implied the commander in chief's authority. . . . Every future letter will have every form his Lordship wishes." However, André's correspondents usually did the cringing. Typical was one who had sent him some "profiles of fortifications," and then quickly explained that he would not have been so presumptuous "had I known that among your other talents you were a master of this."

When he had merely been one of Clinton's aides, officers had asked him crisply to call this or that to his superior's attention; now they were more likely to write André, "I wish to avoid encroaching upon those moments which you employ so diligently in the public service, but if anything I have said should appear to you worthy of His Excellency's notice, I know you will excuse me." André's official letters—even when addressed to such intimates as Simcoe—contain no charm or unnecessary courtesy; they are unadorned assertions of power. Sometimes, having to remind himself that the authority he wielded was not his own, he added to a letter he had already written in his own person such a phrase as "the commander in chief asks me to tell you. . . ."

In charge of Clinton's entire office, André handed routine intelligence activities over to his friend Oliver De Lancey and kept for himself the specialty that gave him the greatest influence in the army. Managing "military applications"—assignments and promotions—he forced all officers who wished favors to come to him. Most matters he settled at once, and, when he called more important ones to Clinton's attention, he often jogged the commander's elbow by asking "may not" such a thing be done, or "should it not be ordered that . . . ?" Clinton usually answered "yes" or "certainly." As Jones commented, he was the general's "first friend," his "best adviser," his "bosom confidant."

André soon had a chance to play his new role during a major campaign. The 8,500 men who in December 1779 marched into transports were all, in one way or another, subject to his power. Their objective was South Carolina. Stymied in the northern and central states, the British were attacking the South, where patriotism was considered less rampant and the Continental Army was not in residence. Savannah had been captured the year before; now Clinton intended to take Charleston.

After seven storm-tossed weeks on the ocean and a month's wait for reinforcements, the British finally advanced against the city. André, who had suffered so much from the Americans' inept nibbling at St. Johns, had the pleasure of ordering out professional soldiers to begin a scientific siege. But one day a detail that had gathered on the parade ground did not march. While André's back was turned orders had been given—"I know not for what cause . . . I know not by whom"—that Hessian officers command British grenadiers. This started an underground intrigue which produced further mysterious orders, and when the troops were lined up, almost every officer present found cause to be offended. The Hessians shouted in their best gutturals; the British responded with Anglo-Saxon profanity; and "General Leslie, who commanded the whole, was concerned to see so much displeasure." Everyone turned on the deputy adjutant general, and long-suppressed resentment came out in charges that "I supinely decree fatigues I am unacquainted with." Attracted by the noise, Clinton appeared, and for once he did not support his favorite. This, he said, was what came of André's foolish idea that special detachments be organized for special work, rather than having brigades go out under their own officers.

Back in his quarters, André started to write Clinton: "For my own part I have seldom suffered so much anxiety. I feared I might be the source of every misapprehension and dreaded—" He stopped, scratched out the too emotional words, and substituted, "These are matters which gave me much anxiety." He insisted that he had not known of the changes in command that had made the trouble and argued that special detachments for special work made possible a more equitable distribution of unpleasant tasks. Far from living at ease while others labored, he had not for seven weeks slept one night in two. The commander in chief was mollified.

There can be no foundation for the legend that André dressed up as a Rebel militiaman and slipped into Charleston; the adjutant considered such routine spying far beneath his social station; and he had more important things to do. Trained in Germany as a military engineer, he directed the approach of trenches toward the city walls, the safe advance of cannon, the protection of work parties. He set up an office to screen inhabitants who claimed trust or special privileges because they were Tories; he established policies for commandeering cows and encouraging slaves to leave their masters; he untangled supply lines, improvised hospitals, and ironed out squabbles on every level from lieutenants to generals.

Clinton was on bad terms with his associates. Moving as cautiously through rival headquarters as a cat in a strange backyard, André tried to mediate between high officers many years his senior. Even the staid *Dictionary of National Biography* describes the autonomous naval commander, Admiral Marriot Arbuthnot, as "a coarse, foul-mouthed, blustering bully"; Clinton considered him senile. André spent hours edging the suspicious sailor toward some desired decision only to have Arbuthnot forget the next morning that the interview had ever taken place.

Another difficulty endangered André's future as well as his general's. Although Clinton, who had repeatedly asked to be relieved of the ungrateful American assignment, had received no hint that his resignation had been accepted, his second in command, Lord Cornwallis, had been interfering so aggressively in top policies that Clinton suspected Cornwallis had heard from London that he was to succeed to the high command. In a memorandum which reveals that Clinton shared his most intimate worries with André, the aide agreed that, if Cornwallis were about to take over, his approval should be secured for every move, so that, should he later botch the siege, he could not blame his own failures on Clinton's previous maneuvers. If, on the other hand, Cornwallis were not to be promoted, Clinton could ignore his advice.

Cornwallis, so André's memorandum continued, had suddenly changed his tack, offering no further suggestions, disclaiming responsibility for those he had already given, and hinting that he would like to undertake some expedition on his own. Clinton seems to have feared that his second in command had some secret reason for regarding the Charleston siege as a failure and was trying to get out from under. André tried to reassure his ever-apprehensive commander. It was unlikely, he wrote, that Cornwallis had "begun to despond," or that "he wishes to be exempted from relieving Your Excellency from a portion of your cares." Rather, he "has been influenced *hitherto* by a degree of ambition industriously set in motion," and realized that he was opening himself to "*future inquiries*" on his insubordinate behavior. He wished only to pull in his horns and undertake "particular points of attack or particular marches" with a self-contained force. André advised Clinton not to try to get rid of Cornwallis completely, but to use him for what he was worth.

The siege went well. One evening a British shovel, digging into a wall, created a cascade and changed the American moat into an English trench. Soon the defenses were so undermined that, without waiting for an assault, General Lincoln acknowledged the superiority of British military science by surrendering the city and a considerable portion of the Rebel army.

André thereupon outlined for his commander the steps that he believed would end the war. In a passage that might have been written by Arnold, he discounted the idea that idealism could be a major motivating force: "Fear, interest, and family ties are the main springs of men's actions. . . . I ascribe to local circumstances and the want of interior resources the friendship of the Americans." Thus, he pointed out, the areas around New York that, although behind the Rebel lines, were accessible to British arms, "contain many active friends," while the far side of unfordable rivers "breathes the rankest rebellion."

As a whole, the northern Colonies were too well protected by their geography to be "wantonly" invaded. Assured of a safe retreat, "perfidious thousands . . . singly take the field against us from every tree and house and . . . though driven from our front, close with redoubled inveteracy on our flank and rear." In this area, the operations called for were "excursions of partisans, devastation to give us a frontier, and, lastly, a rapid movement to bring Washington into action."

The Carolinas, Virginia, and southeastern Pennsylvania presented a more favorable aspect. Once the coast was seized and the rivers used by the British navy to break up inland communication, trade would be annihilated and "nakedness must ensue. . . . Their property [slaves] we need not seek; it flies to us and famine follows." The inhabitants, knowing they were helpless, would be quiet under British garrisons while the main army extended its conquests. To complete this attractive picture, André's mind ran to West Point: "Should we be able to add to our other advantages the possession of the Highlands, the communication of supplies as well as the junction of force would be still further impeded." New England would be virtually cut off from the central colonies.

André proposed the establishment of two British armies, "each inferior in numbers to Washington yet supposed equal to receive his attack," one operating from the South, the other from New York. This would leave the Continental Army "the choice of attacking one corps and exposing their communications to the other, of starving within their stronghold, or of fighting our joint force."

As always, André urged a more violent conduct of the war. To "military prudence" and the welfare of the army "every ancient principle of forbearance toward the inhabitants must give way." Only if the Rebels were treated not as legitimate soldiers but as traitors would the British be enabled to "move through the country without the disgraceful annoyance that the peasants have dared to give them." When an area was under attack, should any groups "dare to remain in arms—much more, should any parties of single men dare to infest the roads and communications—fire and sword should cut them off, or civil justice bring the desperate subjects to the gallows."

The gallows: for peasants, they were a terrifying possibility; for gentleman soldiers, a joke. Some months before, André had mocked the official documents he prepared all day with a super-official document in French. "The undersigned, John André," he began, and repeated all the titles for himself he could think of; mentioning Clinton, he added another string of titles; and then he certified "to all those to whom it appertains that the Chevalier de l'Anos is a tremendous crook, etc., etc. In the testimony of which we have sealed this document with our seal of arms." To the laughter of his companions, André sketched for himself a comic seal. He drew a circle and in it a man hanging from a gibbet.

One day before André had set out for South Carolina, on December 23, 1779, Arnold's court martial had finally convened at Morristown. As the date approached, his spirits had lifted—he told Peggy that he expected a quick acquittal—and the pain went out of his leg until he could limp, on his high-heeled shoe, with an approximation of his old energy. Nor, as the trial progressed, did he find much cause for worry. His enemies had failed to unearth, in support of the four charges under consideration, any evidence against which he did not feel sure he could defend himself.

The argument on the *Charming Nancy* pass ran on whether or not the boat's owners were "disaffected persons," a matter easily confused. Concerning the charge that he had speculated when the shops were closed, the prosecution—ignorant of his contract with the clothiers general—could cite nothing but his agreement, which predated the closings, to back purchases made by Franks; and Franks testified he had made no purchases. The question whether Arnold had imposed menial duties on militiamen was limited to the furor caused by young Matlack's being sent for Franks's barber, a feeble issue certainly when separated from the explosive tempers that had raised it. The charge that he had used public wagons to carry private property took most of the court's time, and turned on the question whether Colonel John Mitchell, the wagon-master, had done Arnold a favor—in which case the fault was his—or had been obeying the orders of his superior officer when he sent out the teams.

Acting as Arnold's agent in Philadelphia, Peggy tried to get Mitchell to testify, but he was determined not to be involved. "You mention Sunday for your return," she wrote her husband. "I will not flatter myself I shall see you even then if you wait for Colonel Mitchell. . . . I never wanted to see you half so much. . . . Farewell, I need not say how affectionately." Securing an adjournment, Arnold made a flying trip to Philadelphia and brought the recalcitrant witness back with him. However, Mitchell was little help to either side: he said that Arnold had requested, not ordered the wagons—but he had felt it his "duty" to comply.

In his summary for the defense, Arnold, who had once regarded his honor as his proudest possession, denied "on the honor of a gentleman and a soldier" that he had bought when the shops were closed. If it had been unwise to grant the *Charming Nancy* pass, that was no more than "an error in judgment." The militia charge was achieved by "a strained construction of the sentiments I expressed." He had never hidden the use for which he wished the wagons, and it was to the public interest to prevent the property of patriots from falling into enemy hands.

Turning from the four charges on which he was being tried

to the four others published by the Pennsylvania Council, Arnold lied on the *Active* matter, denying that he was financially involved. Now that he was speaking for publication, he did not say, as he had done previously, that he had given Hannah Levy a pass for secret government business: he had wished to help her collect money due in New York to her aged and blind mother. As to the Supreme Executive Council of Pennsylvania, since, "activated by the passions of anger or envy" they used their public power for character assassination, "they must not think it extraordinary if they are not treated with all the deference which they may think their due." He was not warmer to Tories than "was justifiable on the principles of common humanity and politeness." He considered it enough "to contend with men in the field; I have not yet learned to carry on a warfare against women."

More revealing than the substance of his defense are his embellishments: "I was one of the first that appeared in the field," he stated, "and from that time to the present hour have not abandoned her [America's] service." Describing himself as a hero "charged with practices the soul abhors," he read what had been his prize possessions, letters from Washington and resolutions of Congress in praise of his patriotism. Was it probable, he asked, that a man so honored "should all at once sink into a course of conduct equally unworthy of the patriot and the soldier?" No! "My conduct from the earliest period of the war to the present time has been steady and uniform." He charged that this could not be said for Reed, who was rumored to have wanted to sell out when Washington was fleeing across New Jersey. Although Arnold had recently sent information on Washington to the enemy, he shouted, "I can say I never basked in the sunshine of my general's favor and courted him to his face when I was at the same time treating him with the greatest disrespect and vilifying his character when absent."

If he had speculated while the shops were closed (as he knew he had done), "I stand confessed, in the presence of this honorable court, the vilest of men. I stand stigmatized with indelible disgrace, the disgrace of having abused an appointment of high trust and importance to accomplish the meanest and most unworthy purposes; the blood I have spent in the defense of my country will be insufficient to obliterate the stain."

These words that seemed to his hearers self-righteous eloquence were to his inner ear the most frightful self-accusations. Why did he speak these terrible words; they were not essential to his defense? Was he posturing before the court, or defying his own conscience?

Arnold was so convinced that the evidence that had been presented was in no way damaging that he later circulated the proceedings widely, and wished to have them published in France; he awaited "the judgment of my fellow soldiers . . . with pleasing anxiety." On January 26, 1780, he sat cockily in the courtroom, expecting to hear his acquittal; he was rocked back in his chair.

The judges exonerated him of mistreating the militia and buying when the shops were closed, but found him guilty on the other two counts. The *Charming Nancy* pass, they ruled, violated the catchall section in the Articles of War which forbade without specification acts "to the prejudice of good order and military discipline." Although they absolved him of fraudulent intent in his use of the wagons, "considering the delicacy attending the high station in which the general acted, and that requests from him might operate as commands, they are of opinion the request was imprudent and improper." Arnold was sentenced to receive a reprimand from Washington. The muscles in his damaged leg cramped, and the man who had limped briskly into the courtroom hobbled out an invalid.

Congress approved the verdict with only Robert R. Livingston and two other members dissenting. Before Washington took any action, he examined the court record: he saw nothing there that indicated more than bad judgment or that impugned Arnold's future usefulness. Phrasing his reprimand as gently as he could, he wrote that he would have been "much happier in an occasion of bestowing commendations on an officer who has rendered such distinguished services to his country as Major General Arnold; but in the present case a sense of duty and a regard to candor oblige him to declare that he considers his conduct in the instance of the permit as particularly reprehensible, both in a civil and military view, and in the affair of the wagons as 'imprudent and improper.' "

Benedict had made his great social splash as resident in the Penn mansion; he had brought his bride there to share its glories. Now Jean Holker, the French consul general, who had used his official position more successfully in speculation, moved into the great rooms where the Arnolds had entertained. The impoverished Arnolds retired to a simple house that was one of Edward Shippen's real-estate speculations.

Since the quickest of all ways to make money was to capture naval prizes, Arnold proposed to the Board of Admiralty that he command a fleet of frigates operating from New London. He wrote Washington that he needed four or five hundred soldiers to man the boats. Although his stiff ankle still barred him from military duty, "my surgeons flatter me" that a sea voyage "will be of great service in strengthening my leg and relaxing the muscles which are greatly contracted." If Washington could not spare the soldiers, Arnold wanted a leave of absence until he was well enough "to take command of a division of the army."

After Arnold had prodded him with two letters, Washington wrote that he had sent his answer, as was proper, directly to the Admiralty Board. The answer was no. Arnold's alternate scheme, which was to command a privateer fitting in Boston, also came to nothing.

Little Edward Shippen Arnold was now screaming from his crib, another son to provide for, when the general put on his best uniform and called on the new French minister, La Luzerne; if George III would not buy his services, perhaps Louis XVI would. His financial difficulties, he told the diplomat, were becoming so great that he would have to leave the army. But a French loan would keep him available to the common cause and also encourage a gratitude to France which he would seek every opportunity to repay. Trying not to look at Arnold's short leg or smile at the thought of buying such damaged merchandise, La Luzerne read Arnold a lecture on the virtue required of public servants. No wonder, when Arnold's "private correspondence" was rifled after his treason, it was found to contain "the most sarcastic and contemptuous expressions of the French nation" and particularly of La Luzerne.

While his mind dashed in every direction that might offer escape from his predicament, Arnold, it is said, dreamed, as so many

American misfits have done, of opportunities beyond the furthest frontier. He would strip off the laces of the polite world that had served him so badly; wearing feathers and wampum he would gather the Indians together into a great confederation. As thousands of muskets and scalping-knives under his command made the poltroons in Congress tremble, he would stop the encroachments of unworthy politicians on the land of noble warriors. Moving in his chair with excitement, he felt pain in the shortened leg that could never again run on Indian trails.

Finally, there separated from the despairing thoughts that jumbled through Benedict Arnold's mind a single sharp vision: the vision of West Point.

CHAPTER TWENTY-THREE

Lust for West Point

A YEAR had passed since Arnold had made his first offer to become a traitor. During that time he had vacillated, hoping sometimes to convince himself that his earlier belief in independence had been justified; hoping that a turn of the cards would enable him to achieve once more fame and wealth as a patriot. But early in May 1780, he began, through a Loyalist merchant in New York, to shift his movable assets to London.

Arnold expatiated to Schuyler on his desire to be assigned West Point as a post suited to a man not well enough for active service; Schuyler, who was on his way to see Washington at Morristown, promised to use his influence. Although this command would present a patriotic soldier no opportunities for fame, it would give Arnold something of great value to sell. Control of the fortress would enable Clinton to cut the United States in half at the Hudson River.

Once more Peggy's head leaned against Arnold's own as they prepared a new offer to the British high command. Deciding not to mention West Point for the moment, as Arnold might fail to get the assignment, they stated that, after a brief business trip to Connecticut, he would remain at Washington's encampment "in a military capacity," and that he "particularly desires to have a conference with an officer of confidence." He could help in an attack on Boston, Philadelphia, "or any other place. . . . Were it not for his family," Arnold "would without ceremony have thrown himself into the protection of the King's army." As it was, he wanted to be guaranteed "in case of emergency" £10,000, one half to indemnify him for the loss of his private fortune, the other half for his expectations from the American government: the old demand.

After Stansbury had begun another perilous journey to British headquarters, Arnold sent to American headquarters a letter reminding Schuyler of his interest in West Point. "Though my wounds make it very painful for me to walk or ride," he explained, he wished "to render every service in my power."

When Stansbury did not return in time, Arnold postponed his Connecticut trip: he had "a very violent cold." His courier finally appeared with a message. It was not from Clinton and André, who were still in South Carolina, but from Wilhelm von Knyphausen. The Hessian general could do no more, in the absence of his commander, than express his belief in Arnold's "rectitude and sincerity"; and pay out small sums for the expenses of the intrigue. To assist communication, he sent a pocket dictionary on which to base a code, and one of two identical rings. The other would be on the finger of a man who would meet Arnold at Washington's encampment.

During the previous negotiations, when Arnold had not been certain of his direction, such a reply would have discouraged him; now he was urged to greater zeal. He had on his desk a proclamation to be printed in French; Washington had sent it to him with many cautions of "secrecy" lest it give away an American plan to invade Canada. On the same day that he reassured Washington, Arnold sent the proclamation to Knyphausen with further information wormed from the French minister: 8,000 troops were expected from France to join in the northern campaign. Arnold gave the British an itinerary of his own Connecticut trip: "If I meet with a person of my mensuration [he would deal with no subordinates], who has the token agreed upon, you may expect every intelligence in my power."

This letter was on the road when Arnold heard from Schuyler that Washington would not commit himself on West Point, but "expressed himself with regard to you in terms such as the friends who love you could wish. . . . He expressed a desire to do whatever was agreeable to you, dwelt on your abilities, your merits, your sufferings, and the well-earned claims you have on your country." (Washington later claimed that he had not delivered this panegyric; perhaps Schuyler, sensing Arnold's peculiar state of mind, was trying to encourage him.) The State of New York, Schuyler continued, "will wish to see its banner entrusted to you. If the command of West Point is offered, it will be agreeable; if a division in the field, you must judge whether you can support the fatigue."

Any qualms these expressions of patriot affection gave Arnold were only momentary. When he reached headquarters early in June, he asked questions so that he could betray the answers. He jotted down more information about the projected invasion of Canada, and that "six French ships of the line, several frigates, and a number of transports with 6,000 troops are expected at Rhode Island in two or three weeks." A postscript implied an encouraging talk with Washington: he expected "to have the command of West Point offered him on his return." Arnold managed to send this message directly from Morristown to New York, but it could not have been by a comparison of rings with Knyphausen's representative, since the British remained unsure that their correspondent was really Arnold.

On his way to Connecticut, the traitor stopped off to examine the fortifications he hoped to command and betray. General Robert Howe showed him around with pleasure, and from nearby Fishkill, Arnold wrote the British that the garrison was mean and too badly provisioned to withstand a siege; the chain which was supposed to block the river could be broken by "a single ship, large and heavily loaded, with a strong wind." The works were "wretchedly planned"—he told the British exactly how best to storm them —and, if attacked before expected reinforcements arrived from Albany, would undoubtedly fall.

The day after this letter was written, Clinton and André sailed into New York. They had wanted to complete the conquest of the South, but Admiral Arbuthnot was afraid of the French navy, and Clinton, who could not separate the main army from its transports, was forced to join the retreat, leaving Cornwallis to continue the campaign.

Had Clinton and André desired to follow Arnold's advice by making an immediate attack on West Point, they could not have done so, for "to our great surprise," as André wrote, they "found General Knyphausen, with every soldier he could squeeze from New York and its posts, in Jersey." The Hessian had been told that Washington lacked horses to withdraw artillery and stores, and that the Continental Army were "so dissatisfied they would desert and crumble into our hands." This, André moralized, was due to incautious intelligence work, to believing "anonymous letters," "sanguine enthusiasts," and people who for their own purposes "are ever stimulating deep play. . . . It exposed the troops in a march of a day to a loss of more men than Carolina cost us, and, as we went to demolish an army we could not get at, so we went to receive the submission of a country we could not protect, and, of course, a country inimical."

As soon as the renewed overtures were reported to him, André dispatched two spies to check Arnold's movements with the itinerary sent in Arnold's name. The traitor did not keep to his schedule, which must have created confusion, but André received word from a Jersey outpost that "our friend is certainly traveling in Connecticut."

Preparing for a switch of sides, Arnold was trying to change his property and prospects into cash. He wanted rapid payment from the legislature at Hartford, which had agreed to indemnify him with the other Connecticut soldiers for depreciation in the value of their salaries; he hoped to secure state backing for his Connecticut protégés in the *Active* case. When he found nothing could be done at once, he entrusted both matters to an agent and hurried for New Haven to sell his house. He asked £1,000 in gold or "good sterling bills on France, Holland, or England," but, "as I have an opportunity of making a purchase that is convenient for me," would take half the sum in paper. Again he did not wait for the deal to go through. Fearing that the West Point assignment might be lost through default, he posted back to Washington's encampment as quickly as his wound would allow.

In Philadelphia, Peggy had induced the susceptible congressman, Robert R. Livingston, to write Washington that New York State lacked faith in the present commandant at West Point: "the post might most safely be confided to General Arnold." Thanking Livingston for his friendly advice, Washington replied that he would gladly give Arnold the assignment "if the operations of the campaign are such as to render it expedient to leave an officer of his rank in that command." He doubted that this would be the case. When Arnold reappeared at headquarters, Washington pointed out, with the most exasperating consideration for what he assumed would be his subordinate's feelings, that West Point would not suit so energetic a general, "as I should leave none in his garrison but invalids, because it would be entirely covered by the main army."

Entering his Philadelphia house after more than a month's absence, Arnold could hardly wait to get rid of the servants so that he could find out what word had come from the British. Peggy reported that there had been no word. (Clinton and André had been too busy extricating Knyphausen from New Jersey.) Arnold notified Stansbury that he himself would write another letter, but found his thoughts so confused they would not go down on paper. About midnight, he sent for the go-between to receive a verbal message.

Arnold wanted "a very explicit answer" on payment; he wanted a conference: "General Phillips might come out to negotiate an exchange of prisoners, or his own for Lincoln." He reported that while at camp he had penetrated into the very center of secret councils to discover that the preparations for a Canadian campaign, which he had previously reported, were a ruse to draw Clinton from New York City, the true objective when the French troops arrived. Two or three of the British spies on West Point were also in the pay of the Americans, to whom they often gave "important intelligence," a matter which should be remedied since, so Arnold stated with inaccurate optimism, he had been promised the command there. He was sure he could show "the proper officer" how the British could take the fortress "without loss."

After Stansbury had bowed his way out, smooth and sugary as ever, Arnold began to wonder whether the go-between had repeated the British messages as they had been written. Perhaps he had edited them to serve some deep purpose of his own. The more Arnold thought about it, the more convinced he became that this explained the strange indifference with which such invaluable offers had been received. He called in Samuel Wallis—how he got wind of André's other secret agent history records not—and persuaded the treacherous back-country militia colonel to carry to New York a letter phrased like an ordinary business document, and written in a disguised hand.

If "a mutual confidence between us is wanting," Arnold stated to André, ". . . our correspondence ought to end," but perhaps "the persons we have employed have deceived us." Then he upped his financial demands, asking that "£10,000 sterling, with near an equal sum of outstanding debts" be "put into stock [paid down] and the profits arising be equally divided [additional payment be made to him for future services]." The bearer should be given a thousand guineas, "on receipt of which I will transmit to you their full value in good French bills [news of the French fleet and army]." He again asked a conference.

As he tossed in bed that night, Arnold had a further frightening inspiration. Although he knew he had been in touch with André during the abortive negotiations of the previous year, he had no proof that any of his recent notes had been delivered in New York. Perhaps he was in contact only with Stansbury's crockery shop! As soon after dawn as one of his servants could move through the streets without attracting attention, he sent again for Wallis. He gave him a restatement in code of the intelligence he had dispatched through Stansbury. The mysterious numbers also revealed that suspicions of his new agent, as well as the old, had assailed Arnold in the dark hours. Wallis, he had decided, should be entrusted with only 200 guineas, and the rest of the thousand paid to "Captain A——." (Was Arnold so ill-informed about British affairs that he did not know his correspondent was now deputy adjutant general with the rank of major?) He urged Clinton to threaten the messenger with British "resentment in case he abuses the confidence placed in him—which will bring certain ruin on me."

Arnold added a passage to show Clinton that such a coup as he could deliver against the United States might really be the *coup de grâce:* "The mass of the people are heartily tired of the war and wish to be on their former footing. . . . The present struggles are like the pangs of a dying man, violent, but of short duration."

Behind his exaggeration lay considerable truth. Inflation and civilian apathy were rising to such a height that Washington had written Reed, "Every idea you can form of our distresses will fall short of the reality. There is such a combination of circumstances to exhaust the patience of the soldiery, that it begins at length to be worn out and we see in every line of the army the most serious features of mutiny and sedition. All our departments, all our operations, are at a stand." Washington felt that the country was "in such a state of insensibility and indifference to its interests" that "I have almost ceased to hope." Some of the forces that were pushing Arnold were pushing others; no one knew how many traitors were wearing Continental uniforms.

French action was the principal hope of the Americans and fear of the British. Although still not absolutely certain that Arnold was "the person who was writing," Clinton was inclined to "risk action" on his correspondent's report that the French were due at Rhode Island. He wished to retake the area before the enemy could arrive, but Arbuthnot "would not think this information good." He refused to supply transports.

Arnold's most recent communications through Stansbury and Wallis had not arrived when André made a further effort to determine exactly who his correspondent was. Spies confirmed that Arnold would certainly "be again employed." Allowing himself to nurture great hopes, Clinton confided to William Smith that "the rebellion would die with a crash." Smith, who was not in on the secret, "told him my opinion that it would die of consumption."

At long last, André was allowed to write Arnold a truly enthusiastic letter. Clinton was "much obliged to you for the useful intelligence" and convinced "of your desire to assist him." He was in favor of Arnold's delivering up West Point, and "could point out such plausible measures as would ward off all blame or suspicion." Arnold was to come to some place on the lines "which a flag of truce could reach" and then, on the excuse of sickness, wait for a British envoy. "Upon effective co-operation you shall experience the full measure of the national obligation," and, meanwhile, an "ample stipend" would be paid him.

313

When the messages Arnold had given Stansbury and Wallis, in which he definitely stated he would command West Point, finally reached André, the adjutant replied that he himself would meet Arnold at some secret place near the fortress.

Clinton, despite his misgivings, had agreed to let his inexperienced favorite conduct the negotiation. General Phillips was no longer available, and André pleaded hard because he had desperate need of a personal triumph. Lord Germain, Secretary of State for Colonies, had written Clinton, "The King, always desirous to show attention to your recommendation, is graciously pleased to approve of your appointing your own adjutant general, and also of Captain John André acting as deputy adjutant general; and with respect to his having the rank of major, had also consented to his promotion if he was found to be an old captain, and commanded me to consult Lord Amherst upon that appointment." Germain enclosed a letter from Amherst reporting that the only Andrés on the military list were young captains whose brevity of service made them ineligible for advancement. Germain assumed "some mistake has been made in the name," and added, "until that is set right, nothing further can be done in the matter."

The long-range advantage André had expected from his onerous post on the staff of a commander who might be recalled at any moment was that his provincial rank of major be confirmed in the regular service, securing him an important promotion "at small expense." Now the money he had given his predecessor in the adjutant's office seemed wasted, and the higher office he had hoped to secure from Clinton blocked. "I am deputy adjutant general still," he complained, "and without confirmation of rank. I do not, however, despair of its being granted me." No one could deny him if he arranged the capture of West Point.

The next communication from Arnold was disappointing. André's honeyed letter, with its vague promises of payment, had only annoyed the traitor into upping his financial demands. He wished to have assured him, whatever the outcome of their plot, £10,000 and an annual stipend of £500. In addition he wanted £20,000 for "West Point, the garrison, etc. . . . I expect a full and explicit answer." He said he was about to set out for the for-

314

tress, which he asserted he would command, but indicated his displeasure by sending no intelligence at all.

Clinton permitted André to meet these curt demands only in part. Although Arnold would not "be left a victim," the adjutant wrote, no huge sums could ever be promised irrespective of "services done." However, Clinton had allotted him £500 (half of what Arnold has asked) for the intelligence he had already sent, and was willing to meet Arnold's request for £20,000 for West Point, provided 3,000 men and a great quantity of artillery and stores were captured with the fortress.

Lest the traitor be too discouraged, André and his colleagues worked out a method to give him further assurances without committing the high command. Clinton, Odell wrote Stansbury, permitted him to say that he only objected to "indemnification as a preliminary. . . . In every possible event" Arnold would have no "cause to complain, and essential services *shall* be even profusely rewarded, far beyond the stipulated indemnification, etc." All matters would certainly be settled to "mutual satisfaction" at the meeting which André "is willing himself to effect" either under a flag of truce "or in whatever manner may at the time appear most eligible."

After the French had landed safely at Newport, Clinton and André embarked with 6,000 men on transports and sailed up Long Island Sound to attack the intruders. Washington countered by marching for the Hudson. Although Arnold had not received André's letter accepting his price for West Point, he hurried out from Philadelphia to secure that command.

From camp he wrote Peggy a letter which, if intercepted, would seem suitably patriotic, but which contained information useful to the enemy. He was "sorry to say" that Washington was not strong enough to attack New York City, even in Clinton's absence, but further French reinforcements were on the way that might make their fleet superior to the British. "So that, upon the whole," he wrote for different eyes to interpret different ways, "our affairs, which do not wear a pleasing aspect at present, may soon be greatly changed." Peggy handed the letter to Stansbury who hurried it across New Jersey.

Eager to hear confirmation of his West Point assignment, Arnold rode up as Washington, from a height near Stony Point, watched the Continental Army crawl in barges across the broad Hudson. He "asked me," the commander is reported to have remembered, "if I had thought of anything for him?" Yes, yes, Washington replied with a smile that anticipated Arnold's pleasure; he was to have "a post of honor." Arnold smiled back, and then Washington told him he was to lead the left wing of the Continental Army. "Upon this information his countenance changed, and he appeared to be quite fallen; and instead of thanking me, or expressing any pleasure at the appointment, never opened his mouth." The commander suggested that Arnold go to his headquarters and await him there.

As Washington returned, his aide, Tench Tilghman, intercepted him to say that Arnold was limping back and forth, dissatisfied and uneasy, insisting that, as his leg kept him from remaining long on horseback, only at West Point would he do justice to himself and the army. Since Arnold did not seem as crippled as he said, Washington reasoned that years of sickness and civil bickering had broken his proud spirit. With pity, with grave courtesy, he tried to awaken the warrior's martial fire, but Arnold showed fire only in expatiating on his ill health and his eagerness for a granny's post. Washington could not bear to give in to such tragic depression; he finally said he would think the whole matter over.

The command of the left wing was a dashing assignment, but it would keep Arnold under Washington's surveillance, and it failed to offer so tangible a piece of merchandise as the West Point fortress. That the chance to fight again, to regain his role as a major founder of the new nation, did not appeal to Arnold shows how far gone he was in his determination to turn traitor. He hated Washington and Congress and all the canting patriots who had made him miserable; he would destroy them all by a move as personal as a duelist's pressure on a trigger. In so doing, he would earn wealth and the approbation of Peggy, his gold and white Peggy, who would forever wear lace and perhaps walk at his side as a countess. He so missed his wife that in a few weeks he was to burst out most inappropriately to the bachelor General Howe:

"Be assured, sir, no sensations can have a comparison with those arising from the reciprocity of concern and mutual felicity existing between a lady of sensibility and a fond husband. I myself had enjoyed a tolerable share of the dissipated joys of life, as well as the scenes of sensual gratification incident to a man of nervous constitution, but, when set in comparison with those I have since felt and still enjoy, I consider the time of celibacy in some measure misspent."

Since the condition of his wound was now the issue, Arnold was careful to hobble around camp most pitifully—but Washington was only more convinced that he needed a forceable lift to his morale. On August 1, the general orders put him in command of the left wing.

Back in Philadelphia, Peggy was attending a party at Robert Morris's mansion. Dinner was over, and she was glittering in candlelight, as always the center of admiring cavaliers, when a newcomer hurried up to offer her his congratulations. Stopping her fan, her mobile features alive with interest and pleasure, she asked for what? Why because her husband had been appointed leader of the left wing. "This information affected her so much as to produce hysteric fits." When arguments that the command was much more honorable than garrison duty at West Point failed to calm her, everyone assumed that the soft woman was terrified because her husband would be exposed to danger. And after her mind returned to control, she wept more becomingly, encouraging this idea.

Arnold was pretending that he could hardly bestride his horse when Washington learned that the British had abandoned their expedition to Rhode Island. (Arbuthnot had decided it was too risky.) Since Clinton was returning to New York, the city could not be stormed, and the campaign would not be active after all. Giving in to the strange preference of the subordinate he trusted, Washington added a postscript to the general orders of August 3, 1780: "Major General Arnold will take command of the garrison at West Point."

CHAPTER TWENTY-FOUR

Dizzy Height and Desperate Hollow

NEAR the village of Haverstraw and overlooking King's Ferry, the Hudson crossing guarded by fortresses at Stony and Verplanck's Points, rose the mansion which has gone down in history as "treason house." Its occupant, Joshua Hett Smith, "spread my table with cheerfulness" for Arnold's entertainment. He fawned on the new commander, eager to make a good impression: many patriots suspected his loyalty because William Smith, Tory propagandist and chief justice of British-held New York, was his brother. As the bottle went round and round, Smith exhibited a childish relish for intrigue and explained, with a mingling of mystery and giggles, how he had collected intelligence for Arnold's predecessor. He would be glad to do the same for the new general.

Arnold listened and wondered and then decided to test the young man out. Becoming affability itself, he "ludicrously mentioned that he had been styled by some of the American army a jockey and horse-dealer," although, of course, he had been an important merchant. His autobiographical narrative soon brought the general to denunciations of the Pennsylvania Council, and Smith, now deep in liquor, was lured into expressing fear that a continuation of the war might throw gentlemen like himself and Arnold irrevocably into the power of the lower orders. Arnold smiled with interior satisfaction: this man, who lived close to the British lines, was energetic, confused, and stupid, the perfect dupe to carry out missions he did not comprehend.

A. Conftitution Ifland, on the eaft fide of the river.

B. A chain, fufpended on pontoons, reaching quite acrofs Hudfon's **River,**
there about 450 yards wide.

C. Fort Clinton, the principal work, intended to **annoy any naval force**
that might attempt the paffage.

D. Fort Putnam, a very ftrong fortrefs on the fummit of a **mountain,**
about half a mile from the point, and which commanded all the
plain beneath.

Befides thefe, there were a chain of forts reaching far weft of Putnam ;
two confiderable redoubts on mountains on the eaft fide of the river ; and
a number of batteries nearly level with the river.

West Point as it appeared at the end of the Revolution, from the *New-York Magazine and Weekly Repository*, March, 1791, which also published the following "Explanation of the Plate." *Courtesy of the New-York Historical Society, New York City.*

Where Washington mourned and Peggy ranted. "Robinson's House," Arnold's head-quarters at Garrison, New York, across the river from West Point. From a photograph taken before the building burned down in 1892. *Courtesy of the New-York Historical Society, New York City.*

In command of the area from the American outposts some fifty miles upriver to Fishkill, Arnold imitated his predecessor, General Howe, by establishing his headquarters on the opposite side of the river from West Point in a mansion that had been confiscated from Beverley Robinson, a Loyalist now in New York. The convivial Smith considered it "a dreary situation, environed with mountains," and the physician, James Thacher, wrote that it would only appeal to someone "guided altogether by a taste for romantic singularity and novelty. It is surrounded on two sides by hideous mountains and dreary forests, not a house in view but one within a mile." However, "the Hudson which washes the borders of this farm affords a facility of communication."

The desolation accorded with Arnold's mood. Although he now controlled West Point, as the weeks passed no word came from the British accepting his offer to sell the fortress for £20,000. (André's letter had reached Peggy in Philadelphia, but she could find no safe way to send it on.)

Arnold had brought Franks with him as his aide; the fop got on his nerves. Wishing soberer company, he asked Richard Varick to be his secretary. The aggressive patrician, who had fomented the historic break between his general and Gates, arrived bursting with efficiency and officiousness. He was annoyed to discover that Arnold was now "very tenacious of ordering and attending to everything himself."

Although much nearer the British lines than he had been in Philadelphia, Arnold was nonetheless cut off from André by his lack of messengers. When Joshua Smith wrote him that his predecessor had, on his own authority, given civilians passes to go through the lines, Arnold was delighted—but Varick read Smith's letter with disgust, exclaimed that Smith was a damned Tory, and forced Arnold to ask Governor George Clinton of New York what was the correct procedure. The Rebel Clinton replied that all passes had to be initiated by civilian authority. Visibly put out, Arnold puzzled Varick by refusing to explain why.

Arnold's next effort was to locate American spies in the habit of sneaking through the line; the area commander could easily make them carry messages the full purport of which escaped them. But Lafayette refused to identify Washington's agents; and Arnold's

319

predecessor, Howe, wrote that his spies had denied permission to be named. Even the usually pliable Smith found an excuse for keeping his correspondents secret. Arnold's British speculation had come to an exasperating standstill.

His efforts to turn his American assets into cash were no more successful. His Hartford agent died; the new agent could promise nothing. His New Haven representative failed to dispose of his house, and the man who bought his china asserted that he could not pay because the money had been stolen by the British. When a dispute developed over Arnold's share in the sloop *John*, the desperate man, who expected to have no time for litigation in American courts, could not relieve his feelings in a typical roar of rage. Mildly, he suggested immediate arbitration—to no avail.

Arnold could only try to make a few dollars from his command. When Varick first reached the post, Franks complained that there were more stores in the house than could be carried away in case of attack. Varick did not hesitate to remonstrate with his superior, but Arnold replied that he was owed 10,000 rations for which Congress refused adequate compensation; he intended to leave no more supplies due him in public hands. He wrote Peggy to "draw all she could from the commissary and sell or store it"; and himself disposed of a barrel of wine for 4,560 inflated Continental dollars. Varick kept him from delivering some rum to a Hudson River skipper by charging that the trader was a Tory, a designation about which Arnold could not be too careful. Later Varick happened into the room when Arnold was selling three barrels of pork and protested that his general would "incur disgrace," since the army was short of meat. Arnold made a pretense of giving in, but, as soon as his secretary's back was turned, completed the deal in a "singularly low" voice.

No man was ever lonelier than Benedict Arnold. All through every long day he had to hide his deepest thoughts, his most important actions. All through every long day he had to play a part. Soon ill health confined him to his gloomy house; "my leg," he wrote his old friend Lamb who commanded the actual fortress across the river, "being a little inflamed has kept me from coming over." When he could visit the works, he tried to occupy his mind by studying out the best route for a British attack. However, the questions he asked were strangely confused. The artillery major, Sebastian Bauman, noted that Arnold had "but a poor idea of this place, *which I can assure you*, after all his inquiry of its particular strength, and the weakest part of it. For his head appeared to me bewildered from the very first moment he took command here."

Back in Philadelphia, Peggy was in an agony of nervousness. Her husband's letters showed him—in sister Hannah's opinion— "a perfect master of ill nature." When the letters were confiscated after the treason, they were discovered to be full of "libelous abuse" of eminent personages and "the most sarcastic and contemptuous expressions of the French nation" (which had failed to take Arnold into its pay). Each successive missive told Peggy that nothing had yet happened, but her husband's state of mind was not reassuring.

Seeking release from her anxiety, she gave "one large and two or three small" parties; she spent the rest of her time rushing around town to the horror of citizens who felt that in her husband's absence her place was at home. Robert R. Livingston was her perpetual companion. Although policy may have motivated this flirtation more than pleasure, Hannah suspected the worst. Arnold's aging sister and oldest friend suffered, indeed, from a perpetual sense of horror—she knew something was terribly wrong, but could not be sure exactly what. Perhaps it was her sister-in-law's ridiculous absorption in fashions—"I have no use for such knowledge"—or the perpetual "scandal" Peggy and her friends talked. Perhaps the menace hung over her two nephews, sons of Benedict's previous marriage, who were away at school. She decided they were so unhappy that they would do something desperate. "If they should, 'tis not so much to be wondered at. They have always been used to the greatest kindness and to having their necessary wants supplied, which, I dare say from concurrent testimony, is not now the case." And all the while the heat made Hannah feel so miserable "that it has been as much as I can do to live."

The spinster, ashamed of hating her sister-in-law, tried to make up for it by being as sweet as saccharine, crooning over the baby, patting the "little dog," but her strain heightened the perpetual nightmare of suspense through which Peggy moved. At any moment, an anguished message or casually dropped word might drive a dagger through all Peggy's hopes. When she finally found a safe way to send her husband André's acceptance of his price for West Point, she added that she would like to join him and be there for the kill.

The long delay in the treason plans did not disturb Clinton and André. After it had become clear that Arnold was actually in command at West Point, almost all their worries as to the true identity of their correspondent had vanished, making them confident that the fortress would be delivered at any time they pleased. They were content to await the perfect moment which they saw ripening.

Arnold and other spies reported that Washington had drawn up a new plan of attack; he intended to strike at New York City from the mainland while the French bore down on the British stronghold through Long Island. To carry out this scheme, the Americans would have to bring up their scarce military equipment, and "it is beyond doubt," Clinton wrote, "that the principal Rebel depot must have been made at West Point." The British tactic was to wait until the irreplaceable ordnance had been placed in the trap and the enemy armies were advancing. To take West Point "at this instant of time" would give "every advantage which could have been desired"; Washington, with his rear exposed, would have to retire into New Jersey, and the French troops, left unsupported, would fall "into our hands." Clinton prepared "everything which my reflection could suggest as necessary upon the occasion, and there were vessels properly manned and of a particular draft of water [for the Hudson] ready to have improved the designed stroke to the utmost." The success of his plan, Clinton flattered himself, would have "infinite effect."

Meanwhile, André began *The Cow Chase*, a mock epic celebrating the defeat of a Rebel attempt, commanded by General Wayne, to gather provisions on Bergen Neck. He wrote the poem in sections, as he found time, and the first canto appeared by itself in the *Royal Gazette*.

André started by expressing his perpetual amusement that a tanner like Wayne should pretend to be a general:

Dizzy Height and Desperate Hollow

To drive the Kine, one summer's morn
The Tanner took his way,—
The calf shall rue, that is unborn,
The jumbling of that day.

And Wayne-descending steers shall know
And tauntingly deride;
And call to mind, in every low,
The tanning of his hide.

Having described in language comically grandiloquent the gathering of the Rebel forces, André wrote a speech for Wayne in which the commander told his troops how easy it would be to defeat the Loyalists "and ravish wife and daughter." Wayne personally would "drive away the cows."

For well you know, the latter is
The serious operation:
And fighting with the Refugees
Is only—demonstration.

His daring words from all the crowd
Such great applause did gain,
That every man declared aloud
For serious work—with Wayne.

They all had another drink.

But here—the muse has not a strain
Befitting such great deeds,
Huzza, they cried. Huzza for Wayne!
And shouting—did their needs.

Did André feel ashamed when he received a pitiful message from Peggy Chew, who loved him but with whom, it seems, he had not bothered to communicate since he had failed to involve her in Arnold's treason? She wished, poor girl, simply "to be remembered to you."

On summer nights, he frequented the brightly lighted mall which had been built in front of the burned-out ruins of Trinity

Church. Sentries kept the common people at a distance, regimental bands played soft music; and the "officers' women" tripped out of the houses across the way which had been rebuilt to accommodate them. Soon the walk became too narrow for all the pleasures it witnessed; André's commander and intimate ordered that it be extended out over the graves. "Such things," wrote a pious American, "make us sigh to the Lord that He have mercy on this land."

André accompanied Clinton on outings to Easthampton. Of their visits there, impossible stories are told,[1] but we may believe that one evening, as oceans of flip bubbled around a red-hot poker, André entertained the company "with a masterly recital of the inimitable *Ballad of Chevy Chase*" (on which his own *The Cow Chase* was based). In fine weather, the officers hunted deer on Gardiner's Island; in bad, ruined the floor of Abraham Gardiner's house by playing quoits with rough Spanish dollars.

André was in fine fettle. "Good fortune," he wrote his mother in the elegant hand he usually reserved for official documents, "still follows me. The commander in chief has raised me to the first office with the army, if that of most confidence and least profit is to be styled so. I am adjutant general. The rank of lieutenant colonel, which usually attends the post, is not given me on account of the difficulties made at giving me rank of major, but I may nourish hope of obtaining it hereafter." He could "hardly look back at the steep progress I have made without being giddy. The having exercised the duties I am called to for near a twelvemonth gives me a greater confidence in myself than I should else have; and the thought that in acquiring this much experience I have not been guilty of great omission, etc., makes me trust in my ability to fill the place with reputation. . . . I am in very good health, though the great quantity of business which assails me sometimes affects my spirits. Exercise, however, infallibly restores me."

On August 30, 1780, three days after Clinton announced André's appointment, Arnold too was given a lift. He received from Philadelphia André's acceptance of his price for West Point, and Peggy's message that she wished to join him. With great eagerness, Arnold prepared to receive his bride. As fresh food was scarce—when Colonel Lamb came to dinner, Arnold could serve only salt cod—

he offered to exchange staples for meat, vegetables, and a milch cow. Varick was instantly at his elbow protesting: when high officers used some of their many rations for barter, farmers refused to accept the commissary's paper money, and the troops went hungry. This time, Arnold ignored his aide; Peggy needed the best.

He sent Franks galloping to Philadelphia to bring her back. "You must by all means," he admonished his wife, "get out of the carriage crossing all ferries or going over all large bridges, to prevent accidents." She should bring her own sheets, since those provided on the road might not be clean; she should carry wine for herself and "spirit for the people"; she should send "your light horseman" ahead every morning to order her dinner. The wagon, with a feather bed placed over the seat, would be more comfortable in the hot weather than the chariot, and easier on the horses. He suggested stopping places for each of six nights: "Let me beg you not to make your stages so long as to fatigue you or the dear boy [even] if you should be much longer in coming."

The next essential was to arrange a rendezvous with André. As he was scratching his head for a messenger, William Heron, a former Connecticut assemblyman, appeared with a recommendation from General Samuel Parsons that he be allowed through the lines to collect a debt. Arnold looked Heron over, disappeared for two hours, reappeared, dictated to Varick the necessary pass, and then called Heron into his private chamber. A letter, the general explained, had been given him for delivery in New York; he had opened it and satisfied himself that it was on civilian business. Would Heron please deliver it to the Reverend Mr. Odell? Heron agreed.

"As soon as I received the letter," he said later, "and viewed the superscription, which was written in a feigned hand, I must confess that I felt a jealousy or suspicion that I had never before experienced concerning any person of his rank." He noted that it had been sealed twice to give the impression that it had been opened, but that neither seal was broken.

In a secret place, Heron broke the seals. He read that Mr. M——e (Moore, one of Arnold's pseudonyms) was eager to arrange an interview "to settle your commercial plan" with someone fully authorized to treat, and still felt that his first proposal was reasonable and would be agreed to. "A speculation might at this time be easily made to some advantage with *ready money*, but there is not the quantity of goods *at market* which your partner seems to suppose, and the number of speculators below, I think, will be against your making an immediate purchase. I apprehend goods will be in greater plenty and much cheaper in the course of the season." (Only André would understand the true meaning of this passage: the British might attack at that time, but there were fewer supplies and men at West Point than Clinton supposed, and Washington's army was uncomfortably close in lower New Jersey. The fortress might be more profitably captured later in the campaign.) The letter ended by stating that Mr. M——e hoped to see his correspondent within ten days and that he wished £300 given to S——y (Stansbury).

Arnold had hidden his meaning too well. Five months before in New York, William Smith had moved "to open a correspondence" with Heron; now, Heron was on his way to exchange treasonous intelligence for British pounds. Had he understood Arnold's letter, he would certainly have delivered it, but, assuming that the general was engaged in nothing more illegal than speculation, he saw an opportunity for a patriotic gesture that would disarm the suspicion of the men he was betraying. He handed the letter to General Parsons.

Parsons, who was in immediate charge of the troops between West Point and the British lines, had already played a major role in the career of the area commander; by repeating at Hartford information Arnold had given him during the first days of the war, he had set in motion the rival expedition against Ticonderoga that had been the start of all Arnold's troubles. The two men were now on "a most friendly footing." Puzzled by the letter Heron gave him, Parsons decided to do nothing that would raise an issue: he would hand it casually to Washington the next time he saw His Excellency. The paper that might have tipped off the treason disappeared into Parsons's desk.

Arnold, who did not know that he had failed to reopen contact with André, must have received a shock when Washington ordered him to put West Point "in the most defensible state which is possible" since the British were preparing an important movement that might carry them that way. As soon as he was capable of calm thought, however, he realized that Clinton would not conceivably expect him to surrender the fortress until ways and means had been worked out in a conference. He dictated orders which drew from Washington the comment that he "perfectly comprehend[ed] my ideas of the rule of conduct which is to be observed should the enemy come up the river in force."

For 160 years, Arnold has been accused of trying to bleed his command by sending away troops and failing to procure necessary supplies. Actually, his problem could not be so simply solved. Since Clinton had agreed to pay him £20,000 only if he delivered in addition to the fortress 3,000 men and innumerable stores, his need was not to deplete the post but to strengthen it. The most he could do was to spread the garrison out in such a manner that battalions could be cut off piecemeal. However, any orders which tended toward this objective had to be carried out under thousands of patriot eyes by subordinate officers of loyalty and skill. Thus, when Arnold sent 200 men to Fishkill to cut wood in preparation for winter, Lamb protested that, if such drafts on the main garrison continued, "we shall neither be able to finish the works that are incomplete nor [be] in a situation to defend those that are finished." But Arnold had carefully already got Washington's approval for what was, at least on the face of it, a completely reasonable action. During those ticklish weeks, he warded off suspicion by consulting his chief, in a manner quite out of his own character, on the most trivial decisions. As an American general, he often leaned over backward to be scrupulously attentive to details that were to his disadvantage as a traitor.

Legend has authoritatively reported that Arnold tried to weaken the chain which blocked the Hudson by removing a link; actually, he tried to strengthen the chain, following the advice of a French engineer Washington had detailed to assist him. When the necessary materials did not arrive, he sent out requisition after requisition. Indeed, the general debility of the American cause served his ends as effectively and more safely than overt action would have done. Visiting West Point before he took over the post, he found the fortress "totally neglected" and "most wretchedly planned."

Efforts to remedy the situation failed under his orders as they had under the orders of his predecessors.

After the discovery of his treason clothed Arnold's every deed in black, patriots from Washington down blamed him for the ancient weakness of the post, and even for the mistakes of subordinates who were not in his confidence; yet he seems to have carried out the normal duties of his command with at least routine efficiency. Whether he could have done more at that time is doubtful, since his mind was confused and clogged with anxiety.

Arnold's eagerness to get in touch with André made him open up more lines of communication than prudence might have dictated. He asked the commander of the American outposts, Colonel Elisha Sheldon, to forward by flag to Major Oliver De Lancey (the officer in specific charge of British intelligence) a letter Peggy had sent from Philadelphia which requested that Major Giles be allowed to send her some "trifling articles" of finery. Although Sheldon complied, his worry about the reaction of his own immediate superior forced Arnold to write Parsons, "I am told there is a general order prohibiting any goods being purchased and brought out of New York, but as the goods were bought many months before the order was issued, I do not conceive they come under the intentions or spirit of it. However, I would not wish my name mentioned in the matter, as it may give occasion for scandal."

When Mary McCarthy, the wife of a captured British soldier, turned up, bearing a pass from Governor Clinton, Arnold seized this opportunity too. He gave her, for delivery in New York, a letter couched "in a mercantile style," which asked André to appear, at the outpost commanded by Sheldon, in the character of a surreptitious trader.[2] Although Arnold assured André that he had "hinted the matter" to Sheldon, his confusion of mind was so great that he allowed four days to pass before he notified that officer to expect a stranger who, he stated, was a secret agent in the American service.

As he spun more threads that might lead some patriot into the deadly center of the web, Arnold's anxiety spilled over into "a thousand fancied disasters" which might have overtaken his Peggy. He sent a dragoon to seek her at all the stopping places he had recommended as far as New Brunswick, and to ask "any gentle-

man or express you may meet if they had seen her on the road."
A few days later, he sailed down to King's Ferry in the hope that
she might be there. Having spent a disconsolate hour staring in
the direction of Philadelphia, he returned home, where he found
a most frightening letter.

Arnold's suggestion that André sneak disguised into the American lines had not pleased General Clinton, who did not wish his
beloved adjutant general to behave like a spy and face execution
on the gallows. Signing himself "John Anderson," André had
written Sheldon, "I am told my name is made known to you." He
intended to come with a flag to Dobbs Ferry at noon on September 11 to meet Mr. G—— (Gustavus, another of Arnold's pseudonyms). "Should I not be allowed to go, the officer who is to command the escort, between whom and myself no distinction need
be made, can speak on the affair." In other words André would
be that officer. He did not wish to "assume a mysterious character
to carry on an innocent affair, and, as friends have advised, get to
your lines by stealth."

In forwarding this letter to his commander, Sheldon had expressed no suspicions, but Arnold was horrified: it made no sense
that a British officer, coming under an official flag of truce, would
be an American agent. How could André have been so indiscreet!
Although he had no messenger at hand, the traitor relieved his
feelings by writing, "You must be sensible my situation will not
permit my meeting or having any private intercourse with such
an officer." He again pressed on André "getting to our lines by
stealth. . . . I will engage you shall be perfectly safe here." It is
indicative of the confusion under which Arnold labored that,
when opportunity came to dispatch this letter some days later, he
did so, although by then the situation had changed to give it no
meaning.

His immediate problem was to lull Sheldon. This he tried to do
by writing that the letter signed "John Anderson" was so "mysterious" that he assumed his correspondence with the American
spy had been "interrupted"; the implication was that British
counter-intelligence had intervened. If Anderson should nonetheless "find some means to come to your quarters," a fast rider should
be sent to notify Arnold, while the agent followed under escort.

Arnold stated that his leg would not let him ride the whole distance; he would meet the party on the road. (This was a safer spot for the conference than his headquarters, where Varick was always interfering.) Should Anderson not appear, "I am determined to go as far as Dobbs Ferry and meet the flag."

In New York, Clinton had again become apprehensive about entrusting the difficult mission to his young favorite. He had hit on a more experienced man who had an obvious reason for conferring with the traitor: Colonel Beverley Robinson, the Tory in whose confiscated house Arnold was living. André remained, however, in need of a personal triumph that would impress the war office in London. His promotion to full adjutant general had only carried him to a dizzier height from which he would be toppled should Clinton be recalled. Still suffering the "mortification to see the rank of major objected to," he was "yet uncertain" whether his new appointment would succeed in lifting him from his junior captaincy in the regular establishment. He put his needs forward so strongly that at last Clinton wrote him a short, grudging note: "Colonel Robinson will probably go with the flag himself. As you are with him at the forepost, you may as well be with the party."

That September was extremely hot. While eight soldiers rowed Arnold down the Hudson on the afternoon before the rendezvous, the green and red Highlands cut off all wind, and the water looked oily in the burning haze. For eighteen miles, the oars struck and rose. In the stern, with his damaged leg up on a thwart, sat the once heroic major general. Many patriots saw him pass, but no one suspected his errand. Rage and fear coursed through his blood, and perhaps regret—but the die was cast. Two and a half years of military glory, two and a half years of sick disgrace lay behind him; now he would grasp his future with both hands. The oars beat and the flanking hills moved by, and then he saw Joshua Smith awaiting him on the Haverstraw landing. He spent the night in "treason house," a dozen miles above Dobbs Ferry.

The next morning, Arnold resumed his journey, his oarsmen sweating in the heat. Suddenly there streaked from the shadows by the shore a British gunboat. Arnold's unarmed vessel turned and fled upstream. The British followed, and cannon balls dashed around the general's barge. Since patriots were certainly watching from the surrounding hills, the traitor did not raise the flag of truce he carried. He faced the cannon with his old bravery. When his strong oarsmen pulled him to safety, Benedict Arnold lost his chance to die a hero.

He paused and then set out again. This time the gunboat did not appear until he had gone so far that his barge was able to dash under the protection of an American blockhouse that guarded the western ferry landing. Arnold gossiped uneasily with the officers stationed there, and wrote Washington a letter, meticulously headed "Dobbs Ferry," explaining that he was at the post to arrange defensive measures "in case the enemy came up the river." He expected André to call off the gunboat, which was now prowling like a terrier in front of a rat hole, and cross the Hudson under a flag of truce.

Since the navy was not in Clinton's confidence, André had set out from the British lines at Kingsbridge on horseback. Accompanied by Robinson and probably guarded by dragoons, he proceeded along the eastern shore of the Hudson through a bleak no man's land. When the party approached Dobbs Ferry, they halted a little inland, so that they would not be visible from the river. They must have reached their stopping place after the chase in which cannon were fired, for they did not know that a gunboat had intervened. They expected Arnold to come to them. Hour after hour, André's ears strained for the sound of the traitor's footsteps crackling in dead leaves.

The broad river flowed between them; hot afternoon waned into steaming evening. Darkness fell. When the gunboat merged invisibly with the water, Arnold limped into his barge and returned upstream. Mounting his horse, André rode back to the British lines.

CHAPTER TWENTY-FIVE

Toward a Dark Appointment

ARNOLD'S next trip down river was to meet his Peggy who, with Franks, had reached King's Ferry. They all stayed at Joshua Smith's. Now, at long last, Arnold had a strong and beloved mind to help him plan the next step. The time had come, they agreed, to make use of Smith's energy and foolishness.

While Peggy regaled Mrs. Smith with chatter about the latest fashions, Arnold took her husband aside and whispered to him portentously. The beaming dupe agreed to undertake, in six days' time, a midnight escapade by water. He would fetch Arnold's secret agent, and bring the exciting visitor to his own house, which he would empty for the occasion by sending his family visiting and his servant on long errands.

Finally, Peggy and Benedict yawned and went upstairs, but they did not go to bed. With his bride smiling over his shoulder, Arnold wrote André that, if he preferred "your former plan" (which was really Arnold's own), he was to come in plain clothes to the posts of either Sheldon or Major Benjamin Tallmadge; both officers had been alerted. Otherwise, Arnold would on the night of the 20th send a man to Dobbs Ferry, "who will conduct you to a place of safety, where I will meet you. It will be necessary for you to be disguised." André was to admit his true business to no one; "I have no confidants. I find I have made one too many already, which has prevented several profitable speculations." (He

332

may have referred to his mistake in bringing Varick to the post.) Using mercantile metaphor that André would understand, Arnold revealed that there were only 1,000 men at West Point, but he could collect 1,500 more in a few days. Perhaps it was Peggy who urged him to end the letter with an assurance of personal friendship.

At headquarters the next morning, Varick received Peggy enthusiastically—"Mrs. Arnold's presence here makes the family happy"—and then confided to Franks that he was worried because Arnold was corresponding with a John Anderson behind the British lines. Franks laughed and said it was nothing new: while in Philadelphia, Arnold had secured intelligence through Anderson. Varick was reassured.

A letter from Washington was awaiting the conspirators. It stated that in forty-eight hours he would cross the river at King's Ferry and that he would spend the night at Peekskill (between the Arnolds and the British lines). This opened up both opportunities and dangers. If the Arnolds could arrange to have Washington killed or captured, they could secure a great deal of money; but one of the many public steps Arnold had taken to re-establish contact with André might come to Washington's attention. (They would have been even more worried had they known that Parsons was exhuming from his desk, for delivery at Washington's headquarters, Arnold's letter which Heron had failed to give the British.)

"I want to make my journey a secret," Washington had written Arnold. Arnold wrote André, "General Washington will be at King's Ferry Sunday evening next on his way to Hartford where he is to meet the French admiral and general. And will lodge at Peek's Kill."

In New York, Clinton had decided that the time to take West Point was at hand. There was no longer any reason to await a combined American and French attack on Manhattan, since a cloudlike spread of sails, moving through the Narrows, had heralded the arrival of British naval reinforcements under Admiral George Rodney, the father of André's Göttingen friend. When Rodney reported that the expected French reinforcements were blockaded in Brest, it was clear that the balance of power had so changed that the French would have to stay in Rhode Island and no major enemy action was likely that autumn.

Not even in the disastrous winter of 1775 had the patriot cause looked blacker. The French were proving no help; and Gates had suffered at Camden a defeat so disastrous that the power of the South to resist further invasion seemed completely shattered. (Arnold wrote delightedly that his hated rival had branded himself with "indelible infamy.") Few militiamen were willing to join Washington, and he had to send home those that came because he had no way to feed and supply them. Since the bankrupt Congress could not pay the Continental Army, this mainstay of the rebellion seemed on the point of breaking up. Even the death penalty did not keep enlisted men from deserting, and Washington expressed fear that his officers would resign in a body. (Arnold was helping things along by suggesting to his fellow generals that 1,000 to 1,500 men from all ranks of the army march on Congress.) The loss of the Hudson River and the Rebels' most famous fortress, which had cost $3,000,000 and three years of unremitting labor, might easily make the French withdraw from their unprofitable alliance and destroy what was left of the American will to resist.

There was only one check to Clinton's jubilation. Ignorant that a British gunboat had prevented Arnold from keeping his appointment with Robinson and André, he returned to his fears that the entire negotiation had been a hoax. "It became at this instant necessary," he wrote, "that the secret correspondence under feigned names . . . should be rendered into certainty, both as to the person being Major General Arnold, commanding at West Point; and that in the manner in which he was to surrender himself, the forts, and the troops to me, it should be conducted under a concerted plan between us, as that the King's troops sent upon this expedition should be under no risk of surprise or counterplot." Everything depended on a personal meeting with Arnold.

André, who had been preparing himself for the mission by drawing maps of the West Point area, was struck, perhaps because of excitement, with "a disorder in my stomach." Glad to consider his adjutant incapacitated, Clinton put the matter entirely in the hands of Colonel Robinson.

Arnold was suffering many tribulations. He had received from

Hannah a letter which, although obviously inspired by spite, was not calming. His sister asserted that his older children were being maltreated at school; and that she herself was being cut dead in Philadelphia by old friends: "there's policy in war, you know." Concerning the one human being now close to her brother, Hannah wrote, "As you have neither purling streams nor sighing swains at West Point, 'tis no place for me—nor do I think Mrs. Arnold will long be pleased with it, though expect it may be rendered dear to her (for a few hours) by the presence of a certain chancellor [Livingston], who, by the by, is a dangerous companion for a particular lady in the absence of her husband. I could say more than prudence will permit. I could tell you of frequent private assignations and of numberless billets-doux, if I had an inclination to make mischief, but as I am of a very peaceable temper, I'll not mention a syllable of the matter. . . . For news of any kind I must refer you to Mrs. Arnold and Major Franks. If they have none, they can make you a little, my word for it."

Arnold had hoped that Peggy's presence would rest his nerves. On the contrary! She was, Franks remembered, "subject to occasional paroxysms of physical indisposition, attended by nervous debility, during which she would give utterance to anything and everything on her mind. This was a fact well known among us of the general's family, so much so as to cause us to be scrupulous of what we told her or said within her hearing." Peggy's hysterics were, of course, an old story, and during them she had never, as far as Arnold knew, lost the core of discretion that had kept her from babbling out the one secret she must not betray—yet her increasing strain worried the traitor who teetered so dangerously between a British peerage and an American gallows. Arnold found it wise to keep her away from headquarters as much as he could, sending her on day-long picnics in the woods with Franks and a female attendant. His foppish aide was for her the safest companion, since, as Jefferson was to remark, "in the company of women . . . he loses all power over himself. . . . His temperature would not be proof against their allurements, were such employed as engines against him." If Peggy dropped an indiscreet word, she could erase it from Franks's mind with a stare of girlish admiration.

His aides got on Arnold's nerves: Varick was a busybody, Franks a fool. He was ruder to the Jew than to the New York patrician, yet both were resentful. When, on the morning of the day Washington was due at King's Ferry, Smith burbled in like the most welcome of guests (he was emptying his house by taking his family to Fishkill), Varick, who had warned Arnold against Smith as a "damn Tory and snake in the grass," took his arrival as a personal insult. They all sat down to lunch in some irritation.

The meal was interrupted when Arnold was handed a packet landed by flag of truce from the sloop whose meanderings up and down the Hudson extended or contracted the extreme point of British penetration; the *Vulture* was now off Teller's Point, only six miles below King's Ferry where Washington was to cross.

With admirable calm, Arnold broke the seal in everyone's presence. Two letters came apart in his hands, one addressed to General Putnam and the other to Arnold himself. He opened his own. Robinson wrote that if Putnam were not there (clearly the other general was included as a blind) he hoped Arnold would demonstrate "the humane and generous character you bear" by according him an interview. The Tory had thrown in the name "James Osborne" (code for the go-between Odell) to show Arnold the direction in which his business lay. Everyone else was supposed to conclude that Robinson wanted to negotiate about his confiscated property, which included the very chairs in which the company sat.

Having put the papers in his pocket, Arnold remarked to the silent table that Robinson wanted to see him, he did not know why. Outrage instantly poured from Colonel Lamb: how dare Robinson make such a suggestion! Arnold could not confer with the villainous Tory without raising "suspicion of improper correspondence." But fortunately, Lamb continued, Washington would arrive at the post that afternoon; Arnold should show the letters to him. Remarking mildly that if Robinson had something to say, he would have to start somewhere, Arnold changed the subject.

Lunch finally over, Arnold said he would join Washington. He did not take his barge to King's Ferry, where the British might make a dash up the Hudson at the general he had betrayed; he rode with Franks to Peekskill. At every turn of the road his heart contracted—was it with fear or remorse or eagerness?—lest he see before him an anguished messenger, lest he hear a shout that Washington was dead or captured. As the afternoon dozed undisturbed in a soft, autumnal haze, Arnold subjected Franks to "repeated insults."

Washington was at Peekskill, as friendly as ever. (There had been no alarm at King's Ferry, and Parsons had failed to deliver the intercepted letter.) Arnold punctiliously showed his commander the communications he had received from Robinson, and agreed that it would be unsuitable for him to grant the Tory an interview. That night he stayed in the same house with Washington.

The situation at Arnold's headquarters had remained explosive. As Varick was working in his office, Smith had drifted in. Varick moved to the dining room but Smith followed, at which Varick "declared in an angry tone of voice that there was no such thing as doing business without being interrupted by one puppy or another." Smith was too full of the importance of his projected mission to take offense, and at the supper table too full of liquor to resist saying that the Americans might have had an "honorable peace" by accepting the British offer of 1778. Varick was instantly in a towering rage. Peggy, who knew Smith's importance to their plans but did not wish to increase Varick's suspicions, tried every feminine wile to separate them. Finally, she soothed Varick down by complimenting him as "a warm, staunch Whig."

After breakfast, Washington jogged off for Hartford and Arnold rode home with a dangerous fact burning in his mind. The commander was planning to return in five days; he intended to spend the night at Arnold's house and inspect West Point. Only the most subtle changes could be made before then in the fortress and the disposition of the troops. And the schedule had been tightened: André would have to be brought from the British lines and returned ere Washington reappeared.

No sooner had Arnold reached his headquarters than Franks told Varick that he had been insulted and intended to leave. Varick replied that he too would resign, lest he be treated in the same manner. Marching into his general's office with blood in his eye, Varick objected that Arnold's letter refusing to meet Robinson sounded as if it were written to a friend not a miscreant. Arnold rewrote it, probably comforting himself by imagining what Varick would think if he could see the other communications he slipped surreptitiously into the packet that would go off by flag of truce.

A letter to Robinson completed the plans for one of the most fateful meetings in American history. Arnold offered to send his representative on the night of the 20th directly to the *Vulture*, but objected to transacting his business with Robinson. (The Tory was so well known in the region that he might easily be recognized.) The traitor hoped that André would "be permitted to come at the time mentioned." Directly to that officer, he sent a copy of his previous letter about the rendezvous, adding a postscript urging the adjutant to be there, disguised for a trip into the American lines.

The morning of the 20th, Smith left his family at Fishkill and started for home, managing on the way to see Arnold without Varick's knowledge. The general gave him a pass that would enable him that night to bring "John Anderson" from the *Vulture* to his own house. Since André would know that he was the man intended, Arnold gave Smith to understand that by "Anderson" he meant Robinson. The Tory landowner, he explained, was bringing, in his desire to get back his confiscated estate, peace terms better than those of 1778. Arnold commented that he himself was "heartily sick of the war," and Smith agreed.

All the communications to the British Arnold had written since Peggy's arrival, including the statement that Washington would cross the river on the 17th, had reached New York by different means on the 18th. Since Arnold made it clear that he was determined to meet with André, Clinton was forced to agree that his favorite undertake the mission, but he still hoped that the more experienced Robinson would go along.

During André's last days before his departure,[1] he completed *The Cow Chase*, revealing again his strange fascination with the gallows, his murky gift for prophecy. In expressing amusement at the Puritan names of the Rebel dead, he asked:

Toward a Dark Appointment

But, ah, Thadaeus Posset, why
Should thy poor soul elope?
And why should Titus Hooper die,
And die—without a rope?

The poem ends:

And now I've closed my epic strain,
I tremble as I show it,
Lest this same warrio-drover Wayne
Should ever catch the poet.

Clinton was worried by his favorite's exuberance; he put him "in possession of every necessary caution that became the dignity of a command and the milder affections of friendship." In particular, he ordered his adjutant not to place himself in the position of a spy by changing his uniform for any other costume or by entering an enemy post. He assumed that André would meet Arnold on disputed ground under a flag of truce. A third prohibition which Clinton later claimed he had made—that André should carry no incriminating papers—was not recalled by his subordinate, and was, indeed, hardly necessary if the first two were obeyed.

André rode to Dobbs Ferry where he boarded a small sloop that sped before a favorable wind to the *Vulture*. In his eagerness, he did not deliver Clinton's orders that the *Vulture* drop back to Dobbs Ferry—Arnold had made this suggestion—but kept the boat off Teller's Point. He could not know that this anchorage was irritating Colonel James Livingston, who regarded it as an insult to his post on the shore, and was collecting cannon and shot with which to give the warship a surprise.

Toward midnight, when Arnold's representative was due, André came on deck and walked back and forth under brilliant autumn stars. Once he would have rhymed on them to his blonde Honora; now "he expressed much anxiety for the arrival of the flag." But the only movement he saw was the dance of the water; when he heard a splash, it was a fish or diving bird. Finally, lest his continued presence on deck arouse the curiosity of the sailors, he was forced to go below.

Earlier that evening, Smith had asked one of his tenants to row "a piece" down the river. Samuel Cahoon replied he "had no mind to go," and Smith, himself tired by his ride down from Fishkill, hardly argued. He said that Cahoon would, in that case, have to carry a message to Arnold. The yokel had no mind for this either, but Smith bundled him off. While André stared over the water in expectation of a flag, the only movement on the American end of the treason had been the slow shamble northward of a work horse bearing a sleepy and resentful farmer.

"Just after sunrise," Cahoon delivered Smith's note at Robinson's house to a gentleman who said that Arnold was still asleep. The general, convinced his importance was so great that the British emissary should serve his comfort, had intended André to spend the night hidden at Smith's house; he himself would appear at his leisure in the morning. When he awoke ready for the adventure, he was enraged by Smith's letter. If only great affairs did not have to be carried out by feeble instruments! No longer trusting Smith to achieve anything without supervision, he ordered out his barge and started for King's Ferry.

When André awoke, he was in a quandary. "This," he wrote privately to Clinton, "is the second excursion I have made without ostensible reason, and Colonel Robinson both times of the party. A third would infallibly fix suspicions." The adjutant general was so conspicuous an officer that, should he return to headquarters, he could not set out again to meet Arnold; nor could he, without explanation, stay on board the *Vulture*. In a second letter to Clinton, which he showed to the ship's officers (only the captain, Andrew Sutherland, was in on the secret), André stated that he had "caught a very bad cold, and so violent a return of the disorder in my stomach" that it was unwise for him to move.

In his role as an invalid, he could not stay on deck, watching for developments. Immured in his cabin, he fidgeted and listened for unusual sounds, "full of fears," so Sutherland tells us, "lest something should have happened" to Arnold's emissary.

Finally he remembered that, on the previous day, one of the *Vulture*'s boats had been lured to shore by a white flag and then fired on: what could be more in order than to prepare a formal protest to Arnold, the commander, in his own hand, which Arnold, the traitor, would recognize. Robinson slipped into the packet a second note, expressing regret that Smith had not appeared and stating that, with his partner (André), he was ready to attend the agent "to any convenient and safe place." Not above violating the rules of war in their protest against such a violation, they dispatched the letters under a flag of truce.

Arnold was proceeding down river. He ostentatiously inspected the fortifications he passed; Colonel Livingston, who handed him the packet from the *Vulture*, considered him "a good deal reserved." However, the general did not hide his intention to send Smith out that night on a secret mission. Finding that his feckless agent had failed to secure a suitable boat, he openly requisitioned one and sent his barge to get it. Since he had not told Varick that he intended to spend the night on the lines, the conspirator, whose original plan had been to sleep at home while Smith got André, may not have been certain that he would have to change his plan until he discovered how woefully incompetent his agent had been. In any case, he did not return to his headquarters but repaired to Smith's house.

As the sun dipped behind the Highlands, Smith intercepted Samuel Cahoon, who was on his way to get the cows, and brought him up to a second-story bedroom, where the famous General Arnold waited. The general smiled, and told Cahoon that he was to row out on the river that night. Cahoon raised one foot a little and then put it down, raised the other foot, twisted his cap in his hands, and replied that the guard boats were dangerous, and, in any case, he was too tired. Arnold was in no mood for such foolishness, but he smothered his irritation and said that the mission was important for the patriot cause—certainly, Cahoon was a patriot?

The farmer finally asked where he was supposed to go. On board the *Vulture*, said Arnold, to pick up a secret agent. Cahoon looked shrewd and volunteered that the agent could probably wait till morning. In a most serious voice, Arnold confided that the business was so momentous that it had to be accomplished in the dark. Cahoon went into his shuffling dance again, and then said he could not row that far alone. When Smith told him to get his brother Joseph, he left the room.

In a few minutes he came back, but without his brother. He had, he explained, spoken to his wife, and she had forbid his going. He would not go. Springing up, Arnold smashed his fist on the table and said he would arrest both brothers as "disaffected men." Grumbling to himself, Samuel Cahoon agreed to fetch Joseph. This time Smith accompanied him downstairs.

Arnold fidgeted for half an hour, and then Smith reappeared to say that the second brother had merely abetted the first; they were standing in the yard repeating that they "did not choose to go." Hurrying downstairs, Arnold tried to calm the Cahoons by asserting that the mission was only secret to "the inhabitants and common men"; it was known to the water guard. He offered them a gift of flour and insisted, "It must be done for the good of the country." The brothers reluctantly agreed, but it then developed that the rowboat had not arrived. Smith's colored boy was sent to investigate, and Arnold went back upstairs.

Joseph Cahoon soon followed. He handed Arnold a letter, saying the rowboat was on the way, and then stood there, fidgeting; he was "afraid to tell the general of it." Finally, "I acquainted him I had no mind to go, as it was late, and said I would rather go in the morning." Arnold made as if to call the guard to have the brothers arrested as traitors. Joseph wandered downstairs again, and in a few minutes Smith appeared to say that he had given the brothers a stiff drink and that they were again willing. Limping out the door, Arnold slapped the Cahoons on their backs, had a moment's private talk with Smith, and then watched the three set out for the landing place.

Smith's gay chatter did not amuse the brothers who followed him in sullen silence. When he ordered them to muffle their oars with sheepskins, their suspicions returned, but a patriotic harangue from Smith (and probably fear that Arnold would arrest them) finally got them into the boat. "The night was serene," Smith remembered, "the tide favorable, and the silent manner in which we passed the fort at Stony Point" attracted no attention. "In short, although the distance was nearly twelve miles, we soon reached the ship. . . .

"I was heartily assailed with a volley of oaths, all in the peculiarity of sea language, by the officer commanding the watch on the quarter-deck, and commanded instantly to haul alongside, or he would blow us out of the water. Upon coming alongside, I was saluted with another discharge of the same nautical eloquence; and orders were given to hoist the Rebel rascal on board, which was prevented by my climbing up a rope fastened to the main chains." When Smith explained that he carried papers for Sutherland and Robinson, the officer was unmoved, "but he poured on me torrents of abuse, threatening to hang me at the yardarm, as he said another Rebel had been a few days before." Smith shouted his reply, hoping to be overheard in the cabin. A boy appeared to say, "The captain orders the man below."

In the cabin he recognized "a venerable looking gentleman . . . dressed in a regimental uniform," as Robinson. Having been introduced to Sutherland, who was ill in his berth, Smith presented the papers he had brought. There was an unsealed letter from Arnold to Robinson, intended to lull the suspicion of prying eyes, saying that Smith would conduct him "to a place of safety. . . . I take it for granted Colonel Robinson will not propose anything that is not for the interest of the United States as well as himself." There were two passes, one for Smith, three men, and a boy; the other for Smith, two servants, and John Anderson. Finally there was a scrap of paper on which Arnold had scratched the countersign "Gustavus to Anderson." Robinson gathered up the documents and excused himself.

As a light flicked in the doorway of his stateroom, André "started out of bed and discovered the greatest impatience to be gone." However, Robinson pointed out that neither of the two passes called for more than one full-grown man in addition to Smith and his servants; they could not, as intended, set out together. For twenty minutes, the agents discussed which should be left behind. "Major André," Robinson wrote Clinton, "thought it was best for him to go alone," since "it appeared to him as, indeed, it did to me that Arnold wished to see him."

André dressed in his uniform, threw on a long blue coat that completely covered it and followed Robinson into the main cabin. Neither he nor Smith remembered that they had dined together almost five years before. This, Robinson explained, was Mr. John Anderson, who would confer with Arnold, since he himself was indisposed. "It made no difference to me," Smith wrote, "who bore me company, so that the object of my mission was fully answered. . . . There seemed no reluctance on the part of Anderson to supply Colonel Robinson's place." Sutherland noted that André did not "betray the least doubt of his safety or success." He stated that "he had not the smallest apprehension on the occasion, and that he was ready to attend General Arnold's summons when and where he pleased."

Although, by wearing his uniform hidden beneath his voluminous coat, André was obeying one of Clinton's commands, the aide was ready to disobey the order that he visit only territory which could be considered no-man's-land. It was understood by all present that, should the business with Arnold not be completed before dawn, André would spend the night at Smith's house. If any of them had doubted that Smith's house, on a commanding eminence only two and a quarter miles from the fortress at Stony Point, was within a Rebel post, they need merely have asked Smith, who had no reason to avoid a truthful answer. André was fully prepared to sneak into the American lines.

There was some talk of assisting the Cahoons with British sailors, either a pair to help row the boat or a whole crew in a navy barge to tow it, but this, it was agreed, would make trouble if they met American guard boats. Relying on Arnold to return André under another pass when their business was completed, the British made no plans to pick up their adjutant general.

The party all went to the rail. After some British sailors, who had been gossiping with the Cahoons, climbed back up the side of the warship, André and Smith climbed down. They sat side by side in the stern; Smith grasped the steering oar. The Cahoons let go, and, with effortless smoothness, André parted from the English world.

Arnold was alone at Smith's house except for a colored boy who had not been banished with the other servants (as a slave, he could not testify in a court of law). When the general's impatience became too great, he called for horses, and trotted, with the boy beside him, down a steep driveway to the river road. After they had gone a mile or so down river, they passed the American outpost; in another few miles, the boy reined in and pointed to an inky wall of evergreens. This, he said, was the place where Mr. Smith wanted General Arnold to wait.

Toward a Dark Appointment

The horses reared at being pulled into the woods, but after they were tied they became somnolent. The boy lay down and slept. Beneath high branches, Arnold groped to the edge of a bluff. He peered out over a dimly-visioned beach to the river surging, powerful and dark. Soon restlessness mastered him. As he paced in the gloomy forest, the long heel on his shrunken leg bit into the floor of needles. Sometimes he thought he heard a sound; he would hurry to the edge, but saw only the Hudson sweeping by under a myriad stars. When there came at last the unmistakable groan of wood on sand, Arnold so forgot his discretion that Samuel Cahoon heard "the noise of a man on the bank above."

With a rattle of falling pebbles, a figure scrambled up into Arnold's darkness. It was Smith, who whispered excitedly that Robinson had refused to come; he had brought John Anderson instead. Arnold was careful to express "chagrin" and say quite casually that, since Anderson was there, he would see him. Smith went down again, and then there showed for a moment, rising above the bank and dark against the stars, a tall, graceful silhouette. In utter blackness, John André groped toward Benedict Arnold.

CHAPTER TWENTY-SIX

Errand with a Fool

THE CAHOON brothers slept in the boat as the broad
waters of the Hudson sank to ebb and then began to flood
again, the tidal current moving ever more strongly away
from the British warship André had left. Smith was "greatly mortified at not being present at the interview, to which I conceived
myself entitled from my rank in life"; he fidgeted and was racked
by the ague to which he was subject. From the black woods overhead, he could hear no sound.

Sitting with their backs to fir trees, Arnold and André spoke in
a half-whisper. They were sizing each other up as best they could
in absolute darkness. Arnold's voice was more cultured than might
be expected from an apothecary upstart; André's efficient and
military for a playboy scene painter. If they ventured into humor,
Arnold was sardonic, André playful. Each tried to impress the
other.

When they got down to business, Arnold stated that he would
not even discuss betraying his command until his request for a
£10,000 indemnity, win or lose, was acceded to. André replied
that he was empowered to offer only £6,000. This induced from
Arnold a whispered tirade in which he was solicitous about his
family responsibilities (were it not for Peggy and the children he
would make no financial demands at all); confidential about the
vast rewards he would receive if independence were established;
and proudly angry at the thought that the British did not consider

André's voyage to the fatal rendezvous. A sketch André drew from memory on the day before his execution. It was found, after he was dead, in the room where he had been imprisoned. Engraving after the lost original. *Courtesy, Emmet Collection, New York Public Library.*

Where the Voyage Began and Ended: UPPER: Here the *Vulture* was anchored when André descended into a rowboat to meet Arnold and his destiny. The Hudson River looking south from Teller's (Croton) Point. LOWER: In utter darkness, the keel of André's boat ground here on sand. He groped his way into woods on the right, where Arnold waited. *Both: Courtesy of the photographer, Richard J. Koke.*

Treason House. A gay nineteenth-century lithograph of Joshua Hett Smith's house, where Arnold and André conferred and André was forced to make himself incontrovertibly a spy by changing his uniform for civilian clothes. *Courtesy of the New-York Historical Society, New York City.*

"The André Window," through which he saw the British warship on which his escape depended being fired on and disappearing down the river. Photographed in 1899. *Courtesy of the New-York Historical Society, New York City.*

his services worth a few paltry pounds. Having tried to stem the flood in other ways, André finally agreed—so Arnold later insisted —that he would urge Clinton "to allow the sum I proposed." The adjutant hinted that his influence over his chief was so great that what he recommended would certainly be granted.

Then they discussed how best to give up and capture West Point. The question whether the attack was to be made while Washington was there, on his way back from Hartford, has been argued by generations of historians. Clinton later dreamed that the invaluable American might have been included in the bag, but it must have been clear to the traitor and the spy that Washington's presence at the fortress would ruin everything, since he would assume the command and override Arnold's orders. The only practical possibility would be to cut him off by a sudden raid on an outpost. Although Arnold was eager to notify André should this opportunity occur, such a raid could not have been planned as a part of the major action. For one thing, Washington might escape and rally the troops; for another, communication through the lines was too uncertain to permit of opportunist changes in a large scheme. Since it would be foolish to sacrifice to an outside chance of destroying Washington their practical certainty of overwhelming the post when he was too far away to meddle, the invasion would have to be postponed for a week or ten days.

Neither negotiator wished to lessen the bag by emptying the post of troops and munitions. Arnold outlined how, just before the attack, he would gather in the troops at Fishkill and other too distant places, bringing the vulnerable force to a few men above the 3,000 for whom Clinton had offered £20,000. The method of cutting off this large army, only part of which would be behind the walls of West Point, carried then into extended discussions of strategy.

Arnold had to confess that he could not rely on such explicit obedience to orders as the British officer assumed; American troops would not carry out commands which seemed to them silly. The post would have to be lost by co-ordinating each step of the British advance with an American counterstep that would seem, on the face of it, aimed effectively at defense. This involved an explanation from Arnold of the terrain, the construction of each

347

strong point, the location and nature of each detachment. After André had outlined the men, ships, and ordnance the British could bring to bear, the movements of the two armies had to be worked out step by step. Since forces allotted to one maneuver later seemed better suited to another, the whole plan had to be reconsidered again and again.

It was a long conference as Smith, shivering with ague, realized. After two or three hours, the eastern mountains began to take on height and shape, but the change was invisible to the men in the firs. Glad to get again into the act, Smith climbed up the bank and told the conspirators of approaching dawn.

Because later events make the true explanation seem incredible, legends have grown up to explain why André was not returned at once to the *Vulture*. The facts are that Arnold asked Smith to row "Mr. Anderson" there. Smith relayed the request to the Cahoons, but they said they were too tired. When Smith repeated their refusal to Arnold, the conspirators did not argue. No pressure, so the brothers remembered, was placed upon them: "Mr. Smith said that if we could not go we must do as we thought best, and would leave it to us; but made us no offer to return on board the vessel that night."

Although Arnold and André had brought their business to a possible end, they could profit from further conversation. In particular, Arnold wanted to show the Englishman some papers, which he had left behind because they would be useless in the woods unless the conspirators lit a dangerous lantern. Both officers expected the *Vulture* to remain at its anchorage; and, since dawn was coming, ferrying might well be safer on the following night. Uncertain what was the wisest move, the principals allowed a most crucial decision to be made by the comic relief.

Arnold and André set out together on horseback for Smith's house. In the open, with dawn sliding in overhead, they became increasingly visible to each other; each stared without seeming to do so. Hawk-nosed warrior and gracious aide, they were both handsome men. Arnold was businesslike and grim, hiding nervousness, perhaps even hiding remorse—but André was in the best of spirits. His fine horse moved through the awakening day like a charger out of chivalry. Here was the Meshianza not in play but in reality; here was such an adventure as ancient bards extolled!

They had not gone very far before a sentry's challenge and Arnold's reply revealed to André that, in contradiction of Clinton's orders, he was tightening a possible noose about his neck by entering an American strong point. Later, when he was fighting for his life, the Englishman wrote Washington, "Against my stipulation, my intention, and without my knowledge beforehand, I was conducted within one of your posts. Your Excellency may conceive my sensation on this occasion." As a matter of fact, André had from the first intended, should circumstances make it advisable, to stay at Smith's house. The added danger merely heightened his joy.

In the thin light, the autumn foliage burned dimly. The farms Arnold and André passed were unresponsive to cockcrow, and the road was deserted. Turning into a driveway, they climbed to a plateau below which the Hudson, four miles broad at Haverstraw Bay, stretched salmon-colored under the ever-brightening sky. As they savored the view that was like the birth of a new world, rumbling reverberated between the hills. Looking down river, they saw smoke rise from Teller's Point, opposite the spidery shape which was the *Vulture*. Smoke responded from the vessel; the noise augmented; a cloud of burnt powder pinkened with the dawn and obscured the scene. Calling impatiently on André to enter Smith's house, Arnold hurried him upstairs to the secrecy of a second-floor bedroom.

When the firing began, Smith and the Cahoons were on the river, rowing to a mooring. They realized that, had they set out with Mr. Anderson for the *Vulture*, they would have been caught in the middle of a battle. Smith, to whose heated imagination the warship "appeared to be set on fire," lost all his taste for midnight expeditions on the river. He did not even mention to the brothers the plan for returning André that night which André assumed was a foregone conclusion.

Finally, the three tired men toiled uphill to the farm. Joseph Cahoon saw Arnold "come out of Mr. Smith's house and go to the necessary house. He walked lame and had on a blue coat and white breeches."

Excited as a beagle on a hot scent, Smith charged upstairs to participate, at long last, in Arnold's exciting intrigue; but when he saw his visitor, he recoiled. André had thrown off his long coat and was sitting there in the uniform of a British staff officer. Arnold whispered that Mr. Anderson was only a merchant who "from pride" had borrowed the coat of an officer in New York. Gratified with this confidence, Smith agreed that less perceptive men than he was might misunderstand, and that Anderson had better be kept in strict hiding.

After Smith had prepared breakfast in the servantless house, the three men ate and discussed inconsequential subjects; the rumbling continued down river. Finally a tremendous explosion—the Rebel magazine had blown up—brought them all to the window. The firing now ceased, but when the smoke cleared they saw the *Vulture* under sail, retiring toward the British lines. Perhaps this was the moment when André first felt fear; Smith never forgot "the impassioned language of his countenance, and the energy with which he expressed his wish to be on board."

Although the firing on the *Vulture* is one of the most celebrated incidents in American history, exactly what happened is far from clear. Colonel Livingston had planned to attack with a single four-pounder, and he is said in hundreds of books to have done so, but Lamb warned him that using so small a ball—an inch and a half in diameter—was "a waste of powder," and it seems from the result that Livingston had collected heavier artillery. The British judged they were attacked by a six-pounder and a howitzer—certainly shells struck as well as balls—and, although the only casualty was Sutherland, who was nicked in the nose by a splinter, they justified their retreat by asserting that the *Vulture* was hulled six times, the boats, booms, and rigging damaged. Not wishing to get too far from André, they anchored off Sing Sing, a few miles below their former station.

Having managed to shake Smith, Arnold showed André the papers he had prepared: a detailed list of the ordnance available and the number of men needed to protect each fort, the artillery commander's plans in case of attack, a confidential statement of Washington's military intentions, and a rough accounting of the 3,086 men Arnold hoped to deliver for death or capture. Since

Arnold had not taken these documents to the riverside rendezvous, and since, when he had copied some of them out, he had not troubled to disguise his handwriting—as he had always done on communications meant to go through the lines—he clearly had not intended them to be carried to New York. But the conspirators lost their presence of mind: André said he wished to show the papers to Clinton, and Arnold, although with misgivings, agreed.

In his later defense of his actions, André asserted that Arnold "made me put the papers I bore between my stockings and feet. While he did it, he expressed a wish that in case of any accident befalling me, that they should be destroyed, which, I said, of course would be the case, as when I went into the boat I should have them tied about with a string and a stone. Before we parted, some mention had been made of my crossing the river and going by another route, but I objected much against it, and thought it was settled that the way I had come, I was also to return."

André would have to wait for nightfall before he could be ferried back to the *Vulture*, but Arnold rode off "in the morning" to King's Ferry where his barge awaited him. To Smith, who accompanied him, he gave two passes, one permitting the agent to return Mr. Anderson by water, the other by land; they were to take the route that seemed safest at the time. Smith carried off both papers, but he had no doubts which one he would use. The Cahoons were to go back and forth with their cows uninterrupted. Smith made not the slightest preparation for another jaunt on the river.

At his headquarters, the traitor found Peggy flushed, his aides sullen. When, on the previous evening, Varick had discovered that Arnold was not coming home to sleep, he guessed at once where his general was staying. He told Franks that he "considered Arnold's treatment of me in keeping his connection with Smith, in opposition to the warning I had given him, as very ungenteel; and I was resolved to quit his family." Franks replied that Arnold was "an avaricious man" and that Smith was probably his agent for illegal trading through the lines with the New York merchant, John Anderson. The aides decided to "prevent further intimacy [between Arnold and Smith] by alarming Mrs. Arnold's fears."

Peggy raised surprised eyes as the young men expressed their suspicion that Arnold was with the villainous Smith. The general, she replied, would never do anything dishonorable. However, she had a low opinion of Smith "both as a gentleman and a man of sincerity"; she would use her influence to keep Arnold from seeing him any more. During this interview, she labored to appear only slightly concerned, but when she reached the privacy of her bedroom, she was less calm. Her husband and her dear friend were on the point of meeting. What would happen at that secret interview?

On his return, Arnold reported that everything had been happily settled. In a few days West Point would be delivered; in a few weeks they would be rich: in a few months—who knows—titled British aristocrats. If, since he had no reason to trust Smith's diligence, Arnold had any dark premonitions, they are not recorded.

Sitting in a second-story bedroom with nothing to do, André became "disconsolate"; he mounted to the roof, stared in the direction of the *Vulture* and his friends in New York. Smith watched him covertly, enjoying the excitement. When, in mid-afternoon, a dealer delivered two cows, and "desired him to go into the road and see them," Smith whispered melodramatically that he could not leave the house because Arnold's secret agent was upstairs.

Toward evening, Smith remarked to his guest that it was too dangerous to row back to the *Vulture*. If Mr. Anderson would discard the army coat he had borrowed and return to the civilian clothes suited to the merchant he was, they would cross the river together, and he would start him in the direction of the British lines. André protested violently, but could not voice true objections, and Smith, "to my great mortification," merely smiled at his arguments. In the end, André was forced to disobey the second of Clinton's orders by substituting for his uniform a claret-colored coat with gold laced buttonholes which Smith lent him. Since his boots, his nankeen breeches, and his waistcoat were not conspicuously military, he continued to wear them. A round civilian hat completed his disguise.

"At the decline of the sun," André wrote, "I set out on horseback." Beside him rode Smith, and behind, the colored boy who had been Arnold's companion the night before. Smith bubbled with high spirits. When they began to catch up to an American officer, André's heart contracted, but Smith shouted, spurred his horse, and encouraged Major John Burrowes to ride between them. Offering the Rebel pasturage for his horses, Smith asked him to drop in for tea; the officer made polite replies; André was silent. His heart lifted a little when the enemy trotted off down a side road.

However, Smith remarked that they were approaching the fortress at Stony Point, and tried to draw André out about its capture and subsequent loss by the British; he "found my fellow traveler very backward in giving any opinion or saying much about it." Reminded that, as he had personally negotiated the American surrender, his face was familiar to Rebels who might have escaped from imprisonment and be again garrisoned there, André noted with apprehension, when they descended steeply toward the ferry, a tent by the side of the road, with officers sitting before it, passing a bowl from hand to hand. They shouted a greeting. André shrunk his chin into his collar, bowed quickly from the saddle, and rode on at a steady pace; but from the corner of his eye he saw Smith rein in. Soon his companion's high, foolish voice was protesting that the bowl was empty.

André was forced to wait by the steps of the ferry, the colored boy impassive behind him. Smith was now shouting hints that he was engaged on a mission of great importance: "What do you think, Daddy Cooley, of being in New York in three weeks' time?" There was a whoop of good-humored laughter, and a cracked voice replied, "No, I'm afraid, Master Joseph." The hilarity continued for many minutes before Smith rode up to André, still giggling a little.

They pulled their horses after them into a longboat manned by four oarsmen and a coxswain. Instantly, André went to the rail and stared where the bright colors of expiring day faded into leaden water; Smith postured in the bow for the amusement of the boatmen. André walked over to him and whispered of haste. With an expansive gesture, Smith offered the men "something to revive our spirits" if they would row faster. The oars groaned a little more rapidly.

When they finally reached the eastern bank, André could not dissuade Smith from calling on Colonel James Livingston, the commandant there. He again waited on the road, glad that it was now really dark. However, Smith's loud voice began boasting of his intimacy with Arnold, and that he was escorting a gentleman on a mysterious errand. A quieter voice asked Smith to call his companion in for some grog and dinner. André could hardly bear the suspense until Smith replied that they were in too much of a hurry. Livingston would not accept the refusal; he argued. But for once Smith's sense of importance stood André in good stead; his business, he insisted, promised too much for the American cause to be delayed.

Now the countryside emptied out. Houses were few and often deserted; Smith's chattering and the beat of hooves were the only sounds as they moved rapidly between dark trees under a sky of stars. Coolness came with night, and Smith thought that his companion "grew more cheerful." They had covered six miles in less than an hour, when a voice cried from the darkness, "Who goes there?"

"Friends," Smith answered.

With his musket in readiness, a Rebel sentry stepped into the road and commanded one rider to dismount. As Smith handed his reins to his companion, he noticed that "Mr. Anderson seemed very uneasy." Smith talked to the sentry for a minute, and then Captain Ebenezer Boyd appeared. He was the first man they had met who proved suspicious. For ten minutes, he cross-questioned Smith about their identity, where they had come from, where they were going. Smith insisted they were on an important mission for General Arnold.

Boyd vanished and reappeared with a light which revealed such a stubborn Scotch-Irish face as had, ever since his tribulations at Carlisle, haunted André's dreams. Smith walked over to him, and André could see, silhouetted against the light, their two heads bobbing over Arnold's pass in emphatic discussion. Then Smith came back to say that Boyd advised them to spend the night nearby, since a band of cowboys, the pro-British raiders, were on the prowl. André would have been delighted to fall into such hands, but he could not tell Smith, and thus his arguments that they should go on lacked weight. "I accordingly returned a short distance to look for night quarters," Smith wrote, "and my companion reluctantly followed."

Smith knocked on Andreas Miller's door. When there was no response, André brightened—perhaps they would have to continue their journey—but Smith, whose own comfort and safety were involved, became, for once, persistent. Pound, pound, pound he went in the silent night until the family, who were trembling within for fear of raiders, dared remain silent no longer. Miller pulled back the bolts. The whole family followed the intruders around suspiciously until they entered a bedroom; then Miller slammed the door and André heard a key turn in the lock. He lay down beside Smith on the one bed.

"I was often disturbed," Smith wrote, "with the restless motions and uneasiness of mind exhibited by my bedfellow." At the first streaks of dawn, André sprang up and summoned Smith's boy to prepare the horses. He looked, Smith noticed, "as if he had not slept an hour during the night. He was, at first, much dejected, but a pleasing change took place in his countenance when summoned to mount his horse."

As they rode through the gray light of dawn, alien hooves sounded and a solitary rider came in view. André recognized Colonel Samuel B. Webb, a Rebel who knew him well. "The colonel stared at him and he thought he was gone," so André had later confided to an American officer, "but they kept moving and soon passed each other. He then thought himself past all danger."

Pine Bridge, the Croton River crossing supposed to be the limit for Rebel patrols, was only a few miles away. As the rested horses advanced rapidly, André amazed Smith by bursting into speech. He out-talked his loquacious companion, his body, no longer rigid in the saddle, swaying to the rhythm of his eloquence. He spoke of history, of the American war, of his hopes for an early peace; he spoke of verse and music and painting; when from the hilltops he could see the Hudson running blue between orange-tinted hills "he descanted on the richness of the scenery around us . . . by adopting the flowery coloring of poetic imagery. . . . The pleasantry of converse and mildness of the weather so insensibly beguiled the time that we at length found ourselves at [close to] the bridge before I thought we had got half the way."

They stopped at a one-story farmhouse for breakfast. Since a border band had robbed her the night before, the Dutch *vrou*

355

could offer them little except some Indian meal boiled with water to make *suppon*. André had mocked this humble dish in *The Cow Chase*, but now he ate heartily, as he had been supperless the night before.

Smith announced that he would go no further: he was afraid of the Tory irregulars who operated on the far side of the Croton. André did not argue with his frustrating companion, but merely borrowed a few Continental dollars; he had brought no money with him, even as he had brought no weapons. When Smith refused to take his gold watch as security, he was pleased, for he could not foresee the future.

The thundering of his horse on Pine Bridge made André's heart leap; he was crossing into British-dominated territory. True, the royal outpost at White Plains was still fifteen miles away, but he had nothing to fear from Loyalist patrols, and, should any Rebels be operating so far off base, he only had to show them Arnold's pass. His dangerous mission was, he believed, successfully completed.

Arnold had been begged by the inhabitants of the region between the lines to suppress the Loyalist cowboys and the Rebel Skinners—lawless ruffians of uncertain allegiance who often co-operated for their basic purposes of loot—but he had not bothered because he could see no way in which they menaced his plans. So great had been their deprivations that the farmhouses which André passed were desolate, the fields overgrown, the orchards loud with wasps eating fruit no hand dared gather. Legends exist of children who gave André fresh water from cool wells, of maidens who patted back their hair as the gallant rode by; but the signs of human life were more likely to have been a door closing quietly and eyes peering with fright from shuttered windows. The occasional yokels he met on the road kept to one side and looked away.

André believed that he carried in his mind the knowledge, under his feet the papers, that would put an end to all this agony. Soon the war would be over and his Loyalist friends would reclaim their broad estates on the banks of the Hudson. Under the rule of well-bred and cultivated gentlemen, the American peasantry would return to their appointed tasks and prosper. An aristocratic government, with His Majesty at the top and the better people ranked round him, would make the Colonies and the world forget the unnatural upheaval which had seemed to him once, when he had been a prisoner at Carlisle, about to destroy everything the world possessed of value. So he dreamed, until roused by a shout. Three ragged knaves, their firelocks upraised, barred his way; and one grabbed his horse's bit.

He was near Tarrytown, André realized, "far beyond the points described as dangerous"; (and, if rumor is to be believed, one of the intruders wore a torn Hessian coat). "Gentlemen," he said, and smiled at the word, "I hope you belong to our party."

"What party?" asked a spare, ungainly giant who seemed older than his companions.

"The lower party." When the giant nodded, André rattled on, "I am glad to see you. I am an officer in the British service, and have now been on particular business in the country, and I hope you will not detain me. And for a token to let you know that I am a gentleman—" He pulled out his gold watch.

The giant looked unimpressed and gruffly ordered him to dismount. Suspecting that these were not Loyalists but Rebels, André gave his best theatrical laugh and said, "My God, I must do anything to get along!" He handed the leader General Arnold's pass. The giant mouthed as his slow-moving eyes encountered each word. Then he repeated his order for André to dismount.

Leaping from his horse, André registered unconcern. "Gentlemen," he said, "you had best let me go, or you will bring yourselves in trouble, for, by your stopping me, you will detain the general's business."

Here the testimony given by André's captors, from which the preceding quotations were taken, starts to differ from a statement André is remembered to have made. John Paulding, the gigantic leader, swore, and was backed up by David Williams who was, with Isaac Van Wart, his companion, that "I told him I hoped he would not be offended, and I told him we did not mean to take anything from him, and told him there were many bad people going along the road, and I did not know but perhaps he might be one, and I asked him if he had any letters about him." According to André, his captor shouted, "Damn Arnold's pass! You said you was a British officer. Where is your money?"

"Gentlemen, I have none about me."

"You a British officer, and no money! Let's search him!"

André was led to a gate. His captors would not let him pull a rail down lest some inquisitive person notice and follow; he was forced to squeeze through. When they were all deep in a thicket, he was ordered to undress. Each garment was snatched from him as it came off and thoroughly searched. By the time he was nude, except for his boots and the stockings that contained the incriminating papers, his tormentors had found his gold watch and chain and the Continental dollars he had borrowed from Smith. For a moment it looked as if they were satisfied, but then, so Williams remembered, "We told him to pull off his boots, which he seemed indifferent about, but we got one boot off, and searched in that boot, but could find nothing; and we found there were some papers in the bottom of his stocking, next to his foot, on which we made him pull his stocking off, and found three papers wrapped up." Of his captors, only Paulding could read. As the naked royal officer watched anxiously, the gigantic yokel labored through the documents. "This," he cried, "is a spy!"

André was allowed to get dressed. He regained hope when Williams, as Williams himself testified, asked him "whether he would give up his horse, bridle, watch, and 100 guineas, upon which he said, 'Yes,' and he told us he would direct it to any place, even if it was to that very spot, so that we could get it. I asked him whether he would not give us more. He said he would give us any quantity of dry goods or any sum of money, and bring it to any place that we might pitch upon, so that we might get it."

Here the two sets of accounts deviate once more. Paulding claimed that his patriotism inspired him to cry, "No, by God, if you give us 10,000 guineas, you should not stir a step!" Although "one of the young fellows winked at me, who had a mind to find out a little more," he was adamant in his virtue.

André asserted that, noticing their "thirst for money," he asked them to name their sum to deliver him to Kingsbridge. They answered that when they all got there, he would have them arrested, "and you will save your money." André then suggested that two of them guard him, while the third go to the British lines with a note that would procure them five hundred or even a thousand guineas. "They held a consultation a considerable time," but finally told him that "a party would be sent out to take them and then they all should be prisoners."

They finally resolved to deliver their prisoner to the American authorities. Prodded by muskets in the unwashed hands, André started back along the way over which he had so recently ridden in expectation of triumph. His captors were soon joined by four companions who had been watching a different road. The seven men were delighted with their bag and in high spirits. Williams remembered that he asked André "if he would not get away if it lay in his power."

André answered, "Yes, I would."

Williams laughed. "I told him I did not intend he should."

It was annoying to be taunted by peasants, but André's mind was busy with the next step. Although he had suffered a misfortune, he felt far from defeated. When delivered to a Rebel outpost, he would continue to play the role of Mr. John Anderson, secret agent to the area commander. The papers that had been found in his stockings might, it is true, be hard to explain, as they contained intelligence only useful to the British, but no wonderings could damage him unless some subordinate officer became suspicious of Arnold, so suspicious that he risked censure for insubordination by going over his own general's head and reporting directly to Washington. The commander of an outpost was more likely to suspect André of spying simultaneously for both sides, and to send him for punishment to Arnold. Arnold would, of course, see that he got safely to the British lines.

André reasoned that his mission had been checked but not defeated: West Point would still fall, making his fortune, pulling down with it the Rebel cause.

CHAPTER TWENTY-SEVEN

Chariot of Fire

WHEN his rough captors delivered André to the American outpost at North Castle, he was pleased to see that the commander, Lieutenant Colonel John Jameson, was a Virginia gentleman to whom another gentleman could talk. "John Anderson" produced Arnold's pass and stated negligently that, of course, he would be released to continue his important mission as a patriot agent. Although Jameson listened with polite gravity, the Rebel was clearly puzzled. True, Arnold had notified him that, should a Mr. Anderson appear from the British lines, he was to be sent on to headquarters—but this man had been captured going in the wrong direction and carrying papers which Jameson considered "of a very dangerous tendency." Furthermore, some of the secret information about West Point was written in the same hand as Arnold's pass. For the first time in any loyal American mind there flared a fear that the hero was a traitor.

However, this seemed incredible, and, should Jameson's suspicion prove unfounded, he would be guilty of the rankest insubordination if he did not send Anderson on as ordered. The agreeable dark-eyed prisoner was showing no anxiety. Jameson went off by himself to think. Finally, he ordered that the captive be delivered to Arnold. André successfully hid his relief.

He would have had less relief to hide had he known that Jameson had compromised by sending a messenger with the incriminating documents to meet Washington on the Danbury road, over which

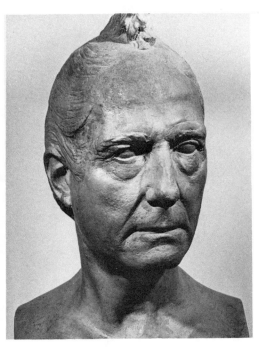

David Williams

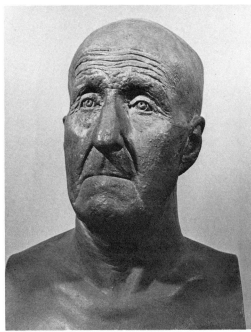

John Paulding

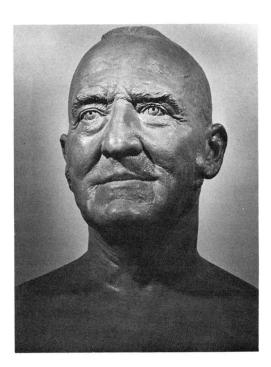

Isaac Van Wart

André's captors as old men. Casts taken from their living heads by John H. I. Browere, who almost killed Jefferson when he applied the same process. *Courtesy, New York State Historical Association.*

André as a prisoner awaiting execution. A self-portrait, expressive of the composed and calm front the doomed man presented, with amazing self-control, to his captors. *Courtesy, Yale University Art Gallery.*

the commander was supposed to be traveling on his way from Hartford to the Hudson. This decision was certain to tip off the treason in the end, and seemed likely to assure the safety of West Point; but the safety of the traitor and the spy depended on the outcome of a three-cornered race which Jameson had set in motion.

The outpost commander had written Arnold of Anderson's capture, and also that the papers found on him had been forwarded to Washington; this letter was confided to the officer who was to take the prisoner northward. If André, with or without the letter, were delivered to Arnold in time, both conspirators could escape. If André were long delayed on the road and the letter to Arnold went ahead without him, the American might achieve safety while the British agent was sacrificed. But if Washington received the incriminating documents first, and had time to take action, both Arnold and André would suffer the consequences of their plot.

Danbury, where at the furthest the messenger hoped to meet Washington, was almost exactly the same distance from North Castle as Arnold's headquarters, but the messenger to Washington started in the afternoon and rode a fast horse, while the party conducting the prisoner and the letter to Arnold set out at nightfall and proceeded on foot.

André walked with soldiers on the four sides of him; one held a strap which bound his arms together behind his back. Towering over the rest of the detachment, for he alone was on horseback, Lieutenant Solomon Allen brandished his sword and shouted that he would run Anderson through if he made the least effort to escape. Far from being frightened, the prisoner, Allen noticed, trudged along "with much cheerfulness." Since he was sure that release by Arnold lay at the end of the march, he could almost enjoy his romantic predicament. For some two hours the party moved through the dark countryside, and then a dragoon galloped up with a dispatch.

Jameson had been pacing his quarters, wondering whether he had acted wisely, when his ranking subordinate, Major Benjamin Tallmadge, returned from an expedition toward the enemy lines. Tallmadge agreed that it looked bad for Arnold, but, so Jameson wrote a few days later, was "clearly of the opinion" that they could not risk the insubordination of failing to notify the general.[1]

He did, however, suggest a way to circumvent Arnold's orders that Mr. Anderson be sent to headquarters: pretending that they had heard rumors of enemy patrols above them, they would call the prisoner back on the pretext that they were protecting him from capture.

Jameson decided that even if Arnold had turned traitor and was warned by the note telling him of Anderson's capture, he would be unable to escape: "I did not think of a British ship being up the river." He assumed that Arnold would try to cross the lines, and "would come down to the troops in this quarter, in which case I should have secured him." Washington was to conclude that Jameson and his fellow officers were "lost in astonishment"; yet, whether by chance or by plan, they increased the lead of the messenger carrying the documents that would give the plot away. They ordered Allen to bring the letter that would alert Arnold back with him when he delivered André to South Salem, a post they fixed on because it was further inland and thus less eligible to an enemy raid than North Castle. Then Allen was to start out again for Arnold's headquarters.

On receiving Jameson's orders, André's guard drew up by the roadside. When Allen announced that, as the enemy were operating above, they were to turn back, the prisoner was dumbfounded. However, he was immediately given new hope by the soldiers, who stated "there was no danger, and it would be best to proceed." (They were eager to join their companions at West Point.) Blessing the bad discipline of the Rebel army, André "seconded the proposal." A spirited argument ensued, yet authority finally triumphed. André found himself plodding away from sanctuary.

Smith dropped in at Arnold's headquarters to report that he had escorted André almost to the British-dominated territory beyond Pine Bridge. Although this news gave Arnold "apparently much satisfaction," Varick and Franks were not pleased to see Smith's hated face. The aides were smoldering with resentment when, at the dinner table, Peggy asked for some more butter. The servant told madam that there was none left.

"Bless me," cried Arnold, "I had forgot the oil I bought in Philadelphia." On the oil being produced, he remarked that it had cost eighty dollars.

"Eighty pence," interpolated Smith, implying that a Continental dollar was worth no more than a British penny.

"You are mistaken!" Varick exclaimed, in a voice that convinced Lamb he intended to be insulting. Smith, with the excitement of his adventure still upon him, did not back down, and Franks joined in the argument on Varick's side. At first, Arnold said nothing, perhaps calming himself with the thought that both his aides would soon be in a British prison. When Smith tried to prove his superiority by speaking in French, Franks answered in the same language; and the shouting rose in intensity until Arnold's inflamed nerves could stand it no longer. Seeing that her husband's control was about to break, Peggy "begged that the dispute might be stopped as it gave her great pain."

After they had risen from the table, Arnold took Franks aside and said, "If he asked the devil to dine with him, the gentleman of his family should be civil to him." Franks replied that had it been in any other house than Arnold's, he would have "sent the bottle" at Smith's head. Then Varick interposed. Assuming that Arnold did not attack him personally because he came from a great New York family, he took credit for starting the argument, and warned Arnold to be careful if he "wished to stand well in this state." Franks, Varick remembered, "went out of the room in a passion and to Newburgh on business. . . . The dispute between me and Arnold continued very high. I cursed Smith as a damned rascal, a scoundrel, and a spy."

Arnold finally got himself half under control, and said "that he was always willing to be advised by the gentlemen of his family, but, by God, would not be dictated to by them." Some hours later, he apologized and promised Varick "he would never go to Smith's house again or be seen with him but in company." After all, he would have to curb his proud spirit for only a few more days.

Smith had gone on to Fishkill to pick up his family. He found Washington there with Lafayette, Knox, and their aides. Instead of taking, as Jameson had counted on their doing, the lower route through Danbury, they had taken the upper one, intending to spend the night with the Arnolds. However, they had met La Luzerne on the road, and turned back. They lodged at Fishkill, supping at the same table with Smith, who saw nothing ominous in the information that the commander in chief intended to break-fast the following morning with Benedict and Peggy Arnold.

When Jameson's messenger had reached Danbury, he had been unable to secure any news of Washington. Not knowing what else to do, he returned with the deadly papers toward the outposts to which André and the note to Arnold were also retreating. The entire race was now running backward.

At South Salem, André was delivered to Lieutenant Joshua King, who locked him in a small bedroom with mounted guards at the door and window. His prisoner, King remembered, "looked some-what like a reduced gentleman," his coat worn and his hat "tar-nished." His face was covered with a black stubble—he had not been shaved in several days—and his clothes were soiled. When King's barber took the ribbon from his queue, "I observed it full of powder," which made the lieutenant suspect "I had no ordinary person in charge." Uncomfortable in his shabbiness, the prisoner "requested permission to take the bed while his shirt and small clothes were washed." King lent him clean ones. Then the two men paced together "in a spacious yard" surrounded with sentries. The captive walked silently, in deep thought, and said at last that he must make a confidant of somebody. After a moment of renewed hesitation, he announced that he was not Mr. John Anderson, an American agent, but Major John André, adjutant general of the British army.

André had given up hope that he would be sent to Arnold, and realized that a man of his prominence must soon be recognized. Imposture could serve his ends no longer. Needing some more subtle stratagem, he called for pen and paper, and wrote Washington:

"What I have as yet said concerning myself was in the justifiable attempt to be extricated; I am too little accustomed to duplicity to have succeeded. I beg Your Excellency will be persuaded that no alteration in the temper of my mind, or apprehension for my safety induces me to take the step of addressing you, but that it is to rescue myself from an imputation of having assumed a mean char-acter for treacherous purposes or self-interest, a conduct incom-patible with principles that actuated me, as well as with my condition of life. It is to vindicate my fame [from any suspicion that he had acted as a spy] that I speak, and not to solicit security."

André then presented the argument on which he had been meditating ever since the trip to Arnold's headquarters had been interrupted. To influence an "adversary is an advantage taken in war." On such a mission, he had come ashore; "I was in my regimentals and had fairly risked my person." However, his unnamed military correspondent had forced him, against his will, to enter the American lines. He was thus made a prisoner of war. A prisoner of war had a right to attempt an escape wearing civilian clothes.

"In any rigor policy may dictate," he hoped to be treated as a gentleman who had done nothing dishonorable. He wanted permission to notify Clinton of his plight and to write his friends for clean linen. Next came an offer and a threat. Some South Carolinians, he pointed out, had conspired against the Crown when "either on parole or under [British] protection. . . . Though their situation is not similar, they are objects who may be set in exchange for me; or are persons whom the treatment I receive might affect."

Although Arnold was not mentioned by name, this letter would hardly contribute to the general's security. Perhaps André knew that the plot was as good as discovered anyway, for the messenger, who had failed to find Washington at Danbury, showed up at South Salem. André's letter was added to the other incriminating documents, and the horseman set out once more, this time for Arnold's headquarters, where it was assumed Washington would be.

Since Allen had been on the road for some hours, the messenger to the commander in chief had fallen behind the messenger to Arnold—yet the late starter could move more quickly. Allen, although also mounted, had with him an enlisted man on foot.

Unconscious of the world-shaking race in which they were engaged, the expresses failed to move with purposeful speed. Taverns that offered refreshment to road-weary men, pretty girls leaning over fences, delayed them both. The messengers, having been on the road since the previous evening, turned in at two separate points for the night. More than thirty-six hours had passed since André was captured and Arnold suspected, yet—inconceivable as it may seem—the news was still restricted to a handful of American soldiers manning extreme outposts.

As the Hudson Valley darkened and whitened again, Washington slept unconcernedly at Fishkill. Arnold and Peggy tossed fitfully in their feather bed fifteen miles away; but, as the time was not ripe for the British attack, they expected no immediate crisis. After he had dispatched his letter to Washington, André no longer "appeared downcast"; he drew for his jailers a comic picture of himself being escorted down the road by his ridiculous captors; and then, with the passion of a completely exhausted man, he slept. The greatest activity was on board the *Vulture*, which still rocked off Sing Sing; Robinson and Sutherland leaned over the rail, scanned the water for small boats, strained their ears for a shout. In the end, Robinson wrote Clinton, "It is with the greatest concern that I must now acquaint Your Excellency that we have not heard the least account of him since he left the ship. . . . I shall do everything in my power to come at some knowledge of Major André."

On the historic 25th of September, Washington's party set out early for their breakfast with the Arnolds. However, they halted to inspect some fortifications on the upper river. When Lafayette objected that Mrs. Arnold was waiting the meal for them, Washington commented good-humoredly that all his young officers were half in love with her. He sent two aides, Majors Samuel Shaw and James McHenry, to tell his hostess to begin.

They found that she was still upstairs, but Arnold sat with them at the breakfast table. After a few minutes, he excused himself to give some orders. He walked into the buttery and was there accosted by an extremely dusty lieutenant and an equally dusty enlisted man. They handed him a dispatch from Colonel Jameson. He opened it negligently, but read: "I have sent Lieutenant Allen with a certain John Anderson taken going into New York. He had a passport signed in your name. He had a parcel of papers taken from under his stockings, which I think of a very dangerous tendency. The papers I have sent to General Washington." Arnold glanced quickly at a second document, which explained that Mr. Anderson had been returned to the outposts.

Although "thrown into great confusion," he managed to tell

366

Allen to wait for an answer. He limped rapidly out into the yard, commanded that his horse be saddled, and sent a servant down the steep slope to the river with orders that his barge crew stand by. Then he returned to the house and passed through the dining room where McHenry "observed in him an embarrassment and agitation so unusual that I knew not to what to attribute it."

Peggy was sitting up in bed in an excellent humor. Some young officers had gone to the orchard to get her peaches; she was pleased by the attention and looking forward to the fruit. Arnold's desperate entrance was completely unexpected. He whispered that all was lost; she gave a cry; and then a low knock thundered on the closed door. With unbelievable calmness, Franks's voice sounded through the wood reporting that Washington's servant had just appeared to say, "His Excellency is nigh at hand." Peggy fell back in a faint.

Arnold bolted from the door, almost knocking Franks down. As he shouted over his shoulder that he was on his way to West Point to prepare a reception for Washington, the aide noticed his "great confusion." However, not knowing what it all portended, Franks stood aside.

Arnold's light eyes gleamed as he saw his horse waiting in the stable yard. He leaped into the saddle and rounded the corner of the barn only to find his road blocked by four of Washington's light-horsemen. His hands dropped to his pistols, but, when one of the men spoke, it was respectfully. The commander in chief, said the dragoon, was right behind. Arnold told the horsemen to stable their mounts in the barn. Then he dug in his spurs, bounded across the little plateau in front of the house, veered to the left, and "galloped almost down a precipice" to the river bank.

People do strange things in moments of great emotion. Arnold, who was leaving everything he owned behind him, felt it necessary to save his saddle. While the oarsmen waited, he unbuckled it, and threw it, with his pistols still attached, into the barge. He leaped on board and "desired the men to pull away for Stony Point." He was, he explained, in a hurry as he was "anxious to return to meet His Excellency."

At that very moment a boat from West Point approached the landing. Arnold shouted that the crew should "go up to the house to get refreshment," and tell Washington that he would be back before dinner. The sailors seemed to accept his message, but "he was not three hundred yards from the wharf when he saw the armed vessel put after him." He ordered his men to hoist their sails, and soon left the boat far behind. (Only in his imagination was it chasing him.)

When his barge was off Stony Point, he told his bargemen that he had "particular business from His Excellency to the captain of the *Vulture*." This change of story elicited a terrifying hesitation in his crew, but when he promised them two gallons of rum their faces cleared. The boat continued down river, tacking in the face of a head wind, and assisted by oars. They moved slowly, but the water was now empty of any vessels that might be following them, and Arnold's most anguished stares could discern no unusual activity on shore. Occasional horsemen visible through breaks in the forest moved with stolid slowness; farmers, as they watched the general's barge go by, leaned laxly on their spades. The landscape slumbered in autumnal peace.

Storm raged only in Arnold's skull. All the darker emotions—fear, hate, rage, disappointment, anguish—swirled there like clouds driven by a hurricane, drawing back only occasionally to show the solid peaks of his actual situation. He had been forced to leave his wife and baby behind, yet, unless Peggy gave herself away in hysteria, his family was secure. No patriot knew of her complicity in the plot, and who would wantonly harm a delicate young mother? He had himself effected his escape. To André's plight he gave, almost certainly, little thought: the catastrophes of subordinates were the necessities of war.

True, he had failed to deliver West Point. Yet, so he reassured himself, he was not without valuable resources. He carried with him his personal prestige as a great hero, his skill as a great soldier. Peggy would join him, and they would build themselves a new life under the benign effulgence of the British Crown. As the *Vulture* loomed ever nearer, so close that he raised a flag of truce, his practical mind faced the necessity of making a good impression when he first stepped into the world where his destiny lay. Surely, he would be welcomed with open arms!

On the *Vulture*, Robinson and Sutherland were leaning over the rail, flooded with blessed relief at the sight of the general's barge. André, they at first assumed, was coming back. When Arnold climbed agilely up the side, they greeted him with consternation. After he had "unfolded all," they demanded to know why he had not, as had been agreed, sent their adjutant back by water. They did not hide their concern at what Clinton's reaction would be.

Eager to demonstrate at once that his powerful example would generate a great wave of American desertions, Arnold led the way to the deck where his bargemen were gossiping with British tars. They came to negligent attention, expecting orders to row back up river, but Arnold announced dramatically that he had recognized the evils of the Rebel government and was now a British general empowered to raise a Loyalist brigade. "If you will join me, my lads, I will make sergeants and corporals of you all; and for you, James," he continued to the coxswain, "I will do something more."

"No, sir!" the coxswain exclaimed. "One coat is enough for me to wear at a time." The nine patriots looked at Arnold with horror. For a few minutes, in increasing rage, the traitor argued. Then he turned to Sutherland and demanded that his servants be thrown into the hold as prisoners of war.

On recovering from the swoon in which Arnold had left her, Peggy heard the voices of men coming up from downstairs; she could distinguish the calm, firm tones of Washington. Her whole body contorted into a scream that seemed about to explode into the air—but it must not, she could not. Her husband needed time to escape. Since she and her baby were helpless in the Rebels' hands, no one must guess her part in the conspiracy. She dug her nails in her palms and silenced her sobbing by piling pillows over her head.

Washington had been surprised that Arnold had not waited for him, but not displeased that his thoughtful subordinate had gone to West Point to prepare a suitable reception. After a leisurely breakfast, the commander's party started across the river. The fortress, which capped the opposite hills, gleamed in the sunlight, a tranquil symbol of the cause they all served. Washington, so it is reported, half suspected that, despite the shortage of powder, Arnold would honor him with a formal salute of cannon. But no booming drowned out the gurgle of water against the sides of his boat. When the landing came in view it was empty except for the usual guards, who sprang to attention with surprise on their faces. Down the hillside, Lamb appeared at as fast a pace as was dignified for a colonel; if only he had been notified, he would have prepared a reception for His Excellency. When Washington expressed surprise that Arnold had not told him, Lamb replied that he had not seen Arnold that day.

Back at Robinson's house, Varick lay in Arnold's ground floor office, suffering from a high fever. Shortly after Washington's departure, the window over his bed was opened from the outside. Franks popped in a frightened face to whisper that Allen had reported John Anderson had been arrested as a spy. Arnold, he exclaimed, was "a villain and a rascal." Varick also damned the general, but as the two aides talked the matter over, they concluded there must be some innocent explanation for Arnold's connection with Anderson. After all, Arnold was "a gentleman and a friend of high reputation." Franks withdrew his head, and Varick "lay down secure in the high idea I entertained of Arnold's integrity and patriotism."

His thoughts turned pleasantly to Peggy, who had, the day before, "made tea for me, and paid me the utmost attention in my illness." He was anticipating another visit from "the amiable lady" when the housekeeper came in to say that Mrs. Arnold wondered how he did. Varick's message of thanks to the "good woman" was never completed.

"I heard a shriek to me," he wrote, "and sprang from my bed, ran upstairs, and there met the miserable lady, raving distracted . . . with her hair disheveled and flowing about her neck. Her morning gown, with few other clothes, remained on her, too few to be seen by a gentleman of the family, much less by many strangers. . . . She seized me by the hand with this, to me distressing, address, and a wild look, 'Colonel Varick, have you ordered my child to be killed?'

"Judge you of my feelings at such a question from this most amiable and distressed of her sex, whom I most valued. She fell on her knees at my feet with prayers and entreaties to spare her innocent babe. A scene too shocking to my feelings, in a state of body and nerves thus so weakened by indisposition, and a burning fever. I attempted to raise her up, but in vain. Major Franks and Dr. [William] Eustis soon arrived, and we carried her to her bed, raving mad. . . .

"When she seemed a little more composed, she burst again into pitiful tears and exclaimed to me, alone on her bed with her, that she had not a friend left here. I told her she had Franks and me, and General Arnold would soon be home from West Point with General Washington. She exclaimed, 'No, General Arnold will never return. He is gone. He is gone forever, *there, there, there,* the spirits have carried him up there; they have put hot irons on his head'—pointing that he was gone up to the ceiling. This alarmed me much."

When, in mid-afternoon, Washington returned, Hamilton handed him a newly arrived packet of papers. His party separated to prepare for an early dinner, but Lafayette had hardly begun to "arrange my clothes" when Hamilton threw open the door in great agitation; he begged the marquis to attend on His Excellency. Lafayette found Washington holding documents in trembling hands. "Arnold," he cried, "has betrayed us! . . . Whom can we trust now?"

With a pounding of hooves in the courtyard, Hamilton and McHenry galloped for King's Ferry in the hope they could gather in the traitor for hanging. A few minutes later, footsteps echoed on the second floor of the house. Rushing from Peggy's room, Dr. Eustis begged Varick and Franks "for God's sake" to send for Arnold, "or the woman would die." The aides pulled Eustis into a corner and whispered that Peggy's behavior made them suspect that, in the brief interview with her before he vanished, Arnold had confessed to the innocent, patriotic girl that he was in British pay; her husband and their general had "destroyed himself or gone off." The three were so frightened by their suspicions that they decided not to tell Washington, but to let him see Peggy and judge for himself.

Peggy also wanted to see His Excellency. There was a hot iron on her head, Varick remembered she shouted, and no one but General Washington could take it off.

"I attended him to her bedside," Varick wrote, "and told her there was General Washington. She said, no, it was not. The general assured her he was, but she exclaimed, 'No! that is not General Washington! That is the man who is going to assist Colonel Varick in killing my child.' She repeated the same sad story about General Arnold: poor, distressed, unhappy, frantic, and miserable lady."

Washington walked out of the chamber visibly upset, but made no comment. When the uneasy group were gathered in the living room, he remarked, "Mrs. Arnold is sick and General Arnold is away. We must therefore take our dinner without them." Lafayette is quoted as remembering, "Never was there a more melancholy dinner. The general was silent and reserved, and none of us spoke of what we were thinking about. . . . Gloom and distrust seemed to pervade every mind, and I have never seen General Washington so affected by any circumstance."

Eventually a dispatch came from Hamilton enclosing three letters which had been sent ashore from the *Vulture*. One was from Robinson defending André; the others were addressed in Arnold's familiar hand to Washington and Peggy.

"The heart that is conscious of its own rectitude cannot attempt to palliate a step which the world may censure as wrong" were the traitor's words to the commander he had betrayed, "I have ever acted from a principle of love to my country." The same principle "actuates my present conduct, however it may appear inconsistent to the world, who very seldom judge right of any man's actions." He had "too often experienced the ingratitude of my country" to ask any favor for himself, but he wished Washington to protect Mrs. Arnold; "she is as good and as innocent as an angel and is incapable of doing wrong. I beg she may be permitted to return to her friends in Philadelphia, or to come to me, as she may choose." Arnold added in a postscript that Smith, Franks, and Varick were "totally ignorant" of his actions.

Washington, the ever courtly, sent Peggy's letter upstairs without opening it, and also the message that, although it had been his duty to try to capture Arnold, he was happy to relieve her anxiety by telling her that her husband was safe.

The commander in chief had learned of Arnold's treason at about 4 P.M. A strong wind that was blowing up river was favorable to the British fleet should they try that afternoon to snap shut the treasonous trap. Yet Washington's only official act had been to send McHenry and Hamilton on their vain mission to head off Arnold. From King's Ferry, Hamilton on his own authority advised General Greene in New Jersey to put the Continental Army "under marching orders," and to dispatch a brigade to the Hudson.

Not until he had heard from Hamilton that Arnold had escaped, did Washington send out his first directive. At 7 P.M., after three hours had passed, he confirmed Hamilton's suggestion to Greene; relieved James Livingston, who might possibly be in on the treason, of command of the outposts; called all available troops in from the countryside; and notified the ranking officer at West Point to prepare for an attack. Since everything took time, it was 2 A.M. on the following morning before the fortress was ready.

The most rational explanation of Washington's delay, during which he kept Varick and Franks ignorant of what he knew, is that he was avoiding any move that would alert possible accomplices, or the traitor himself in the unlikely possibility that, despite his unnatural early morning departure, he did not know of his danger and was engaged in some unexplained business within the American lines. Washington may have assumed that, since André had been stopped, no word had got through to the British and that thus it was safe to delay unless he discovered, as he now had done, that Arnold had got safely to New York City. Yet more than two days had passed since André's mission had been interrupted and there was no way of knowing how far the ramifications of the plot extended; there had been no way to be sure that the British would not advance that very afternoon. Perhaps Washington, for once, had not thought with calm rationality. Treason was so alien to his nature that the treason of a fighter he had admired, a man he had trusted, shook his being to its very foundations. He seems to have risked the loss of West Point and his own capture on an outside chance that he could keep the foul betrayers from going free.[2]

When Hamilton returned from King's Ferry, he found Peggy still raving. That her hysterics had at first been genuine there is no reason to doubt, although she gave her husband time to escape before she signaled his treason, and never divulged the slightest hint of her own guilt. Nervous crises came naturally to her, and she had always shown an ability to keep, beneath her wildest rantings, her secrets inviolate.

However, as the hours passed, the fire in her brain seems to have burned down, permitting her to notice that her wild talk was winning sympathy. From Hamilton's own account, we suspect that, by the time she worked on his emotions, she was consciously playing a role: "One moment she raved, another she melted into tears. Sometimes she pressed her infant to her bosom and lamented its fate occasioned by the imprudence of its father, in a manner that would have pierced insensibility itself. All the sweetness of beauty, all the loveliness of innocence, all the tenderness of a wife, and all the fondness of a mother showed themselves in her appearance and conduct. . . . It was the most affecting scene I ever was witness to."

"This morning," Hamilton went on, for he wrote on the 26th, "she is more composed. I paid her a visit and endeavored to soothe her by every method in my power, though you may imagine she is not easily to be consoled. Added to her other distresses, she is very apprehensive the resentment of her country will fall upon her (who is only unfortunate) for the guilt of her husband. I have tried to persuade her that her fears are ill-founded, but she will not be convinced. . . .

"She received us in bed, with every circumstance that would interest our sympathy, and her sufferings," Hamilton continued to his own fiancée, "were so eloquent that I wished myself her brother to have a right to become her defender. As it is, I have entreated her to enable me to give her proofs of my friendship."

While her old friend, John André, paced back and forth under the unblinking eyes of guards; while her husband slunk into New York, an exile whose plot had failed, Peggy was surrounded with love and pitied by everyone from Washington to the lowest stable boy. Everyone in the house vied to do her "the most delicate attentions"; everyone was convinced that she had known nothing of the treason until Arnold had informed her the instant before he fled.

CHAPTER TWENTY-EIGHT

Human Sacrifice

ARNOLD'S escape and Peggy's successful hysterics had left André the only conspirator in extreme danger. Yet the drama that had rocked Robinson's house and bounded across the river to West Point and down to the decks of the *Vulture*, disturbed not at all the tranquility of his South Salem prison. He could only imagine what had happened to General and Mrs. Arnold, or what his own fate would be. The idea that the adjutant general of the British army could be viewed in the "mean character," as he put it, of a common spy seemed to him preposterous; the penalty for spying—to be hanged by the neck until dead—had no reference to a high officer and a fine gentleman. General Clinton held many important Rebels, captured under equivocal circumstances, whom he would gladly offer in exchange. It seemed only a matter of time until André was restored to his friends in New York.

However, the general orders announcing his capture called him a spy; and Captain Shaw thus expressed the sentiments toward him of the army: "His military knowledge, his address and talents, were so exceedingly necessary to Sir Harry [Clinton] that nothing of any consequence was undertaken but by his concurrence and approbation. It is said he was the soul of the army. However, were he ten times more than he is, the fate of a common spy will be his fate."

Unfortunately, André had been unable to inform his friends of the line he had adopted in his defense. No sooner had Robinson cross-questioned Arnold in the *Vulture*'s cabin than he sent Washington a contradictory story. In his own letter to the same commander, André had stated that he had "fairly risked my person" on a warlike mission; Robinson insisted that he had gone ashore under a flag of truce. André had claimed that he was forced behind the American lines, becoming a prisoner of war; Robinson stated that he had willingly put himself under Arnold's orders. André argued that, as a prisoner, he was justified in using any means to escape; Robinson argued that, in all his acts—assuming a feigned name, putting on civilian clothes, carrying papers—André had been acting as an obedient subordinate to the legally constituted American commander of the area. "Under these circumstances," Robinson concluded, "Major André cannot be detained by you without the greatest violation of flags. . . . I must desire you will order him to be set at liberty and allowed to return immediately."

Sending no answer to Robinson, Washington wrote a subordinate, "I would not wish Mr. André to be treated with insult, but he does not appear on the footing of a common prisoner of war, and therefore he is not entitled to the usual indulgences they receive, and is to be most closely and narrowly watched."

After being shunted around for a few days, André was finally imprisoned at Tappan, near the headquarters of the Continental Army. His bedroom was a shed under a sloping roof, but his living room was large. From its windows, he saw a little church and some houses with overhanging eaves, a tidy lane so reminiscent of Holland that it seemed a perverse vision there among the wild hills of wild America. André was barred from entering this Old World scene. He was kept indoors, watched by pairs of New World officers who relieved each other every few hours all day and all night long.

Washington had agreed to Arnold's request that Peggy be permitted to choose whether she would join her husband in New York or her father in Philadelphia. She was pro-British; she had urged Arnold into the treason; she knew that the man who had always been dependent on her would need her even more in desperate exile. On the other hand, the young officers, who clustered around her bed, begging to be sent on errands, pitied her for the villainy of her husband and urged her to leave him. "Could I forgive Arnold for sacrificing his honor, reputation, and duty," wrote Hamilton, "I could not forgive him for acting a part that must have forfeited the esteem of so fine a woman. At present, she almost forgets his crime in his misfortunes, and her horror at the guilt of the traitor is lost in her love of the man. But a virtuous mind cannot long esteem a base one; and time will make her despise if it cannot make her hate."

Peggy vacillated, but not for long. Deep in her heart, the twenty-year-old wife did not wish to share her husband's failure and disgrace; she wanted to be a child again in her father's house. Two days after the discovery of the treason, she set out for Philadelphia with her "nursemaid" Franks.

As soon as she left the courtly atmosphere of Washington's military family, she discovered that to be forgiven would not be easy. She could not have hysterics before the whole population; she could not let the army, regiment after regiment, see her becomingly distraught in bed. In a nation already riddled with discouragement and suspicion, the treason had raised great waves of fear. "Heavens on earth!" wrote Arnold's old subordinate Colonel Scammell, "we are all astonishment, each peeping at his next neighbor to see if any treason was hanging about him; nay, we even descended to a critical examination of ourselves. The surprise soon settled down to a fixed detestation and abhorrence of Arnold" as "the veriest villain villain of centuries past." And here was the traitor's wife, accompanied by his dandified aide, jogging down the road behind fine horses as if nothing had happened!

When, a few weeks before, she had traveled toward West Point dreaming of a British title, the sun had shone. Now rain poured down, seeping through the curtains of the light wagon prepared for a summer journey. This had one advantage—it kept the roads empty—but occasionally they met a militia company marching soddenly along, or were stopped by a sentry. Then the belle who had never desired anonymity, prayed that she would not be recognized: everyone stared at Mrs. Arnold with such hatred. Franks would stand out in the rain, arguing with the soldiers, until at long last the horses were whipped up once more.

At nightfall in the hamlet of Cachats, they knocked at many doors before they found anyone "who would take us in . . . or give our horses anything to eat." Franks was in perpetual terror that Peggy would take off again: "Mrs. Arnold, thank God, is in tolerable spirits," he wrote Varick, "and I have hopes to get her home without any return of her distress in so violent a degree."

Although it was only a short trip to Paramus, they decided to spend the next night there, since they knew they would be welcomed by Theodora Prevost, the widow of a British officer. When they arrived, company was in the drawing room, and Peggy behaved quite frantically, but once alone with Mrs. Prevost, she "became tranquilized." To this first Tory she had encountered since tragedy struck four days before, Peggy, for the only recorded time in her entire life, confessed the truth. She assured Mrs. Prevost that she was "heartily sick" of the "theatrics" that were perpetually forced upon her. She had long been "disgusted" with the patriot cause, and had, "through great persuasion and unceasing perseverance" convinced her husband to correspond with the British. Mrs. Prevost repeated the conversation to Aaron Burr, whom she later married, and Burr kept the secret until both Arnold and Peggy were dead.

At Philadelphia, her family received Peggy with sympathetic tears. Edward Shippen was "fully convinced" she had "never participated in the guilt of her perfidious husband." He pointed out that Washington, "who happened to be an eyewitness of her condition and conduct at the most critical time, declares, in the pass he gave her to proceed hither, that 'there is every reason to believe she is only unfortunate in the late unhappy affair of her husband,' and recommends it 'to all persons to treat her on the journey with the delicacy and tenderness due to her sex and virtues.' " Edward Burd considered that "so delicate and timorous a girl as poor Peggy" could not have been "the least privy or concerned in so bold and adventurous a plan. . . . It is impossible she should be engaged in such a wicked one."

Franks wrung all hearts with his account of her hysterics at Robinson's house, but, in the safety of her home, she abandoned hysterics and "fell into a kind of stupor. . . . The consequences of these violent transitions from one kind of grief to another,"

Burd wrote, "I am a trifle apprehensive of. . . . She keeps her room and is almost continually on the bed. Her peace of mind seems to me entirely destroyed."

With violence and unanimity, the family excoriated Arnold for what he had done to their delicate flower. "The sacrifice was an immense one," Burd continued, "at her being married to him at all." Edward Shippen considered that "if she were again put into the hands of so bad a man, her mind might, in time, be debased, and her welfare, even in another world, endangered by his example."

The Shippens noted that Peggy was disturbed by their endless diatribes against her husband's treason. She wished "to be persuaded there was some palliation of his guilt, and that his conduct had not been so thoroughly base and treacherous as it was generally thought." They attributed this not to its true cause, but to her "affectionate disposition." She was, they reasoned, "dotingly fond of her husband," and they were terrified lest she wish in the end to return to him. However, she did not let them worry for long. Docilely, she signed a statement "engaging not to write General Arnold any letters whatever, and to receive no letters without showing them to the council, if she was permitted to stay" in Philadelphia.

A movement to force her by law to join her husband in exile had been set in motion by the results of a sentimental mistake Peggy had previously made. When the Arnolds had burned all their correspondence with the British, Peggy had rescued from the pyre the letter André had written her offering her his services in New York as a milliner. Since the council's first move on learning of the treason had been to seize the Arnolds' papers, the document was now in unsympathetic hands.

Its existence disproved, so the *Pennsylvania Packet* argued, "the fallacious and dangerous sentiments so frequently avowed in this city that female opinions are of no consequence in public matters. . . . Behold the consequence! Colonel Andrie [*sic*], under the mask of friendship and former acquaintance at Meshianzas and balls, opens a correspondence in August 1779 with Mrs. Arnold, which has doubtless been improved on his part to the dreadful and horrid issue." The Shippens swore that this was the only communication she had received from André, and that it referred exclusively to feminine matters, but, as Burd admitted, "the letter is an unfortunate one."

Arnold's other papers, according to the *Packet*, "disclose such a scene of baseness and prostitution of office and character as, it is hoped, this new world cannot parallel." They revealed his financial involvement in the *Active* case, and that he had bought goods when the shops were shut. From Burd we learn there was also a description Peggy wrote Arnold of a concert at the French Minister's "in which she is free in her observations upon several of the ladies there, and which has given them much offense."

In the rising controversy over Peggy, the same group that had supported her husband against the council supported her. Robert Morris wrote, "Poor Mrs. Arnold: was there ever such a villain?" and John Jay added, "His wife is much to be pitied. It is painful to see so charming a woman so sacrificed." But Arnold's old enemy Wilkinson was "ready to burst with indignation" that Peggy should be in Philadelphia; his agitation to have her deported was assisted by "the popular clamor."

Edward Shippen threw all his long-stored prestige into the balance. "She is very young," he wrote the council, "and possessed of qualities which entitle her to a better fate" than being forced to live with a monster. Indeed, she seemed every day to become younger. As the men she had influenced suffered exile or imprisonment, as the backwash of the treason she had fomented rocked the land, as patriot leaders wrangled over her fate in legislative halls, she returned in her father's house to the tears and dependence of a little child.

At New York, Arnold had waited eagerly for his dearest friend, his support in the world, his beloved Peggy to come through the lines. He told the Loyalist, Andrew Elliott, "he hopes to get his family in," and, as the days passed with no word from his wife, he was increasingly tortured by fears. Had her guilt been discovered; was she in danger of her life? Or had she decided not to share with him the tribulations resulting from their common deeds?

Arnold's first appearance at British headquarters had elicited "the astonishment of all here." Clinton hardly listened to his aggressive statements of how he could, if permitted, singlehandedly pull down the Rebel cause. He was only interested in having him write Washington in André's behalf. Obediently, Arnold stated that all André's acts had been carried out under his orders and with the protection of passes he had given, "which I then had a right to do, being . . . commanding general at West Point." The British commander added a curt note demanding his adjutant's "return to my orders."

To his own government, Clinton wrote, "The general has escaped to us, but we have lost—how shall I tell it to you—poor André. I am distressed beyond words to describe." He was anxious to convince himself that the tragedy was not his own fault, that, as he put it, "I have nothing to reproach myself with." His emotional state would not permit him to blame the beloved friend whom he might never see again. Who else was there to blame but Arnold? The story which Robinson had concocted placed the deserter in a very peculiar light. As Judge Jones wrote, "If the major went on shore *'under the sanction of a flag,'* and this Arnold in a letter to Washington positively asserts, why in the name of God could he not return on board again under the same *'sanction'?*" Clinton and his associates suspected that Arnold had risked André's skin by being too careful of his own.

Although Clinton's personal feelings were close to hatred, policy dictated that he honor Arnold in order to encourage other Rebel desertions. In this quandary, he did what was typical of his vacillating nature: he worked out a strange compromise. He appointed Arnold a brigadier in the provincial service and allowed him to wear the uniform, but he did not mention the appointment in his orders or give Arnold any command. Although the Rebel press was screaming about the treason, exposing Arnold's every villainy and attributing to him a thousand other evil deeds, Clinton would not allow the Tory press to welcome the turncoat or even to mention that he had entered the British lines. He wished, Clinton explained, to do nothing that would further endanger his dear André.

Of course, the famous newcomer attracted attention on the street. "The people," William Smith noted, "exult much, but it is not known yet that André was catched." Arnold's peers, who did know, were anxious to treat him in whatever way would please

Clinton. Since that commander was "so much affected that none chose to speak to him except on affairs of consequence," friendliness to Arnold seemed impolitic—and, in any case, no one desired to be friendly. The Loyalists attributed his defection not to principle but to "avarice," and, being as snobbish as all exiles with nothing left except their social position, they despised the lower-class merchant risen to eminence by military services in a cause they considered evil. Their whisperings were not lost on the officers of the British army, who expressed great displeasure at having a horse-jockey turned Rebel turned traitor placed among them as a brigadier. In many a mess room, English aristocrats agreed that they would refuse to serve under the low-born, dishonorable Benedict Arnold.

In this situation, the traitor tried to behave with dignity that would in the end win him esteem: he spoke "handsomely" of Washington and the other Rebel generals (always excepting Gates) and "he does not scruple to mention the inactivity of our [the British] army at certain periods in former campaigns." However, everything possible was interpreted to his disadvantage. Wishing to have some prisoners in New York to exchange for André should opportunity offer, Clinton rounded up about twenty noncombatants on the charge of espionage. Although Arnold had no part in this action, the rumor circulated that he had betrayed his friends. To have done so would have been a service to the Crown, yet—and this showed Arnold how hard it would be for him ever to earn credit—Tories and British soldiers were alike horrified.

It became gradually clear to Arnold that, unbelievable as it seemed, people of his "mensuration" in New York felt that they had made a bad bargain in exchanging the boyish major, whom Arnold had regarded merely as a pawn in great events, for the strong fighter and powerful leader he considered himself to be. If André were released, Arnold might still win Clinton's favor. If André were hanged—but that must not happen. To his own amazement, the traitor found himself greatly worried about the fate of the spy.

At liberty in a brigadier general's uniform, Arnold passed through sneers and frowns; in his prison, André was surrounded with love. By contrast with the traitor, the young man, who was in such desperate danger because of loyal service to his King, seemed to the officers who guarded him an unfortunate victim of circumstance. Alexander Hamilton wrote, "There was something singularly interesting in the character and fortunes of André. To an excellent understanding, well improved by education and travel, he united a peculiar elegance of mind and manners, and the advantages of a pleasing person. . . . His knowledge appeared without ostentation, and embellished by a diffidence that rarely accompanies so many talents and accomplishments, which left you to suppose more than appeared. His elocution was handsome; his address easy, polite, and insinuating. By his merit, he had acquired the unlimited confidence of his general."

As the seriousness of his predicament became clear to him, André labored to keep up a bold front, and never has a doomed man played to so sympathetic an audience. Imprisoners and imprisoned alike were caught up in a tragic drama almost unbearably poignant because it was real. The victim around whom everything circled, André played his heroic role with such grace and fortitude that he became in the minds of his companions a symbol of the courtly civilization for which he had fought. He was a symbol being carried to death by soldiers who wept for what they were destroying, but saw another, brighter image for which they were forced to make the sacrifice.

Even Washington, whose duty it was to preserve stern impartiality, found "much in his character to interest," and considered André "a gallant and accomplished officer." The prisoner wrote, "I receive the greatest attention from His Excellency, General Washington, and from every person under whose charge I happen to be placed."

On September 29, five days after André was captured, all the general officers at headquarters, with the exception of Washington, convened as a board. André was allowed to walk down the Old World lane he had viewed from the window and into the little Dutch church, where his trial was held. At the request of the judges, he acknowledged the letter to Washington in which he had asserted that he had been made a prisoner of war, and in the evidence he subsequently gave, he tried to back up this contention. Ignorant of the conflicting argument put forward by Robinson,

Clinton, and Arnold, he did not realize what was involved when he was asked whether he had left the *Vulture* under a flag of truce. "He said," the official report reads, "that it was impossible for him to suppose he had come on shore under that sanction; and added that, if he had come ashore under that sanction, he might certainly have returned under it." Since his own line of defense was not taken seriously, and he innocently denied the line on which the judges were trying him, they considered that "the unhappy prisoner . . . confessed everything." They were not obliged to call witnesses.

Unable to recognize the places where André lied—his insistence, for instance, that Arnold had forced him behind the American lines against his will—the judges concluded that, while he "carefully concealed everything that might involve others," he frankly acknowledged "all the facts relating to himself." They were much impressed by his "candor and firmness, mixed with a becoming sensibility." And the courtly young man, eager to avoid (as his British friends later pointed out) "the apprehension even of meanness," made no emotional plea in his own defense. He stated merely that he left the evidence "to operate with the board."

Through the years, there has been much controversy over André's guilt. His own contention that he was made a prisoner of war has been ignored (a tendency which has made writer after writer misunderstand his actions at the trial), but much support has been given to Clinton's position that he came in under a flag and subsequently obeyed orders Arnold had a right to give. However, flags do not cover the suborning of treason; had André been acting legally, he would have had no need for an assumed name. An officer is not obligated to obey an enemy's orders, and, in any case, it is no defense from conscious complicity in treason to assert that you were carrying out a superior's commands.

Called back before the board, the prisoner was read the judges' decision: "Major André, Adjutant General of the British Army, ought to be considered a spy from the enemy, and that, agreeable to the law and usage of nations, it is their opinion he ought to suffer death." There is no record of André's behavior as he listened to his doom, but, after he was returned to his prison, he commented "with manly gratitude" on the "generosity" with which the board had treated him, by giving him "every mark of indulgence," and not pressing him to answer questions which could "embarrass his feelings." If he had ever felt, he stated, any prejudice against the Americans, his "present experience must obliterate them."

Dashing out of André's prison, Tallmadge wrote, "By heavens, Colonel Webb, I never saw a man whose fate I foresaw whom I so sincerely pitied. He is a young fellow of the greatest accomplishments, and was the prime minister of Sir Harry on all occasions. He has unbosomed his heart to me, and, indeed, let me know every motive of his actions. . . . He has endeared himself to me exceedingly. Unfortunate man! He will undoubtedly suffer death . . . and, though he knows his fate, seems to be as cheerful as if he was going to an assembly. I am sure he will go to the gallows less tearful of his fate and with less concern than I shall behold the tragedy. Had he been tried by a court of ladies, he is so *genteel, handsome, polite* a young gentleman I am confident they would have acquitted him."

During the hours Hamilton spent with the prisoner, André broke down only once. "I foresee my fate," he said, "and, though I pretend not to play the hero or to be indifferent about life, yet I am reconciled to whatever may happen, conscious that misfortune not guilt has brought it upon me. There is only one thing that disturbs my tranquility. Sir Henry Clinton has been too good to me. . . . I would not for the world leave a sting in his mind that should embitter his future days." André could scarce finish the sentence, "bursting into tears despite his efforts to suppress them, and with difficulty collected himself enough" to ask that he be permitted to write Clinton. Permission was granted.

"Your Excellency," André wrote, "is doubtless already apprised of the manner in which I was taken and possibly of the serious light in which my conduct is considered and the rigorous determination that is impending." He wished "to remove from your breast any suspicion that I could imagine I was bound by Your Excellency's orders to expose myself to what has happened. The events of my coming within an enemy's posts and of changing my dress, which led me to my present situation, were contrary to my own intentions, as they were to your orders, and the circuitous route which I took to return was imposed (perhaps unavoidably) without alternative upon me.

"I am perfectly tranquil within my mind, and prepared for any fate to which an honest zeal for my King's service may have devoted me. In addressing myself to Your Excellency on this occasion, the force of all my obligations to you, and of the attachment and gratitude I bear you, occurs to me. With all the warmth of my heart, I give you thanks for Your Excellency's profuse kindness to me, and I send you the most earnest wishes for your welfare which a faithful, affectionate, and respectful attendant can frame.

"I have a mother and three sisters to whom the value of my commission would be an object, as the loss of Grenada has much affected their income; it is needless to be more explicit on this subject: I am persuaded of Your Excellency's goodness."

On the day after the trial, Washington approved the sentence and ordered "that the execution of Major André take place tomorrow, at five o'clock, P.M."

"When his sentence was announced to him," Hamilton wrote, "he remarked that since it was his lot to die, there was still a choice in the mode, which would make a material difference to his feelings, and he would be happy, if possible, to be indulged in a professional death." Wishing to be shot like a gentleman and an officer, not hanged like a peasant and a spy, he wrote Washington, and signed himself with his proud title, "Adjutant General of the British Army":

"Buoyed above the terror of death by the consciousness of a life devoted to honorable pursuits, and stained with no action that can give me remorse, I trust that the request I make to Your Excellency at this serious period, and which is to soften my last moments, will not be rejected.

"Sympathy toward a soldier will surely induce Your Excellency and a military tribunal to adapt the mode of my death to the feelings of a man of honor.

"Let me hope, sir, that if aught in my character impresses you with esteem toward me, if aught in my misfortunes marks me as the victim of policy and not of resentment, I shall experience the operation of these feelings in your breast by being informed that I am not to die on the gibbet."

Washington did not stop the carpenters who were erecting a gallows, and Hamilton for once criticized his commander: "I urged compliance with André's request to be shot," he wrote his fiancée, "and I do not think it would have had an ill effect; but some people are only sensible to motives of policy. . . . When André's tale comes to be told and present resentment is over, the refusing him the privilege of choosing the manner of his death will be branded with too much obstinacy." Actually, Washington had no choice. If André were to be executed at all, he had to be executed as a spy, and the prescribed mode of death for spies was hanging. Any change would seem to admit a doubt of André's guilt on which the British propaganda machine would seize.

André was not notified of Washington's decision. However, word came that his execution had been postponed for a day. This reprieve reflected frantic British efforts to save him.

At first, Clinton had known no more of his adjutant's plight than Arnold had been able to tell. When, after two days, no further news had come through the American lines, the British commander sent for William Smith and begged to be assured that his favorite could not legally be considered a spy. He talked so much, blaming "Arnold for not sending André back by water," that Smith hardly had a chance to give him "the consolation" he desired.

Three more days passed, and then Clinton received his friend's farewell note and an equally terrible letter from Washington, which stated that André had been employed in measures which flags "were never meant to authorize or countenance in the least degree"; that André had "with great candor" confessed he had not been under the sanction of a flag; and that a board of general officers had sentenced André to death as a spy.

Clinton was suffering acute distress when an officer appeared from the lines with a strange message. The Rebel colonel, who had delivered the letters, had hung around with seeming aimlessness, and finally let drop, as if casually, that should Clinton "in any way suffer General Washington to get within his power General Arnold, then Major André should be immediately released." (Colonel Aaron Ogden had been sent by Washington, whose official position barred him from making such a proposal, to Lafayette, who instructed Ogden to insert the idea in British minds.) Although Clinton was sorely tempted, agreement would destroy all further efforts to win over Rebels. "A deserter," he stated firmly, "is never given up."

Clinton called into conference his seven generals and the leading Loyalist officials of New York. They found him "much affected." When he laid André's situation before them, several asked questions which revealed their fears that the adjutant had actually been a spy. But the doubters, seeing that this "distressed him more," lapsed into prudent silence. The meeting voted unanimously that André was being illegally held. Clinton thereupon drafted a protest to Washington, but his subordinates considered its pleading note undignified, particularly in "a compliment to Washington's humanity." General James C. Robertson was allowed to prepare "a shorter and more peremptory note" which stated that, since Washington had been misinformed, Clinton was sending a delegation "to give you the true state of the facts." The mission was entrusted to the civil officials of New York: Robertson, Governor; Andrew Elliott, Lieutenant Governor; and William Smith, Chief Justice.

The same express that had informed Clinton of André's danger brought Arnold his first letter from Peggy. The troubles under which he himself was laboring had, he gathered, not afflicted his co-conspirator; she was being caressed by Washington and Washington's aides. Although she expressed concern for her husband's welfare, she did not intend to share his trials; she would wait to join him until he could give her more information about his situation in New York. His wife planned to set out for Philadelphia and her father's house. Although Arnold had asked Washington to open this possibility to her, he could not have been pleased that she had embraced it. He was deep in depression when, about midnight, he received a peremptory order to attend on Clinton.

Even as Washington had used Lafayette and Ogden to make a suggestion he could not officially countenance, so Clinton asked Arnold to make threats that would be unsuitable for a British commander. Grimly, Arnold agreed and wrote his former friend and chief that, should the Americans not release André, he would be bound "by every tie of duty and honor to retaliate on such unhappy persons of your army as may fall within my power, that the respect due to flags and to the law of nations may be better understood and observed." He added that Clinton held forty South Carolina gentlemen to whom clemency could no longer be extended if André suffered. "I call heaven and earth to witness, that Your Excellency will be justly answerable for the torrent of blood that may be spilled in consequence."

Elliott considered this letter a proof of Arnold's courage, since Peggy and his children were in Washington's power, but the traitor trusted the gentlemanliness of the man he had tried to betray. In any case, he may not have been, at that dark moment, overly concerned with the safety of the wife who seemed to have deserted him. If he were sentenced to live with the British alone, he might as well live happily, and André's execution would cast a deep shadow over his future career.

Clinton forwarded Arnold's letter to the delegation, which set out by boat the next morning, and anchored in the Hudson a few miles from André's prison. Although they were met by Greene, that Rebel general said he could not receive them officially, since British interference with American justice could not be tolerated—he would speak to Robertson only as a friend. Replying that it was immaterial in what light he was received, the English envoy argued from Arnold's evidence that André had in his confession given a "wrong idea." Arnold, Greene answered, was "a rascal" and André "a man of honor who he believed"; the case was closed. However, so William Smith's account continues, "Greene hinted that André might be safe if Arnold was given up, and talked of satisfying the army. Robertson answered with a look."

Robertson then stated that Clinton, because of his personal emotions, would repay many times over clemency to André; on the other hand—he showed Greene Arnold's threatening letter. Would it not be fair to appoint the two foreign generals, Rochambeau and Knyphausen, mediators? Greene promised no more than to repeat the conversation to Washington, yet Robertson was "so well satisfied with the interview that the strongest hopes were received of having a favorable answer."

As the negotiators talked, Robertson's aide, who was walking apart with Hamilton, was suddenly conscious that something had been slipped into his pocket. It proved to be a note, written in a disguised hand, saying "there is great reason to believe" that Arnold had "meditated double treachery" and had sacrificed André to his own safety; it would thus be fair to save André by handing over Arnold. Hamilton had resisted pressure that he suggest such an exchange to André, certain that the gallant officer would merely think the less of him—"I have the weakness to value the esteem of a dying man because I reverenced his merit"—but now he was doing his best.

The next morning, "Light-Horse Harry" Lee wrote from Washington's encampment, in answer to an appeal from Simcoe, that André would probably be saved. However, before Lee could dispatch the letter, he was forced to add a postscript: "I find that Sir Henry Clinton's offers have not come up to what was expected, and that this hour is fixed for the execution." The Americans seem to have hoped till the very end that, by delivering up the traitor, the British would rescue André.

"Arnold or he must have been the victim," Hamilton wrote; "the former was out of our power." To this Washington added, "The circumstances he was taken in justified it, and policy required a sacrifice, but as he was more unfortunate than criminal in the affair . . . while we yielded to the necessity of rigor, we could not but lament it." Arnold's treason had shaken the patriots as no other event had ever done: civilian distrust of the army, the common soldiers' suspicion of their more conservative officers were heightened until the Loyalists in New York crowed with joy. Should no punishment ensue, it would be interpreted as halfheartedness in the high command; it might sink the foundering cause. Washington, who had ordered thousands of men to die for an ideal, could not endanger it to save one life, however charming. As Hamilton wrote, "the authorized maxims and practices of war are the satires of human nature."

The delegation Clinton had sent to save André still rocked in the Hudson, a few miles distant, when the prisoner was informed that the sentence would be carried out that day, October 2, at noon. In contrast with his guards, who were afflicted with silent depression, André showed no emotion. He spoke quietly and raised his voice only when his servant, who had been allowed in from the

British lines, burst into sobs: "Leave me until you can show your-self more manly!" He ate his breakfast, was shaved, and then dressed with unusual care in "the rich uniform of a British staff officer." Finally, he laid his hat on the table and said to the guard officers, Captain John Hughes and Lieutenant Burrows, "I am ready at any moment, gentlemen, to wait on you."

There was the sound of music and a large detachment drew up outside the prison. Linking his arms with Hughes and Burrows, André pulled them into a run that carried the three out the door, down the stoop, and into the center of the parade. Fife and drums struck up the death march. As André strode in step, a spectator noted that he seemed less concerned with death than "a dignified deportment."

"I am very much surprised," he said in a clear voice, "to find your troops under such good discipline, and your music is excel-lent."

The procession moved along a country road, mounted a hill, and turned into a field that was wriggling with massed spectators. A line of soldiers sagged as the mob closed in, but André proceeded with such composure that all shrunk back again. His calmness seemed horrible to the pious because, as a freethinker who had refused to be attended by a minister, he was "setting the Almighty and His vengeance at defiance at the time of his execution." Others were awed to see him walking to his death as if to a ballroom. John Hart, who noted that he seemed "the most agreeable, pleasing young fellow I ever saw, the most agreeable smile on his counte-nance," added that never "had I such disagreeable feelings at an execution: to see a man go out of time without fear, but all the time smiling, is a matter I could not conceive of." So great was the concentration of the crowd that one soldier, who had taken off his shoes to reach a vantage point in a tree, forgot to keep his eyes on them, and, as a result, had to walk barefoot all the way back to Pottstown, Pennsylvania.

The general officers who had pronounced the death sentence rose above the mob, a knot of men on horseback. With "a com-placent smile on his countenance," André bowed to each in turn. They bowed back. Then the victim looked up and saw, topping a little rise, "a very high gallows made by setting up two poles or crotchets, and setting a pile on top." Realizing for the first time that his request to be shot like a gentleman had been denied, André "involuntarily stepped backward, and made a pause."

"Must I then die in this manner?"

When he was told it was unavoidable, he said so loudly that the words remained in hundreds of memories, "I am reconciled to my fate, but not to the mode." He strode with his head up toward the gallows.

Once in the gibbet's shadow, he waited for the executioner to center under the protruding pole the wagon that was to act as a drop. Dr. Thacher's scientific eye observed that André revealed "some degree of trepidation, placing his foot on a stone and rolling it over, and choking in his throat as if attempting to swallow." Another spectator noted how "he bowed his head a little down, viewed his feet, and so up until his head rose to its natural position; at which time I discovered a small flush moving over his left cheek. I suppose at the time he looked at the gallows and viewed himself from the feet upwards, that he was reflecting upon the untimely end he had come to."

When the cart was in place, and the horses that were to pull it away stood indifferently between the shafts, André stepped quickly to the tailboard, put his hands upon it, and made a motion as if intending to jump. He did not leave the ground. Then he put a knee on the wagon and lifted himself up. Now that he was in plain view of all, a murmur arose. He shrank back, but instantly straightened and said in a firm voice, "It will be but a momentary pang."

He took off his hat, which he gave to his loudly lamenting servant, and revealed, a private noticed, "a long and beautiful head of hair, which, agreeable to the fashion, was wound with a black ribbon and hung down his neck." He placed his hands on his hips, and walked back and forth, casting up his eyes to the pole over his head.

Colonel Scammell (who considered André "perhaps the most accomplished officer of the age") read the death sentence in as steady a voice as he could muster. The prisoner listened, standing quietly with his hands still on his hips. "Major André," Scammell concluded, "if you have anything to say, you can speak, for you have but a short time to live."

"I have nothing more to say, gentlemen, but this: you all bear me witness that I meet my fate as a brave man." A wailing arose from the crowd.

Up into the wagon leaped the hangman, "a frightful-looking creature," unshaven, his face covered with soot "taken from the outside of a grease pot." When this personification of all worsted-stocking knaves tried to put the noose over his head, the finely dressed officer made "a moderate snatch" and pulled the rope from the dirty hand. André took off his neckcloth and put it in his right coat pocket; after which, with the forefinger of his right hand, he turned down the collar of his shirt. He opened the halter, put it over his head, and drew the knot close on the right side of his neck. Then he tied a white handkerchief over his eyes "without the least tremor or appearance of fear."

Scammell said "in a rather loud voice, 'His hands must be tied.'" André at once pulled down the handkerchief with which he had just covered his face, and, extracting another from his pocket, handed it to the executioner. After he had rebandaged his eyes, the hangman tied his arms together, just above the elbows, behind his back. Then the greasy-faced functionary sprang into violent action. He shinnied up a gallows post and tied the other end of the rope to the beam. The crowd swayed and yelled with hysteria. André stood motionless.

Dropping lithely to the ground, the executioner hurried to the horses. He had a whip in his hand. The whip descended, the wagon moved, and the world sprang out from beneath John André's feet.

The Long Way Down

ARNOLD was in William Smith's office when news arrived that André had been hanged: "He is vastly discon-certed," Smith noted, "and retires on the chariot's coming for him from General Robertson."

Having no further excuse for delay, Clinton announced that Arnold had been appointed a colonel with the provincial rank of brigadier; but in the same general orders he gave three times as much space to mourning the execution which had been the bitter price of the new officer's arrival. Arnold tried to capitalize on Clinton's emotion by writing that the dead adjutant had promised him £10,000. Clinton granted him only the £6,000 (with additions of expenses) which André had been authorized to offer. However, Arnold's prosperity depended in the long run less on his grieving superior than on his own ability to attract the some thousand deserters needed to fill the regiments of foot and of horse he had been empowered to raise. With Smith's help, he prepared statements and proclamations. Everyone in New York expected important results.

Discontent had long been rife in patriot territory, and many a man there had suspected his neighbor. Furthermore, conservative leaders whom the radicals hated (and for whom the British were angling) had been embarrassingly friendly with the traitor. The stage seemed set for a witch hunt that would foster disunion—yet wisdom prevailed. Reed made no effective political capital out of the support innocently given Arnold by Jay, Livingston, and Schuyler; Varick and, by implication, Franks were exonerated by a court martial; a civilian trial found Joshua Hett Smith a fool not a villain. When it became clear that Arnold, far from heading a widespread cabal, had been a lonely individual, the treason backfired on the enemy. American confidence in American unity mounted. Furthermore, the slender chance by which André had been captured and West Point saved convinced many patriots that God had intervened in support of their cause. Congress set a day for national thanksgiving.

Arnold was scowling down the streets of New York, depressed that he had inspired so few desertions, when he was stopped by the former sergeant major of "Light-Horse Harry" Lee's crack dragoons. John Champe explained to the delighted traitor that he had been induced to change sides by the example of the hero he most admired. After Arnold had appointed him to a place of trust, he secretly wrenched palings from the fence around the general's house and then tacked them back so lightly that they would give way when he dragged Arnold, gagged and tied, from the personal garden into the anonymous street. Champe had been commissioned by Washington to kidnap the traitor. He intended to support Arnold to the water front, explaining, if the watch intervened, that he was conveying a drunken sailor to the guardhouse. Although an accomplice had prepared a rowboat in which to hurry Arnold off to New Jersey for hanging, Champe never found an opportunity to carry out his sensational scheme.

Another recruit brought to Arnold by his proclamations was his wife: Reed's council was outraged into exiling her from Pennsylvania. That she was "obliged, against her will, to go to the arms of a man who appears to be so very black" shocked Edward Burd. Peggy's own apprehensions can be imagined. Had rumor reached Arnold—who certainly knew she was being forced to him by law—that she had wished to leave him forever, had even agreed to show his letters to his bitterest enemies? How would she be received by the violent man whom she had urged into treason and whom she had now offered to betray?

Her dear, conservative father rode with her to the American lines; then she proceeded alone through strange faces to join the husband who had to stay far back for fear of capture—the patriots had put a price on his head. He met her with his habitual courtliness. During the rest of his life, he permitted her to be pitied as an innocent angel tied to a monster; he never revealed her part in his treachery. Yet in the privacy of their bedroom there must have been tensions.

Peggy, a Loyalist lady reported, "is not so much admired for her beauty as one might have expected. All allow she has great sweetness in her countenance, but wants animation, sprightliness." However, she "had every attention paid to her" at a headquarters ball "as if she had been Lady Clinton." Englishmen anxious to encourage Americans "to follow Arnold's example" found it less repugnant to honor her than the known traitor. Caught up in gaiety, she soon became the subject of "strange stories" which a Quaker considered an effort "to blacken her character in a way which her uncommon affection for the general renders very improbable."

That no leading Americans had followed Arnold through the lines, that he had recruited only forty deserters, might, the British realized, be blamable on the fact, discouraging to Rebel waverers, that he had been kept in ignominious idleness. Clinton publicly entrusted Arnold with an expedition to Virginia, but privately empowered Simcoe and another lieutenant colonel at any moment to displace him from the command. Arnold was ordered to make a few raids, and then hole in for the winter, thus taking pressure off Cornwallis in South Carolina by pinning the Virginia militia down. Among the 1,500 soldiers who were marched on transports was Sergeant Champe. (He soon escaped to patriot territory.)

By a quick maneuver on his arrival at the James River, Arnold took Richmond before the Rebels could gather to fire a shot. Having burned public warehouses, he obediently retired to Portsmouth, where he chafed in inaction. When spring opened the possibility of further campaigns, reinforcements sailed in—but also a superior officer. General Phillips, the man who had once been Clinton's candidate to arrange the treason, was now in charge.

Moving in their fleet on intricate watercourses to destroy many Rebel installations, the British army kept the defenders so off balance that no effective opposition was possible. (These were the tactics André had recommended for harassing the South.) A few skirmishes did develop, but Arnold failed to attempt the feats of personal heroism which had once been his emotional release and his glory. Since the enemy had been ordered to bring him in alive, he foresaw, in case of catastrophe, not an honorable death on the battlefield but a noose tightening around his neck in the presence of cheering thousands.

Arnold was making money—in partnership with the agent of transport, he leased eight vessels to the Crown, securing in two months £6,066 from an investment of £1,148—yet his frustration was so obvious that, when Phillips was taken ill, the rumor circulated that the traitor had poisoned the British general to secure the command. Phillips did die, but Arnold's leadership lasted for only the week before his army was merged with Cornwallis's.

Returning to New York, he agitated for an expedition under his leadership that would bring West Point at last to heel. However, Clinton did not forget that Arnold's moment in the sun had failed to encourage Rebel desertions. Becky Franks, exiled from Philadelphia and now an intimate of Clinton's circle, noted that she had not seen or heard of Peggy "these two months. Her name is as little mentioned as her husband's."

"Chagrined beyond expression," Arnold offered to raid the privateering port of New London, only a dozen miles from his birthplace. Perhaps because he was so familiar with this territory, Clinton agreed. As Arnold sailed up the Sound, a British brigadier in control of impressive armament, he intended to force admiration and fear on the neighbors who, by undervaluing him, had first made him experience the injustice of the world.

He landed troops on both sides of the Thames. The column he himself led marched easily into New London, but Fort Griswold, high up on the far bank, was strongly defended. Standing on a hillside above the city, Arnold watched the desperate British assault he would have so loved to lead. It went badly. Frightened at last by the number of redcoated figures he saw fall, he ordered his troops to retire, but, before his messenger could get across the Thames, they breached the walls. Arnold had not foreseen what happened then. The defenders, having shed the blood of almost a hundred Englishmen who lay dead or writhing on the approaches to the fortress, were eager, now that they themselves were in desperate danger, to surrender—but the British could not forget their comrades. When Colonel Ledyard offered his reversed sword to the British commander, it was driven into his bosom. This was the signal for massacre. Arnold reported that eighty-five Rebel dead were found in the fort, and sixty wounded, "most of them mortally."

Arnold did not prevent his soldiers from looting New London, but he had ordered that only warehouses and public buildings be burned. From his high perch, he saw the flames cast a wild light on the streets of residences where he had so often walked as a boy. Suddenly a warehouse—"unknown to us," Arnold wrote, it contained powder—exploded. Burning brands cascaded on the town. "Notwithstanding every effort to prevent it," much of New London "was unfortunately destroyed."

It was useless for Arnold to deny responsibility for the burning and the bloodshed. Among his childhood companions, the rage was indescribable; and the British army was horrified by its own losses. Clinton was not sorry to conclude that any further trust put in the traitor would encourage disunion in his own ranks, angry unanimity among the Rebels.

However, Arnold had never relied too heavily on André's friend. From his first arrival in New York, he had gone over Clinton's head, writing the ministry in England urgent appeals for independent Tory action under his leadership. When, shortly after his return from New London, Cornwallis surrendered at Yorktown, he was delighted to assume that Clinton had been discredited. By "artfully" promising to push for reinforcements that would neutralize the disaster, he finally secured permission to sail "home." His real objective, he told Smith, was to secure for himself Clinton's command.

He was so hated that he would only be safe on a warship, but Peggy felt she would be more comfortable in a merchantman. As a last gesture with which to dazzle the land he had betrayed, Arnold bought out the entire cabin so that his wife could choose her own shipmates. A catty observer commented, "I do not hear of any females but her maid." The traitor left America on December 15, 1781.

Peggy Shippen Arnold in England with the treason behind her. The child is believed to be Edward, who became a British cavalry officer, but experienced his most celebrated moment when an almost naked infant. That was when Peggy, in her successful hysterics, shielded him from Washington, whom she insisted was an assassin come to murder her child. Painted in England, c. 1783–1784, by David Gardner. *Courtesy, Historical Society of Pennsylvania.*

"I saw Mrs. Arnold a few days after her arrival in town," a Tory soon wrote from London, "and was really pleased she looked so well, as general expectation was raised so high by the incessant puffers of the newspapers and the declaration of Colonel Tarleton that she was the handsomest woman in England. . . . They have taken a house and set up a carriage and will, I suppose, be a good deal visited." Arnold was attacked in the Whig press and hissed at the theater, but the cabinet considered him "a very sensible man"; he had "many private conferences with the King and was seen walking with the Prince of Wales and the King's brother in the public gardens. . . . The Queen was so interested in Mrs. Arnold as to desire the ladies of the court to pay much attention to her." Although the top American command proved beyond Arnold's possibilities, "I received notice from Lord Amherst that His Majesty wished me to return to America, and it was promised me that I should be promoted." Not for years had the desperate soldier's fortunes looked so rosy.

Then the Tory government fell: "From the present administration, who are most of them violent republicans, I have little to hope." Peace was soon solemnized, and Arnold became a retired colonel on half pay. He agitated for a berth in India, but was told that, despite his "very superior military character . . . no power in this country" could put him in an important situation.

Although Arnold's perpetual complaints about the great American prospects he had sacrificed brought him only minor financial concessions, Peggy was given a pension of £500 (which she resolved to save for her children). "By all accounts she is an amiable woman," a banker wrote, "and, was her husband dead, would be much noticed." In glittering London, Arnold was placed in the position which had tortured his father in provincial Norwich: his wife, like his mother, was pitied for the man she had married.

Arnold had yearned for a peerage; André's brother was made a baronet. Among the British heroes in Westminster Abbey rose a memorial to the spy whom the traitor had considered so expendable. (When an American visitor saw the Arnolds conversing before André's tomb, he turned away in disgust.) Anna Seward's sentimental *Monody to Major André* deluged the nation in tears. If Peggy also wept, it was not in her husband's presence, nor did

399

she show Arnold her cherished lock of the handsome Englishman's hair.

At the age of forty-four, Arnold, all his prospects blasted, bought a brig and sailed away to explore the ports of Canada in search of a new career. He was received everywhere with astonishment and disapproval, but settled at last in St. John's, New Brunswick. Finding what comfort he could in the arms of the woman who bore him the son he called John Sage, he embarked on the type of trading which he had practiced in New Haven and had hoped was forever behind him. He built a store and set off to the Indies for merchandise.

In London, Peggy was playing the role that his unhappy first wife had so resented: she had "all the general's business to transact," and was "harassed with a troublesome and expensive lawsuit." Lonelier than Peggy Mansfield Arnold had ever been, she complained, "I am in a strange country without a creature near me that is really interested in my fate." When a rumor reached her that Arnold's ship had been lost, she sank into a frenzy of anxiety over "the fate of the best of husbands."

Arnold reached the Indies safely and then zigzagged to England, picking up Peggy and their three children. At St. John's, the family was swelled by Hannah and his older sons. They lived ostentatiously; although the community was largely made up of Tory exiles, Arnold was greatly disliked. To frowns he responded with haughty reserve; to accusations of dishonesty, with his old New Haven weapon, a suit for libel. Although he won it, the jury considered his injured honor worth only twenty shillings. "I have met with so much unmerited reproach from the world," he wrote, "that it has taught me to become a philosopher [how he had once hated this word!] in my own defense. . . . I care little what the herd of mankind say or think of me." However, he was pitifully effusive in his thanks to anyone who was kind to him.

Peggy visited her family in Philadelphia. Although some of her old friends thought "she would have shown more feeling by staying away," she expanded into happiness. In a quiet drawing room, shielded from the clamors of the world, she renewed her intimacy with the father who was so different from the man she had married. They discussed investments, and agreed that Arnold's mind had a dangerously speculative turn. Alone in frightening exile, she had considered him "the best of husbands"—but she did not miss him now. She mourned that her pension, which supplied the only money she could protect for her children, would cease if she stayed in the United States. After she had returned to her husband, she wrote her family that she would never visit them again: the inevitable parting was too painful.

The French Revolution brought to Arnold's nostrils the scent of possible war; he wound up his unsuccessful affairs in Canada and hurried to London, hoping for a military command. However, the conservatives who had formerly been his supporters were so worried about Jacobins in the English army that the very thought of treason made them shake in their shoes. "I am without rank or consequence," Arnold soon complained, "and without friends or connections that have the power to be of any service to me." Then suddenly, during a debate in the House of Lords, he was given the opportunity for such a feat of personal violence as had in the old days rescued him from his troubles: the Earl of Louderdale referred to him rhetorically as the epitome of treason. He gleefully challenged the radical earl, but on the morning of the meeting Peggy felt it necessary to feign sleep lest her agitation "unman the general." The opponents were to fire simultaneously. Arnold's once steady hand shook so that he missed; Louderdale refused to fire. After the matter had been arbitrated by the seconds, Arnold felt he had vindicated his honor. Yet his urgent pleas still failed to secure him a command in the war that broke out with France.

As he had done near Saratoga, he hurried to the battlefront, commission or no commission. Turning so many of his assets into cash that Peggy had to move to a smaller London house, he sailed his own boat to the Indies and engaged in deals, as dangerous as they were lucrative, under the very guns of the opposing fleets and armies. On Guadeloupe, he was thrown into a French prison ship. Why did he choose "Mr. Anderson" as an alias to give his captors —the name under which André had been caught? If he wished to prove his superiority to the dead man who was now more revered than he, to show how much more effectively he could escape, he proved his point. Having pried loose some boards, he tied them together into a raft, and then dropped noiselessly over the vessel's side. Soon he was on the headquarters ship of Sir Charles Grey, André's former general.

After serving briefly as a volunteer, Arnold continued his commercial wanderings among the war-torn islands. From Martinique he wrote that he was "considerably improved in fortune and infinitely more in health than when I left England." But Grenada, the island that had been the graveyard of André's fortune, proved damaging to his own. Having lost £3,000, he returned downcast to England.

The perpetual uncertainty of her life churned up in Peggy nervous tempests that blew for weeks at a time. "My reason," she often wrote, "was despaired of." She would apologize for sending a letter when her mind was so confused that she could not put two consecutive thoughts together—but the letter would be efficient, logical, and lucid. With a combination of tantrum and mental power, she goaded Arnold to provide for their children.

The "ambition" to which she confessed centered on elevating her daughter and four sons to the great role in the world she was now certain her husband would never achieve. For this, the first requisite was "keeping up an appearance": a coach with footmen, a fine house, expensive wine in the cellar. Although she warned the boys against their father's propensity for "scheming," she schemed perpetually to get them the protection and countenance of the great; she charmed and coaxed generals and noblemen. While her husband was in the Indies, she secured for her four oldest children pensions of £100 a year.

However, the governmental favors which the Arnolds periodically secured were not great enough to compensate for the traitor's inability to earn anything considerable. As the Napoleonic wars unrolled, he offered "to risk and, if necessary, to sacrifice in the defense of the country and for the benefit of my numerous family that are unprovided for, the remains of a life rendered unfortunate by my attachment to the government and constitution of Great Britain." He would destroy the French fleet in a mad dash of fireboats; he would lead a native revolution to "liberate Chile, Peru, and both Mexicos from Spain." Always he was pushed aside.

Despite his wife's "forebodings," he invested their savings in a privateer. At sixty, he was too feeble to command the vessel himself; she sailed under a hired captain to misfortune. Each new communication from what Peggy called "that vile ship" contained a new flock of bills, until at last Benedict was forced to sell the lease to their house. Peggy saw "ruin staring me in the face"; her "agonizing state of mind" made a further drain on her husband.

"The disappointment of all his pecuniary expectations," she eventually wrote, "with the numerous vexations and mortifications he has endured, had so broken his spirits and destroyed his nerves that he has been for a long time past incapable of the smallest enjoyment. . . . His legs swelled greatly and his difficulty of breathing was at times so great, particularly at night, that he could scarcely lay down. . . . This painful sensation was always brought on by any agitation of mind. . . . Every alarming and distressing symptom rapidly increased and, after great suffering, he expired Sunday morning, the 14th of June [1801] at ½ past six in the morning, without a groan." Although the doctors had diagnosed dropsy brought on by gout, his wife believed that Benedict Arnold "literally fell sacrifice" to a "perturbed mind."

When bills came in that would wipe out every cent her husband had ever made, Peggy desponded as she had never done: "I fancied that nothing but the sacrifice of my life would benefit my children, for that my wretchedness embittered every moment of their lives; and, dreadful to say, I was many times on the point of making the sacrifice." Yet she took on herself the settlement of his estate, paying somehow every debt until, for the first time in her married life, her affairs were completely shipshape. She boasted to Edward Shippen of her success, and, to her amazement, found herself, although sentenced to a small house and no carriage, "contented, if not happy."

Employing the imaginative frugality her father had taught her, she managed to move in society enough to help her children, and she saw before her a vision the more splendid because it was not troubled by the angry hero she had married, the broken traitor she had watched die. Her sons—she warned them against encumbering the family team with wives—would draw each other along "the road to advancement." At last "crowned with laurels," they would "by tender and affectionate attentions" render "my declining years more comfortable than those of my youth have been. . . . Mine," she wrote, "has been an eventful life, and I may yet ascend nearer the top of the wheel."

But for Peggy the wheel soon stopped turning; she was stricken with cancer of the womb. On August 24, 1804, when she was only forty-four years old, her wild career ended.

The perfidious beauty, the traitor, and the spy: they are immortal, but not for evil alone. Their names have gone down in history because Peggy Shippen was once fair and innocent, because John André possessed nobility, because Benedict Arnold flamed for a while, a hero. Pure villainy lies forgotten, while we mourn a broken sword, tarnished honor, the glory that descended.

ACKNOWLEDGMENTS
NOTES
STATEMENT ON SOURCES
SOURCE REFERENCES
INDEX

ACKNOWLEDGMENTS

I AM GRATEFUL to The New-York Historical Society—Fenwick Beekman, M.D., President; R. W. G. Vail, Director; and Dorothy C. Barck, Librarian—for hospitality extending over several years. I have received invaluable assistance from E. Marie Becker and other members of the Society's staff: Wayne Andrews, Charles E. Baker, Geraldine Beard, Arthur B. Carlson, Betty K. Ezequelle, Louis J. Fox, Richard J. Koke, Wilmer R. Leech, Oscar Wegelin, and William D. Wright.

Mrs. Dorothea K. André, James André, and Group Captain A. R. Arnold have made available to me their invaluable collections of family objects and documents.

Among the many institutions which have placed at my disposal manuscripts and other materials are: British Museum; William L. Clements Library, University of Michigan; Colonial Williamsburg; Historical Society of Pennsylvania; Houghton Library, Harvard University; Library of Congress; Massachusetts Historical Society; New Haven Colony Historical Society; New York Public Library; Public Archives of Canada; Public Records Office, London; Somerset House, London; Universitätsbibliothek, Göttingen; and Yale University.

It would be impossible to thank all the scholars, librarians, and manuscript collectors who have come to my assistance. To name a few among many: Theodore Bolton, Miss Marjorie Case, Brigadier D. F. Campbell, Edward C. Childs, Samuel Chew, Robert J. Christen, J. G. Cuyler, Mrs. Langston Douglas, George W. Dyson, Dr. Joseph Fields, C. P. G. Fuller, Fred C. Haacker, Robert W. Hill, Fiske Kimball, David Kirschenbaum, Milton Kline, William K. Lamb, Foreman M. Lebold, Vera J. Ledger, Richard M. Loewenberg, David C. Mearns, Edward B. Morrison, Mrs. Vernon Munroe, John Marshall Phillips; Dr. Davis Reichart, Stephen T. Riley,

ACKNOWLEDGMENTS

Lady Robertson, Rosenbach Company, Charles Coleman Sellers, Mrs. Rutherford M. Shepard, Colton Storm, D. W. Thompson, Justin G. Turner, Nicholas Wainwright, Edith M. Wakefield, Philip L. White, R. Norris Williams, Marya Zaturenska.

NOTES

Benedict Arnold, engraved at Paris in 1781 by Bénoit Louis Prévost after a drawing executed at Philadelphia, probably during 1779, by André's friend Pierre Eugene Du Simitière: Collection New-York Historical Society.

This engraving, which was frequently pirated, is the only authentic likeness of Arnold, since the many other prints published during his lifetime were imaginary portraits.

Peggy Shippen, pencil drawing made by John André, probably at Philadelphia in 1778-1779: Collection Yale University Art Gallery.

A gouache and crayon portrait of Peggy with one of her children was painted in England, is attributed to Daniel Gardner, and belongs to the Historical Society of Pennsylvania.

John André, watercolor miniature probably drawn on the Continent, 1772-1774: Collection James André, Esq., South Australia.

Likenesses said to be of André should be viewed with suspicion since for a century and a half it has been common practice to assume that almost any picture of a handsome young British officer represented the popular hero. The several portraits by Reynolds are now considered by students of that artist's work to show other sitters; they do not resemble André. The pencil self-portrait at Yale, which he drew during his captivity, may be accepted. The James André family owns several other miniatures, probably by his hand and representing John André or his brother. A lost self-portrait was engraved for the *Political Magazine*, 1781, II, op. p. 171.

CHAPTER ONE

1. Most accounts of Arnold's childhood are based on a chapter in Sparks, *Arnold*, which was in turn based on letters from James Lanman and James Stedman, who during 1834 collected information for Sparks in Norwich. Lanman had talked with "ancient and respectable neighbors"; he described Benedict as a blusterer, but gave him credit for ability and told no damaging anecdotes. Stedman, who consulted two octogenarians, Deacon Caleb Huntington and Ezekiel Huntley (the latter became the Lathrops' gardener

shortly after Benedict left them), is the source for the stories of Arnold's cruelty which have been repeated over and over. While with the Lathrops, Benedict is supposed to have whipped small boys and strewn broken glass to cut their bare feet. Had he done such things, the benevolent Lathrops would never have continued to encourage and employ him.

Although information about Arnold's childhood is scattered in many places, the only other detailed independent source is Caulkins's *Norwich*. Like Sparks's informants, Miss Caulkins relied on the memories of old inhabitants, but she consulted many people over a long period of years. She refers to Sparks, but tells no anecdotes of cruelty.

2. All three of the basic sources on Arnold's childhood tell of Arnold's first enlistment, which ended in his being sent home. (Both Lanman and Stedman give the date as 1755; why Sparks moved the incident on to 1756 is not clear.) However, the only Norwich source for the desertion story is Stedman, the least reliable of the informants, and even he regarded it as an uncertain rumor.

The Benedict Arnold who was in 1759 advertised for as a deserter served in the New York Regiment in 1758, and was back again in 1760. During the first two of these years, he was described in three separate records as a "weaver," a trade the future general never followed, and in 1760 was demoted to "laborer," an appellation he would have considered insulting. The deserter was of the same age as the future general. However, his birthplace is given in the 1758 roll as "Norwalk."

During the eighteenth century there lived at Norwalk, Conn., a line of Benedict Arnolds whose relationship to the traitor is not clear. A man of that name died there in the 1730's, another was born in 1784. The family is so obscure that only fragmentary records of the intervening generations remain, yet there is a piece of circumstantial evidence that links Benedict Arnold, the deserter, with the Norwalk Benedicts. On the 1758 roll, which is not alphabetical, the deserter's name appears directly under "Robert Arnod" who enlisted on the same day, was also a weaver, and came from Stratford, a few miles from Norwalk. This young man was in all probability the Robert Arnold who was son to John Arnold, of Stratford, and grandson of a Benedict Arnold of Norwalk.

Had the Revolutionary general, who was well supplied with enemies, actually been a deserter from an earlier army, this fact, which would have been well known in Norwich, would certainly have been used against him in his lifetime, instead of waiting to be published by Sparks half a century later. Furthermore, the deserter served in the New York Regiment during three years; no source ascribes to the future general any such extensive break in his apprenticeship to the Lathrops, or any battle experience before the Revolution.

CHAPTER THREE

1. Anna Seward published in her *Monody* (29-47) what purported to be three letters written her by André in 1769. However, an undated letter from John to Anna which appeared recently in the New York autograph

market (*Collector*, 1951, lxiv, 14) contains in a slightly different form some but not all of the letter Anna quoted under the date October 3 and additional passages which Anna did not quote. She seems to have selected from André's correspondence the parts she liked best, edited them a little, and then combined them under three dates.

Where in the original John referred to himself as "a poor novice of nineteen," Anna changed his age to eighteen. It was partly on the basis of this garbled passage that André was said to have been born in 1751.

CHAPTER FOUR

1. André was too young and obscure an officer to serve as an official emissary of the Crown, and, had he been engaged on a surreptitious mission, he would not have crossed the ocean with Smith, who knew he was a royal officer and was himself an ardent patriot. That André hoped to publish his journal is shown by his referring to his drawings as "cuts."

CHAPTER SEVEN

1. There is no independent evidence to show that André brought Honora's miniature with him to America, and, in any case, he could not have been stripped of everything but the miniature since he kept his military diary and his illustrated account of his travels. In the bitter summary of his captivity he wrote his mother after his release, André stated that the surrender terms, which were violated by the brutality with which the prisoners were treated, "had this good effect that they secured the garrison's effects from plunder."

However, several months before his release, he drew up a protest to the patriot authorities, which was signed by all the officers interned at Carlisle, in which they hinted that, because the prisoners' baggage had been rifled "on the way down from Canada," they might consider themselves no longer bound by their paroles. An explanation for this contradiction is supplied by Schuyler's statement that the British officers sought every excuse to break their paroles, and that Captain Dundee was the ringleader. Significantly, Dundee, not André, originally complained that the baggage of the Royal Fusiliers had been plundered. André subsequently joined the other quartermasters in a protest to Wooster. We gather that the charges were based on technicalities and dusted off whenever the prisoners saw an opportunity to gain a point. André could do no less than go along with his companions.

CHAPTER ELEVEN

1. Writers have commonly confused John Despard with his brother, Edward Marcus Despard, who attempted to assassinate George IV.

CHAPTER THIRTEEN

1. Whether Gates or Arnold advocated the best way to fight Burgoyne can be argued endlessly, since it is impossible to be sure how the campaign would have turned out had it been differently fought. The victory actually was achieved by a mixture of both strategies: Gates never permitted Arnold to engage the entire army, and Arnold forced Gates to fight more violently than he had intended.

2. There are no reliable eyewitness accounts of Arnold's actual appearance on the battlefield. Frank Moore, it is true, quotes in his *Diary of the American Revolution* what purports to be the account of someone who, while he himself did not see Arnold at the battle, was told by "S." that "Arnold rushed into the thickest of the fight with his usual recklessness and at times acted like a madman." No date or author is given for this document which is ascribed merely to "the Churchill Papers."

The recollections of Ebenezer Wakefield also place Arnold at the battle, but they were written at least thirty-five years after the event and are so full of demonstrable inaccuracies that no reliance can be put upon them.

Major William Hull's recollections (edited by his daughter and published seventy-one years after the engagement) show Arnold giving orders at an advanced post a quarter of a mile from headquarters, but do not in any way imply that he rode on to the battle.

Evidence for Arnold's physical participation has been manufactured by a consistent misreading of contemporary documents. Thus the matter is considered proved by such statements as that in the diary of Hezekiah Smith, chaplain of Nixon's regiment: "A warm battle was fought between General Burgoyne and one division of our army commanded by General Arnold." This need mean nothing more than that the left wing was officially under Arnold's command.

Strange meanings have also been found in the many statements which gave Arnold credit for the victory because the writer believed that the battle was fought at Arnold's urging. This was, for instance, the reason General Burgoyne praised Arnold. "Another disappointment," Burgoyne is reported to have told the House of Commons, "proceeded from the enemy. Gates would receive the attack in his lines. Arnold chose to give instead of receiving the attack."

The most common (and amazing) source of error is the tendency to read the word *send* as if it meant *lead*. In defending the importance of his participation, Arnold wrote Gates, "You desired me to *send* Colonel Morgan and the light infantry and support them. I obeyed your orders, and, before the action was over, found it necessary to *send* out the whole of my division to support the attack." (Italics here and hereafter are mine.)

Varick and Henry Brockholst Livingston insisted, of course, that all the credit should go to Arnold, but they never state or imply that he was on the battlefield. Livingston wrote Schuyler that if Gates had "had the direction of the battle" he would have allowed the riflemen to be cut off, but

"Arnold *sent* out most of his division before he received orders to the contrary." To his brother, Robert R. Livingston, Brockholst added, "General Arnold was the *adviser* of the late battle." To Schuyler, Varick describes Arnold not as leading the troops but as *"ordering them out."*

Wilkinson's account, although not published until 1815, is for the most part accurate in details that can be checked. He wrote, "Not a single general officer was on the field of battle . . . until the evening, when General Learned was ordered out." He described Gates and Arnold as together during the action: "The orders went out in detail from headquarters where they were worked out by both commanders. It is not known what conversation passed between the generals."

On January 12, 1778, Robert R. Livingston wrote Washington urging the promotion of James Livingston: "I take the liberty to enclose Your Excellency an extract of a letter written to him under General Arnold's direction by a gentleman of his family, he being unable to hold the pen himself. After a warm commendation of his conduct both in the camp and the field, and giving him and his regiment a full share of the honor of the battle of the 19th, in which, General Arnold, *not being present*, speaks only from the report of those that were, he adds, 'On the 7th of October your corps fell more immediately under the inspection of General Arnold.'"

CHAPTER EIGHTEEN

1. Silas Deane had played a part in starting Ethan Allen's expedition against Ticonderoga, but, as one of the more conservative Connecticut revolutionaries, he had been impressed by Arnold's efforts to keep order in the garrison and protect private property. He took Arnold's side in the resulting controversies, and was his active supporter in Congress until he failed of reappointment for the year 1776.

2. Anne Hollingsworth Wharton published in her not too scholarly book, *Through Colonial Doorways*, a story which, if it could be substantiated, would cast a strange light on Arnold's character. She states that Arnold used substantially the same letter in which he proposed to Peggy Shippen for a proposal to a Miss A., whom she tentatively identifies as Miss Amile. If Mrs. Wharton did not repeat a confused rumor about the letters Arnold wrote to Miss De Blois, it means that he used the same phrases not to two ladies, as has been believed, but to three.

3. In a later letter to Governor Clinton, Arnold gave more details. He preferred Johnson's 130,000 acres on the Mohawk and offered to sell enough land in fee simple to induce 130 families to settle within three or four years of the peace. The rest of the area would, we gather, be farmed by his tenants.

CHAPTER NINETEEN

1. Years later, Richard Peters who had been a member of the Board of War, claimed that when the Americans first regained Philadelphia, he had entrusted Arnold with $50,000, which Arnold had appropriated, using some of it to buy Mount Pleasant. Furthermore, "Colonel Pickering and I detected him ordering stores and provisions out of the public magazines" to fit out privateers and embellish his own table. Peters continued that his attempts to stop this robbery produced "an open quarrel with Arnold," and that he had complained in writing to headquarters. There is no record of this complaint in Washington's papers and neither Peters nor Pickering testified at Arnold's trials. After Arnold had been proved a traitor, many a man who had harbored vague suspicions translated them in memory to certainties.

CHAPTER TWENTY-ONE

1. We know that in Arnold's absence Peggy handled the treason correspondence with complete knowledge of its contents; several of the letters Arnold signed contained messages from her to André. It seems a safe assumption that Arnold's adviser, co-conspirator, and beloved bride, who alone of the pair was personally acquainted with the British agent, would have helped draft the difficult communications to him.

CHAPTER TWENTY-TWO

1. Arnold owned shares in several privateers operated by Isaac Sears, a former New Haven neighbor, and undoubtedly in other boats as well.

CHAPTER TWENTY-FOUR

1. André is supposed to have known that a Rebel officer, Abraham Gardiner's son, was skulking in the cellar, but said nothing till the enemy departed, when he expressed his regret that "their respective stations" had prevented him from making the young gentleman's acquaintance. Such behavior on the part of the officer in charge of counter-intelligence would, if discovered, have ended his career.

Such impossible stories are common in Winthrop Sargent's biography of André, as are other stories that might possibly contain some truth: André, Sargent tells us, happened on some fifteen-year-old lads being hustled to prison because they had been captured bearing arms. "My boy," he asked one of them with sensational stupidity, "what makes you cry?" It seemed the children missed their mamas. Almost in tears himself, André rushed off and returned with pardons. "Run home," he exclaimed, "to your fond parents and be good boys. Mind what they tell you, say your prayers, love one another, and God Almighty will bless you." This speech is completely out of character—André made not one religious reference in all his surviving letters—yet, because no military advantage was lost, he might have permitted himself the luxury of releasing small boys.

Sargent, incidentally, suppressed the ribald ending we have quoted of the first canto of *The Cow Chase*.

2. Although Mary McCarthy later claimed a British pension because she had carried Arnold's letter "at great hazard of her life," it is improbable that she knew the importance of the document which she delivered to General James Robertson, the royal governor of New York.

CHAPTER TWENTY-FIVE

1. There are fashions in legends as in every other form of human adornment, and one promoted by Morton Pennypacker in his *Gen. Washington's Spies* (Brooklyn: 1939, 114-9, 137-8) is becoming so chic that notice must be taken of it. According to Pennypacker, André stayed at the Townsend House in Oyster Bay after the abortive Dobbs Ferry interview. Sarah Townsend saw "a supposed Whig" hide in a kitchen cupboard a letter addressed to James (or John) Anderson. She watched as André "searched through the closets." Having "hastily concealed" the letter on his person, he hid some doughnuts in the cupboard "as an excuse for entering the forbidden precincts of the kitchen." Sarah then listened "to a whispered conversation in Colonel Simcoe's room," and heard West Point mentioned. She rushed through patriot secret service channels a message to Tallmadge that was responsible for Tallmadge's suspicions of André after his capture.

This story is told in such detail that many documents would be needed for substantiation; Pennypacker cites no sources. Furthermore, the anecdote does not stand to reason. When the plot in which he longed to play a part was coming to fruition, André, even if he had been feeling ill, would not have retired from Clinton's headquarters to Simcoe's outpost. And why should a messenger use as a hiding place a cupboard in a part of a patriot-owned house which the British lodgers did not frequent? "A supposed Whig" could have found a thousand safe pretexts for walking openly into André's presence.

Pennypacker states that Arnold's letter to Anderson of September 15 never reached Clinton's headquarters, but that a copy was delivered at Oyster Bay by a treasonous crew member of a Connecticut privateer. The letter is in the British headquarters files now at the Clements Library, still bearing its original address: "to be left at the Rev. Mr. Odell's in New York." Arnold tells in a later letter that it was carried to the British lines at Kingsbridge at the tip of Manhattan Island. Had the message been forwarded from there to Oyster Bay, it would have been by official messenger.

Another favorite legend is based on Major Tallmadge's statement, written when he was senile, that André had claimed that Clinton promised to let him lead the party that would capture the principal fortification at West Point. Had Clinton attempted to give the most conspicuous command in a major operation to a favorite who was still, as far as anyone knew, a junior captain in the regular service, he would have started a near mutiny among his own officers. Clinton wrote Germain that he intended to lead the attack in person.

CHAPTER TWENTY-SEVEN

1. When Tallmadge was in his eightieth year, Jared Sparks asked him why the stupid mistake had been made of notifying Arnold. The old gentleman defended himself by stating that he had begged Jameson not to do so, and then launched into reminiscences which have become the most fertile source of error about André's last days. Tallmadge's memory had obviously become senile since, when his statements can be checked with truly contemporary documents, they are almost always wrong. There is no record that at the time Tallmadge denied Jameson's statement that he had agreed to sending on the letter to Arnold.

2. The theory that not until evening had Washington "known enough about the situation to take action" seems untenable: his two most important letters, those he eventually sent to Greene and the ranking officer at West Point, are so undetailed that they could have been sent out at once. Furthermore, Lamb, who was at Washington's side, was as familiar with the local situation as anyone.

Other facts imply that Washington was stunned. It seems strange that he did not order Hamilton to do what Hamilton did spontaneously: notify Greene from King's Ferry (which was on the road to the Continental Army) should it become clear that Arnold had escaped. The accounts of the drama at West Point which Washington wrote during the succeeding few days are contradictory in detail.

STATEMENT ON SOURCES

Since in the story of the traitor and the spy historical fact has been obscured by prejudice and legend, I have based my study on letters, records, and diary references written at the time the events took place, and on eyewitness accounts prepared when the memories of the participants were still fresh. Secondary sources have been used rarely and with caution.

The principal groups of manuscripts I have consulted are: the André Papers (here used for the first time) belonging to Mrs. J. Louis André, Sussex, England, and James André, South Australia; John André's "Narrative of the Siege of St. Johns" (here first identified) and other papers in the Public Archives of Canada; André's "The Mischianza, Humbly Inscribed to Miss Peggy Chew" and other papers belonging to Samuel Chew, Pennsylvania; papers dealing with Arnold's career after the treason belonging to Group-Captain A. R. Arnold, London; the British Headquarters Papers from the files of Sir Henry Clinton and other papers at the William L. Clements Library, University of Michigan; the British Headquarters Papers from the files of Sir Guy Carleton belonging to Colonial Williamsburg (consulted in a complete set of photostats at the New York Public Library); the Horatio Gates and Joseph Reed Papers and other collections at The New-York Historical Society; the Philip Schuyler Papers, William Smith's *Diary*, and other papers at the New York Public Library; the Shippen Papers and other collections at the Historical Society of Pennsylvania; Revolutionary War papers at the Library of Congress; various materials at the Public Record Office, the British Museum, and Somerset House, London; the Henry Knox and William Heath Papers and other collections at the Massachusetts Historical Society; the Jared Sparks Papers and other collections at the Houghton Library, Harvard University. Arnold's files left at West Point are with the

Washington Papers in the Library of Congress; his Philadelphia files have vanished except for a few documents in the Joseph Reed Papers at The New-York Historical Society; his New Haven files have passed through the autograph market and are scattered among more institutions and autograph collectors than can be listed in this brief statement. A group of his early business papers have found their way into the New Haven Colony Historical Society.

The printed compendia of manuscripts I have found most useful are: documents dealing directly with the treason transcribed by Howard Peckham from the Clinton Papers and published as an appendix to Carl Van Doren's *Secret History of the American Revolution*, 1941; Thomas Balch, *Letters and Papers Relating Chiefly to the Provincial History of Pennsylvania*, 1885; Edward Burd, *Letters, 1763-1828*, ed. by Lewis Burd Walker, 1899; Edmund C. Burnett, ed., *Letters of Members of the Continental Congress*, 1922-33, vols. ii-vi; *Journals of the Continental Congress*, 1904-12, vols. i-xxi; Connecticut Historical Society *Collections*, 1860-1949, vols. i-xxvi; John C. Fitzpatrick, ed., *Writings of George Washington*, 1931-37, vols. iii-xxiii; Peter Force, ed., *American Archives*, 1839-46, 4th ser., vols. ii-vi, 1848-53, 5th ser., vols. i-iii; Massachusetts Historical Society *Collections*, 1792-1914, vols. i-lxxix, and *Proceedings*, 1879-1945, vols. i-lxvii; The New-York Historical Society *Collections*, 1868-1946, vols. i-lxxix; *Pennsylvania Archives*, 1852-56, 1st ser., vols. i-xii; *Pennsylvania Colonial Records*, 1851-53, vols. vii-xvi; *Pennsylvania Magazine of History and Biography*, 1877-1953, vols. i-lxxvi; Kenneth Roberts, ed., *March to Quebec: Journals of the Members of Arnold's Expedition*, 1938; Jared Sparks, ed., *Correspondence of the Revolution*, 1853, 4 vols., and *Writings of Washington*, 1837, vols. i-xii; Benjamin F. Stevens, ed., *Facsimiles of Manuscripts in European Archives Relating to America, 1773-1783*, 1889-98, vols. i-xxv.

Other important publications of original documents are: Ethan Allen, *A Narrative of Col. Ethan Allen's Captivity*, 1779; John André, *Journal from June 1777 to November 1778*, 1903, 2 vols.; *The Case of Major John André*, 1780; *Proceedings of a Board of General Officers . . . Respecting Major John André*, 1780; "An Authentic Account of that Greatly Lamented Officer, Major John

André," *Political Magazine*, London, 1781, ii, pp. 171-73; *Proceedings of a General Court Martial . . . of Major General Arnold*, 1780; Thomas Jones, *History of New York During the Revolutionary War*, 1879, 2 vols.; Samuel A. Peters (?), "An Account of Major General Benedict Arnold," *Political Magazine*, London, 1780, i, pp. 690, 740-48; Anna Seward, *Monody on Major André, To Which Are Added Letters Addressed to Her from Major André in the Year 1769*, 1781; Joshua Hett Smith, *An Authentic Narrative of the Causes which led to the Death of Major André*, 1808; "Trial of Joshua Hett Smith for Complicity in the Conspiracy of Benedict Arnold and Major André," *Historical Magazine*, 1866, x, suppl., pp. 1-5, 33-38, 65-73, 97-105, 128-38; *The Varick Court of Inquiry*, 1907; James Wilkinson, *Memoirs of My Own Times*, 1816, 3 vols.

Carl Van Doren's *Secret History of the American Revolution* contains a learned, well-balanced, and extremely useful account of the situations and negotiations that led directly to the treason. Isaac Arnold's *Benedict Arnold*, although published in 1880, has remained the best life of the traitor; see also Malcolm Decker, *Benedict Arnold, Son of the Havens*, 1932, and Jared Sparks, *The Life and Treason of Benedict Arnold*, 1835. Winthrop Sargent's *Life and Career of Major André*, 1861, is the only useful biography of that officer, although it is based on uncritical and inadequate research. For Peggy Shippen see the laudatory account published by her kinsman, Lewis Burd Walker, in the *Pennsylvania Magazine of History and Biography*, 1900, xxiv, pp. 257-66, 401-29, 1901, xxv, pp. 20-46, 145-90, 289-302, 452-97, 1902, xxvi, pp. 71-80, 224-44, 322-34, 464-68. William Abbatt's *The Crisis of the Revolution*, 1899, contains a detailed description of André's last days, in which legend is mixed with useful fact.

NOTE FOR THE NEW EDITION

Since the original compilation of this statement on sources, only two books of any importance concerning the subject of this volume have been published: Willard Mosher Wallace's *Traitorous Hero: The Life and Fortunes of Benedict Arnold* (New York, 1954) is a solid and effective biography that cites, in addition to original sources, the conclusions on key events that have been reached by previous distinguished historians. Since this book was in the process of publication when *The Traitor and the Spy* appeared, neither work influenced the other. Dr. Wallace's primary concern with Arnold cast Peggy and André as supporting characters, but he gave more space than my intentions allowed to Arnold's post-treason years. Concerning these years, we both found sources unknown to the other.

Richard J. Koke's *Accomplice in Treason: Joshua Hett Smith and the Arnold Conspiracy* (New York, 1973) is a lucidly written and scholarly life of a key figure in the unfolding of the treason. Describing events both before and after those climactic days, the book gives a fascinating picture of the problems faced by the New York patricians who, like Peggy's Philadelphian father, did not really favor either side and were thus primarily concerned with saving as much of their own property as they could without endangering their own skins. Smith himself is revealed as a man by nature overenthusiastical who had been forced by his indecision into doldrums. He was enchanted to the point almost of idiocy by the opportunity Arnold gave him of getting into the action close to the top.

With the author's kind permission and assistance, Mr. Koke's volume has been a useful source of illustrations to this edition.

SOURCE REFERENCES

KEY TO ABBREVIATIONS USED
IN SOURCE REFERENCES

Source references are grouped together under identifying headings and placed in the order in which the material appears in the body of the book. Sources for statements in the Notes will be found in a position equivalent to where the note elucidates the main text.

Complete consistency in presentation has been sacrificed to conciseness and clarity. Proper names and the titles of publications are given often in abbreviated form. The name of the author and the title of a magazine article are omitted when a reference to the title, date, volume, and page of the periodical seems adequate. Unless this leads to ambiguity, places of publication are omitted. Sources often cited are referred to by abbreviations for which full references are given in the alphabetical Key which follows.

For the convenience of scholars, citations to original documents which have been published in accurate form are made to the most widely available printed text; usually space has not permitted an additional statement of the location of the original manuscript.

When, in the abbreviation of dates, no century is given, the references are to the 1700's. Thus, 1/1/76 means January 1, 1776; the date of a century later would be stated as 1/1/1876.

Abbatt, William, *The Crisis of the Revolution*, 1899
Allen, Ethan, *A Narrative of Colonel Ethan Allen's Captivity*, 1779
(André, *Case*) *The Case of Major John André*, 1780, original John Carter Brown Library; ms. copy NYHS
(André, *Journal*) André, John, *Journal from June 1777 to November 1778*, 1903, 2 vols., original Huntington Library, San Marino, Calif. Although the authorship of this journal has sometimes been questioned, it can be definitely ascribed to André on the basis of internal evidence, of handwriting, and the similarity of the maps to those in the André Papers.
(André, *Mischianza*) André, John, "The Mischianza, Humbly Inscribed to Miss Peggy Chew," 6/2/88, *Century Magazine*, xlvii, 1893–94, 687–91, original ms. in collection of Samuel Chew, Pa.
(André, *Mischianza Letter*) André, John (?), "Particulars of the Mischianza . . . A Letter from An Officer in Philadelphia," 5/23/78, *Gentleman's Magazine*, xlviii, 1778, 353–57. The earliest statement I have found of the traditional attri-

bution to André is a notation, on a clipping of the letter in MHS, written by Israel Mauduit, who died in 1787: "This account and the poetry is supposed to have been written by Maj. André." Mauduit published an attack on the Meshianza in 1779.

(André, *Narrative*) André, John, "Narrative of the Siege of St. Johns," National Archives of Canada. This ms. journal is here first ascribed to André on the basis of internal evidence, of handwriting, and of the similarity of the map to that in the André Papers.

(AP) André, John, *Papers*, Dorothea K. André, Sussex, England. This important group of manuscripts, which has come down in the André family, has not previously been known.

(André, *Proceedings*) *Proceedings of a Board of General Officers . . . Respecting Major John André*, 1780, republished by H. W. Smith, 1865(?)

(Arnold, *Arnold*) Arnold, Isaac, *Benedict Arnold*, 1880

(Arnold, *Proceedings*) *Proceedings of a General Court Martial . . . of Major General Arnold*, 1780

(Arnold, *Regimental*) Arnold, Benedict, "Regimental Memorandum Book Written While at Ticonderoga & Crown Point," *PMHB*, viii, 1884, 363–76

(ArP) Arnold, Benedict, *Papers*, Group-Captain A. R. Arnold, London. These voluminous and valuable documents deal with the careers of Benedict Arnold's family after the treason.

(*Authentic Account*) "An Authentic Account of that Greatly Lamented Officer, Major John André . . . Solely Composed from Material Supplied by the Late Major's Most Intimate Friends both in this Country and in America," *Political Magazine*, ii, London, 1781, 171–73

Balch, Thomas, *Letters & Papers Relating Chiefly to the Provincial History of Pennsylvania*, 1885

Benson, Egbert, *Vindication of the Captors of Major André*, 1865

Burd, Edward, *Letters, 1763–1828*, ed. by Lewis Burd Walker, 1899

Burnett, Edmund C., ed., *Letters of Members of the Continental Congress*, 1922–33, ii–vi

(CaP) Carleton, Guy, *Papers, Including Files of the British Headquarters in America*, Colonial Williamsburg; complete set of photostats NYPL

Caulkins, Frances M., *History of Norwich, Connecticut*, 1874

(CCJ) *Journals of the Continental Congress*, 1904–12, i–xxi

(CHS) Connecticut Historical Society, Hartford, Conn.

Codman, John, *Arnold's Expedition to Quebec*, 1901

(CP) Clinton, Henry, *Papers, Including Files of the British Headquarters in America*, William L. Clements Library, University of Michigan. The documents dealing specifically with Arnold's treason were transcribed and collated by Howard Peckham, curator of manuscripts, and published as an appendix to Van Doren, *op. cit.*, 439–95

Decker, Malcolm, *Benedict Arnold, Son of the Havens*, 1932

Dexter, Franklin Bowditch, *Biographical Sketches of Graduates of Yale College*, October, 1701–May, 1745, 1885

Fitzpatrick, John C., ed., *Writings of George Washington*, 1931–37, iii–xxiii

Force, Peter, ed., *American Archives*, 1839–46, 4th Ser., ii–vi; 1848–53, 5th Ser., i–iii

Foucher, Antoine (?), *Journal tenu pendant le siege du Fort St. Jean en 1775*, National Archives of Canada. Only a small part of this fascinating document has been published. The authorship by Foucher is presumptive.

(HL) Houghton Library, Harvard University, Cambridge, Mass.

(HMC) Historical Manuscripts Commission, *Mss. of Mrs. Stopford Sackville*, 1910, ii. The Germain Papers, here calendared, are at the Clements Library.

(HSP) Historical Society of Pennsylvania, Philadelphia, Pa.

Source References

Jones, Thomas, *History of New York During the Revolutionary War*, 1879, 2 vols.

Lanman, James, *Letter to Jared Sparks*, 4/7/1834, HL

(LC) Library of Congress, Washington, D.C.

Mahan, A. T., "Military History of the Royal Navy, 1763-1792," in Clowes, William L., *The Royal Navy*, 1898, iii, 353–564

(MHS) Massachusetts Historical Society, Boston, Mass.

(NHCHS) New Haven Colony Historical Society, New Haven, Conn.

(NYHS) New-York Historical Society, New York City

(NYPL) New York Public Library, New York City

(*PA*) *Pennsylvania Archives*, 1852–56, 1st Ser., i–xii

(*PCR*) *Pennsylvania Colonial Records*, 1851–53, vii–xvi

Peters, Samuel A. (?), "Account of Major General Benedict Arnold," *Political Magazine*, i, London, 1780, 690, 746–48. Here attributed to Peters because of similarities in subject matter with his *History of Connecticut*, 1781. The *Political Magazine* and the *History* were both published by J. Bew; extracts from the *History* and a plug for it were published in the *Magazine*, ii, 1781, 648, 680. The account of Arnold's New Haven years, although spiteful and containing some slanders, can be checked in so many particulars that it must have been written by someone very familiar with that city.

(*PMHB*) *Pennsylvania Magazine of History and Biography*, 1877–1953, i–lxxvi

Roberts, Kenneth, ed., *March to Quebec: Journals of the Members of Arnold's Expedition*, 1938

Sargent, Winthrop, *Life and Career of Major André*, 1902. This biography of André, first published in 1861, has remained the standard, although it is based on superficial and uncritical research.

Seward, Anna, *Monody on Major André, To Which Are Added Letters Addressed to Her from Major André in the Year 1769*, Lichfield, 1781

(Smith, *Authentic*) Smith, Joshua Hett, *An Authentic Narrative of the Causes which Led to the Death of Major André*, 1808

(Smith, *Diary*) Smith, William, *Diary*, 7 ms. vols., NYPL

(Smith, *Fourteenth*) Smith, Justin H., *Our Struggle for the Fourteenth Colony*, 2 vols., 1907

(Smith, *March*) Smith, Justin H., *Arnold's March from Cambridge to Quebec*, 1903

(Smith, *Trial*) "Trial of Joshua Hett Smith for Complicity in the Conspiracy of Benedict Arnold and Major André," *Historical Magazine*, supplement, x, 1866, 1–5, 33–38, 65–73, 97–105, 128–38

(Sparks, *Arnold*) Sparks, Jared, *The Life and Treason of Benedict Arnold*, 1835

(Sparks, *Correspondence*) Sparks, Jared, ed., *Correspondence of the Revolution*, 1853, 4 vols.

(Sparks, *Writings*) Sparks, Jared, ed., *Writings of Washington*, 1837, i–xii

Stedman, James, *Letter to Jared Sparks*, 4/8/1834, HL

Stevens, Benjamin F., *Facsimiles of Manuscripts in European Archives Relating to America, 1773–1783*, 1889–98, 25 vols.

Taylor, J. G., *Some New Light on the Later Life of Benedict Arnold*, 1931

(Tomlinson) Parke-Bernet Galleries, *Tomlinson Sale Catalogue*, 1/20–21/1947

(Varick) *The Varick Court of Inquiry*, 1907

Van Doren, Carl, *The Secret History of the American Revolution*, 1941. The most basic printed source on Arnold's treason.

Walker, Lewis B., "Life of Margaret Shippen," *PMHB*, xxiv, 1900, 257–66, 401–29; xxv, 1901, 20–46, 145–90, 289–302, 452–97; xxvi, 1902, 71–80, 224–44, 322–34, 464–88

Wilkinson, James, *Memoirs of My Own Times*, 1816, 3 vols.

SOURCE REFERENCES

CHAPTER ONE

COURAGE: George W. Corner, ed., *Autobiography of Benjamin Rush* (1948), 158

ANCESTORS: Elisha Arnold, *Arnold Memorial* (1935); Decker, 1–5

CHILDHOOD IN GENERAL: Lanman; Stedman; Caulkins, 409–15; *Vital Records of Norwich* (1913), i, 153; Arnold, *Arnold*, 19–26; Decker, 5–17; Peters, 690; see text note one

COGSWELL: Dexter, 701–04; E. O. Jameson, *Cogswells of America* (1884), 117–18; Ellen D. Larned, *History of Windham, Connecticut* (1874), i, 412–13

MOTHER'S LETTERS: *Historical Magazine* (1860), iv, 18; Decker, 9–10; Caulkins, 410

ARNOLD ON DEATH: Decker, 41

FATHER'S TROUBLES: Warrant for his arrest, 11/4/54, and Arnold, Sr., to John Frebody, 3/10/57, HL; *PMHB* (1898), xxii, 124–25

LATHROPS: Dexter, 483–84, 741–42; Lydia Huntley Sigourney, *Sketch of Connecticut Forty Years Since* (1824), 4–9, 139–40, and *Letters of Life* (1866), 6–12, 66–67

FORT WILLIAM HENRY: CHS *Collections* (1860), i, 324–26 (1903), ix, 236–37

DESERTION PROBLEM: Lanman; Stedman; Sparks, *Arnold*, 6–7; *New York Gazette*, 5/21/59; *Annual Report of the Historian of the State of New York, 1896* (1897), 877, 930, *1897* (1898), 609; Samuel Orcutt, *History of Stratford* (1886), 1116; Augustus G. Golding, "Family Records of Norwalk, Connecticut," typescript, NYPL; Spencer P. Mead, "Abstract Probate Records of Fairfield, 1704–1757," typescript, NYHS, 5; Caulkins, 412

LATHROPS' GIFT TO ARNOLD: Caulkins, 412, denies this gift, but Wilkinson, i, 58, and Smith, *Narrative*, 391–92, state that Arnold spoke of it. See also Peters, 690

TO ENGLAND: Peters, 690; Caulkins, 413; trade sign, NHCHS

CHAPTER TWO

LONDON AND DEBTORS' PRISON: Peters, 690

STORE: Sign and broadside, NHCHS; *Magazine of History* (1924), extra no. 104, xxvi, 366

BUYS AND SELLS HOMESTEAD: Deed, 10/4/63, HSP; deed, 3/31/64, copy HL; Caulkins, 410

FRENCHMAN: Lanman; Caulkins, 412–13

VOYAGES: Arnold letters, bills, invoices, in NHCHS, HSP, NYHS, private collections; Peters, 690; NHCHS *Papers* (1882), iii, 112–13. Arnold's business letters are numerous and widely scattered.

JOCKEY: *Canadiana* (1889), i, 187–89; John Hart to Abraham Gould, 10/4/80, collection of Mrs. Rutherford M. Shepard; *Connecticut Gazette*, 1/24/66

ENGLISH DEBTS: J. Thomas Longman to Bernard Lintot, 7/7/66, HSP; indenture, Lintot and Arnold, 5/9/67, NHCHS; Decker, 30; Wilkinson, i, 58

ANGRY LETTERS: Decker, 31–33

BEATS INFORMER: *Connecticut Gazette*, 2/14/66; papers dealing with Arnold's arrest, 1/29/66–2/3/66, NHCHS; Lawrence Henry Gipson, *Jared Ingersoll* (1920), 115, 233–36

MARRIAGE: H. Mansfield, *The Descendants of Richard and Gillian Mansfield*

Source References

(1885), 14, 24–26; Dexter, 542–43; Ezra Stiles, *A History of the Three Judges of Charles I* (1794), 198; Stedman; Arnold ledger pages, NHCHS; Peters, 690

PROBLEMS WITH WIFE: Arnold to wife, 8/8/68, 8/13/68, 10/5/73, HSP, 6/22/72, Rosenbach collection; Arnold to B. Douglas, 6/9/70, HSP

SLANDER SUIT: Arnold to McKensie and Campbell, and to Capt. Dobson, 1/7/71, NHCHS; Roger Sherman, summary of his speech on Gouverneur Morris, King Papers, NYHS

ON WEATHER: Arnold, notation in log, 11/2/70, NHCHS

CROSKIE: Arnold, *Arnold*, 30–32

BOSTON MASSACRE: Arnold to B. Douglas, 6/9/70, HSP

ATTACKS PETERS: Peters, 690; Samuel A. Peters, *General History of Connecticut* (1877), 267–69

MILITIA CAPTAIN: Jason P. Thompson, *Digest of the History of the Second Company, Governor's Foot Guard of Connecticut* (1898), 3–7; Gipson, *op. cit.*, 337–38; Edward E. Atwater, *History of the City of New Haven* (1887), 42–44

BUILDS HOUSE: Arnold to Enoch Brown, 6/5/80, HSP; Peters, 690

CHAPTER THREE

ANDRÉ'S LETTERS TO SEWARD: See text note one

ANDRÉ DESCRIBED: *Authentic Narrative*, 172; *Political Magazine*, London (1780), i, 688; André, *Major André's Journal* (1930), caption on frontispiece

SEWARD AND HER CIRCLE: Anna Seward, *Memoirs of Dr. Darwin* (1804); Margaret Ashmun, *The Singing Swan* (1931); George Warren Gignilliat, Jr., *The Author of Sanford and Merton* (1932); Richard Lovell Edgeworth, *Memoirs* (1844)

ANDRÉ FAMILY: MHS *Proceedings* (1875–76), xiv, 217–22; Huguenot Society of London *Proceedings* (1912–14), x, 485–90; Joseph Lemuel Chester, *The Marriage, Baptismal, and Burial Records of Westminster Abbey* (1875), 497–98; *Gentleman's Magazine* (1869), xxxix, 216

ANDRÉ'S BIRTH AND BOYHOOD: *Register of the Church of St. Martin Orgars*, Publications of the Huguenot Society of London (1935), xxxvii, 23; *Authentic Narrative*, 171; *Political Magazine, op. cit.*; Anthony André, will proved 4/26/69, Somerset House; André drawings among AP; P. E. Du Simitière to Henry Clinton, 11/10/80, LC

SEWARD AND HONORA: Hesketh Pearson, ed., *The Swan of Lichfield* (1936), 41–42; Seward, *Letters* (1811), iv, 217–18, v, 258

ANDRÉ AND HONORA: Seward; Ashmun, *op. cit.*, 34–38; Edgeworth, *op. cit.*, 152–55, 161, 163, 214, 234, 237, 558; *Central Literary Magazine*, Birmingham (1911), xx, 50–57; Seward, *Letters* (1811), iii, 260

ENLISTS: *A List of General and Field Officers, 1771* (n.d.), 77

CHAPTER FOUR

PROMOTION: *A List of General and Field Officers, 1772* (n.d.), 61

GÖTTINGEN: Göttinger Matrikel; *Authentic Account*, 171; Karl Weinhold, *Heinrich Christian Boie* (1868), 36, 75; information from Ludwig Ullman and Universitätsbibliothek, Göttingen

MINIATURES: Collection of James André, South Australia

FAREWELL TO GÖTTINGEN: *The Literary World*, Boston (12/3/1881), 446–47

HONORA MARRIES: Seward; Seward, *Letters* (1811), iv, 217–18; *American Bibliopolist* (1870), ii, 190; Margaret Ashmun, *The Singing Swan* (1931), 63

PARTING: Ms. in Göttingen Universitätsbibliothek

JOHANN ANDRÉ: *Notes and Queries*, London (1854), ix, 111

GOTHA: *American Historical Review* (1944), xlix, 260–61; Otto Dencke, *Lichtenberg's Leban* (1944), i, 198–99; Rudolph Schloesser, *Friedrich Wilhelm Gotter* (1895), 83

TRIP TO CANADA: *Authentic Account,* 171; André to mother, 12/17/76, AP; *Historical Magazine* (1870), 2d ser., vii, 81, 83; Benson, 108–09

ILLUSTRATED JOURNAL: André to Mary André, 3/5/75, AP; P. E. Du Simitière to Henry Clinton, 11/10/80, LC

LIFE IN QUEBEC: André to Mary André, 3/5/75, AP

DRAWING OF INDIANS: AP

CHAPTER FIVE

MARCH TO CAMBRIDGE: Jason P. Thompson, *Digest of the History of the Second Company, Governor's Foot Guard of Connecticut* (1898), 7–13; *Record of the Services of Connecticut Men in the Revolution* (1889), 17–18

COMMISSIONED BY MASSACHUSETTS: 4 Force ii, 450, 485, 748–50

RIVAL EXPEDITION: CHS *Collections* (1860), i, 163–74, 181–82; Smith, *Fourteenth,* i, 113–17, 121–33; 4 Force ii, 557–60

TICONDEROGA TAKEN: Allen, 3–5; Allen French, *The Taking of Ticonderoga* (1928); Smith, *Fourteenth,* 132–40; CHS *Collections* (·860), i, 163–88 (1870), ii, 246–49; 4 Force ii, 556–59, 584–85, 1085–88

RAID ON ST. JOHNS: 4 Force ii, 645–46; 693–94; Arnold, *Regimental,* 367–68; Allen, 6

ARNOLD ACTIVE: Arnold, *Regimental;* CHS *Collections* (1870), ii, 246–49

POLITICS INTERVENE: 4 Force ii, 645, 676, 724, 808–09, 1382–83, 1833

HARASSES ST. JOHNS: Arnold, *Regimental,* 371–73; Leiter Sale, 12/6/1928, Parke-Bernet Gallery, i, 3

FIGHT WITH EASTON: Arnold, *Regimental,* 373; 4 Force ii, 1085–88

PLANS CANADA ATTACK: 4 Force ii, 732–34, 976–77

HINMAN CONTROVERSY: *Ibid.,* 676, 986–88, 1539–41, 1592–93, 1595–99; Arnold, *Regimental,* 375–76

ARNOLD'S CONDUCT SUMMARIZED: 4 Force ii, 1088; Arnold, *Arnold,* 47–48

BACK IN NEW HAVEN: Arnold, *Arnold,* 47; CHS *Collections* (1870), ii, 252, 356–57

CHAPTER SIX

ACCOUNTS SETTLED: CHS *Collections* (1870), ii, 354–57; 4 Force iii, 344; Van Doren, 149

STUART ON WASHINGTON: James Thomas Flexner, *America's Old Masters* (1939), 289

EXPEDITION IN GENERAL: Roberts; Smith, *March;* Codman

EXPEDITION PLANNED: Smith, *Fourteenth,* i, 495–516; *Historical Magazine* (1857), i, 372; 4 Force iii, 442–43; Fitzpatrick, iii, 436–38; NYPL *Bulletin* (1920), xxiv, 490–92

EXPEDITION STARTS: Roberts, 67; Peters, 746; Fitzpatrick, iii, 491–92

PREPARATIONS ON KENNEBEC: Smith, *March,* 74–89; Roberts, 45–47, 73, 511–12; 4 Force iii, 947–48, 960–61

UP THE KENNEBEC: Roberts, 46–49, 69–72, 514, 582

THREE PONDS: *Ibid.,* 51

FLOOD: *Ibid.,* 53–55, 208–10, 254–55

COUNCIL OF WAR: *Ibid.,* 55–56, 210

ENOS TURNS BACK: *Ibid.,* 210–13, 254–55

ARNOLD ON HEIGHT OF LAND: *Ibid.,* 56–59, 77–79

ON CHAUDIÈRE: *Ibid.,* 60–61

TROOPS IN TROUBLE: *Ibid.,* 216–18, 522–29

ARNOLD TO THE RESCUE: *Ibid.,* 218–20, 347–48, 529–30

MARCH TO PT. LEVI: *Ibid.,* 200–22; Codman, 125

MUSTER: Roberts, 558

Source References

CHAPTER SEVEN

ST. JOHNS DESCRIBED: *PMHB* (1898), xxii, 29–31; Smith, *Fourteenth*, i, 344–46; André, *Narrative*, 1–2, map opposite 49
AMERICANS APPEAR: André, *Narrative*, 1–4
FIRST BATTLE: *Ibid.*, 4–7
JITTERY SENTRIES: *Ibid.*, 8–9
DAILY CANNONADE: *Ibid.*, 17
ALLEN CAPTURED: *Ibid.*, 17; Smith, *Fourteenth*, i, 371–99
HOPE FOR ACTION: André, *Narrative*, 18
NO WORD FROM CARLETON: *Ibid.*, 46
REBEL INCOMPETENCE: *Ibid.*, 47–48
THE SOW: *Ibid.*, 21–22
REBELS MARCH BY: *Ibid.*, 25–27
MORE CANNONADING: *Ibid.*, 28–33
CHAMBLY SURRENDERS: *Ibid.*, 34–35; Foucher, 31–32
MORE DAMAGE AND NEW HOPE: André, *Narrative*, 36–39
FINAL DESTRUCTION: *Ibid.*, 40–42; Smith, *Fourteenth*, i, 418
ANDRÉ'S MISSION: André, *Narrative*, 43; Foucher, 42
SURRENDER: André, *Narrative*, 45; André to mother, 12/7/76, AP; 4 Force iii, 1394; Smith, *Fourteenth*, i, 460–66; Seward, 16
WAS BAGGAGE PLUNDERED: André to mother, *op. cit.*; André and others to Cumberland Committee, 8/1/76, LC; 4 Force v, 520
TRIP TO MONTREAL: Montgomery to Schuyler, 11/8/75, Preston to Schuyler, 11/11/75, and A. Gordon to Schuyler, 11/12/75, NYPL; 4 Force iii, 1343, 1603
SUMMARY OF SIEGE: André, *Narrative*, 45–48

CHAPTER EIGHT

CROSSES ST. LAWRENCE: Roberts, 87–88, 224–25, 264, 351–52
QUEBEC UNPREPARED: *Ibid.*, 352–53; *Remembrancer* (1776), i, 130–31
DRILL BENEATH WALLS: Roberts, 87–88, 353–54
RETREAT: *Ibid.*, 90–94
ARNOLD LOOKS BACK: *Ibid.*, 96–99
MONTGOMERY: *Ibid.*, 108–10, 270; *New York Genealogical and Biographical Record* (1871), i, 129–30; 4 Force iv, 189
ESCALADE CALLED FOR: 4 Force iv, 288–89; 4 Force iii, 1638–39; Roberts, 94, 101–02
HANCHET AND BROWN: J. E. A. Smith, *History of Pittsfield, Massachusetts* (1869), i, 259; Smith, *Fourteenth*, ii, 121–22; 4 Force iv, 464–65; Roberts, 119–20, 231, 269–70; Goelet Sale, Part II, American Art Association (1/24–25/1935), 153
ATTACK ON QUEBEC: Smith, *Fourteenth*, ii, 117–47; 4 Force iv, 480–81; Roberts, 102–03, 108, 189–92, 275–76, 375–77, 536–39, 564–66, 590
IN HOSPITAL: Roberts, 102–06, 113, 233–35
RENEWED SIEGE: 4 Force v, 549–51; Roberts, 108–23
CATHOLICS: MHS *Proceedings* (1872), ser. 1, xii, 276–77; Roberts, 118; Helena O'Reilly, *M. de St.-Vallier et l'hôspital général de Québec* (1882), 410–13
PROMOTION AND REINFORCEMENTS: 4 Force iv, 1639; 4 Force v, 549–51
WOOSTER ARRIVES: 4 Force v, 845–46, 1098–99
COMMISSIONERS: Kate Mason Carroll, *Charles Carroll of Carrollton* (1898), i, 152–53
THE CEDARS: 4 Force, vi, 595–97; Wilkinson, i, 44–47
MONTREAL GOODS: 4 Force vi, 579–81, 796–97, 924; Wilkinson, i, 48–49
RECOMMENDS RETREAT: 4 Force vi, 796; 5 Force i, 165
HAZEN: André, *Narrative*, 7, 22; Foucher; Philippe Demers, *Le Général Hazen* (1927)

LEAVES CANADA: 4 Force vi, 930; Wilkinson, i, 51–55; HMC, 39
REACTIONS TO DEFEAT: 4 Force iv, 192, 874; 4 Force vi, 649, 925–26

CHAPTER NINE

ARNOLD TAKES COMMAND: 5 Force i, 649, 747, 952
AMERICANS BUILD FLEET: Howard I. Chapelle, *The History of the American Sail-ing Navy* (1949), 99–114; 5 Force i, 511, 680, 1033
HAZEN AND MONTREAL CHARGES: 5 Force i, 810, 1268, 1272–75; 5 Force ii, 224, 294–95, 334
ARNOLD SAILS: 5 Force i, 826–27, 901
JOKE ABOUT DOCTORS: *Ibid.*, 988–89
ARNOLD'S ANXIETY: 5 Force ii, 223–24, 251, 481, 531–32, 834–35, 982
COMMENT ON FALL OF NEW YORK: *Ibid.*, 933
NAVAL BATTLES: *Ibid.*, 1038–39, 1079–80, 1224; Mahan, 363–70; Friedrich A. Riedesel, *Memoirs, Letters, and Journals* (1868), 70–74
ARNOLD PRAISED AND CRITICIZED: 5 Force ii, 1080, 1143, 1224; 5 Force iii, 527; Mahan, 369–70; Wilkinson, i, 92–93
FEARS ABOUT PROMOTION: 5 Force i, 1267
HAZEN AND BROWN: Brown, charges, 12/1/76, Huntington Library; 5 Force iii, 1042–43, 1219–20; Arnold, *Arnold*, 102–04
MARCH TO JOIN WASHINGTON: Wilkinson, i, 98–111; Arnold to Schuyler, 12/1/76 and 12/14/76, NYPL; *PMHB* (1888), xii, 395; 5 Force iii, 875, 1124, 1217–18, 1258, 1313
WITH WASHINGTON: Arnold to Schuyler, 12/28/76, NYPL
VISITS NEW HAVEN: Arnold, orders, 1/6/77, HSP; Decker, 201; Peters, 690; Isaac Q. Leake, *General John Lamb* (1850), 147–50
PROVIDENCE COMMAND: Fitzpatrick, vi, 428, vii, 115–16; Arnold to Schuyler, 2/7/77, NYPL; Sparks, *Correspondence*, i, 326–28, 334–36, 353–56, 359–60; Arnold to Gates, 3/8/77, NYHS; Ezra Stiles, *Literary Diary* (1901), ii, 147–48
IN BOSTON: Arnold to Revere, 3/1/77, MHS; Arnold to Gates, 3/8/77, NYHS; Sparks, *Correspondence*, 353–56
DE BLOIS AND BRIMMER: Anon., *The Motley Assembly* (1779); *New England His-torical and Genealogical Register* (1857), xi, 75–76; Arthur W. H. Eaton, *The De Blois Family* (1913), 1–5; List of Boston Whigs, MHS; MHS *Proceedings* (1928–29), lxii, 21; Lucy Knox to Colonel Knox, 4/31/77, MHS
NAVAL AMBITION: Arnold to Schuyler, 3/8/77, NYPL; Arnold to Gates, 3/8/77, NYHS
NOT PROMOTED: Fitzpatrick, vii, 233–34, 251–52, 352–53; Sparks, *Correspondence*, 353–56, 359–60; Arnold to Gates, 3/25/77, NYHS
REASONS NOT PROMOTED: Burnett, ii, 261–63, 269, 287–88, 311
SPY HUNT: Arnold to William Heath, 5/2/77, MHS; Oswald to Lamb, 5/11/77, NYHS; Prof. Woolsey to Sparks, received 2/15/1834, HL
DANBURY INVASION: James Montgomery Bailey and Susan Benedict Hill, *History of Danbury, Connecticut* (1896), 60–102; George L. Rockwell, *History of Ridgefield, Connecticut* (1927), 103–19; Hugh Hughes to Gates, 5/3/77, copy NYHS
MADE MAJOR GENERAL: CCJ, vii, 323; Fitzpatrick, viii, 16
WASHINGTON BACKS ARNOLD: Fitzpatrick, viii, 47–48
RUSH: George W. Corner, ed., *Autobiography of Benjamin Rush* (1948), 158
VOTED HORSE: CCJ, vii, 372–73
BROWN'S CHARGES TRIED: J. E. A. Smith, *History of Pittsfield, Massachusetts* (1869), i, 270–73; CCJ, viii, 382; Arnold, *Arnold*, 134–35; Richard Henry Lee, *Memoir of Richard Henry Lee* (1825), ii, 38; Charles Francis Adams, *Familiar Letters of John Adams* (1876), 276
ACCOUNTS: Sparks, *Arnold*, 95–97; Van Doren, 255–57

Source References

ARNOLD SEES GATES: Arnold to Gates, 8/6/77, NYHS
GOWNS: Lucy Knox to Colonel Knox, 6/4/77, MHS
PERMITS TO PASS LINES: Fitzpatrick, viii, 198; Arnold, pass to Thomas Riché and family, 6/24/77, HSP; Decker, 31–32
NEW JERSEY CAMPAIGN: *CCJ*, viii, 432, 467; *Remembrancer* (1777), v, 267–68; Sparks, *Correspondence*, i, 384–86; Fitzpatrick, viii, 259–62
ARNOLD RESIGNS: Burnett, ii, 442; Arnold to Congress, 7/11/77 and 7/12/77, LC; *CCJ*, viii, 545, 549
CALLED NORTH: Fitzpatrick, viii, 376–78; *CCJ*, viii, 545

CHAPTER ELEVEN

LEAVES ST. JOHNS: Charles Preston to Schuyler, 11/11/75, and A. Gordon to Schuyler, 11/12/75, NYPL
KNOX: Sargent, 92–93; Noah Brooks, *Henry Knox* (1900), 41–42
IN ALBANY: André, portraits of Mr. and Mrs. Cuyler, collection of J. G. Cuyler, South Australia; Maud Churchill Nicoll, *The Earliest Cuylers* (1912), 31–32; *American Bibliopolist* (1870), ii, 103; 4 Force vi, 1072–73; André to Schuyler, 6/1/76, collection of Justin Turner
TRIP TO LANCASTER: André to mother, 12/17/76, AP; Smith, *Narrative*, 295; 4 Force iv, 542
IN PHILADELPHIA: American Jewish Historical Society *Publications* (1897), vi, 41; Walker, xxv, 29
SITUATION OF LANCASTER PRISONERS: 4 Force iv, 371, 561, 619, 801, 1213–14; *PA* (1890), 2d ser., xiii, 507–08
ANDRÉ IN LANCASTER: André, parole, 2/23/76, HSP; Lancaster County Historical Society *Papers* (1903), viii, 142–64, (1914), xviii, 129–55; 4 Force v, 848–49
DISCIPLE: André, watercolor, HSP; John Jay Smith, *American Historical and Literary Curiosities* (1860), 2d ser., iv, 1–4, plate 27; Oliver Cope, *Cope Family* (1861), 26, 32–33
FULTON AND BARTON: James Thomas Flexner, *Steamboats Come True* (1944), 113; Lancaster County Historical Society *Papers* (1924), xxviii, 60
LEAVES LANCASTER: 4 Force iv, 1213–14; 4 Force v, 725; *PA, op. cit.*, 512–15
LETTERS TO COPE AND MICHAEL: John Jay Smith, *op. cit.*, 1–4; Lancaster County Historical Society *Papers* (1914), xviii, 129–55
LIFE IN CARLISLE: J. A. Murray, *André and Despard at Carlisle* (1902); Conway P. Wing, *History of Cumberland County, Pennsylvania* (1879), 86; Thomas G. Tousey, *Military History of Carlisle* (1929), 71–73; 5 Force i, 158–69, 327–28, 759–60
DESPARD: *Gentleman's Magazine* (1829), xcix, pt. 2, 369–70
ANDRÉ MALTREATED: André and others to Cumberland Committee, 8/1/76, LC; George Stevenson to Congress, 8/17/76, LC; André to mother, 12/7/76, AP
ANDRÉ IN ROOM: *Notes and Queries*, London (1854), x, 79

CHAPTER TWELVE

ANDRÉ EXCHANGED: André to mother, 12/17/76, AP; Conway P. Wing, *History of Cumberland County, Pennsylvania* (1879), 93; *PCR* (1852), xi, 64; *A Centennial Memorial of Christian and Anna Wolff* (1863), 42–45; Historical Society of Montgomery County, Pennsylvania, *Sketches* (1905), iii, 338–44; Fitzpatrick, vi, 327; Sargent, 103–05
RETURNS TO NEW YORK: André to mother, 12/17/76, AP; *Authentic Narrative*, 171; Sargent, 108–11
STATEN ISLAND: André to Charles Preston, 7/16/77, collection of Foreman Lebold; Charles Gilbert Hine and William T. Davis, *Legends of Old Staten Island* (1925), 86, 122

JOINS GRAY: *Authentic Narrative,* 171; André to mother, 10/28/77, AP; André, *Journal*

ANDRÉ'S WILL: NYHS *Collections* (1900), xxiii, 138–39

IN NEW JERSEY: André, *Journal,* 35–48; André to Preston, 7/16/77, *op. cit.; View of Evidence Relative to the Conduct of Sir William Howe* (1779), 19

AGAIN IN NEW YORK: André, *Journal,* 48–50; André to Preston, 7/16/77, *op. cit.;* André to mother, 12/17/77 and 9/28/77, AP

FROM ELK TO BRANDYWINE: André, *Journal,* 50–84; André, account of campaign, 9/28/77, 1, 6, AP

BRANDYWINE: André, *Journal,* 84–88; André, account, *op. cit.,* 1–4; André to mother, 9/28/77, 1–2, AP

PAOLI MASSACRE: André, *Journal,* 92–96; André to mother, *ibid.,* 3; André, account, *op. cit.,* 4–5; *New York Gazette and Weekly Mercury,* 12/1/77, 3; J. Smith Further and Gilbert Cope, *History of Chester County, Pennsylvania* (1881), 83–90

CHEW: André, epigram, collection of Samuel Chew; *Century Magazine* (1893–94), xlviii, 685–87

GERMANTOWN: André, *Journal,* 98–115; André to mother, 9/28/77, 1–4 and postscripts 10/8 and 10/14/77; André, account, *op. cit.,* 6–8

VIEWS ON WAR: André, memorandum, 11/20/[77], AP

CHAPTER THIRTEEN

ARNOLD GOES NORTH: *CCJ,* viii, 545, 549, 553; Fitzpatrick, viii, 427

CLARKSON: *The Clarksons of New York* (1876), ii, 8–17

ARNOLD JOINS SCHUYLER: Schuyler to Washington, 8/1/77, NYPL; Arnold to Gates, 8/5/77, NYHS

SCHUYLER'S TROUBLES: Schuyler to Washington, 7/26/77, and Schuyler to Congress, 7/15/77, NYPL

STANWIX IN GENERAL: John Albert Scott, *Fort Stanwix and Oriskany* (1927); Hoffman Nickerson, *The Turning Point of the Revolution* (1928), 193–213, 269–76; William L. Stone, *Lieutenant General John Burgoyne and Lieutenant Colonel Barry St. Leger* (1877)

ARNOLD UNDERTAKES RELIEF: Schuyler to Washington and Schuyler to Arnold, 8/13/77, NYPL; Fitzpatrick, viii, 459–60

ARNOLD'S EXPEDITION: Gates to Arnold, 8/19/77, Arnold to Schuyler and report of council of war, 8/21/77, Arnold to Gates, 8/23/77, NYHS; Scott, *op. cit.,* 273–74

HON YOST SCHUYLER: William L. Stone, *Life of Joseph Brant* (1838), i, 256–62; George W. Schuyler, *Philip Schuyler and Family* (1885), ii, 463, 473–77; Timothy Dwight, *Travels in New England and New York* (1822), iii, 196–98

ST. LEGER FLEES: Peter Gansevoort to Arnold, 8/22/77, NYHS; Scott, *op. cit.,* 282–87

COVETS KINGSBOROUGH: Arnold to Schuyler, 11/30/78, collection of Justin G. Turner; Arnold to Schuyler, 2/8/79, NYPL

SENIORITY NOT RESTORED: *CCJ,* viii, 623–24; Burnett, ii, 442–43, 445, 448

FIRST SQUABBLE WITH GATES: Arnold to Gates, 9/22/77, NYHS; Varick to Schuyler, 9/12/77, NYPL; Wilkinson, i, 254–55

LIVINGSTON JOINS ARNOLD: Edwin B. Livingston, *The Livingstons of Livingston Manor* (1910), 250

VARICK JOINS ARNOLD: Varick to Schuyler, 4/10/77 and 9/16/77, NYPL; 5 Force i, 1033

CONGRESS DENOUNCED: H. B. Livingston to Schuyler, 9/11/77, NYPL

HELPS KOSCIUSZKO: Washington Irving, *Washington* (1856), iii, 226

RECONNOITERING: Varick to Schuyler and H. B. Livingston to Schuyler, 9/15/77, NYPL; H. B. Livingston to Schuyler, 9/17/77, NYPL

Source References

FREEMAN'S FARM: Wilkinson, i, 234–55; Arnold to Gates, 9/22/77, NYHS; Varick to Schuyler, 9/19/77, 9/21/77, 9/22/77, 9/25/77, NYPL; H. B. Livingston to R. R. Livingston, 9/25/77, NYHS; H. B. Livingston to Schuyler, 9/25/77, NYPL; R. R. Livingston to Washington, 1/12/78, NYHS; *Magazine of American History* (1880), iv, 186–87; Reuben Aldridge Guild, *Chaplain Smith and the Baptists* (1885), 209; Maria Campbell, *Revolutionary Services of General William Hull* (1848), 92–98; *PMHB* (1880), iv, 389–90; HMC, 114; Arnold, *Arnold*, 163–90; Isaac N. Arnold, *Arnold at Saratoga* (1880); Frank Moore, *Diary of the American Revolution* (1865), i, 497–98

CHAPTER FOURTEEN

DAY AFTER FREEMAN'S FARM: Varick to Schuyler, 9/25/77, NYPL; H. B. Livingston to R. R. Livingston, 10/4/77, and Arnold to Gates, 9/22/77, NYHS; Wilkinson, i, 249–52

OPEN BREAK WITH GATES: Arnold to Gates, 9/22/77 and 9/23/77, NYHS; Varick to Schuyler, 9/22/77, NYPL; Gates to Congress, Gates to Arnold, 9/23/77, NYHS; Wilkinson, i, 257–58

GATES'S STRATEGY: Gates to wife, 9/22/77, Gates to George Clinton, 10/4/77, and Gates to Washington, 10/5/77, NYHS

CONTINUING CONTROVERSY: Varick to Schuyler, 9/24/77, 9/25/77, and 9/26/77, H. B. Livingston to Schuyler, 9/24/77, 9/25/77, and 9/26/77, NYPL; Arnold to Gates, 9/27/77 and 10/1/77, Gates to Arnold, 9/28/77, NYHS; Wilkinson, i, 258–60

SCHUYLER ON CONTROVERSY: Schuyler to Varick, 9/21/77 and 9/25/77, NYPL

BATTLE OF BEMIS HEIGHTS: Arnold, *Arnold*, 196–209; Wilkinson, i, 267–79; Hoffman Nickerson, *The Turning Point of the Revolution* (1928), 357–68; William L. Stone, *Lieutenant General John Burgoyne and Lieutenant Colonel Barry St. Leger* (1877), 56–66, 322–26, 371–75

CHAPTER FIFTEEN

FLEET ENTERS PHILADELPHIA: *PMHB* (1877), i, 31–32

PEGGY'S BIRTH: Walker, xxiv, 406

SHIPPEN FAMILY: John W. Jordan, *Colonial Families of Philadelphia* (1911), i, 96–109; *PMHB* (1883), vii, 11–34; Balch, v–xli; *Portfolio*, New York (1810), iii, 1–7; Walker, xxiv, 257–66; Charles P. Keith, *Provincial Councillors of Pennsylvania, 1733–1776* (1883), 54–59

FATHER'S CULTURAL IDEAS: Balch, 20–21; *PMHB* (1883), vii, 16

PEGGY'S BUSINESS ABILITY: Walker, xxv, 459, 483, xxvi, 227

TIMOROUS GIRL: *PMHB* (1916), 380–81; Balch, li

STAMP ACT: Walker, xxiv, 419–21

IMMIGRANTS NATURALIZED: Burd, 9–10

WASHINGTON DINES: John C. Fitzpatrick, ed., *Diaries of George Washington* (1925), ii, 165

AGAINST BURD'S MARCHING: J. Bennett Nolan, *Neddie Burd's Reading Letter Book* (1927), 63–64

SHIPPEN WORRIES: Edward Shippen, Jr., to Jasper Yeates, 9/19/75 and 6/23/76, HSP; *PMHB* (1883), vii, 24–26

SERENADE: *PMHB* (1887), xi, 281–82

TO NEW JERSEY: Edward Shippen, Jr., to Yeates, 5/9/76, and to Joseph Shippen, 6/23/76, Joseph Shippen to Yeates, 7/3/76, HSP; Burd, 89

PEGGY ON RURAL LIFE: Walker, xxv, 480

FLIGHT FROM NEW JERSEY: Balch, 252; *Acts of the General Assembly of New Jersey* (1777), 2–6

TO SCHUYLKILL FALLS: Balch, xxxiv, 255; *PMHB* (1885), ix, 193

BROTHER CAPTURED: Balch, 255–56; Edward Shippen, III, to Edward Shippen, Sr., 3/11/77, HSP; *PMHB* (1884), viii, 260 (1885), ix, 193

SHIPPENS' PLIGHT: *PMHB* (1885), ix, 195–96; Balch, xxxiv, 252–59

WASHINGTON AND HOWE AT SCHUYLKILL FALLS: *PA*, v, 469, 478, 502–03; *PCR*, xi, 269; *PMHB* (1885), ix, 284, (1892), xvi, 28–41; Fitzpatrick, ix, 20–21; Joseph Galloway, *Letters to a Nobleman* (1779), 42

CHAPTER SIXTEEN

BEFORE HARBOR OPENED: André, *Journal*, i, 100, 135; André to mother, 10/14/77, AP

THEATER: Thomas Clark Pollock, *The Philadelphia Theatre in the 18th Century* (1933), 34–35, 130–32; George O. Seilhamer, *History of the American Theatre* (1889), ii, 16–32; Sargent, 169–75; John F. Watson, *Annals of Philadelphia* (1891), ii, 292

PEGGY BURSTS FORTH: Balch, 266–67; *PMHB* (1892), xvi, 216–18; Watson, *op. cit.*, 293; Decker, 293; Johann Heinrichs, *Extracts from Letter Book* (n.d.), 3

BRITISH IMMORALITY: Jones, i, 351, ii, 86; Ethel Armes, *Nancy Shippen, Her Journal Book* (1935), 91; D. A. Story, *The De Lanceys* (1931), 90

ANDRÉ'S ACTIVITIES: P. E. Du Simitière to Henry Clinton, 11/10/80, LC; André, "Return Enraptured Hours," collection of Library Company of Philadelphia; *Century Magazine* (1893–94), xlviii, 284–86

SILHOUETTES: *Connoisseur* (1926), lxxvi, 209–18; André, silhouettes, collections of Library Company of Philadelphia and Harry Du Pont

ANDRÉ AND PEGGY: Pownoll W. Phipps, *The Life of Colonel Pownoll Phipps* (1894), 88; André, drawing of Peggy, Yale University Art Gallery

MESHIANZA: André to Peggy, 8/16/79, NYHS; André, *Mischianza Letter*; André, *Mischianza*; Anon., "Account of Mischianza," Beekman Papers, NYHS; Israel Mauduit, *Strictures of the Philadelphia Mischianza* (1779); *PMHB* (1889), xiii, 307, (1936), lx, 179–80; J. Thomas Scharf and Thompson Westcott, *History of Philadelphia* (1884), i, 381; Walker, xxiv, 427–28

VALLEY FORGE: Harry Emerson Wildes, *Valley Forge* (1938), 235–36

RAID ON OUTPOSTS: Scharf and Westcott, *op. cit.*

ATTACK ON LAFAYETTE: *Ibid.*, 382; *PMHB* (1936), lx, 176–78

STEALS FROM FRANKLIN: *PMHB* (1884), viii, 30; *Pennsylvania Packet*, 9/6/81; Carl Van Doren, *Benjamin Franklin's Autobiographical Writings* (1945), 700–01, 760; *Letters to Benjamin Franklin from His Family and Friends* (1859), 77–78

BRITISH DEPART: André. farewell to Peggy Chew, collection of Samuel Chew; Sargent, 150, 185; *PMHB* (1889), xiii, 306, (1936), lx, 175

CHAPTER SEVENTEEN

IN ALBANY HOSPITAL: James Thacher, *Military Journal* (1854), 103; Varick to Schuyler, 10/30/77, 11/1/77, 11/5/77, 11/8/77, 11/12/77, 11/16/77, and 12/1/77, NYPL; Oswald to Lamb, 12/18/77, NYHS; *New England Historical and Genealogical Register* (1864), xviii, 34; George Clinton, *Papers* (1900), 430; *Freeman's Journal*, Philadelphia, 7/18/81

ARNOLD AND GATES: Gates to Congress, 10/12/77, NYHS; *Remembrancer* (1781), xi, pt. 1, 100

ACTION CONCERNING COMMISSION: *CCJ*, ix, 861, 981; Fitzpatrick, x, 324–25; Arnold to Washington, 3/12/87, LC

TO MIDDLETOWN: MHS *Proceedings* (1885–86), ser. 2, ii, 444; Edward A. Collier, *History of Old Kinderhook* (1914), 370–71

IN MIDDLETOWN: Louis F. Middlebrook, *History of Maritime Connecticut During the American Revolution* (1925), ii, 97–98; *Naval Records of the American*

Source References

Revolution (1906), 311; James Otis, bill, 4/10/78, and Samuel Goodrich, bill, 11/30/78, NHCHS

DE BLOIS: David S. Franks to Lucy Knox, 12/11/77, Arnold to Elizabeth De Blois, 4/8/78 and 4/26/78, ring, MHS; *New England Historical and Genealogical Register* (1857), xi, 75–76; Arthur W. H. Eaton, *The De Blois Family* (1913, 5; Decker, 285–88

BACK IN NEW HAVEN: *Connecticut Journal*, New Haven, 5/6/78; Colonial Society of Massachusetts *Publications* (1902–04), viii, 234–35; Fitzpatrick, xi, 359–60; Francis S. Drake, *Henry Knox* (1873), 56

AT VALLEY FORGE: Fitzpatrick, xii, 94–95; *PMHB* (1904), xxviii, 249–50; Arnold, *Proceedings*, 8–11; William Constable to William Duer, 6/13/78, NYHS; New Hampshire Historical Society *Collections* (1931), xiv, 61

FRANKS: Paul L. Ford, *Writings of Jefferson* (1894), iii, 310, iv, 365–66; *Magazine of History* (1906), iv, 63–72; NYHS *Collections* (1889), 530; American Jewish Historical Society *Publications* (1893), i, 58, 76, (1894), ii, 7, (1897), v, 187–89, (1902), x, 101–05

CONTRACT WITH FRANKS: Arnold, *Proceedings*, 10–12, 26, 43

ARNOLD ENTERS PHILADELPHIA: Sally Wister, *Journal* (1902), 184–85; Decker, 300

CONTRACT WITH CLOTHIERS: Arnold, James Mease, and William West, Jr., agreement, 6/12/78, copy NYHS

CLOSES SHOPS: *PCR*, xi, 522–23, 540; Arnold, *Proceedings*, 9–10, 26–27, 31–32

MCLANE: McLane, note on copy of agreement, *op. cit.*

ARNOLD ENTERTAINS: Arnold, *Proceedings*, 27; Arnold to Congress, 3/?/79, NYHS

TORY PROPERTY: Arnold, *Proceedings*, 9–10; Fitzpatrick, xii, 94–95; *PMHB* (1931), lv, 36, 38, 48, 51–52; Charles C. Sellers, *Charles Willson Peale* (1947), i, 185–86

TORY GIRLS: Walker, xxiv, 417; Charles J. Stillé, *Anthony Wayne* (1893), 153–54, 161

CHAPTER EIGHTEEN

REED WARNS DEANE: NYHS *Collections* (1890), xxiii, 380

ORDERS TO GARRISON: Arnold, broadside, 7/7/78, HSP

ARNOLD'S ESTABLISHMENT: *PMHB* (1900), xxiv, 368; Arnold to William Heath, 10/23/79, MHS

NAVAL AMBITIONS: John J. Meng, ed., *Dispatches and Instructions of Conrad Alexandre Gérard* (1939), 159–60, 283; *CCJ*, xiii, 855–56; Fitzpatrick, xii, 161, 269–70

BUSINESS DEALS: John R. Livingston to four New York merchants and his agreement with Arnold, 7/18/78, HL; George Clinton, *Papers* (1902), vi, 428–29; American Art Association Catalogue, 1/12/1932, pp. 2–3; *PA*, viii, 73; *Yankee Clipper* (1937), v, 767–68; William Constable to William Duer, 6/13/78, NYHS

BORROWS WAGONS: Arnold, *Proceedings*, 15–19, 23, 28–30, 32, 38; Arnold, receipt to Stephen Collins, 11/24/78, HSP

PASSES AND HANNAH LEVY: *CCJ*, xi, 779, xiii, 455–56; Fitzpatrick, xiv, 101; George Bryan to Arnold, 10/22/78, NYHS; *PCR*, xi, 676; *PA*, vii, 223–24

ARNOLD AND PEACE PROPOSALS: Arnold, Memorial to Commissions on Tory Losses, ?/?/84, ArP; Arnold, *Arnold*, 228; Gouverneur Morris to Reed, 4/9/79, NYHS

INFLATION AND LUXURY: George Washington Greene, *Nathanael Greene* (1871), ii, 103, 169; Fitzpatrick, xiii, 462–68; Charles J. Stillé, *Anthony Wayne* (1893), 161–62; MHS *Proceedings* (1909–10), xliii, 334; *CCJ*, xii, 1018; *Letters to Benjamin Franklin from His Family and Friends* (1859), 84–85

REED ON EXECUTIONS: Reed to ?, 10/23/78, NYHS; NYHS *Collections* (1873), iii, 245–53

SHIPPEN ON COSTS: Balch, 266–69

ARNOLD'S FLIRTATIONS: Anne H. Wharton, *Through Colonial Doorways* (1893), 194–95, 223; *PMHB* (1879), iii, 377

BREAK WITH DE BLOIS: Arthur W. H. Eaton, *The De Blois Family* (1913), 5; John Q. Adams, *Life in a New England Town* (1903), 135–36

ARNOLD PROPOSES: Arnold, *Arnold*, 228–29; Balch, lvii; Decker, 285–88

ARNOLD RECOVERS: Arnold to Lamb, 8/29/78 and Oswald to Lamb, 10/15/78, NYHS

ARNOLD AND PEGGY'S CIRCLE: *PMHB* (1878), ii, 162–63; Max J. Kohler, *Rebecca Franks* (1894), 20; Esther De Berdt to Reed, 9/28/65, NYHS; *Pennsylvania Packet*, 1/1/78

PEGGY CHEW: *PMHB* (1931), lv, 39, 53

DEANE CONTROVERSY: *The Clarksons of New York* (1876), ii, 29–33; NYHS *Collections* (1887), xx, 481; Jared Sparks, *Gouverneur Morris* (1832), i, 202

LAMB, OSWALD, AND MANSFIELD: Arnold to Lamb, 8/29/78, and Samuel Mansfield to Lamb, 11/9/78, NYHS; Joseph T. Weller, *The Maryland Press, 1777–90* (1938), 22–27

ACTIVE: *PMHB* (1892), xvi, 385 ff.; Van Doren, 176; Arnold, *Proceedings*, 46; *Pennsylvania Packet*, 11/12/79

MATLACK AND BARBER: Arnold, *Proceedings*, 12–15

BURD WEDDING AND ARNOLD COURTSHIP: Walker, xxv, 32–40; Grace Galloway to Elizabeth Galloway, 2/12/79, HSP; Burd, 104–05; Matthew L. Davis, *Aaron Burr* (1852), ii, 34; NYHS *Collections* (1873), vi, 270–71

NEW YORK LAND SCHEME: Arnold to Schuyler, 11/30/78, collection of Justin G. Turner; Jay to George Clinton, 1/31/79, Jay, William Floyd, James Duane, and Francis Lewis to George Clinton, 2/3/79, HL

ACTIVE CASE CONTINUES: Arnold, *Proceedings*, 45–47; *PMHB* (1892), xvi, 388–90

PENNSYLVANIA OPENS ATTACK: Matlack to Clarkson, 1/25/79 and 1/27/79, Clarkson to Matlack, 1/26/79, Pennsylvania Council, unsent draft to Washington, 1/31/79, NYHS; *PA*, ix, 34, 179; *CCJ*, xiii, 115, 131, xiv, 574–77; Arnold, *Proceedings*, 7, 51–52

RELINQUISHES PRIVATEER: New London Historical Society *Collections* (1933), ii, 122

PUBLISHED CHARGES: Arnold, *Proceedings*, 4–5

ARNOLD'S TRIP: Sparks, *Writings*, vi, 517; Fitzpatrick, xiv, 80; Arnold to George Clinton, 2/8/79, Rosenbach collection; Arnold to Schuyler, 2/8/79, NYPL; *Pennsylvania Packet*, 2/13/79; Christopher Marshall, *Extracts from Diary* (1887), 211; Arnold to Peggy, 2/8/79, NYHS

CHAPTER NINETEEN

CONGRESS REFERS CHARGES TO COMMITTEE: *CCJ*, xiii, 184, 188–89; Burnett, iv, 71

CONSERVATIVES SUPPORT ARNOLD: Council to Washington, 5/8/79, NYHS; Francis S. Drake, *Henry Knox* (1873), 60; Reed to Gouverneur Morris, 4/16/79, NYHS; *PA*, ix, 179

COUNCIL *vs.* COMMITTEE: Council to William Paca, 2/20–23/79, Council to Washington, 5/8/79, Paca to George Bryan, 3/4/79, Bryan to Paca, 3/5/79, Paca to Bryan, 3/9/79, NYHS; *PA*, vii, 230; Arnold to Paca Committee, 3/?/79, NYHS; *PA*, vii, 230

BROWN CHARGES REVIVED: *Pennsylvania Packet*, 2/27/79, 3/4/79, and 3/6/79; *PA*, vii, 226–27

CONGRESS ACTS ON ACTIVE: *CCJ*, xiii, 281–86

COMMITTEE REPORTS: *CCJ*, xiii, 324–26; Arnold, *Proceedings*, 52

RESIGNS COMMAND: *CCJ*, xiii, 337

CONGRESS COMPROMISES: Francis Lewis to George Clinton, 3/8/79, HL; Charles Pettit to Nathanael Greene, 3/29/79, NYHS; Congressional Society Report, 3/23/79, NYHS; *CCJ*, xiii, 378, 391, 412–17; Burnett, iv, 135

REACTION OF PEGGY'S CIRCLE: Walker, xxv, 36, 39

Source References

BUYS MOUNT PLEASANT: Pettit to Greene, 3/29/79, NYHS; Harold D. Eberlein and Cortlandt V. Hubbard, *Portrait of a Colonial City* (1939), 341–53; Pennsylvania Museum, *Mount Pleasant* (1927)

PETERS'S CHARGES: Nellie P. Black, *Richard Peters* (1904), 73–74

CHILDREN'S SCHOOLING: J. C. Williams, *History of Washington County, Maryland* (1906), i, 70–71; Helen A. Hays, *Antietam and Its Bridges* (1910), 99–101

MARRIAGE: Walker, xxv, 34–40

SMITH WRITES ARNOLD'S PROCLAMATION: Smith, *Diary*, 10/3/80, 10/4/80, 10/5/80; Arnold, To the Inhabitants of America, ArP

ARNOLD SUPPORTS FRENCH ALLIANCE: Arnold to Schuyler, 12/28/76 and 3/8/77, NYPL

ON CATHOLICS: Arnold, statement, 12/9/96, ArP

ARNOLD'S SELF-INTEREST: Arnold, *Proceedings*, 13; Williams, *op. cit.*

ON BRITISH INDUCEMENTS: Arnold to Germain, 10/28/80, ArP

JURY BACKS ARNOLD: Arnold, *Proceedings*, 45–46

NEW PLEAS FAIL: Arnold, *Proceedings*, 52–53; Sparks, *Writings*, vii, 517–18; *PA*, viii, 347–50; *CCJ*, xiii, 457–58, xiv, 511, 529–32; Fitzpatrick, xiv, 418, 420, 443

CHAPTER TWENTY

CLINTON: Jones, i, 132, 319; Thomas J. Wertenbaker, *Father Knickerbocker Rebels* (1948), 130, 157–58, 247

RETREAT TO NEW YORK: André, *Journal*, ii, 3–17

AT BEDFORD: Henry B. Stiles, *History of the City of Brooklyn* (1867), i, 320–21, ii, 176

RAIDING EXPEDITION: André, *Journal*, ii, 21–30; André to uncle, 9/12/78, AP

SURPRISES BAYLOR'S VIRGINIANS: André, *Journal*, ii, 46–47; Jones, i, 286

CLINTON'S VICES: Jones, i, 341

ANDRÉ AS AIDE: *Political Magazine*, London (1780), i, 688; Wertenbaker, *op. cit.*, 247

OPPOSES GRAFT: André, incomplete letter, 11 or 12/?/79, AP; André, undated memorandum, CP

RAID ON CONNECTICUT: Smith, *Diary*, 7/3/79, 7/16/79, and 8/1/79; André (?), "Address to the Inhabitants of Connecticut," *Royal Gazette*, New York, 7/17/79

LOYALIST NEGOTIATIONS: William Franklin to André, 5/29/79 and 11/10/79, second letter enclosing draft by André, CP; André to [Henry Banney], 11/13/79, CP; Wertenbaker, *op. cit.*, 247

THEATER AND WRITING: Smith, *Diary*, 4/24/79; André, "Prologue," *Royal Gazette*, 1/13/79; André, "Dream," *Royal Gazette*, 1/23/79; *Memorial History of the City of New York* (1833), i, 567–68; I. N. Phelps Stokes, *Iconography of Manhattan Island* (1926), v, 1081; André, "The Frantic Lover," CP; *Pennsylvania Packet*, 9/6/81

HANDBALL: William Dunlap, *History of the American Theatre* (1833), i, 80–81

ILLNESS AND SIMCOE: Maggs Bros. Catalogue No. 429 (1922), 80–81; Simcoe to André, two undated letters, CP; Harold D. Eberlein, *Manor Houses and Historic Homes of Long Island and Staten Island* (1928), 148–53

EXCHANGE NEGOTIATIONS: Documents, 4/8/79–5/11/79, CP

PUT IN CHARGE OF INTELLIGENCE: Date based on nature of correspondence in CP

CHAPTER TWENTY-ONE

FIRST DAYS OF TREASON: Taylor, 55; Fitzpatrick, xiv, 457–58; Sparks, *Writings*, vi, 522–23

ANDRÉ HEARS FROM ARNOLD: Van Doren, 439–40

SOURCE REFERENCES

CORRESPONDENCE WITH WASHINGTON: Sparks, *Writings,* 523–26; Fitzpatrick, xv, 13, 85–86

PEGGY CHEW: *PMHB* (1931), lv, 78; Van Doren, 440–41

ARNOLD REPLIES: Van Doren, 441–42

RUINED LETTER: *Ibid.,* 442–43

GO-BETWEENS CORRESPOND: *Ibid.,* 442–46

ARNOLD AT HEADQUARTERS: Deane to Greene, 5/29/79, Greene to Reed, 6/2/79, NYHS; Arnold, *Proceedings,* 1–4; Fitzpatrick, xx, 370; Van Doren, 448–49

INTELLIGENCE WORK: André, undated memorandum re Brink, Christopher Sower, memorandum, 5/1/80, André to Dr. Stevenson, 9/15/79, with memorandum, CP; Van Doren, 220–28

FORT LA FAYETTE: André, surrender terms, 6/1/79, NYHS; *New Jersey Gazette,* 12/29/79; Stevens, x, 999

ANDRÉ REPLIES TO ARNOLD: Van Doren, 446–48; Henry Clinton to Germain, 10/11/80, CaP

ARNOLD ANNOYED WITH BRITISH: Van Doren, 449–52

GILES: Eliza Shipton to Giles, Tuesday Morning, NYHS

ARNOLD APPROACHES WASHINGTON: Sparks, *Writings,* 527; Fitzpatrick, xv, 441–42

BRITISH WILL NOT STEP DOWN: Van Doren, 451–53

ARNOLD NOT SATISFIED: *Ibid.,* 453–55

ANDRÉ AND PEGGY: *Ibid.,* 454–55; André to Peggy, 8/16/79, NYHS

CHAPTER TWENTY-TWO

PRIVATEERS: *PMHB* (1900), xxiv, 367

ARNOLD'S ACCOUNTS: James T. Austin, *Elbridge Gerry* (1828), 316–18; Van Doren, 177, 254–57; *CCJ,* xv, see index, xvi, 393 ff.; Arnold to William Heath, 10/23/70, MHS

JAY NOMINATES: *CCJ,* xv, 1027

RIOTS: *PMHB* (1893), xvii, 348–49; Balch, 280; Burnett, iv, 476–77

SCIENTIFIC MACHINES: Taylor, 54; Oswald to Lamb, 11/22/80, NYHS

ANDRÉ BECOMES ADJUTANT: André, incomplete letter, 11 or 12/?/79, AP; André to Stephen Kemble, 9/16/80, CP; Amherst to Germain, 12/4/79, CaP; NYHS *Collections* (1883–84), xvi and xvii, see index; *Pennsylvania Packet,* 9/6/81

ACTIVITY AS ADJUTANT: André, correspondence in general, André to Lord Cathcart, 3/11/80, Robert Donkin to André, 3/14/80, André to ?, 11/13/79, André, memorandum to Clinton, [1780], André, Activities of Clinton's Aides, 1780, CP; Jones, i, 382; *Authentic Narrative,* 171–72; Patrick Ferguson to André, 12/10/79 and 2/?/80, CP

SNAFU: André, memorandum, 4/3/80, CP

ARBUTHNOT AND CORNWALLIS: André, memorandums, 4/2/80 and undated [1780], CP; Stevens, x, no. 1043

SPY IN CHARLESTON: Benson, 123–28

PLAN OF WAR: André, memorandum [3/?/80], CP; *Clinton–Cornwallis Controversy* (1888), i, 213–15

PREMONITION: Document, CP

ARNOLD'S COURT MARTIAL: Arnold, *Proceedings;* Peggy to Arnold, 1/4/80, Matlack to Reed, 1/20/80, NYHS; *Rules and Articles for Better Government of Troops* (1776), 36; NYHS *Collections* (1889), xxiii, 116; *CCJ,* xvi, 161–63

REPRIMAND: Fitzpatrick, xviii, 127–28, 222–25

FINANCIAL TROUBLES: Peggy to Arnold, *op. cit.;* Tomlinson, 66

NAVAL EXPEDITION: Sparks, *Letters,* ii, 409–11; NYHS *Collections, op. cit.,* Fitzpatrick, xviii, 114–15, 173–74; Charles O. Paullin, *Out-Letters of the Continental Marine Committee and Board of Admiralty* (1914), 168–69

OFFER TO FRENCH: Barbé Marbois, *Complot d'Arnold* (1816), 37–48

INDIAN DREAMS: *Ibid.,* 36–37

Source References

CHAPTER TWENTY-THREE

SHIFTS ASSETS: Robert Bayard, account book, collection of Justin G. Turner
SCHUYLER, WASHINGTON, AND WEST POINT: Schuyler to Arnold, 6/2/80, Schuyler to James Duane, 6/5/80, NYHS; Arnold to Schuyler, 5/25/80, NYPL; Fitzpatrick, xx, 213–14
ARNOLD'S OFFER: Van Doren, 458–59
CANADIAN PROCLAMATION: Fitzpatrick, xviii, 476; Arnold to Washington, 6/7/80, HSP; Van Doren, 262–64, 459–60
INTELLIGENCE SENT FROM CAMP: Van Doren, 265–66, 460
VISITS WEST POINT: *Ibid.*, 266–67, 460–61
ANDRÉ ON NEW JERSEY INVASION: André, memorandum, 6/8/80, CP; Maggs Bros. Catalogue No. 429 (1922), 395
ANDRÉ CHECKS ON ARNOLD: Joseph Chew to André, and George Beckwith to André, 6/20/80, CP
CONNECTICUT BUSINESS: Van Doren, 267–69; Arnold to Enoch Brown, 7/25/80, HSP; Arnold to Titus Werner, 7/8/80, collection of Foreman Lebold; Tomlinson, 59–60
RENEWED ATTEMPT FOR WEST POINT: Burnett, v, 233–34; Fitzpatrick, xix, 90–92
RENEWED OFFERS TO BRITISH: Van Doren, 269–73, 461–64
WASHINGTON ON STATE OF ARMY: Fitzpatrick, xviii, 434–35
CLINTON AND ARBUTHNOT WONDER: Henry Clinton to Germain, 10/11/80, CaP; Smith, *Diary*, 9/26/80 and 9/27/80
ANDRÉ RE-ENTERS NEGOTIATION: Van Doren, 464–65
ANDRÉ'S PROMOTION TROUBLES: Germain to Henry Clinton, 12/4/79, CaP; Maggs, *op. cit.*, Stevens, 730
ARNOLD DEMANDS PROMISES: Van Doren, 464–65
MONEY OFFERED FOR WEST POINT: *Ibid.*, 465–66
ARNOLD SENDS INFORMATION TO PEGGY: *Ibid.*, 467–68
ARNOLD GIVEN LEFT WING: Henry B. Dawson, *Papers Concerning Major André* (1886), 139–41; Fitzpatrick, xix, 302
ARNOLD ON PEGGY'S CHARMS: Van Doren, 286–87
PEGGY'S HYSTERICS: Walker, xxv, 183
ARNOLD GETS WEST POINT: Fitzpatrick, xix, 309–11, 313

CHAPTER TWENTY-FOUR

JOSHUA HETT SMITH: Smith, *Authentic*, 15–18, 291–96
ROBINSON'S HOUSE: *Ibid.*, 16; James Thacher, *Military Journal* (1854), 133
VARICK INTERVENES: Varick, 81–96, 173, 186
TRIES TO FIND SPIES: Morton Pennypacker, *General Washington's Spies* (1939), 120–23
BUSINESS AFFAIRS: New London Historical Society *Collections* (1933), ii, 122–24; American Art Association Catalogue, 2/5/1929, 10–11; Van Doren, 292–93
SELLS RATIONS: Varick to Colonel Pickering, 8/16/80, NYHS; Varick, 134–35, 153–58, 183–85; *Pennsylvania Packet*, 9/30/80; Varick to Gouverneur Morris, 10/10/80, NYHS
AILING LEG: Arnold to Lamb, 8/11/80, NYHS
CONFUSED MIND: Sebastian Bauman to Knox, 9/26/80, NYHS
PEGGY IN PHILADELPHIA: Hannah Arnold to Arnold, 9/4/80, collection of C. P. G. Fuller; Arnold, *Arnold*, 233–35; *Pennsylvania Packet*, 9/30/80
BRITISH DELAY: Henry Clinton to Germain, 10/11/80, CaP
COW CHASE: *Royal Gazette*, New York, 8/16/80, 8/30/80, and 9/23/80
PEGGY CHEW: Colin Campbell to André, 8/17/80
LEGENDS AND GAIETIES: Sargent, 259–61, 298–300; David Gardner, *Chronicles of Easthampton* (1871), 107–08; *PMHB* (1886), x, 427, 429

ANDRÉ BECOMES FULL ADJUTANT: Royal Commission, 8/3/80; André to mother, 9/1/80, AP; *PMHB* (1899), xiii, 397

ARNOLD PREPARES FOR PEGGY: Arnold to Mrs. Field, 9/7/80, facsimile in Boston Public Library; Arnold to ?, 9/1/80, collection of Foreman Lebold; Arnold to Lamb, 8/20/80, NYHS; Tomlinson, no. 56

HERON'S MISSION: Varick, 99–106; Stevens, viii, no. 733; Smith, *Diary*, 4/21/80

DID ARNOLD WEAKEN POST: Adrian H. Joline, *Rambles in Autograph Land* (1913), 244–45; New York *Tribune*, 3/6/1857; Franks to Lamb, 8/16/80; Fitzpatrick, xix, 370, 488–89, xx, 10; Van Doren, 290–92

PEGGY'S PACKAGE: Varick, 107–08, 196–98; Sheldon to Arnold, 9/6/80, LC

MCCARTHY: Varick, 171; James Robertson, statement, 2/6/86, NYPL; McCarthy, petition, 8/23/83, CaP; Van Doren, 301

ARNOLD WORRIED ABOUT PEGGY: Arnold to Samuel Rollins, 9/5/80, collection of Joseph E. Fields; Arnold, *Arnold*, 234; Varick, 139

ANDRÉ WRITES SHELDON: Varick, 108, 113, 171; Van Doren, 471–72

ANDRÉ SETS OUT: André to Stephen Kemble, 9/16/80; Van Doren, 472

DOBBS FERRY: Arnold, deposition for J. H. Smith, 12/20/84, ArP; Henry Clinton, note written in Charles Stedman's *History of the Origin, Progress, and Termination of the American War*, John Carter Brown Library; Smith, *Authentic*, 181; Sparks, *Letters*, iii, 80–81; Van Doren, 472; André, *Case*, 4–5

CHAPTER TWENTY-FIVE

ARNOLD MEETS PEGGY: Varick, 122, 136, 139

NEW NEGOTIATIONS: Van Doren, 472

VARICK GREETS PEGGY: Varick to Lamb, 9/15/80, NYHS

FRANKS ON ANDERSON: Varick, 171–72

WASHINGTON COMING: Fitzpatrick, xx, 47–48; Sparks, *Letters*, iii, 90; Van Doren, 473

PAY AND GATES: Arnold to Greene, 8/23/80, LC; Varick, 196–200

BRITISH DECIDE TO STRIKE: Henry Clinton to Germain, 10/11/80, CaP; André, *Case*, 10; André, maps of West Point area, CP

HANNAH'S SPITE: Hannah Arnold to Arnold, 9/4/80, collection of C. P. G. Fuller

PEGGY'S BEHAVIOR AT WEST POINT: Balch, lx–lxi; Paul L. Ford, *Writings of Jefferson* (1894), iii, 310

ARNOLD INSULTS AIDES: Varick, 121, 138–39, 169–70

ROBINSON'S MISSION: Varick, 123–24, 133–34, 149–50; Smith, *Authentic*, 19–22, 194; Smith, *Trial*, 101; Van Doren, 482–84; Sparks, *Writings*, vii, 525–26

ARNOLD MEETS WASHINGTON: Varick, 123, 170; Van Doren, 483

SMITH-VARICK FEUD: Varick, 123–24, 140, 170

ARNOLD REPLIES TO ROBINSON: Varick, 133–34; Van Doren, 483–84; Sparks, *Writings*, vii, 526–29

SMITH AND ARNOLD MAKE FINAL PLANS: Smith, *Authentic*, 20–22; Smith, *Trial*, 99, 101; Van Doren, 319–20

ANDRÉ IN NEW YORK: Simcoe to André, 9/11/80, CP; Anderson Gallery Catalogue, 5/26/1928, 3; André, *Case*, 9–10; *Royal Gazette*, New York, 8/30/80 and 9/23/80; Morton Pennypacker, *General Washington's Spies* (1939), 123–43; Sargent, 298–300; Albany *Argus*, 4/21/1848; Van Doren, 484

ANDRÉ WAITS ON VULTURE: Van Doren, 474, 484–85; André, *Case*, 10–14; Sparks, *Writings*, vii, 529

UNWILLING BOATMEN: Smith, *Trial*, 2–5

ARNOLD GOES DOWN RIVER: Van Doren, 326–27; Smith, *Trial*, 2, 132–34

SMITH ON VULTURE: Smith, *Authentic*, 23–30, 137, 295; Van Doren, 474, 485, 493–94; André, *Case*, 12–13, 44–46

ARNOLD TO RENDEZVOUS: Smith, *Authentic*, 30–31

MEETING: *Ibid.*, 31; Smith, *Trial*, 9, 11, 23

Source References

STORY ANDRÉ TO LEAD ATTACK: *Magazine of American History* (1879), iii, 755–56; Henry Clinton to Germain, 12/5/80, CaP

CHAPTER TWENTY-SIX

INTERVIEW: Smith, *Trial*, 3, 5, 38, 101; Smith, *Narrative*, 30–33; André, *Proceedings*, 11–14; Van Doren, 480–81

CLINTON ON CAPTURING WASHINGTON: Smith, *Diary*, 9/27/80

ANDRÉ NOT RETURNED TO VULTURE: Smith, *Trial*, 3, 5; Stevens, vii, 739

RIDE TO SMITH'S HOUSE: André, *Proceedings*, 11

FIRING ON VULTURE: Isaac Q. Leake, *John Lamb* (1850), 258; *Mariner's Mirror* (1949), xxxv, 48; Van Doren, 475; Smith, *Authentic*, 33

AT SMITH'S HOUSE: Smith, *Trial*, 3, 5, 37, 69, 97, 99, 104; Smith, *Narrative*, 34–37; Sargent, 393; André, *Proceedings*, 11–14

PAPERS CARRIED BY ANDRÉ: Abbatt, 16–18

AIDES ALARM PEGGY: Varick, 126, 178–89

ANDRÉ'S RIDE: Smith, *Trial*, 33–34, 65–70, 135; Smith, *Narrative*, 37–48; Abbatt, 14–27; *Historical Magazine* (1857), i, 294; Sargent, 393–94

ARNOLD ASKED TO SUPPRESS COWBOYS: George Clinton, *Papers* (1902), vi, 187–88

ANDRÉ CAPTURED: As the years passed, André's captors enlarged on their memories to increase their prosperity and glory; I have relied principally on the testimony given by Paulding and Williams a few weeks after the event in Smith's *Trial*, 70–73. For later accounts see Benson and *Historical Magazine* (1865), ix, 177–80. André's belief that his captors' main motive was robbery was testified to by several officers who conversed with him. The fullest account is that of Joshua King in *Historical Magazine* (1857), i, 293–95. See also Benson and *Magazine of American History* (1879), iii, 747–56

CHAPTER TWENTY-SEVEN

ANDRÉ AND JAMESON: Sparks, *Writings*, vii, 530–31; Sparks, *Letters*, iii, 102; William Allen, *American Biographical Dictionary* (1857), 23–25; Fitzpatrick, xx, 173

TALLMADGE'S TESTIMONY: *Magazine of American History* (1879), iii, 747–56

DISPUTE OVER SMITH: Varick, 127–29, 149–51, 173–77; Smith, *Authentic*, 48–49

SMITH AND WASHINGTON: Smith, *Trial*, 100, 103; Smith, *Authentic*, 49

ANDRÉ AT SOUTH SALEM: Allen, *op. cit.*; *Historical Magazine* (1857), i, 293–95; André, *Proceedings*, 9–13

ROBINSON WORRIED: Van Doren, 474–75

WASHINGTON APPROACHES: Arnold, *Arnold*, 294–95; Douglas S. Freeman, *George Washington* (1952), v, 196–99

ARNOLD FLEES: Stevens, vii, 739; Varick, 129–30; Allen, *op. cit.*; *Pennsylvania Packet*, 10/3/80; Sparks, *Writings*, vii, 530–31; McHenry to ?, 9/26/80, transcript, HL

BOATMEN UNPERSUADED: MHS *Collections* (1816), 2d ser., iv, 51–52; William Heath, *Memoirs* (1904), 269

AIDES AND PEGGY'S HYSTERICS: Varick, 129–32, 142–43, 179–83, 190–93

WASHINGTON LEARNS OF TREASON: Fitzpatrick, xx, 84–94; Lafayette, account given to Mrs. Clement Biddle, HSP; Henry C. Lodge, ed., *Works of Alexander Hamilton* (1886), iii, 15–16; Knox to Sebastian Bauman, 9/25/80, NYHS; Abbatt, 44–45; Freeman, *op. cit.*, 199–204

ARNOLD WRITES WASHINGTON: Sparks, *Writings*, 533

HAMILTON AND PEGGY: Lodge, *op. cit.*, 16–17, 22–23

CHAPTER TWENTY-EIGHT

ATTITUDE TO ANDRÉ: Samuel Shaw, *Journals* (1847), 79; Fitzpatrick, xx, 86–87

TRAVELS BEFORE TAPPAN: Abbatt, 47–56 (to be used with caution)

BRITISH DEFENSE OF ANDRÉ: Sparks, *Writings*, vii, 533–35

PEGGY DECIDES: Henry C. Lodge, ed., *Works of Alexander Hamilton* (1886), viii, 17

PEGGY'S TRIP: Tomlinson, no. 304; Matthew L. Davis, *Aaron Burr* (1852), i, 219–20; *Historical Magazine* (1870), 2d ser., viii, 145

PEGGY IN PHILADELPHIA: Edward Shippen to William Moore, in mirror-writing, 10/5/80, photostat in collection of Mrs. B. Langton Douglas; Burd, 116–17; *PMHB* (1916), xl, 380–81; Robert Morris to Catherine W. Livingston, 10/17/80, MHS; NYHS *Collections* (1878), xi, 453; Balch, lxv; Jared Ingersoll to Reed, 10/4/80, NYHS

ARNOLD FIRST IN NEW YORK: Smith, *Diary*, 9/26/80, NYPL; Stevens, vii, 739, 741; Jones, i, 371–72, 382; Sparks, *Writings*, 534–35; *Political Magazine* (1871), ii, 291; HMC, 183–84; Henry B. Dawson, *Papers Concerning André* (1866), 69

ANDRÉ'S IMPRISONMENT AND TRIAL: Lodge, *op. cit.*, 17–29; Fitzpatrick, 110, 151, 173; Sparks, *Writings*, 537, 543; André, *Proceedings*; Samuel B. Webb, *Reminiscences*, 297; *American Bibliopolist* (1870), ii, 13

MORE NEGOTIATIONS TO SAVE ANDRÉ: Smith, *Diary*, 9/27/80 and 10/3/80; J. G. Simcoe, *Military Journal* (1844), 292–94; New Jersey Historical Society *Proceedings* (1892–93), 2d ser., xii, 23–24; Van Doren, 476; Lodge, *op. cit.*, 17–29; Fitzpatrick, xx, 103–04; Sparks, *Writings*, 539–43; Stevens, vii, 739; André, *Case*, 21–39

ANDRÉ'S LAST HOURS: *Political Magazine* (1780), i, 689; Lodge, *op. cit.*, 27–28; Fitzpatrick, xx, 111, 151

EXECUTION: The eyewitness reports of André's execution are amazingly consistent among themselves, an indication of how deep an impression the scene made; James Thacher, *Military Journal* (1854), 225–33; *Historical Magazine* (1863), vii, 250–52 (1870), 2d ser., viii, 145; *Harper's Magazine* (1855), xi, 419–20; *New England Magazine* (1834), vi, 353–54; John Hart to Abraham Gould, 10/4/80, collection of Mrs. Rutherford M. Shepard; *PMHB* (1896), xx, 313–14; American Art Association Catalogue, 2/5/1929, No. 39; Lodge, *op. cit.*, 25–26; Tallmadge to Heath, 10/10/80, MHS

EPILOGUE

LEARN OF ANDRÉ'S FATE: Smith, *Diary*, 10/5/80 and 10/6/80; *PMHB* (1899), xxiii, 398

ARNOLD PAID: Arnold to William Pitt, 9/8/92, ArP; Van Doren, 384

RECRUITING GOES BADLY: Van Doren, 380

KIDNAP ATTEMPT: *William and Mary Quarterly* (1938), 2d ser., xviii, 322–42 (1939), xix, 548–54; Henry Lee, *Memoirs* (1812), ii, 159–87; Sparks, *Writings*, vii, 544–49

PEGGY EXILED: Walker, xxv, 160–63; Burd, 116–17; *PMHB* (1911), xxxv, 399

VIRGINIA CAMPAIGN: Henry Clinton, orders to Arnold, 12/14/80, ArP; Van Doren, 418–20; Arnold, *Arnold*, 338, 342–48; Alexander Sterling to Samuel Loudon, ?/?/82, NYHS; NYHS *Collections* (1878), xi, 48–50; Steuben to Greene, 1/8/81, NYHS

NEW YORK AFTER VIRGINIA: Smith, *Diary*, 8/1/81; *PMHB* (1899), xxiii, 308–09; Van Doren, 420–21

NEW LONDON: *London Chronicle* (1781), l, 437–38; William Heath, *Memoirs* (1904), 321–23

WISHES TO GO TO LONDON: Clinton to Arnold, 10/15/81, ArP; Smith, *Diary*, 12/8/81; Van Doren, 421–22

SAILS: Stansbury to Arnold, 3/22/82, ArP; Walker, xxv, 163

FIRST IN LONDON: Thomas Glenn Allen, *Some Colonial Mansions* (1900), ii, 163–64; Arnold, *Arnold*, 355–69; Arnold to William Smith, 6/?/82, Peggy, pension warrant, 3/19/82, ArP; *PMHB* (1905), xxix, 303; Walker, xxv, 453–54; Decker, 428–38

ANDRÉ MOURNED: Seward; Germain to Clinton, 12/5/80, CaP; Henry C. Van Schaak, *Peter Van Schaak* (1842), 147; Pownoll W. Phipps, *Colonel Pownoll Phipps* (1894), 88

ST. JOHN'S: J. W. Lawrence, *Foot-Prints* (1883), 70–78; *Winslow Papers*, New Brunswick Historical Society (1901), 270; Arnold to B. Goodrich, 7/27/86, ArP

PEGGY VISITS HOME: Walker, xxv, 168–69, 454–57

BACK IN ENGLAND: Arnold to William Pitt, 9/8/92, ArP; documents on duel, July 1792, ArP; Walker, xxv, 458–63

WAR IN INDIES: Cooper Willyam, *Campaign in the West Indies* (1796), 127; *Gentleman's Magazine* (1794), lxiv, 685–86; Lawrence, *op. cit.*, 76; Decker, 455–61; Walker, xxv, 464

PEGGY INTRIGUES FOR CHILDREN: Peggy to Edward Arnold, 7/16/1802, pension warrant, 7/20/93, ArP; Walker, xxv, 458–72

AFTER INDIES: Arnold, Objects of Expedition, 12/9/96, Arnold to Lord Spencer, 1/14/98, ArP; Walker, xxv, 465–72

ARNOLD'S DEATH: Peggy to Edward Arnold, 7/16/1802 and 10/16/1802, ArP; Taylor, 59–60; Walker, xxv, 472–74

PEGGY'S FINAL AMBITIONS: Peggy to Edward Arnold, 10/16/1802 and 3/20/1803, ArP; Walker, xxv, 474–96; Taylor, 60–67

INDEX

443

Index

Danbury, Conn., 125-6, 360, 363-5
Darwin, Erasmus, 25-6
Davies, William, 270
Dead River, 61, 65-8, 77
Deane, Barnabas, 48, 50
Deane, Silas, 43, 48, 95, 222-3, 227, 237-8, 266, 283, 413
De Blois, Elizabeth, 117-9, 124, 130, 220-1, 235-6, 413
De Blois, Gilbert, 117, 221
De Blois, Mrs. Gilbert, 117-8
Decker, Malcolm, 419
Declaration of Independence, 195-6, 253-4
Defoe, Daniel, 23
De Lancey, Oliver, 205, 297, 328
Delaplace, William, 46
Delaware River, 150, 152-3, 158, 187, 194, 200
Derby, Earl of, 208
Despard, Edward Marcus, 411
Despard, John, 144-5, 411
D'Estaing, Charles H. T., 295
Detroit, Mich., 289
Dictionary of National Biography, 299
Dobbs Ferry, N. Y., 329-32, 338-9
Douglas, Mrs. Langston, 407
Drinker, Mrs. Henry, 214
Drummond, James, 193
Duer, William, 228, 237
Duncan, James, 230
Dundee, Peter, 411
Du Simitière, Pierre Eugène, 23-4, 35, 206, 215, 409
Dyson, George W., 407

Easthampton, N. Y., 324
Easton, James, 43-4, 50, 52-3, 55, 57
Edgeworth, Maria, 29
Edgeworth, Richard Lovell, 29, 33
Edward, Fort, 162
Egg Harbor, N. J., 230
Elliott, Andrew, 388
Eneas, 64, 68
Enos, Roger, 66-8
Eustis, William, 371
Ezequelle, Betty K., 407

Fairfield, Conn., 125, 265
Falls of the Schuylkill, Pa., 196, 200-1
Feltham, Jocelyn, 45-6
Fields, Joseph, 407
Fifty-fourth Regiment, 296
Fishkill, N. Y., 319, 327, 337-8, 347, 363-4
Fitzgerald, John, 223

Fitzpatrick, John C., 418
Flatbush, N. Y., 289
Force, Peter, 418
Foucher, Monsieur, 78, 80
Fox, Edward, 285-6
Fox, Louis J., 407
Francis, Tench, 188
Franklin, Benjamin, 95, 215, 232
Franklin, William, 260, 265-6, 286
Franks, David, 221, 231, 237
Franks, David Salisbury (Solebury), 221-3, 239-41, 302, 319-20, 324, 332-3, 335-8, 351-2, 362-3, 367, 370-3, 377-8, 395
Franks, Rebecca, 139, 203, 205, 225, 237, 289, 397
Frantic Lover, The, 267-9
Fraser, Simon, 182
Freeman's Farm, Battle of, 170-4, 181, 412-3
French Alliance, 207, 210, 253-4, 282
Fuller, C. P. G., 407
Fulton, Robert, 141

Galloway, Joseph, 224, 241, 256
Galloway, Mrs. Joseph, 224-5, 237, 281
Gardiner, Abraham, 324, 414
Gardiner's Island, N. Y., 324
Gardner, Daniel, 409
Gates, Horatio, defense of Lake Champlain, 101-6, 113; and Brown's charges, 115; march through New Jersey, 115, 149, 196-7; Arnold's confidant, 118-21, 130; Saratoga campaign, 162, 164-5, 168-84, 217-8, 228, 412-3; Camden, 334; Arnold attacks after treason, 382; papers, 417
General McDougall, 219
Geneva, University of, 24
Gentleman's Magazine, 24
George III, 314, 399
George IV, 399, 411
George, Lake, 8, 137
Gérard, Conrad Alexandre, 226-8
Germain, George, 100, 257, 314, 415
Germantown, Pa., 155, 157-8, 214
Gerry, Elbridge, 121
Gibraltar, 207
Giles, Aquilla, 289-91, 328
Giradot, Marie Louise, *see* André, Marie Louise Giradot
Goethe, Johann Wolfgang von, 34
Göttingen, Germany, 30-4, 267
Göttingen, Universitätsbibliothek, 407
Göttingen Hain, 30-3

Index

449

Index

A STAGE raised on the body of a cart, on which was an effigy of General ARNOLD fitting; this was dressed in regimentals, had two faces, emblematical of his traiterous conduct, a mask in his left hand, and a letter in his right from Belzebub, telling him that he had done all the mischief he could do, and now he must hang himself.

At the back of the General was a figure of the Devil, dressed in black robes, shaking a purse of money at the general's left ear, and in his right hand a pitchfork, ready to drive him into hell as the reward due for the many crimes which the thief of gold had made him commit.

In the front of the stage and before General Arnold, was placed a large lanthorn of transparent paper, with the consequences of his crimes thus delineated, i. e. on one part, General Arnold on his knees before the Devil, who is pulling him into the flames—a label from the General's mouth with these words, "My dear Sir, I have served you faithfully;" to which the Devil replies, "And I'll reward you." On another side, two ropes from a gallows, inscribed, "The Traitors reward." And on the front of the lanthorn was wrote the following:

"MAJOR GENERAL BENEDICT ARNOLD, late COMMANDER of the FORT WEST-POINT. THE CRIME OF THIS MAN IS HIGH TREASON. "He has deserted the important post WEST-POINT, on Hudson's River, committed to his charge by His Excellency the Commander in Chief, and is gone off to the enemy at New-York.

"His design to hav
vered by the goodnes
his carrying it into ex
Adjutant-General of t

"The treachery of
exposition of infamy;
stance of the interposit

"The effigy of this
Traitor to his native c

The procession bega
Seve

Just before the

The procession was
ter expressing their abh
to the flames, and left
oblivion.